This book sets out a generative structuralist conception of general theoretical sociology: its philosophy, its problems, and its methods. The field is defined as a comprehensive research tradition with many intersecting subtraditions that share conceptual components. The focus is on formalization and unification as processes that can help advance the state of theory today.

An integrative philosophy of the field is set out in terms of a process worldview, a focus on generativity in explanation, and a conception of the structure of theories as hierarchical meaning control systems.

This philosophy is implemented in two phases. In the first phase, Professor Fararo carefully defines the core problems of general theoretical sociology in the context of setting out and illustrating the logic of a nonlinear dynamical social systems framework. A critical analysis of the outcome of this phase then leads, in the second phase, to formal treatments of action principles and structural analysis. A variety of traditions are drawn upon to treat theoretical problems of order and integration, as well as to examine searchingly problems of formalization and unification in theoretical sociology.

Along the way, many conceptual issues and methodological problems in contemporary sociological theory are discussed as Fararo develops the implications of his generative structuralist conception of general theoretical sociology.

The Arnold and Caroline Rose Monograph Series of the American Sociological Association

# The meaning of general theoretical sociology

The Rose Monograph Series was established in 1968 in honor of the distinguished sociologists Arnold and Caroline Rose, whose bequest makes the series possible. The sole criterion for publication in the series is that a manuscript contribute to knowledge in the discipline of sociology in a systematic and substantial manner. All areas of the discipline and all established and promising modes of inquiry are equally eligible for consideration. The Rose Monograph Series is an official publication of the American Sociological Association.



For other titles in this series, turn to page 388.

# The meaning of general theoretical sociology

## Tradition and formalization

**Thomas J. Fararo**
*University of Pittsburgh*

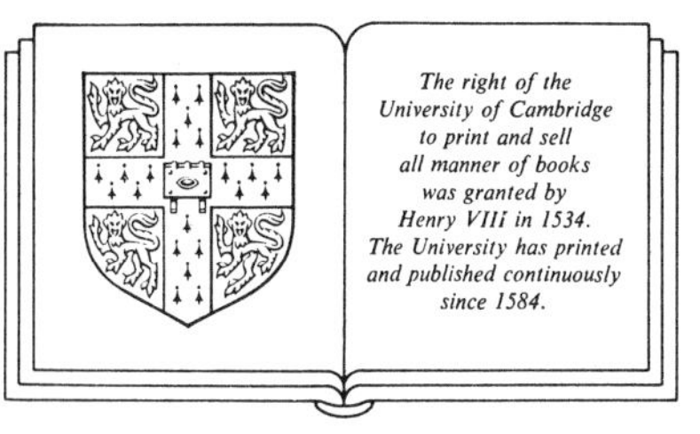
The right of the
University of Cambridge
to print and sell
all manner of books
was granted by
Henry VIII in 1534.
The University has printed
and published continuously
since 1584.

**Cambridge University Press**

*Cambridge*
*New York Port Chester Melbourne Sydney*

Published by the Press Syndicate of the University of Cambridge
The Pitt Building, Trumpington Street, Cambridge CB2 1RP
40 West 20th Street, New York, NY 10011, USA
10 Stamford Road, Oakleigh, Melbourne 3166, Australia



First published 1989

Printed in the United States of America

*Library of Congress Cataloging-in-Publication Data*

Fararo, Thomas J.
The meaning of general theoretical sociology: tradition and formalization / Thomas J. Fararo.
p. cm. – (The Arnold and Caroline Rose monograph series of the American Sociological Association)
Bibliography: p.
Includes index.
1. Sociology. 2. Sociology – Philosophy. I. Title. II. Series.
HM24.F353 1989
301–dc19 89–740
CIP

*British Library Cataloguing in Publication Data*

Fararo, Thomas J.
The meaning of general theoretical sociology: tradition and formalization. –
(The Arnold and Caroline Rose monograph series of the American Sociological Association)
1. Sociology. Theories
I. Title II. Series
301′.01

ISBN 0-521-37258-5 hard covers

# Contents

# Figures and tables

## Figures



## Tables

# Preface

The main objectives of this book are to set out a conception of a comprehensive research tradition I call *general theoretical sociology* and to show how key problems in this field are defined and studied in formal terms. The Introduction presents an overview of the topics treated in sequential terms in four chapters: a philosophy of general theoretical sociology, a dynamical systems formulation of its main problems, formal studies in action theory and social order, and integrative theory construction centered on the analysis of social structure in network terms.

This work represents two tendencies in my thinking emerging over the past decade. On the one hand, there is a continuity of past and present, of traditions in sociological theory. Despite the pluralism, I have come to regard the various traditions as communicating branches of one comprehensive tradition to which each generation makes its contributions. On the other hand, theoretical advance is through a *unification dynamic*. It is not that some static state of integrated sociological theory, wiping out disagreements, is envisioned. The commitment is to a recursive process of unification of otherwise separate contributions. This can occur at a variety of levels and in diverse ways, involving metatheory, principles, and theoretical procedures, a number of which are discussed and exemplified in this book.

Two overall elements of orientation inform the approach taken in this book. First, I treat the vast body of work of the past and present of sociological theory as a compound of general theoretical analysis, world-historical analysis, and normative analysis. In a wider envisagement of the meaning of sociological theory, all three of these elements of its tradition would be treated. This book treats only the component of general theoretical analysis. Hence, the subject matter is the meaning of general theoretical sociology, which is an abstraction from the concrete body of sociological theory. A further element of selection is indicated by the use of the term *general*. These and other matters of orientation are discussed in Chapters 1 and 2 of the book. The point here is that what is involved is an element of value orientation; namely, this book is based on a value commitment to the advance of the general theoretical element in sociological theory.

A second element of orientation informs this book. It is a methodological and sociological approach that I call *generative structuralism.* On the one hand, the approach is based on the idea of generativity. With regard to theoretical method, this amounts to a commitment to the construction of generative theoretical models. Formal elements are intrinsic to this activity. This idea is explicated in Chapter 1. On the other hand, the approach is based on the idea of social structure. Structuralism can mean and has meant many things. In this book, its primary meaning is the treatment of social structure as the problem focus rather than the solution focus for other problems. Whatever else it may mean, the sociology of a phenomenon is its interpretation or explanation in terms of social structure. But general theoretical sociology treats that very resource of explanation in other contexts as the source of its key problems. This idea is explicated in Chapter 2. Accordingly, the generative structuralist approach leads to the view that the meaning of general theoretical sociology is found in the activity of constructing generative theoretical models that answer to problems of social structure.

In a previous book (Fararo, 1973), I advocated and tried to illustrate a set of standards in the use of logic and mathematics in sociological theory. These included, for instance, conceptual clarity, formal consistency, deductive fertility, and empirical meaningfulness. In this book, it has not always proved possible to maintain all these standards. This is true, in particular, of Chapter 3, with its difficult focus on action and order. For instance, some of the formal work does not exhibit deductive fertility. Yet such work may have value in exhibiting a mode of formalization specially adapted to qualitative perspectives and also in its potential to function in unification episodes. In another instance, there is an introduction of primitive quantitative terms without demonstrated empirical meaningfulness as I used this term in the earlier book. This occurs in the mathematical model of dynamic normative control. I doubt that I would have set out this model in a context where we are dealing with the normative meaning of action were it not for the exemplar of David Heise (1979, 1986). Given that his theory rests on a quantitative control systems model supplied with a measurement basis, I feel less uneasy about the problem of empirical meaningfulness than I would otherwise. So one problem for future analysis is to link the normative control model of Chapter 3 to an empirical basis, possibly even the same as that employed by Heise. Another problem is to articulate the two types of theoretical models as such, one addressed to normative meaning and the other to affective meaning. I hope there has been some compensating value in framing the particular model in terms of a process-oriented explication of an important principle of general theoretical sociology.

My aim has been to speak not only to a small circle of committed formalists but also to a broad audience of theorists, teachers of theory, and their students.

Since the use of formal techniques is an intrinsic feature of the approach taken in this book, there is also a substantial obstacle to the realization of this aim. It may be anticipated that not all readers will be able to follow the more technical developments of the ideas. But much of the book is couched at the level of presuppositions and principles and of theoretical procedures that can be implemented in diverse formal ways. These and related discussions should be accessible to readers who are not totally put off by the more formal aspect of the book.

I have been fortunate in the past decade to have had John Skvoretz as a collaborator on a number of formal theoretical studies reported in this book. I am grateful to him for comments on portions of an earlier version of the book and to Kenji Kosaka and John Mellott for their very useful comments. Thanks also go to external reviewers for prompting revisions that, I hope, improved the form and substance of the book; and I am especially indebted to David Willer. He provided an extraordinarily detailed and sophisticated critical commentary, which nevertheless gave the sort of encouragement an author welcomes. My colleague and friend Robert Avery was more valuable to me than he knows in giving me his reactions to some of the ideas expressed here. And for her encouragement and emotional support, my unlimited gratitude goes to my wife, Irene.

THOMAS J. FARARO
*Pittsburgh, Pa.*

# Introduction

The central concern of general theoretical sociology is the construction of frameworks and models by means of which generalized sociological problems can be posed and studied. These problems have their roots in those empirical and conceptual problems that pervade all of sociology. They are general problems at the core of our effort to analyze the social world.

The general empirical problems of sociology concern social structures. How do novel social structures emerge? Under what conditions are they stable? How do we compare social structures? How do social structures change? To say that these are general problems is to say that they arise in any and all more specific contexts of sociological analysis whatever the cultural or physical environment, whatever the institutional setting, and whatever the historical period. To pose and work on these problems in a generalized way, the focus shifts from the actual world to abstract and generalized models. But the models are studied from the point of view of what they imply is really possible under varying conditions in the actual world. The concern is with how bare logical possibility, implied in a conceptual scheme, passes over into real possibility as a consequence of principles and mechanisms.

The general conceptual problems arise within the tradition of attempting to provide answers at the same level of generality as the general empirical problems. For example, if social structure is the focus of analysis, what is or should be the role of cultural concepts in our theories? If we say, with Parsons (1977), that social structure is institutionalized normative culture, what do we make of Blau's (1977) decision to eliminate values and norms in formulating macrostructural theory? And how are these two conceptions of social structure related to the idea that in some sense social structure is constituted by social knowledge, modules of tacit rules that account for the forms of situated interaction? And for that matter, if we begin with the primacy of process, as will be the case in this book, what can structure mean and how can we treat it as at once enduring and changing? What relation will this imply between human actors and the structures they generate in interaction?

Such conceptual problems can lead to further theoretical analyses, often of an integrative kind, and sometimes to improvements in the body of theory. In addition, such problems suggest a gradual passage into broadly philosophical concerns that must not be put aside as "nonscientific." Presuppositions as well as concepts, principles, and models are legitimate concerns for sociological theorists.

This book describes and illustrates an outlook on theoretical sociology. This outlook may be termed *generative structuralism.* The volume begins with the statement of a philosophy of general theoretical sociology and then goes on to employ formal means to state and address generalized empirical and conceptual problems. As a whole, the book suggests a philosophy of the field and an implementation of that philosophy leading to a body of principles and theoretical methods that illustrate how, working within a certain presuppositional basis, one is led to certain results. There is no implication that these results are final or ultimate. On the contrary, a basic idea is that by working on problems generated within the *tradition* of the field, both *formalization* and *unification* are operations leading to transformations of theory structures in an incessant recursive process in which we reapply the operations to any state they may have produced. There is no fixity, but there are theoretical structures generated and transformed over time. Indeed, if in this sentence we change the word *theoretical* to *social,* we obtain two different applications of a single process worldview that is a component of the philosophy of general theoretical sociology and characterizes generative structuralism. Thus, this book is one instance of a phase of theoretical sociology that I have called "neoclassical" (Fararo, 1984a), by which I mean a dual commitment to advance the state of generalized theoretical analysis and to do so on a firm classical foundation.

An overview of the contents of the book will serve to provide a brief introduction to the ideas treated.

Chapter 1 states a philosophy of general theoretical sociology. A number of key questions are posed and addressed by making use of philosophical models. The first question is, How shall we think about the history and current state of the field? Drawing upon a general model of science proposed by a historian of science, the answer proposed is that general theoretical sociology is a single comprehensive research tradition containing a number of communicating subtraditions, each with various branches. As in any sociocultural enterprise, there are competitive as well as cooperative elements. According to the general model, any such scientific research tradition implies a corresponding worldview. So the claim that the field can be modeled, descriptively and normatively, as a single tradition suggests a second question: What philosophical model provides an explicit articulation of its worldview? Idealism and materialism, essentially nineteenth-century movements of ideas, were transcended by the philosophers involved in the classical sociological breakthrough at the turn of the century. A new worldview was born, a process worldview. One aim of Chapter 1 is to describe this process worldview, which then pervades the entire approach of the book.

The philosophy of general theoretical sociology, as further set out in Chapter 1, involves two other key questions: What form should theory take? What is explanation?

The problem of the form of theory will be treated in terms of two philosophical models of theory structure, positivist and instrumentalist. The former arises from the philosophical tradition of logical positivism as modified in later work. In its most sophisticated form, it offers a vision of theory structure in terms of the mathematical axiomatic method, in which a formal theory defines a category of models and studies families of models in that category. The instrumentalist vision of theory structure arises from nonpositivist philosophical traditions, mainly from pragmatism and from Wittgenstein-inspired analyses. In one of its sophisticated forms, it proposes that theory structure is given by a nondeductive hierarchy of meanings. After these two philosophical models have been set out, a synthesis is stated in which the mathematical axiomatic method constitutes an optional and useful substructure of a four-level nondeductive meaning control hierarchy. The crown of this hierarchy is constituted by a set of nonempirical presuppositions, followed in order by what I call representation principles, theoretical models, and invariants.

The problem of theoretical explanation is treated in an analogous way. Two philosophical models are described. Again, positivism provides one definite model of scientific explanation as necessarily involving a relation of deduction between propositions. An alternative philosophical model has been formulated by nonpositivist philosophers, in this case in the realist tradition of the philosophy of science. Some realists stress generative mechanisms; others stress idealized model objects. When the traditional positivist account is modified by reference to the essential role of models, and when we emphasize the importance of generativity in model building, we arrive at a synthesized conception of theoretical explanation.

Given a process worldview and a conception of explanation as involving the construction of generative models, how do we formulate the formal theoretical versions of the main empirical problems of sociology? In short, what form does the framework of general theoretical sociology take?

Chapter 2 provides an answer to this question. The formal aspect of the framework has as its core two types of models: *networks* and *dynamical systems*. A network represents the social units and their interactions, including given and emergent structures of social relations among them. A dynamical system represents the relational processes constituting the network, conceived in terms of states and parameters. In the sociological context, we define a model called a general dynamical social system, which incorporates both the network and the dynamical system representations in a sociological interpretation.

Four types of theorems naturally emerge from the formal study of such models. The operative ideal for theorizing that is formulated is that we should aim toward the construction of theoretical models such that we can derive instances of these four types of theorems. They state general answers to four general problems of theoretical sociology: problems concerned with the emergence, the stability, the comparison, and the change of social structures. To the extent that we can obtain such general results, the main aim of general theoretical sociology is attainable. Nowhere in this book, however, is it claimed that such types of theorems are easy to obtain. They define an ideal that guides the theoretical process and can be used to assess how difficult our theoretical tasks are.

By study of the formalization of Homans's theory accomplished by Simon in the early 1950s, an example can be provided of four definite theorems that realize the theorem types. Then some elements of modern nonlinear dynamic analysis are applied to show that we can formally treat ''structuration'' and ''destructuration'' as (in a technical sense) catastrophes of group process. It will be noted that these are qualitative theorems about the forms of possible outcomes of group process. Although the ideas and techniques of recently developed ''chaos science'' are not used here, they constitute a logical next step in the spirit of adopting nonlinear dynamical systems as a framework for general theoretical sociology.

The formal theory and four theorems that illustrate the idea of the four key theorem types of general theoretical sociology exhibit two conceptual problems, which are framed at the end of Chapter 2 and provide transition to the two subsequent chapters. One conceptual problem leads to the claim that we require, for the purposes of general theoretical sociology, an action framework in the sense of principles that provide a mode of representation of the generation of action by single actors. This problem requires formal work within action theory. The second conceptual problem leads to the claim that we require, for the purposes of general theoretical sociology, a structuralist framework in the specific sense of a sustained focus on the network aspect of the dynamical social system. These two conceptual points are treated, respectively, in Chapters 3 and 4. The spirit of these chapters is that of making contributions in the two directions, action theory and structuralism, not of providing definitive solutions.

Chapter 3 consists of contributions to action theory, understood much more broadly than usual. Three representation principles are stated and explored conceptually and formally. These relate to and in a sense formalize key components of three branches or wings of a broadly understood collection of variants of action theory in sociology. The three branches are analytical action theory, especially the contributions of Parsons; interpretive sociology, a broad set of contributions from such authors as Schutz, Mead, Berger and Luckmann, Blumer, Garfinkel, and Giddens; and the theory of adaptively rational action, which includes the contributions of Homans, Emerson, and Coleman. I am not attempting to formalize extant sociological frameworks as totalities. I am seeking general representation principles, as defined in Chapter 1, implemented in theoretical models of action such that by various procedures one can derive dynamical social interaction system models.

The first branch of action theory treated in Chapter 3 is analytical action theory. Two elements of the theory are studied. The first element is normative control, the second is the AGIL scheme. The element of normative control is treated in terms of a representation principle: The actor in a situation is a dynamical normative control system. From a metatheoretical standpoint, adoption of this principle is a mode of treatment of classical dichotomies (such as voluntarism and constraint) as aspects of a single relational–processual whole. In turn, this leads to two forms of control system models, the first of which is the starting point for the second. The first model is based on a "vertical" coupling of normative control mechanisms to constitute a cybernetic hierarchy generating the behavior of a single actor in a situation. The second model is based on a "horizontal" or social coupling of such cybernetic hierarchy models. The image of social action systems becomes that of a dynamic network of socially coupled hierarchical normative control systems. Thus, a social generator is defined in terms of an action generator. On this basis we are led to a general formulation of the problem of social order. The AGIL scheme is then considered in dynamical system terms. In this context, a general answer to the problem of social order requires a type of theorem that combines two of the theorem types of Chapter 2. Parsons's work is interpreted as suggesting theorem conjectures about the stability conditions of networks based on social couplings of cybernetic actor models. It is here that the conjectured role of types of common value patterns finds its niche as a substantive contribution to action theory.

In analytical action theory, the values of the actors loom large. In interpretive sociology, the second branch of action theory treated in Chapter 3, it is the social knowledge of the actors that takes this dominant role. The key representation principle is that institutions, as schemes of typification, are regarded as classes of generated normal forms of interaction where the generator is a system of *production rules*. The formalism of production rules is used to represent a variety of ideas of interpretive sociology, including the interpretive procedures of ethnomethodology. What is involved here is a combination of philosophical, sociological, and formal ideas that together are taken to define what I call structural–generative action theory. Interpretive sociology plus ideas from analytical action theory function as the ingredient sociology. Thus structural–generative theory is integrative in spirit and provides a second mode of representation of ideas of analytical action theory, especially those concerned with the structure of action systems.

The third branch of action theory treated in Chapter 3 is termed the theory of adaptively rational action. There are actually two types of theories here. One theory starts from a rational choice perspective. It treats change of action in terms of a dynamic utility theory involving the actor's effort to increase utility in a small time interval. The coupling of such adaptively rational actors then yields social generativity with emergent social structures. This theory is illustrated but not treated in detail. The other theory starts from a behavioral foundation. The key principle is that action propensities change as a function of the sanction significance of their consequences for the actor. I adopt a dynamic adaptive model, close in spirit to the approach of Homans and Emerson. Then I specify and apply two theoretical procedures: coupling of actor models to define an interaction model and computer-assisted thought experiments on the interaction model to study its properties. The properties of interest are those concerned with the emergence and stability of social structures, that is, with social order.

Chapter 4 is a contribution to structuralism. My aim is theoretical, not data analytical. The focus is one of formalization of sociological theories and efforts toward their unification. Network analysis is employed in the form of a biased net framework. Sociological ideas are coordinated to the framework in the role of bias parameters over a baseline random network. Throughout the prior chapters, the reader will have noted that integrative processes and substructures play a crucial role in developing the ideas. In this chapter, a biased network model allows a representation of what is called the "dilemma of integration" of a social system. This dilemma arises in the context of formalizing Granovetter's weak-ties theory. The network conception of integration, as connectivity, is related to the normative conceptions of integration studied in Chapter 3. Then macrostructural theory is formalized and synthesized with weak-ties theory. Thus, we begin with two branches of structuralism: social network analysis and macrostructuralism. But the unification episode shows that theories in these two wings of structuralism can be formally articulated within a common framework, one that preserves the network element while being especially suitable for the analysis of large-scale social systems.

An effort is made to preserve the conception of generativity in treating this biased network mode of formalization and unification, but in general it is true that structuralism has been stronger in its data-analytical than in its explanatory

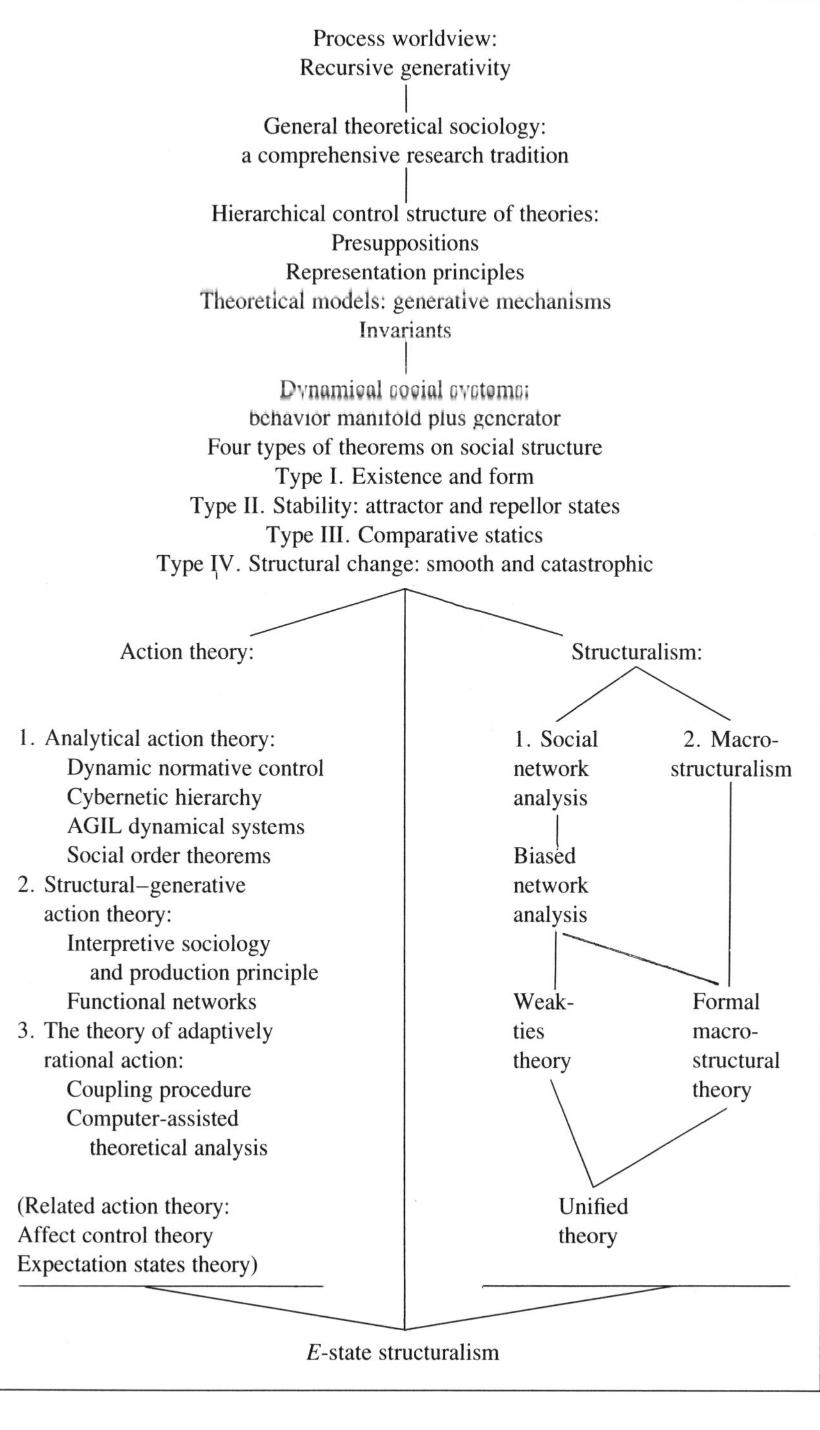

Process worldview:
Recursive generativity
General theoretical sociology:
a comprehensive research tradition
Hierarchical control structure of theories:
Presuppositions
Representation principles
Theoretical models: generative mechanisms
Invariants
Dynamical social systems:
behavior manifold plus generator
Four types of theorems on social structure
Type I. Existence and form
Type II. Stability: attractor and repellor states
Type III. Comparative statics
Type IV. Structural change: smooth and catastrophic
Action theory:
1. Analytical action theory:
Dynamic normative control
Cybernetic hierarchy
AGIL dynamical systems
Social order theorems
2. Structural–generative action theory:
Interpretive sociology and production principle
Functional networks
3. The theory of adaptively rational action:
Coupling procedure
Computer-assisted theoretical analysis
(Related action theory:
Affect control theory
Expectation states theory)
Structuralism:
1. Social network analysis
2. Macro-structuralism
Biased network analysis
Weak-ties theory
Formal macro-structural theory
Unified theory
E-state structuralism

achievements. Both at the micro level and the macro level, we need dynamic models that satisfy the presuppositions of structuralism formulated in the introduction to Chapter 4. Although this book does not attempt to spell out any dynamic macrostructural theory, in the very last section of Chapter 4 it does attempt to combine a number of ideas and procedures that focus on dynamics and on structure in the context of a small network. The treatment is in terms of suggesting and actually applying a general theoretical procedure called *E*-state structuralism, an implementation of generative structuralism that combines features of a specific action theoretical approach with the presuppositions of social network analysis. This is followed by a discussion of how *E*-state structuralism might contribute to further unification within general theoretical sociology.

The book closes with a summary that presents the key ideas in compact outline form.

The chart on page 7 provides a visual overview of the logical structure of the ideas treated. The upper portion shows key topics in Chapters 1 and 2. Then the two branches to action theory and structuralism depict key ideas in Chapters 3 and 4, respectively. The apex of the whole structure is the process worldview, with its conception of a recursively generated actual world exhibiting forms of order. At the bottom of the structure is the theoretical method of *E*-state structuralism, with its convergent relatedness to dynamical social system ideas, theoretical procedures of action theory, and presuppositions of structuralism.

# 1. A philosophy of general theoretical sociology

## 1.1. Introduction

The task of this chapter is to state the main philosophical and metatheoretical elements that form the general presuppositions of generative structuralism, the approach taken in this book. The assumption made is that there is a single time-extended and comprehensive research tradition to which this work aims to be one contribution. This tradition is termed *general theoretical sociology*. Thus, this chapter constitutes a statement of a philosophy of general theoretical sociology.

General theoretical sociology is a research tradition. In fact, I take it to be a *comprehensive* research tradition, within which the familiar paths of sociological theorizing from the classics to the present find their niche. This book both assumes this metasociological proposition and tries to contribute to its further realization. In other words, the claim has normative as well as descriptive significance. It functions both as a premise of the position developed in this book and as a tentative conclusion the work might be seen to make more or less plausible. Research traditions occur within communities of people committed to some more or less articulated *worldview*. This book takes the position that most of the worldviews discussed in contemporary theory, such as idealism or materialism, are simply inadequate as proposed presuppositions of classical theory or contemporary theory. My claim is that the tradition of general theoretical sociology is in fact characterized by what I will call a process metaphysics or worldview. Hence, one task of this chapter is to discuss general theoretical sociology as a comprehensive research tradition with a process philosophical worldview.

General theoretical sociology aims to provide theoretical solutions to a small number of fundamental general problems centered on the concept of social structure, as has been stated earlier and will be elaborated upon in the next chapter. It supplies proposed solutions by constructing frameworks and models based on presuppositions as to what is important and how it should be studied. What I term *representation principles* define frameworks that introduce families of models as modes of representation of social phenomena. Within any one such framework, the construction of theoretical models leads to statements or *theorems* describing the properties of such models. The properties of interest are those that relate to the solution of general problems motivating the construction of the frameworks and the models.

This process of constructing frameworks and models around certain problems is governed by various *operative ideals* as to the form of theorizing and the nature of explanation. Such operative ideals have been the subject of explicit formulations by philosophers as well as by sociologists. Such explicitly formulated ideals for the form of theorizing and explanation I term *philosophical models* of such activity. Another task of this chapter is to spell out how the conception of general theoretical sociology employed in this book is related to more or less familiar philosophical models of scientific activity, such as those associated with positivism, instrumentalism, and realism.

In Section 1.2, the conception of general theoretical sociology as a comprehensive research tradition is discussed. Section 1.3 formulates two philosophical models of theory structure that, as integrated there, function as a philosophical element in my approach to general theoretical sociology. Section 1.4 formulates two philosophical models of theoretical explanation and, again, provides an integral model that functions as an operative idea in this book. Section 1.5 treats the process worldview in relation to general theoretical sociology. Then, with this foundation set out, three familiar philosophical issues are taken up in Section 1.6 in order to state explicitly the viewpoint adopted in formulating the generative structuralist approach to theory in sociology. Section 1.7 sums up these ideas.

## 1.2. General theoretical sociology as a comprehensive research tradition

In this book, contributions are made to a research tradition with many proliferating strands of conceptual schemes and theories. I call it *general theoretical sociology*. In the next chapter, I frame the four central problems of this research tradition and characterize more specifically the aims and procedures it should follow. Anticipating the problem foci: These are the problems of explaining how novel social structures emerge, how given social structures are maintained, how social structures vary with varying cultural or other parameters, and how social structures are transformed over time, either gradually or more abruptly. The procedures to be recommended, based on the philosophical elements explicated later in this chapter, relate to the construction and analysis of theoretical models.

General theoretical sociology is a comprehensive research tradition. What exactly is a research tradition? How can we conceptualize it? According to Laudan's (1977) historical and systematic analysis, it is a set of ontological and methodological conceptions: what entities there are in the empirical domain under investigation, how they interact, and what the proper methods are for theorizing about them, the "do's" and "don'ts" of the tradition. Every research tradition inhabits an intellectual environment comprised of some dominant worldview. Laudan defines worldviews as implicit or explicit systems of ideas that are in the domains of metaphysics, logic, ethics, and theology.

We might think of a worldview as a set of presuppositions associated with one or more frameworks advancing through time. This advance through time, which may or may not be a matter of cumulativeness of knowledge, is what the research tradition concept highlights. In Laudan's model, a research tradition includes a number of distinct theories and formulations of problems. In my own terms, a tradition includes a number of frameworks that, in turn, include specific theories or theoretical models. Then their interpenetration, in terms of conceptual schemes and problems investigated, is what is advancing over time. The unification of such frameworks or the integration of theoretical models under comprehensive theories is a primary mode of advance of a research tradition. In this book, this *unification dynamic* will be partly a programmatic element and partly a demonstration of what is possible, although nothing done will have any claim to finality.

For my formulation of the philosophy underlying this book, a philosophy of general theoretical sociology, it is important to note that Laudan takes a very wide view of what counts as such a tradition. Examples given by Laudan include Aristotelianism, Cartesianism, Darwinism, Newtonianism, and Freudianism. No effort to spell out any such tradition will ever find a total consensus, a pure realization of a single scheme of abstractions slavishly carried forward by puzzle solvers. So it is appropriate to note that we can view general theoretical sociology as a single research tradition with its inner differences of emphasis.

Collins (1985) sees at least three such inner traditions within sociology: the conflict theory tradition stemming from Marx and Weber, the Durkheimian tradition with its functionalist and ritual solidarity wings, and the microinteractionist tradition. From the point of view represented in this book, these three traditions and others like them (such as action theory) are regarded as parts of a more comprehensive research tradition. To emphasize this point, I call them *subtraditions* and, following Collins, call *their* inner variations *wings* or *branches*.

I treat systems thinking, structuralism, and action theory as subtraditions. Each has various branches. In the case of systems thinking, I stress the modern concept of a dynamical system and see the development of ideas from Pareto to (early) Homans to Simon as contributing to a framework of dynamical social systems analysis. The Parsonian wing of systems thinking, also rooted in part in

Pareto, I treat separately and in the context of its wider commitment to action theory.

My treatment of structuralism concentrates on the development of ideas within a probabilistic framework that defines models called biased nets. From a substantive standpoint two main wings of structuralism are treated: the macrostructural wing associated with Blau's later work and the approach of network analysis. The biased net representation allows a unification process to occur in which macrostructuralism and network analysis are integrated.

Action theory is treated in terms of three branches: analytical action theory (e.g., Parsons), interpretive sociology (e.g., Garfinkel), and adaptively rational action theory (e.g., Homans's so-called exchange theory). Many readers may find this grouping of diverse modes of analysis a bit forced. Yet the history of the field is by no means properly recorded in all its patterning of positive and negative lines of influence among its various contributors. Consider the following. Historically, Parsons was a synthesizer who drew upon (among others) Pareto and Weber, both of whom can be called action theorists. Homans was considerably influenced by Pareto as well as by psychological conceptions of *change* of action over time. Garfinkel was a student of Parsons who reacted to how Parsons conceptualized the problem of order and made considerable use of the ideas of Schutz. But Schutz developed his approach by deepening Weber's action foundations of sociology. So we find partial overlapping of intellectual roots traced back to the classical action theorists, Weber and Pareto.

More generally, all the inner traditions and their branches within sociology overlap heavily. For instance, Homans is very much in the Durkheimian tradition defined by Collins (a view I defend in Chapter 2). Because of this extensive interpenetration of the various traditions and their branches, as well as the density of communication among them as contrasted with their communication with other traditions outside sociology, I regard the whole they constitute as a single comprehensive tradition with inner tensions and disputes as well as inner lines of positive influence.

It is vital to this conception of general theoretical sociology that there be some sufficiently general worldview to encompass the whole tradition, capable of being drawn upon by variant elements within it. I shall spell out this worldview in Section 1.5. The effort to articulate an only dimly appreciated unity at the level of worldview is just another aspect of the unification dynamic we must foster within our field. And, in the same spirit, throughout this book, I point to classical ideas that are in this comprehensive tradition and that are responsible for the developments leading to my own formulations.

In another recent mapping of social theory, Wilson (1983) uses Laudan's model to define three worldviews within sociology: sociology as a natural science of social phenomena, sociology as interpretive of a social world of meanings, and sociology as a realist project with respect to the discovery of a deep structure of social life. Parsons's action theory, symbolic interactionism, and historical materialism, respectively, are said to be research traditions based on these three worldviews. A number of other traditions are also allocated to one or another of these three views.

The problem with this mapping of social theory is that, especially in the aftermath of World War II, these traditions have not been isolated but are very much in communication. Influences flow, albeit across certain barriers. More discrete theories of particular phenomena often draw freely upon ideas from traditions that seemingly represent different worldviews. At gatherings of sociologists, as well as in their formal papers and books, communication rests on a common knowledge of, and value placed on, contributions of classical theorists allocated artificially to one or another of these traditions in this metatheoretical mapping.

For these and other reasons, I prefer to treat all these various research traditions as parts of one more comprehensive tradition that, in turn, is grounded in a more comprehensive worldview. In the subsequent chapters of this book, the reader will find work readily recognizable in its classical heritage: Pareto, Durkheim, Marx, Mead, Weber, and Simmel. The work is based on contributions of more contemporary theorists, such as Homans, Simon, Parsons, Schutz, and Blau. It relates to the ideas expressed in recent theory and metatheory writings, such as those of Jeffrey Alexander, Randall Collins, Peter Berger, Anthony Giddens, David Willer, Joseph Berger, and others.[1]

Laudan notes that particular theories will be sources of conceptual problems for investigators if they violate the ''do's'' and ''don'ts'' of the research tradition. Meanwhile some of the theories are really solving empirical and also conceptual problems. Thus, progressive advance of a research tradition occurs if the solution of important empirical problems outweighs the conceptual problems generated within the tradition. By this criterion, it is not clear that sociology, now including relevant empirical research, has exhibited a progressive advance.[2]

It is clear, however, that certain developments are very promising. Some of the do's and don'ts of the general theoretical sociology research tradition are beginning to come into focus more clearly in recent years. For instance, the social network representation of social structures is a vital advance. The requirement, for explanatory intelligibility, of some principle of action is another idea gaining in acceptance. The unification of micro-level theories and macro-level theories of social structure is one area of definite recognition of the importance of a unification dynamic.

Thus, at least the elements of *social network representations,* the explanatory use of *explicit action principles,* and *micro–macro unification* are taking form as do's and don'ts of the comprehensive research tradition of general theoretical sociology.

However, obstacles exist in the effort to advance this tradition. Among these are three that merit our attention. The first obstacle is the misreading of important works we yet might build upon and even the dismissal of vital constructs used in virtually all theoretical sciences. More specifically, the willingness of so many recent theorists to abandon the system construct and its heritage of use in sociology is unfortunate. One can read Chapter 2 as an effort to make the case for the idea of system, in relation to the theoretical model-building element, as a "do" of general theoretical sociology. A second obstacle arises through the failure to recognize and nurture *theoretical methods* as well as empirical methods in sociology. Our methodological thought has been molded along lines suggested by the technical norms of sound empirical research, including forms of data analysis. Corresponding technical norms, especially concerning formalism in theorizing, are underplayed in our teaching and in our actual theoretical work. The entirety of this book is an effort to make a contribution at the level of theoretical procedure, ways of theorizing that are effective for the attainment of our shared goals. For recent statements on the importance of developing theoretical methods in sociology see Freese (1980a,b).

Finally and most significantly, a major obstacle to theoretical advance is the sheer difficulty in maintaining a *general theoretical* orientation. Ours is a subject matter filled with immediate relevance to our contemporary affairs. It is not so much the social problems focus of much of the field of sociology that is the problem here. Theorists already recognize our need to rise above the social problem level of discourse in framing sociological theory. What they seem to find more difficult is somewhat different. The key aspect of this obstacle is the tendency to regard the "substance" of sociology as concerned with the one and only actual path of change of real human societies.

Let us call this viewpoint the *world-historical* image of sociology. It is the image we get from Weber. This focus seems to supply theorists with a set of problems not limited to any one society or even to one time period of history. The problems are big and evidently important in terms of understanding the present human condition and its prospects. They are, in Weber's terms, highly value relevant. For Weber and the world-historical theorists, theoretical sociology is largely a conceptual instrument leading to generalizations about the key tendencies of world history. Analogically, world-historical sociology is the cosmology of the one and only actualized social universe. As such, it definitely requires some explicit theorizing. But the theory it requires should not be limited to conceptual schemes. The main problems of general theoretical sociology do not pertain to the actual history of the social universe but to real possibilities for social order. These problems relate not to the historical universe of actualized social orders but to the conceptual universe of really possible social orders. Although empirical knowledge of realized social structures is relevant, such realized social structures are not the complete domain of interest for general theorizing. Analogically, general theoretical sociology is the theoretical physics of the conceptual social universe.

The position taken here is that Weber's value relevance criterion is an obstacle to the cumulative advance of general theoretical sociology unless the relevant value is internal to the research tradition itself. Within this tradition are certain key problems that have value as objects of cognitive orientation. They are empirical but not limited to any particular empirical referent such as the industrial or postindustrial social structures. They are *general* empirical problems. By virtue of the value relevance of these problems, general theoretical sociology can pursue, in value-neutral mode, its own value-relevant path.

Within the tradition of sociology as a whole – granted that general theoretical sociology is only a part of that advancing whole – Weber's conception of value relevance reapplies in his own intended meaning. All sorts of value-relevant sociological investigations with their own appropriate but more historically specified conceptual schemes are welcome components of the entire *sociological* tradition. Meanwhile, *general theoretical* sociology has its tasks, to be set out in the next chapter. Perhaps it will not, on balance, ever achieve what this author or others consider possible. Yet, we who have staked out our commitments toward its inner advance, for its own sake, have made a Weberian type of value commitment. Part of this commitment involves the recognition that the real situation and the value-defined operative ideal that guides us may never coincide.

Thus, from the present perspective on sociology as a whole, it is useful to map *sociological theory* as an enterprise with three variant and interpenetrating traditions: general theoretical sociology, world-historical sociology, and normative social theory. By the latter, I mean the theoretical analysis of the rational bases for the evaluation of social structures, a task whose philosophical side is typified by the work of Rawls (1971). Sociologists, I believe, ought to contribute to such theory by blending ideas from general theoretical sociology with those of social philosophy to arrive at a more effective normative theory. This is in agreement with the spirit of the remarks by Coleman (1986:Ch. 14) on the potential linkage between social philosophy and sociology. Among the writings of contemporary social theorists, perhaps the work of Habermas (1971, 1981) most clearly focuses on an integration of world-historical sociology and normative social theory with the benefit of ideas from general theoretical sociology. Within this broader domain map of contemporary sociological theory, the present book attempts to clarify and contribute to the meaning of general theoretical sociology. From this perspective, efforts to develop pure theory are thwarted if they start from premises rooted in world-historical interests or normative interests. A certain amount of autonomy of general theoretical sociology is a requirement for its own advance and for its improved capacity to address the problems of the other two components.

The next three sections of this chapter discuss three philosophical elements of general theoretical sociology. The first element relates to the question: What form should theory take? Explicit philosophical models of theory structure are relevant here. In Section 1.3, I define and illustrate two such models and then show how the approach taken in this book involves an integration of these two models. The second element relates to the question: What form should explanation take? Explicit philosophical models of theoretical explanation are relevant to this question also. In Section 1.4, I define and illustrate two such models and then show how the generative structuralist approach taken in this book involves an integration of the two. Finally, the third philosophical element relates to the question, What general worldview provides a metaphysical and epistemological basis for general theoretical sociology as a comprehensive research tradition? Section 1.5 undertakes to spell out such a worldview.

## 1.3. Theory structure

What form should theory take, in the sense of constituting some sort of structure of ideas? Two families of philosophical models of the structure of scientific theories are relevant for general theoretical sociology. The first is the hypothetico-deductive system model proposed by the logical positivists. The particular positivist model that requires discussion involves the conception of the deductive system as axiomatic. The second family of models I call instrumentalist. The particular model of interest to us here posits that theory takes the form of a proposed mode of representation of a body of phenomena such that meaningful ideas are arranged in hierarchical patterns.

In the following paragraphs, I shall outline *versions* of these two models of theory structure that are elements of an integrated conception of the form of theory as employed in this book. Each version has a resemblance to, but also differs from, similar models, positivist or instrumentalist, advocated by certain social theorists, as I shall indicate.

### *1.3.1. A positivist model: mathematical axiomatics*

In the twentieth century, advances in symbolic logic, metamathematical studies, and reflections on the meaning of the new physics all combined to create a conception of the structure of a scientific theory as a formal calculus with an intended interpretation. The logical positivists of the Vienna Circle (e.g., Carnap, 1955) and the Polish logicians who discussed science (e.g., Tarksi, 1946) advanced versions of this idea. Hempel (1952) provided a very cogent analysis of science based on a modification of the earlier viewpoints. In the 1950s, then, the positivist stress on an interpreted formal system evolved into a variety of views about theory structure and functions. During the 1960s, it was clear that the received view in the philosophy of science had been transformed considerably (Suppe, 1977). Related to this transformation were arguments about what was termed the "natural science model" as a canonical way to do sociology. In Section 1.6.1 I discuss this issue as one involving a "realist" critique of the positivist model of natural science. In the present section, the aim is a narrower one of explicating one of the variant images of scientific theory that emerged out of the received view.

Insofar as examples in the behavioral and social sciences are concerned, probably the work of Suppes (1957, 1969) was most important in the 1950–1960s phase of the positivistic philosophy of science. Unlike many other philosophers Suppes became very involved in the construction and empirical testing of formal theoretical models (Suppes and Atkinson, 1960). He showed, both abstractly and by examples, that "axiomatization within set theory" was a simple and elegant procedure of formalization. In Suppes (1957) classical mechanics is axiomatized in this way. In the later work with Atkinson, mathematical psychological theories are axiomatized in the same way. Sets, relations, functions, matrices, directed graphs, probability functions, and other sorts of mathematical objects – all these and much more – are at home within the general set theory framework. A piece of scientific theorizing is formalized by setting down axioms about such mathematical entities and providing an empirical interpretation. The various mathematical entities, taken together, constitute an abstract model.[3] I shall now expand on and illustrate this idea.

To construct a pure or mathematical axiomatic system (for details, see Fararo, 1973:Sect. 4.18), one sets out a primitive basis followed by a deductive elaboration on this basis. The *primitive basis* has two components: a set of primitive terms referring to purely mathematical objects and a set of axioms about these objects. The *deductive elaboration* also has two components: definitions in terms of primitive notions and theorems derived from the axioms and definitions. This whole structure has scientific significance through the *interpretation* of the ideas in relation to the world. Axiomatic systems vary enormously in complexity. It is *not* necessary to envisage that only those axiomatic systems that formalize an entire disciplinary theory or set of theories are worthwhile. Recall that I am not arguing that this is *the* form of theorizing we should utilize. The positivist or axiomatic model for theorizing will be embedded within a broader conception of theorizing, as will be indicated not only for theory structure but also for other elements of theorizing. It is one subordinate *element* in the philosophy of theoretical sociology.

*An example of mathematical axiomatics.* An example of mathematical axiomatics is given that relates two concepts used in the theory of rational choice: preference and indifference. According to the theory, a choice of an action in a given menu of alternative actions depends upon the utilities assigned to the possible outcomes of each action. In the case of uncertainty about outcomes, the relevant principle is that the choice is given by the action associated with the greatest expected utility. But a utility function is a numerical representation of a system of preference and indifference relations over both pure outcomes and probabilistic mixtures of pure outcomes. For pure outcomes only the utilities define an ordinal scale if the preference–indifference structure satisfies order properties. When preferences among probability mixtures also satisfy order properties, the utilities computed through taking expected values define an interval scale. The present aim is to illustrate mathematical axiomatics in a relatively simple context so the axiomatics of expected utility theory is not discussed (but see Fararo 1973:Ch. 20). Aside from its function as a simple example of mathematical axiomatics, the main relevance of what follows is in relation to the idea of adaptively rational action treated in Chapter 3. It also relates to the behavioral theory proposed by Homans (1974), to be treated in detail in Chapter 3, but which I briefly discuss in the next section as an example of axiomatics in sociological theory.

In what follows, the preference and indifference interpretation is first withheld in order to display the purely mathematical structure followed by a discussion of the interpretation.

For primitive or undefined terms take $X$, an unspecified *set* of objects, and two *relations,* denoted $R$ and $E$, between pairs of elements in $X$. The following are the axioms of the theory, stated for any elements $x, y, z$ in $X$:

A1. $R$ is transitive: if $xRy$ and $yRz$, then $xRz$.
A2. $R$ is asymmetric: if $xRy$, then not-$yRx$.
A3. $E$ is transitive: if $xEy$ and $yEz$, then $xEz$.
A4. $E$ is symmetric: if $xEy$, then $yEx$.
A5. $E$ is reflexive: $xEx$ holds for all $x$ in $X$.
A6. If not-$xEy$, then $xRy$ or $yRx$.

Axioms A1 and A2 together say that $R$ is a type of order relation. Axioms A3, A4, and A5 together say that relation $E$ is an equivalence relation on set $X$, thereby partitioning the elements of $X$ into classes. Axiom A6 relates the two relations. It says that if two elements are not equivalent (in whatever sense the interpretation will supply), then they are in relation $R$ in one or the other direction (but never both, by Axiom A2). Note that the primitive notions are the direct subject matter of the axioms construed abstractly. We term the entity ($X$, $E$, $R$), which is a set-theoretical entity consisting of all the mathematical objects designated by the primitive terms, an *abstract mathematical model*. Hence, we think of the axiom set as a definition of an abstract mathematical model

The next step is the deductive elaboration. This consists, first, of definitions within the theory. They are framed in terms of the primitive notions. Definition D1 specifies a relation that holds between $x$ and $y$, in that order, just in the case that neither $xRy$ nor $xEy$ holds:

D1. $xSy$ if and only if not-$xRy$ and not-$xEy$.

Note that the definition is in terms of the two primitive notions of the theory. The second element of the deductive elaboration of the theory consists of proofs of theorems, for which the premises are axioms, definitions, and/or previously demonstrated theorems. The following is a theorem that follows from the above axioms and Definition D1. The logical proof is not difficult but is omitted as unnecessary for my illustrative purposes.

T1. $S$ is transitive: if $xSy$ and $ySz$, then $xSz$.

This deductive elaboration could be considerably extended, but enough has been shown to illustrate the general conception of an axiomatic system. Such a system can be interpreted in different ways, producing different interpreted systems or theories. In particular note the following two interpretations:

(1) Numerical interpretation
  $R$ is "less than"
  $E$ is "equal to"
  $X$ is the set of real numbers
(2) Preference interpretation
  $R$ is a preference relation
  $E$ is an indifference relation
  $X$ is a set of evaluated objects

Each axiom can now be translated into two domains of interpretation.

According to the numerical interpretation, the axioms simply characterize certain of the order properties of the real numbers. The axioms are true in this interpretation. This is so because the axioms that define the abstract mathematical model comprising the system of real numbers either include these order properties or logically imply them. For instance, Axiom A6 states that if $x$ and $y$ are two distinct numbers, then either $x$ is less than $y$ or $y$ is less than $x$. Then Definition D1 defines the relation "greater than" in terms of the two given relations.

The preference interpretation is more interesting. According to it, Axiom A1 says that preference is transitive: If an object $x$ is preferred to an object $y$ and object $y$ is preferred to an object $z$, then object $x$ is preferred to object $z$. Similarly, under this interpretation, the assigned meaning of equivalence is indifference. This implies, by A3, that whenever a person is indifferent between objects $x$ and $y$ and between objects $y$ and $z$, then that person will be indifferent between objects $x$ and $z$.

Given the preference interpretation, the meaning assigned to the primitive terms $R$ and $E$ is intuitively clear and yet by no means definite for scientific purposes. Three possible elaborations of this theory (or, really, any member of a family of theories about preferences) seem to exist in practice: (1) purely empirical, (2) purely normative, and (3) rational choice baseline elaborations. The purely empirical elaboration says that we should aim to test the theory by seeking out its axiomatic or derived claims that might be falsified. Historically and systematically, this corresponds to the point of view of the psychologist. Given the unwillingness to adopt idealized model objects, the traditional experimentalist shows that properties such as transitivity fail and the theory is rejected. The purely normative elaboration says that what the axioms describe is a model of how people should evaluatively orient to the world on grounds such as consistency among choices. It is irrelevant that some axioms do not hold empirically because this only means that people find it difficult to achieve such evaluative consistency. A good example of such an application occurs in the work of John Rawls (1971) in his effort to provide a normative theory of social justice. The rational choice baseline elaboration is a kind of hybrid elaboration. It recognizes that the axioms might well be falsified in careful empirical investigations, yet it regards them as defining an idealized model of action as a starting point for theoretical explanations in a variety of contexts. This is what people in sociology (e.g., Coleman, 1986) mean when they speak of "rational choice theory," since they usually have no interest in the empirical test of the rational choice axioms but considerable interest in their deployment to explain social structural phenomena. I discuss this important interpretation of the theory in the last part of Chapter 3.

There is another aspect to the interpretive problem in relation to axiomatic systems. For empirical testing purposes, any interpretation needs to be supplemented with what are often called *rules of correspondence* or *operational definitions*. These are necessary because the theory leaves open the possibility of diverse operations by which empirical instances of the relations might be identified or produced, all having the same generic interpretation. I shall sometimes speak of this as yielding *empirical identification* of the conceptual entities.[4]

Note that an *interpretation* yields a *general* meaning for the axiomatic definition of a class of abstract mathematical models. By contrast, an *identification* is a *specification* of the general meaning. Rules of correspondence provide a mode of producing such specific instances, or empirical identifications, of the notions of the theory.[5]

To illustrate, for the preference interpretation there are at least two distinct possibilities for modes of empirical identification or correspondence rules. The first I term *algebraic,* the second *probabilistic*. The general difference between the algebraic and the probabilistic correspondence rules is that they specify different ways in which the axioms, now treated as empirical assumptions, can be found to be incorrect.

(a) Algebraic preference correspondence. For a given person under "controlled conditions" – that is, careful research design – ask that person to evaluate every pair of objects in a finite subset of a domain of objects, indicating that the evaluation may be that of preference for one over the other or that of indifference between the two. Then:

$xRy$ if the person prefers $x$ in a comparison of $x$ and $y$
$yRx$ if the person prefers $y$ in a comparison of $x$ and $y$
$xEy$ if the person expresses indifference in the comparison of $x$ and $y$

Under this set of correspondence rules and with the preference interpretation supplying the general meaning of the axioms, it is now possible to state which axioms are eligible for treatment as empirical claims, that is, claims that might be wrong about the world. For instance, Axiom A1 is falsifiable but Axiom A2 is not since we assume only a single comparison opportunity for each pair.

Consider now a falsifiable axiom under the given preference interpretation and the particular correspondence rule, such as Axiom A1. Suppose a single person's evaluative data under these correspondence rules fails to satisfy this transitivity axiom for preference. Do we now revise the axiom? This is rather severe. Do we really want to mean by transitivity that absolutely, in every case, we expect to observe the condition to hold? For instance, suppose we repeat this investigation with the same person and obtain choices that differ between the two occasions, say, $xRy$ at time 1 and $xEy$ at time 2. Do we want to say that the evaluation changed? But suppose the time interval was only 10 minutes. If we believe that evaluations of the domain of objects are not likely to change in small intervals of time, then we will not want to say evaluations changed. We will probably want to say that chance fluctuations are involved.

This leads to the idea that the correspondence of preference relation $R$ and indifference relation $E$ with observations is through patterns or regularities that emerge at the level of repetitions of the basic comparison investigation. This is the basis for the second type of correspondence rule set. We assign a probability $p(x, y)$ to every pair being compared: $p(x, y)$ is the probability that $x$ will be chosen over $y$ in repeated comparisons. Then we set up the following specification of the preference interpretation:

(b) Probabilistic preference correspondence:

$xRy$ if $p(x, y) > \frac{1}{2}$
$yRx$ if $p(x, y) < \frac{1}{2}$
$xEy$ if $p(x, y) = \frac{1}{2}$

In an investigation permitting repetitions – either with one person over occasions or numerous persons on one occasion – we then test the statistical hypotheses embodied in these rules in deciding on the direction of preference. Let us suppose that our aim is to test the axiomatic system as an empirically correct account of human preference. Then the falsifiability of the axioms is of strong interest. Without going through each case, consider again Axioms A1 and A2 with regard to the outcomes of these various statistical tests. Certainly A1 is falsifiable since we can very well statistically accept the hypotheses that $p(x, y) > \frac{1}{2}$ and $p(y, z) > \frac{1}{2}$ but statistically reject the hypothesis that $p(x, z) > \frac{1}{2}$. Axiom A2, on the other hand, is not falsifiable, because pure arithmetic disallows any alternative to $p(x, y) > \frac{1}{2}$ implying that $p(y, x) \leq \frac{1}{2}$, since $p(x, y) + p(y, x) = 1$.

In closing this example, one should note that the fact that we have two different interpretations of a single axiom system, one of which is numerical, is the formal basis of measurement (Fararo, 1973:Ch. 7). In the case at hand, it shows that "utility" is a numerical representation of a system of preferences assumed to satisfy the given axioms or some extended set of axioms to capture probability mixtures of pure alternatives. Within a rational choice framework, we can say that actors choose according to their preferences, whereas it is the analyst who computes with utilities in order to provide an interpretation of the actor's choice situation and behavior (Fararo, 1973: Sect. 22.7). This means that it is misleading to equate a utility theory with any specific motivational orientation, since "utility" is only a numerical representation of a preference–indifference system that might range from highly self-oriented to highly collectivity-oriented.

This concludes my example of some aspects of the logic of axiomatics in a scientific context.

*Axiomatics in sociological theory.* Among important contemporary sociological theorists, perhaps Homans (1974) and Blau (1977) have been most influenced by the positivist conception of scientific theory. Each has taken it as an operative ideal and admitted that, according to this model of theory, their works are in various ways unsatisfactory. Blau's (1977) macrosociological theory is treated in Chapter 4, where its axiomatic element is largely ignored in favor of embedding the approach within a structure of theory best thought of in terms of the integrated philosophical model to be presented in Section 1.3.3. Homans's social behavior approach (Homans, 1974) will be discussed briefly here and more extensively in Chapter 3 where, again, it is best seen in terms of the ideas in Section 1.3.3 coupled with the social structure problem setting for action theory emerging out of Chapter 2.

Homans adopts the positivist model of the structure of theory: His theory is to be seen as a hypothetico-deductive system. The assumed propositions are general statements about acts of individual human organisms. An interaction is (at least) an act related to another act. The central idea is: The assumed propositions are about acts; deductions are about the emergent features of interaction. In particular, the central emergent feature is the endurance of patterns of social interaction. Hence, the primitive basis of any axiomatic system corresponding to this theory will involve terms interpretable as elements of an actor–situation system. The axioms will be interpretable as general modes of relationship among such elements. The deductive elaboration will define social interactive systems and analyze them with a view to deriving theorems about social relations.

When we examine Homans's theory, we see that the fundamental analytical element is the probability of an act. The actor is characterized in terms of a dynamically changing probability of action. It is the *change* of such action propensities, as depending on action–outcome events, that is the core of the theory. Concepts such as *reward* and *value* get their meaning by their embeddedness in the equations of a probabilistic dynamic process (as shown in Chapter 3). Some remarks by Homans (1974:43–46) on rationality have led to the view that his axioms incorporate a rational choice approach. His main point is that preferences, as we draw upon them in sociological contexts, are not ultimate givens but are generated in social interaction. Rationality in relation to preferences and actions, he says, is really a special case of the possibilities permitted by his theory. But this claim is complicated by the differences in presuppositions and representation principles that characterize a formalized theory of adaptive rationality when approached from, on the one hand, a rational choice starting point and, on the other hand, a behavioral starting point. The two types of theories of adaptively rational action will be discussed in Chapter 3.

Now let us turn to the purely axiomatic element and use the preceding account of axiomatics to evaluate the form of theory we find in Homans's work.

The general propositions Homans proposes amount to the following:

A1 (success): If an act is rewarded in a situation, then it becomes more likely in that situation (envisioning repetitions of a type of situation in various occasions).

A2 (similarity): If an act is rewarded in a situation, then similar acts in the same situation and the same act in similar situations also become more likely.

A3 (value): The likelihood of the act in a situation depends positively on the value of the reward.

A4 (satiation, declining marginal utility): The marginal value of the reward declines with increasing amounts of the reward.

A5 (emotion): Expected events or states are compared with actual states or events. If the reward is less in value than the expected amount, the person will be angry; if the reward is at least equal to that expected, the person will be pleased. Also, in the angry state, aggressive acts become more likely; in the pleased state, approving acts become more likely.

Taking the axiomatic model as a standard, we see that the interpretation and the primitive basis are not distinguished. There is no definite axiomatic system to *be* interpreted. The absence of a definite abstract mathematical model, defined by the primitive basis, has as its main consequence that Homans finds it difficult to deductively elaborate the theory. The most frequent empirical criticism of the theory, that it is not really falsifiable, is related to this structural problem. It is argued in Chapter 3 that when a dynamic mathematical model is defined, corresponding to the adaptive or action–change focus of the theory, the deductive elaboration and the interpretation together suggest that falsifiable claims can be derived.

Although much could be said on this subject, let us return to the main line of discussion of two philosophical models of scientific theory structure. We have just looked at a version of the positivist model, one that will function as a subordinate element in the integrated approach to theory structure used in this book. The more inclusive form of theory I use is a version based on the instrumentalist philosophy of science.

### *1.3.2. An instrumentalist model: meaning hierarchy*

According to this second philosophical model of theory structure, a theory is a hierarchical system of meaningful ideas based on a mode of representation of a class of phenomena. As distinguished from the received logical positivist model of science, the claims of instrumentalism are that (1) theory structure is not essentially deductive from axioms to theorems and (2) general scientific statements are not properly regarded as either true or false or even more or less probable; rather, they are instrumental or useful in reasoning from the circumstances of a phenomenon to the form that the phenomenon takes in those circumstances. In this section, I treat instrumentalism as contrasted with positivism on the nature of theory; later, in Section 1.6.2, I shall contrast instrumentalism to realism on the issue of the cognitive status of theories.

A number of philosophers may be regarded as in the instrumentalist tradition in terms of how they regard the structure and function of scientific theory. In America, Dewey (1938) formulated a general model of science along instrumentalist lines and strongly influenced the approach taken by Kaplan (1964). In England, Wittgenstein (1958), in the abandonment of his earlier positivist approach, was influential in the way a number of philosophers began thinking about science, especially Toulmin (1953, 1961).

As in the case of positivism, I shall adopt a version of the instrumentalist model that leans in the direction of recognition of the significance of mathematics for theoretical science. Thus my aim is not to adopt a Wittgensteinian or a pragmatist model of science as a whole but to elucidate how the instrumentalist model, in one of its versions, functions as a more inclusive conception of the structure of theory within which the method of mathematical axiomatics finds its niche as a possibility sometimes in fact used.

The version I have found most effective is presented by Toulmin (1953). Among formal theorists, Willer follows Toulmin's instrumentalist model quite closely both in his methodological writings (Willer, 1984) and in his theorizing (Willer, 1986). As distinguished from his approach, that presented here aims to reconcile the axiomatic and the instrumentalist conceptions of theory structure, in accordance with the general point of view taken by Fararo (1973, 1984a). For this purpose I shall first state Toulmin's model and then show how I adapt it to my purposes.

The model of theory structure we find in Toulmin's account seems to have three levels. The upper level contains the *principles* that define a particular analytical science. For instance, geometric optics is a framework defined by the principle that the phenomena of light are represented in terms of Euclidean geometry and trigonometry. More compactly, the framework-defining principle is that light travels in straight lines. The middle level contains *laws,* which presuppose some mode of formalized representation introduced at the principle level. An example in geometric optics is Snell's law, which describes the form of a regularity in the behavior of light as it passes from one medium to another. The lower level contains *constants,* which presuppose the mathematical formulation of laws. An example in geometric optics is a certain coefficient that appears in the mathematical relationship formulated in Snell's law.

Three points about this conception of theory structure are important to note.

First, the components of the hierarchy are not arrived at by inductive generalization over instances. Principles do not await the cumulation of facts. They are framework-defining statements that establish the way any and all facts within a domain of investigation will be represented.

In Toulmin's terms, the principles introduce an inference technique and a *type of model* (a way of thinking about those phenomena in terms of the inference technique). Laws, too, are not inductive summaries of facts. Rather, they are proposed forms of regularities. Empirical work can discover regularities, but laws are proposals of their explicit forms. To every such formal law, there is an associated statement of scientific experience with it. Also, there is an associated set of empirical findings with respect to the constants appearing in the law. For example, a presentation of optics might note the various pairs of media for which Snell's law is known to provide a good description. It might also note some known departures from the law that are problems for further investigations. Also, for those media that have been investigated empirically with the use of the law, it will report how the constant varied. An important invariance in the case of geometric optics is the fact that for sufficiently pure samples of the same pair of media, the constant in the law remains approximately the same from sample to sample. This is an invariance that could not possibly be discovered without an antecedent law. Scientific handbooks report tables of such discovered invariant behavior of constants in laws for use in basic or applied projects involving the relevant phenomena.

Second, although there is a hierarchy, it is not deductive. It is a hierarchy of meaningful ideas: Constants are meaningful in terms of laws in which they are included, and laws are meaningful in terms of the model-building procedure introduced by the principle.

Third, as implied in the discussion of the first point, another ''axis'' or dimension cross-cuts the levels of the theory; that is, the components of the theoretical structure may be established or may be problematic at a given point in time. Problematic modes of representation, problematic formulations of laws, and problematic assignments of values of constants all are important in defining scientific problems for empirical and theoretical investigation.

### *1.3.3. An integrated model: meaning control hierarchy with embedded optional axiomatics*

As an element of the philosophy of theoretical sociology guiding the work of this book, the instrumentalist depiction of theory structure will be revised somewhat and mathematical axiomatics will be embedded within it as a desirable but not essential feature of a structure of theory. Also, the hierarchy involves control in the cybernetic sense; so it is referred to as a *meaning control hierarchy.*

First, at the uppermost level of a theory structure for sociology I put what

Alexander (1982) calls *presuppositions*. In my usage, this will usually refer to elements of a worldview, although it also includes other philosophical elements of the type being considered here. The recognition of presuppositions as definite elements of a theoretical system is essential. If presuppositions are not made explicit, debates about lower levels of the meaning hierarchy are confused with disagreements as to more general features incorporated into the presuppositional basis.

Second, at the next level down, I place Toulmin's principle level. It is identified by the fact that the statement of principle is *nonhomogeneous:* In subject–predicate terms, the subject is some class of empirical phenomena and the predicate refers to some mode of formal representation. The paradigmatic example is Toulmin's: Light travels in straight lines. In a slightly more general sense, I shall say that this is the *framework* level introduced through what I term a *representation principle,* that is, a nonhomogeneous statement that describes a generalized mapping of an empirical domain into a mode of representation.[6]

Third, within the framework, various families of *theoretical models* may be constructed. A model is constructed to implement and thereby satisfy the defining principle(s) of the framework. Thus a model is always *within* a framework, subordinated to it as a specification of a wider meaning system to some more specific (though perhaps still quite general) domain.[7]

Fourth and last, when significant invariants are discovered in the process of empirically identifying and applying models, we arrive at a lower level presupposing the models constructed within some framework. This is a combination of Toulmin's middle and lower levels of laws and constants, respectively. Both his "laws" and his "constants" are, for me, invariants. I think of these, in their formal aspect, as *within* a theoretical model, but they are not exhaustively characterized by their formal aspects alone.

As a brief example of this four-level theory structure consider the following. Let the presuppositions be based on the worldview that human beings are rational beings whose behavior toward one another must be studied by assuming that they attempt to optimize against intelligent opponents insofar as they can. Let the presuppositions also include the image of good theory as mathematical–axiomatic in form. For the representation principle take the following: A system of interaction of human beings is a game. The predicate *is a game* is precisely a set-theoretical predicate defined when certain intuitive ideas about games were axiomatized by von Neumann and Morgenstern (1947). This representation principle defines the framework level one step down from the presuppositions. Consider as a model a two-person iterated Prisoner's Dilemma game – a specific form of game in the mathematical sense that is played repeatedly by the same set of players. This is at the third level, that of a model constructed within the game-theoretical framework. For the fourth level, consider Axelrod's (1984) discovery that in such repeated plays it seems that tit-for-tat is the best strategy to adopt against all sorts of strategies adopted by the other side (see also Section 3.6.3). It may be still problematic, but in a series of simulation experiments, the invariant element of the optimality of tit-for-tat was observed. The discovered invariance presupposes the model. The model presupposed the framework. The framework is understandable within and constructed because of the ultimate level of presuppositions guiding and giving meaning to the whole enterprise.

This game theory example has illustrated the general way in which the positivist conception of theory structure as hypothetico-deductive fits into the conception of a meaning hierarchy.

> One way in which an analytical science can be defined is to construct a mathematical axiomatic system. The stated general empirical interpretation of the system then functions as the representation principle of a meaning hierarchy.[8]

Within this broader framework for characterizing the structure of theories, axiomatic form is not essential. Short of axiomatics, one can still employ mathematics in formulating theories. Probably most of theoretical physics, historically, has not been explicitly axiomatic, although various reconstructions after the fact are possible. The tendency is to regard axiomatics as a mode of presentation of a theory, an option sometimes taken when it seems useful to do so. Often, the theoretical system of interest has so many proliferating branches of activity and so many approximations in various steps of argument that the axiomatic presentation is foregone in favor of looser structures. Fragments of theory – specific theoretical models – may be axiomatized, others not. In either case, axiomatic or not, the mathematics confers deductive power upon the theory. It is an engine of inference.

Thus any richness of deductive structure is included at the second and third levels. The choice between a hypothetico-deductive image of theory and a meaning hierarchy image need not be made: We embed the former within the latter. When the hypothetico-deductive development instantiates mathematical axiomatics, this is one special case. If the hypothetico-deductive structure is not axiomatic, this is another special case.

What the axiomatic system defines is a *class* of models or a category of abstract mathematical models, such as games. What the model level in the meaning hierarchy involves is the theoretical *construction* or *derivation* of a subclass of such models on the basis of specific assumptions about some class of circumstances within the scope of the framework.

There is an additional complication if we recall that the axis of ''problematic versus established'' cuts across the theory structure. In many instances in science, the representation principle does not establish a nonproblematic mode of formal representation. Mathematical models are in use in such circumstances, but they model this or that process or structure without being instantiations of a *comprehensive theory* (Bunge, 1973) that is *simultaneously both substantive and mathematical.*[9] For such cases, there is still the possibility of work at the framework level in which the aim is to get the generalized approach into formal terms. Such is the situation in the context of the research tradition of general theoretical sociology.

The procedure of this book is to strive toward the statement of representation principles mapping our phenomena, in the fundamental way we understand them, into mathematical terms. In the interest of eventual attainment of explanatory comprehensive theories, all formal work is constrained by the condition that it emerge out of the ideas in the tradition of general theoretical sociology. Since this can only be done for this or that set of ideas within the tradition, the effort must be accompanied by a commitment to a *unification dynamic:* The strands of theorizing are both formalized and unified as a matter of over-time development. Although the gap between the ultimate end and the present state is enormous, we should try to make contributions that narrow it. Thus we have a triple prescriptive emphasis in advancing general theoretical sociology: work on problems emerging within a scientific research tradition, employ formalization in the sense of striving to arrive at effective representation principles, and work in the spirit of unification. Only in Chapter 4 will the unification dynamic prove particularly successful in its outcome. But the recommendation to colleagues is that we all should be committed to the unification dynamic as a high ideal of theoretical science. In this connection, one should note that the emphasis on representation principles in this book is not just pragmatic. It strongly relates to the unification dynamic with its known relationship between beauty and mathematical form (Zee, 1986). In turn, the unification dynamic is essential to the progressive character of scientific research programs, not just *within* a program (Wagner and Berger, 1985) but *between* programs that, in turn, are variant developments of a single comprehensive tradition with highly general and sometimes ill-formed empirical and conceptual problems.

To sum up, as one of the elements of a philosophy of theoretical sociology, a four-level meaning hierarchy image of a scientific theory structure has been proposed:

(I) General presupposition level
(II) Framework level (representation principle)
(III) Theoretical model level
(IV) Invariants level (laws, constants)

How do we link this structure to function? This element of the philosophical model I propose involves a cybernetic element. The meaning hierarchy is associated with a "cybernetic" hierarchy of control involved in framework construction and model building (Fararo, 1973:6). It is a meaning *control* hierarchy. Some problem, which depends on the state of a framework defined by certain representation principles and the knowledge acquired with their use, leads to the building of some theoretical model of the given type. The analytical study of the model aims to study its properties. At some point, this model may be empirically tested by reference to appropriate data, which means data acceptable from the standpoint of the framework and the presuppositions. The comparison of model and data is done within the context of the state of the framework in terms of the significance of any discrepancies or agreements.

Thus, the framework is controlling not only the model building but also the forms of data and the evaluative comparison of the two. But although this creates an interpenetration of the theoretical and the empirical in the specification of data, it does not imply that testing ideas is simply some positivistic myth. It is true that a disagreement between model and data does not imply that we *must* abandon the particular model, much less the framework. What is important is that the control loop passes over into *feedback* to the more conceptual and principled components of the models and the framework from the more empirical components involved in the comparison process. The seemingly one-way control, from the relatively nonempirical toward the empirical, is coupled with a reverse control, provided that the relevant community of investigators treats the theoretical apparatus as a scientific system.

A final question about this four-level meaning control hierarchy is suggested by the situation in general theoretical sociology. If multiple theoretical structures exist, each crowned by its own presuppositions that control its lower levels of development, how can their unification be possible? An example from physics suggests that the meaning components at lower levels may be disengaged from the presuppositions that give rise to them. Namely, in present-day formulations of theoretical ideas that unify relativity and quantum theory, the Einsteinian presupposition that "God does not play dice," which governed his mode of representation in developing relativity theory, is simply ignored. The fundamental indeterminism of quantum mechanics overrides the Einsteinian deterministic presupposition. Similarly, when Homans (1974) adopted the principle of success from Skinner's work on reinforcement, he did not in the least concern himself with Skinner's paradoxical antitheory presupposition. Instead, the fundamental presupposition that theory consists in a hypothetico-deductive structure overrode the Skinnerian presupposition that governed the latter's search for invariants in animal and human behavior. As a final example, consider Blau's (1977) macrostructural theory with its repudiation of values, norms, and other cultural elements. From the standpoint adopted in this book, we can formalize what is valuable in Blau's achievement (as in Chapter 4) without in the least believing that the structuralist presuppositions that led to these theoretical results require us to refrain from later attempting to unify the theory with, for instance, a theory structure based on the principle of dynamic normative control stated in Chapter 3. The upshot of these considerations is that while the theory structure functions as a meaning control system, if we adopt the spirit of unification, we can override high level presuppositions that were helpful for the particular line of theory development but might impede the integration of theoretical systems. This, at least, is one of the high-level presuppositions of the approach to general theoretical sociology taken in this book.

Thus far, this section (1.3) has been an extended discussion of answers to the query: What form should theory take? The *positivist* answer was an empirically falsifiable interpretation of a mathematical axiomatic system. The *instrumentalist* answer was a meaning hierarchy based on a mode of representation. The *integrated model* that constitutes the answer for this book and my approach to general theoretical sociology is essentially instrumentalist, with an embedded positivist option as a desirable but not essential component of theorizing.

*An example: balance theory and the* ABX *model.* My aim here is to provide a sociological illustration of the integrated model of the structure of theory. In particular, I discuss an illustration that includes the axiomatic element within the context of a broader meaning control hierarchy. For the purposes of this brief illustration, both the substance and the mathematics are dealt with in cursory terms.

The illustrative theory structure is in the structuralist subtradition of general theoretical sociology, namely, the balance theoretical approach initiated by Heider (1946, 1958). Within this framework, of particular interest here is the balance model of interpersonal relations (Newcomb, 1953). Balance means a structure of sentiments that is free from any source of tensions. It is this key idea that was formalized in the context of a category of abstract mathematical models. (The reader might want to look ahead to Figures 1.1 and 1.2 to see examples to be discussed.)

The presuppositions of balance theory are twofold. On the one hand, the formal elements were introduced by investigators who assumed that putting theories into mathematical axiomatic form was very important for the advance of the sciences of human behavior. Their worldview was not in any narrow or nineteenth-century sense "positivistic," however. Rather, and this is the second presupposition, in the sense to be used in this illustration, the balance framework presupposes the significance of commonsense constructs. For example, Heider (1958:5) assumes that we "must deal with common-sense psychology regardless of whether its assumptions and principles prove valid under scientific scrutiny. If a person believes that the lines in his palm foretell his future, this belief must be taken into account in explaining certain of his expectations and actions."

The fundamental idea of the theory is that cognitive and social structures exhibit tendencies to balance. In the original work of Heider, this idea is spelled out with numerous examples in terms of a conceptual scheme focused on balance as a kind of psychological equilibrium state. Later, through the formal work of Cartwright and Harary (1956), the balance idea was abstracted from this discourse and treated in terms of mathematical axiomatics.

For later reference in this book as well as present reference, the following is an axiomatization within set theory. There are three primitive notions: a finite set *S* of elements and two relations, denoted *P* and *N*, defined on *S*. The single axiom required is:

*Axiom 1*. *N* and *P* are disjoint.

The structure (*S*, *P*, *N*) satisfying this axiom is an abstract mathematical model. Certain geometric terms are now used in a purely nominal way along with helpful diagrams. The elements in *S* are called *points* (or, sometimes, nodes). The particular instances of relations are called *lines* (or ties, links, connections, etc.). A configuration of points joined by lines is usually called a *graph*.[10] For this present case, there are two types of lines or ties: *P* and *N*. They may be called the *positive* and the *negative* lines, respectively, and these are called the *signs* of the lines. The axiom represents the disjointness of positivity and negativity. (Ambivalent relations are not considered in framing this particular model.)

Given this terminology, (*S*, *P*, *N*) is called a *signed graph*.

As we expect with the axiomatic approach, the next step involves deductive elaboration through definition and demonstration of theorems. It is through the definitions that the balance idea is formalized. For present purposes, let us suppose that *path* has been formally defined as a sequence of distinct lines. Then a cycle is a closed path, so that the initial point of the first line in the path is identical with the final point in the last line of the path. We define the *sign of a cycle* as the product of the signs of the component lines in it. Now we are ready for the definition, which was the first objective of the formalization.

*Definition*. A signed graph (*S*, *P*, *N*) is said to be *balanced* if and only if all its cycles are positive.

Given more rigorous versions of all these definitions, Cartwright and Harary (1956) go on to prove an important theorem:

> *The structure theorem.* A signed graph is balanced if and only if its points can be separated into two mutually exclusive subsets such that each positive line joins two points of the same subset and each negative line joins points from different subsets.

Thus, as brief as it is, this sketch has illustrated all four components of a mathematical axiomatic system. To review, the primitive basis consists of primitive terms ($S$, $P$, $N$) and an axiom that makes ($S$, $P$, $N$) a signed graph; the deductive elaboration consists of the definition (of balance) and the important structure theorem. The next step involves empirical interpretation.

Consider a first interpretation in terms of interpersonal sentiment relations. The elements or points are persons. A positive line means that a positive ($P$) sentiment such as liking exists. A negative line means that a negative ($N$) sentiment such as disliking exists. The absence of a line means neither a positive nor a negative sentiment exists. Balance means that the configuration of interpersonal sentiments contains no source of tensions that might lead to change even without external disturbance. It is an equilibrium condition. From the point of view of this intended interpretation, the definition of balance leads, via the structure theorem, to a definite prediction about the equilibrium structure of interpersonal sentiments, a prediction that could be wrong. In fact, it is almost certainly not the case that every such equilibrium implies that the group can be separated in the manner indicated. As Davis (1967) argues, the empirical regularity seems to involve an arbitrary number of clusters in which positive lines appear only within clusters, negative lines only between clusters. Even this is an idealization, but a more fitting one. Thus, Davis went on to generalize the theory by altering definitions. (I take up this topic again in Chapter 4.)

Now let us consider a somewhat different interpretation that is required if we are to work with the Heider–Newcomb contributions. Newcomb (1953) worked with ideas drawn from Heider (1946). Like Heider, he presupposes that the subjective point of view matters and, in particular, that commonsense beliefs are important to explaining human behavior. In the language developed by Heider, this subjective point of view is called the "$p$-centric" standpoint, where $p$ is some person. But from this viewpoint the sentiments of others appear not as they *actually* are but as they are *believed* to exist. It is readily seen that we can use the graph representation for $p$-centric analysis merely by keeping track of the actual-versus-believed distinction. This can be done by using solid lines for actual relations and dotted lines for "perceived" relations.

Newcomb considered the problem of treating a collective system from this subjective point of view. The simplest case involves two persons, $A$ and $B$, and a common object of orientation $X$. An important instance is the case in which

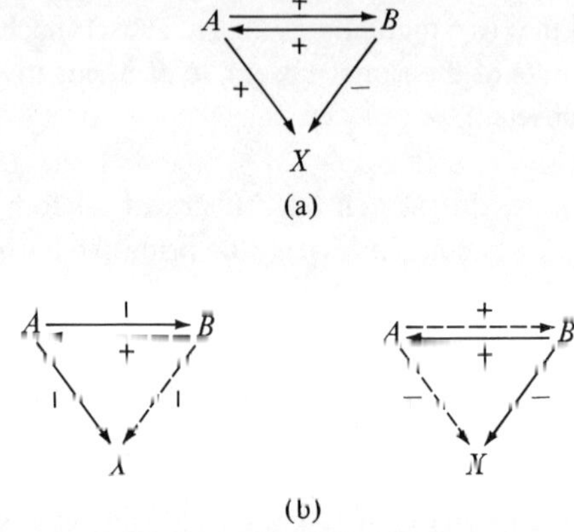


Figure 1.1. Example for *ABX* model

*X* is a normative idea. Common positive sentiments toward *X* by *A* and *B* make *X* a norm for them. Then there are three graphs for any one situation. (See Figure 1.1.)

One graph represents the interpersonal structure of sentiments (Figure 1.1a). In keeping with the usual way one thinks of "actual states of social affairs," these are the sentiments actually felt. The other two graphs are *p*-centric. Dotted lines now represent the beliefs about the sentiments of others, which are not one's own actual sentiments nor the other's actual sentiments. The graph on the left in Figure 1.1b is *A*-centric: The sentiment of *A* toward *B* is actual; the sentiment of *B* toward *A* is perceived. Similarly, the other graph is *B*-centric.

We see that the collective system is not balanced but each *p*-centric structure is balanced. Newcomb's model says that when people communicate about relevant and important items, say, *X*, the sentiments about *X* become overtly expressed. This leads to more veridical perceptions. These changes may imbalance a *p*-centric structure that was balanced through a misperception. In turn, the imbalanced structure may change to a balanced one through a change in an interpersonal sentiment.

Thus, through the communication process, we expect change. In equilibrium, either the balanced graphs will show *A* and *B* in mutual positive linkage with agreement about *X* *or* there will be disagreement about *X* and mutual negative linkage between *A* and *B*. *Both* of these two structures are balanced, as shown in Figure 1.2. (For the moment, attend only to the "stable equilibria" part of the figure, the remainder of which will be discussed below.)

The reader will note that the various inferences made in this discussion of the *ABX* model made use of the definition of balance found in the formal axiomatic

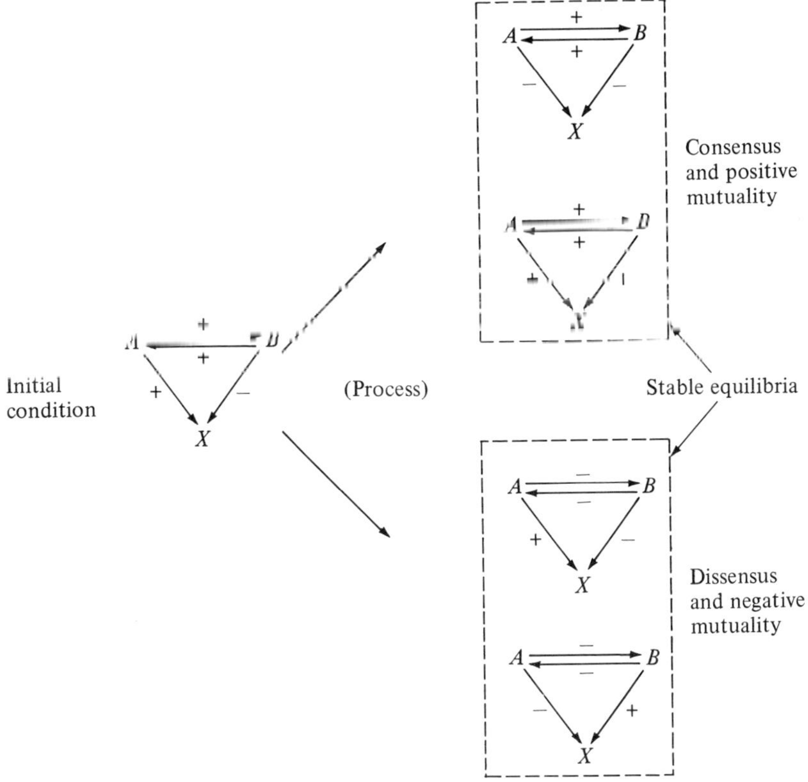


Figure 1.2. Stable equilibria for *ABX* model

theory. The diagrams were drawn and reasoned about by using the formal mode of representation systematized in the axiomatic system. We could say that this version of the *ABX* model was constructed by utilizing the axiomatic system rather than trying to develop further formal definitions and theorems.

To conclude this example, let us sketch (but not with completeness) elements of the theory structure as a meaning control hierarchy:

(I) Presupposition level: Models should be constructed from the subjective point of view of the actor. Such models, where possible, should be based on formalization of intuitive theoretical ideas.

(II) Framework level involving a representation principle: Cognitive and social structures are mapped into signed graphs, and balance is a property definable with respect to such graphs. This leads, in the deductive elaboration, to the important structure theorem.

(III) Theoretical model level: Newcomb's *ABX* model. The model is given in mathematical form, which instantiates the use of signed graphs, the formal concept of balance, and the structure theorem for a particular class of cases.

(IV) Invariants level. A lawlike statement is: In equilibrium, consensus goes with mutual liking and dissensus with mutual disliking.[11]

### *1.3.4. Comments on discussions of theory structure in sociology*

I mentioned earlier that among sociologists Willer (1984) is closest to Toulmin in his approach to theory structure. Alexander (1982) draws upon Toulmin for his image of a "scientific continuum." However, in contrast to Willer, he omits any treatment of formalism, the technique of inference that is the core of Toulmin's account of why and how theoretical physics *works*. It is interesting to note a parallel to an earlier generation. Zetterberg (1966) described and recommended the positivist model of theory structure *minus* the mathematical element (which would then reappear only at the level of operations on data). Alexander describes and recommends the instrumentalist model of theory structure *minus* the mathematical element (which then presumably reappears at the other end of his continuum featuring data).

The lesson is that theoretical sociologists should stop trying to rule formalism out of the game and admit that, whatever their particular substantive inclinations, their theoretical methods would be *more effective* if they adopted operative ideals of science recognizing the enormous significance of mathematical ideas in theoretical formulations. This does not mean that *only* formalized theories count or matter. But surely, we cannot go forward if sociologists begin with the unhelpful presupposition that mathematics is a useful tool for data analysis *and that is all.*[12]

The discussion in this section has concentrated on the elements of theory structure. I have tried to show that by drawing upon two philosophical models of theory structure, we arrive at an integral model of the form of theory. In turn, this philosophical model functions as one element in the philosophy of theoretical sociology that provides the operative ideals for the remainder of this work. But additional elements are involved. Theory is not only a structure. I have indicated briefly how, through a control loop, it is made to function in science to solve various problems. Some of these problems concern explanation. The next section treats philosophical models of this function of theory.

## 1.4. Theoretical explanation

A single structure of theory may be deployed in an unlimited number of explanatory contexts, depending on the empirical problem. In each case we can ask,

What form should explanation take? As in the case of the form of theory, there are two families of philosophical models of scientific explanation that are relevant to theoretical sociology. In the logical positivist philosophical tradition, the claim is made that a necessary condition for the explanation of an event or a law is a deduction of the event statement or the law statement from premises that include some more general principles or laws. This conception is usually called the *covering law model.* A second important philosophical tradition proposes a different conception of scientific explanation. According to this "realist" tradition, explanation requires what I call *generativity*, to be explicated in this section. In short, positivism proposes covering laws and realism proposes generative rules or mechanisms. In what follows, I outline brief versions of these two philosophical approaches and indicate how they function in the integral model that forms one component of the philosophy of theoretical sociology employed in this book.

### *1.4.1. A positivist model*

According to one influential positivist explication (Hempel, 1965), a theoretical explanation involves (at least) a logical deduction in which the conclusion describes facts or laws to be explained and some of the premises are laws or principles. In the case of the explanation of laws, those in the premises must be more general than those to be explained. Note that the deduction of the fact or law is only necessary, not sufficient.[13]

A standard example from physical science is the explanation of planetary orbits by mathematical deduction from Newton's laws. These same laws function as covering laws for many other such explanations of the form that motion takes in various circumstances. Therefore, in any one explanation, the premises are of two kinds: (1) general principles or laws and (2) statements describing the circumstances to which the general statements are applied. The conclusion is the expected form of the phenomenon under those circumstances according to the principles or laws.

The version of this positivist model of explanation underlying this book emphasizes elements often completely neglected in sociological discussions. These arise as soon as we locate explanatory problems within the context of the theory structure outlined in the previous section. These elements are *representation, idealization* and *approximation.*

These three elements are readily seen in the example of explaining planetary orbits. According to the structure of theory being deployed, a fundamental representation principle is that motion is a change in position in Euclidean three-dimensional space. This is the representation element. This element is involved in the data on planetary orbits and also in the model to explain such orbits. At the data level, the observations are recorded as dated points in the geometric model of physical space. Some sort of observed pattern or regularity in the data prompts the explanatory problem, such as: How is it that the data form what looks like an elliptic orbit around the sun? At the model level for the problem at hand, the sun and the planets are treated as occupying points in space. Of course, they actually occupy extended regions, but they are idealized as point masses in the model. In general, the motion of a body is accounted for by proposing a set of forces that act on it. In the model construction for the problem at hand, as a first approximation, one can neglect all but the inertial force and the gravitational force from the sun. In particular, gravitational attraction between planets is neglected. What is done is to insert these forces into the general form $F = ma$. This leads to the differential equations of motion for the particular circumstances as idealized in setting up this model. The solution of the equations is then derived and compared with the orbital data. The orbital data do not fit an ellipse exactly, so the derived ellipse is only a first approximation. By adding forces due to the other planets, a "perturbed model" is obtained with a solution that agrees with the data with better accuracy.

The solution of empirical problems was described in Section 1.2 as the key activity of research traditions. The problems and the frameworks employed in a tradition are interdependent elements of an advancing nexus of scientific activity. In general, an explanatory empirical problem arises in the context of some state of a framework defined or instituted by representation principles. Both the observation and the explanation of the phenomenon or regularity to be explained arise within this framework. A conceptual scheme constructed within the framework defines a space of possible states of the world in the relevant aspects. When the scheme is applied operationally to the phenomena, we have relevant data as a collection of points in the space. When the conceptual scheme is applied theoretically to the phenomena, so that mechanisms or principles are stated and inferences drawn, we have a relevant theoretical model. The model is some definite idealized object with properties to be derived by formal analysis. These properties are compared with corresponding properties of the data. To the extent that there is agreement, the theoretical model may be said to account for the data.

Let us summarize this version of the positivist model of explanation:

> Let $R$ be some statement describing a regularity in a body of data arising within a given framework. Then an explanation of $R$ is given by theoretical analysis leading to a model within this framework such that the relevant

formally derived properties of the model agree well with the data that prompted statement R.

Let us reconsider the balance-theoretical example of the prior section. The regularity *R* takes the form consensus goes with liking and dissensus with disliking. Thinking in terms of the balance-theoretical framework, we envision data in the form of measured attitudes about items *X* of interest to both persons *A* and *B* and also sociometric data as to their sentiments toward each other. It is some body of data of this sort that prompts the regularity statement and the corresponding explanatory problem. We can conceive of a Newcomb type explanatory model constructed within the framework of structural balance theory, that is, using signed graphs and the corresponding exact concept of balance along with the structure theorem. Here we have the representational element in the explanation. The idealization and approximation elements also are clearly present. We treat *A* and *B* and *X* as conceptually isolated from the rest of the universe. In particular, other items and other people are not in the model. Also, in using qualitative signed lines, we are giving a first approximation to a prospectively later model that would quantify the sentiments and attitudes. Nevertheless, we do obtain the conception of an equilibrium of the collective system that has the balance property. The diagrams can be read as directly embodying the statement of the regularity *R* interpreted in a purely qualitative form as a first approximation.

### *1.4.2. A realist model*

Realist models of theorizing begin with an ontological assumption. The ''phenomena'' to be accounted for are the overt manifestations of some real structure constitutive of some actuality. This structure functions as a generative mechanism that produces the phenomena whenever it is triggered into action. Laws or regularities are a consequence of the structure and the pattern of arrival of triggering events. Thus, in a stable environment, the structure may produce phenomena of simple regular form. With irregular inputs, the resulting phenomena may be equally irregular. Yet the structure across the various environments is what accounts for the phenomena.

The realist model of explanation is nicely illustrated in the work of biologist Barbara McClintock, who won a Nobel Prize for her explanation of why maize did not seem to follow the predicted patterns of genetics. The problem was one of figuring out the mechanism that controls the color of maize kernels. The latter is the observable output of the system or structure being investigated. The structure proposed by her model contains various types of genes that control the color.

The model specifies several types, such as activator, dissociator, and structural genes. A process is specified in which impinging events on the activator "turn on" the dissociator, which interrupts the basic activity of the structural gene, thereby suppressing the coloring process. The result is that the kernels are sometimes entirely uncolored, sometimes colored, and sometimes speckled, depending on the sequence of events involving these genetic program elements.[14]

There are various wings of the realist tradition in the philosophy of science. For the present (but see Section 1.6.1) I draw attention to a wing led by the influential British philosopher Harré (1970) (see, also, Harré and Secord, 1973). His position is that models, as understood in terms of a realist ontology, are the key elements of scientific theory. Such models relate closely to analogies since what one does is to conjecture the form of the unknown structure in terms of the properties of a known structure. So each model has a source, from which it is drawn, and a subject, to which it is hypothetically applied. For instance, Harré and Secord (1973) treat Goffman's (1959) dramaturgical model. The constitutive structure of everyday interaction is comprised of rules and roles. To model this structure, the source is the theater and the subject is situated interaction, to which theatrical elements and relations are hypothetically applied. In keeping with Harré's antiformalism, the dramaturgical model is not a model associated with a formalism.

But it is possible to combine generativity based on analogy with the element of formalism.

As an example, consider the cognitive theory proposed by Newell and Simon (1972), which I call upon in a sociological context later in this book. The general class of phenomena that Newell and Simon wish to account for are the cognitive performances of people, especially cognitive problem solving. Clearly they are trying to understand a realist-type structure: the mind. The mind is viewed as a system of processes operating on symbols. But this is what computer software does with respect to input data. A program has a very distinctive ontological character: As a static structure it embodies a potentiality for certain symbol manipulation processes. That is, when it is triggered from a latent to an active state, symbol processing occurs. But the latter is just what mind is, and yet mind must also consist of stable structures with just such potentialities. The concepts of structure, process, and symbols are mutually implied in computer programs. Hence the idea arises of hypothetically applying the structure of computer programming and computation to the mind. This is called the *computational model of mind*. The source of the analogy lies in computer science, whereas the subject is the human mind. To explain cognitive phenomena, one must write down representations of mind in terms of appropriate programs.

Some writers regard Marx as the classic sociologist closest to the realist view

(Benton, 1977; Keat and Urry, 1982; Wilson, 1983). Durkheim, however, is another candidate. The discussion that follows will be drawn upon at a number of points in this book; so it is given in some detail.

Consider the following programmatic interpretation of Durkheim (1915) in which one places the ideas within a generative model-building framework. As interpreted by Parsons (1937) and more recently by Collins (1975, 1985), Durkheim had shown in his earlier work that a stable social system was impossible on the premise that all actors behave rationally in the sense presupposed in economic theory. The problem now was: So what is the nonrational foundation of social life? Some real process is generating or constituting social groups, creating solidary relations under some conditions. What process? Under which conditions?

Durkheim addresses this problem in a realist mode. He models the nonrational structure of society by analogy with a familiar structure, religion. Every religion defines its category of sacred things and its corresponding proper modes of behavior toward such things, that is, ritual behavior. Also, each religion has its set of symbols that express and revivify the special attitudes of respect toward the sacred things. In fact, the symbols become sacred too. To construct a "religious model" of a class of social phenomena, identify the sacred objects and symbols and the corresponding rituals. When you do this, you should also find the source of solidarity. Namely, the ritual occasions create and reinforce a special state of feelings that constitutes the complex of sentiments or values unifying the members. Later, Warner (1959) showed how one could apply these ideas to interpret the symbolic life of modern communities. The sentiment is focused about the "constitutive symbolism" (Parsons, 1977). This will yield the stability presumed impossible in a purely rational action system. Goffman (1967) applied this model to analyze interaction as ritual, and Collins (1981) used the model to treat chains of ritual interactions.

This religious model is one aspect of Durkheim that we are only now beginning to appreciate as his work is disengaged from the evolutionist framework in which it has often been embedded. The new focus is on Durkheim as a theorist of interaction who stresses the role of *sentiments* and *activity expressive of them* in the formation and maintenance of groups. This is still a focus on the integration dimension always associated with Durkheim but more clearly elaborated in the work of Collins (1981, 1988) than we found it developed by Parsons (1937, 1951). I call it *Durkheimian depth sociology*.[15] Throughout this book, I discuss its importance in general theoretical sociology. I especially want to show that the work of Homans (1950) embeds it within a systems framework also attuned to Marxian "materialist" elements.

Although I agree with Harré's restoration of the importance of analogy in theoretical science, I must deny that analogy is always necessary. My version of the realist model emphasizes *generativity* as the key idea rather than analogy. In particular, structural generativity means that a model of a structure has been constructed such that instances of the phenomenon to be accounted for are derived from mechanisms or rules.

In the context of present-day empirical research, a great deal of stress is placed on the specification of variables and "explaining" variation in one variable by appeal to variations in a battery of other variables. This conception of explanation is based on a legitimate *aspect* of the dynamic or process-oriented frame of reference of general theoretical sociology. Namely, as we shall see in the next chapter, as the generative mechanism produces changes of state, it does so under parametric conditions. Variations in parametric conditions, either dynamically or comparatively, thereby produce variations in states *via* the generative mechanism. What is omitted in the usual accounts of "causal models" based on "explaining variation" is the explicit formal representation of process. Here we have a clear case of the way in which a process worldview implemented through a realist model of explanation reaches into the details of research to affect the operative ideals guiding empirical work. (This discussion is amplified in Section 2.10.2.)

*Mechanism* and *rule* define two pure types of generativity (Fararo, 1987b). A *hybrid mode* also can be defined.

1. A generative mechanism implies a *dynamical system,* to be discussed in Chapter 2. In this case, the model recursively generates the over-time development of the state of the system. If a distinction is made among state, input, and output, then both the transition of the state and the output depend on the state and the input.[16]

2. A generative rule system implies operations on symbol structures. It is illustrated by modern formal linguistics with its *generative–transformational grammars*. In these models, certain rules for the formation and transformation of expressions are stated. They are then recursively applied to derive, one says *generate,* all (and only) expressions in an infinite class of expressions constituting a language, formal or natural. As distinct from the generative mechanism type, in this type of model the recursion from expression $E$ to expression $E'$ is not intended to refer to an event in time. It is not that $E'$ temporally follows $E$; it is more like a mathematical expression following from another such expression.

3. The hybrid type of generativity is illustrated in the computational model of mind. This type originates in the twentieth-century breakthrough in computer programming: A program operates on symbols in real time. Hence its operation is akin to a dynamical system in which the system is described in terms of struc-

tures of symbols, which are tacit or conscious knowledge states. In Chapter 3, this hybrid generativity is explored in the context of aspects of human action systems treated in the subtraditions of symbolic interactionism, ethnomethodology, reality construction theory, and structuration theory.

Let us return to the balance example with this realist model of explanation. We assume, as in the case of the positivist covering law model, that we want to explain the regularity that liking tends to go with consensus and disliking with dissensus. In implementing generativity, we employ the process version, seeking a process model that will recursively generate the system states until we arrive at the equilibrium. Now the reader may look again at Figure 1.2 with attention to the initial condition and the "process" link between it and the stable equilibrium structures. What does generativity imply? This realist element adds the following operative ideal to the structural discussion of the prior section: To *explain* why consensus goes with liking and dissensus with disliking, construct a *generating process*[17] as a formal model whose stable equilibrium solutions are those shown in the figure. The key point is that the previous derivation, employing the representation principle that equilibrium structures are balanced, is not as satisfactory an explanation as a derivation that displays such an equilibrium as a special case of a process, showing how it is arrived at.

Thus, compared with the positivist account, the realist account of explanation focuses on generativity. In the form of generative mechanisms, including the hybrid type that operates on symbol or knowledge states, it supplies an operative ideal that calls for definite process models with structural regularities as properties of derived equilibria of such models.

### 1.4.3. An integrated model

The two preceding sections stated, respectively, a positivist and a realist model of theoretical explanation. Combining these two philosophical models yields an upgrading of the standards of our theorizing by demanding more in the way of explanation than is called for by nonprocess orientations. What is the combined model? Essentially it is defined by appending generativity to the positivist statement made earlier. So in the following combined account, statement 1 reflects a positivist understanding of explanation, whereas statement 2 appends a realist conception of it:

1. Let $R$ be some statement describing a regularity in a body of data arising within a given framework. Then an explanation of $R$ is given by theoretical analysis leading to a model within this framework such that the relevant property of the model agrees well with the body of data that prompted statement $R$.

2. The model proposes a generative mechanism (including the hybrid type) such that instances of the regularity to be explained can be derived or generated from it.

It must be emphasized that this statement functions as an operative ideal in the work to follow. One tries to implement it. Also, one checks actual work against this criterion and engages in self-criticism on its basis. Representation principles and models, comprising the core of a structure of theory, may be elegant in some axiomatic sense and yet lack generativity. Conversely, this or that generative model may be constructed without a coherent structure of theory. The problem is to combine these two elements in theoretical practice. In Chapter 4, for instance, the explanatory force of one strand of the work is less than it might be because the approach taken does not feature a generative mechanism. This is not a permanent defect of the structuralism under discussion but a tendency in need of correction from the standpoint of statement 2. A step in this direction is the development of the procedure termed *E*-state structuralism, described toward the end of Chapter 4. In this way, philosophical models function as operative cognitive ideals that guide us in our choice of theory formulations.

To conclude this discussion of integrated models of theory structure and of explanation, another important point requires some discussion. It can be illustrated in reference to the *ABX* model. Recall that it was assumed that the item *X*, such as a normative idea, is jointly relevant and important to *A* and *B*. This implies that possibly with sufficiently low levels of such parametric conditions, the equilibria described by use of the balance principle might not hold. Under some conditions, an equilibrium may not be possible. Under other conditions, an equilibrium may be possible but take another form. Depending on the particular values of the relevance and importance parameters of the process, distinct initial states may give rise to distinct structural outcomes; the dissensus structure might emerge from one class of initial states, and the consensus structure might emerge from another class of initial states. Thus, when a generative theoretical model is constructed, the work of the theorist consists of analytical (and possibly computer-assisted) studies of its properties so as to learn about how variations in outcomes depend on variations in conditions. This is the perspective set out in Chapter 2. We shall see there that another operative ideal is framed: that we should seek to demonstrate various types of theorems about dynamic theoretical models. One such type of theorem is exactly of the sort that answers questions about how the structural outcomes of process depend on the conditions incorporated into a theoretical model.

In setting up such generative theoretical models, a number of methodological rules can be stated that have served to guide the construction or setup of process models expressed in mathematical terms. (See especially Fararo, 1973: Ch. 8.) Four such rules may be stated:

1. Given the constraint of a framework of complex possibilities defined by a representation principle, study the simpler model objects first and then try to generalize the results to more complicated cases.
2. In setting up any particular theoretical model, state simple postulates and derive complex outcomes.
3. Set up the model in the small with implied recursive generativity.
4. Use a state space approach with observables expressed as functions of the state.

The first and second rules are basically self-explanatory. In some but not all contexts of theorizing, the number of persons is a critical element. Then rule 1 might be implemented by studying a three-person model before passing to an $n$-person model. In rule 2, in setting up a particular family of models, the important point is to look for complexity at the level of the derived outcomes, not at the level of the basic mechanisms. The latter should be expressed in relatively simple terms.

Rules 3 and 4 specify how this derived complexity is obtained from premises that describe simple mechanisms. This can be illustrated with a generative mechanism of the type to be explored further in Chapter 4. The mechanism involves the existence and transformation of expectation states or, more abstractly, $E$-states. To indicate the meaning of rules 3 and 4 without getting into the substance at this time, let us employ a simplifying notation for the basic representation of an actor in a situation. Let $E$ be the actor's state. It is assumed to be an unobservable latent state. Let $I$ be some information input to the actor. Let $B$ be the observed behavior of the actor. The recursive generativity of the actor's state ($E$) and behavior ($B$) may be denoted by

$$B = f(E, I)$$
$$E' = g(E, I)$$

The first expression says that the current behavior is a function of the actor's expectation state and information input in a given situation. The second expression says: That same information input, given the situation and the state $E$, transforms the expectation state. This transformation occurs in the small in the sense that the emerging new state is displayed as generated out of the present state and the information input. The recursive character of the process is shown by subscripting with respect to time with zero as the initial time:

$$B_t = f(E_t, I_t)$$
$$= f(g(E_{t-1}, I_{t-1}), I_t)$$
$$= f(g(g(E_{t-2}, I_{t-2}), I_{t-1}), I_t)$$

Continuing the recursion, we eventually obtain

$$B_t = F(E_0, I_0, I_1, \ldots, I_t)$$

This says: The current behavior is a function of the initial expectation state and the complete history of information inputs since the initial time. In turn, what the initial state is doing is summing up the past history of situational information processing. All actors whose past experience leads to the same such state are equivalent so far as the theoretical model is concerned. Thus, we have the form of a state space approach to theorizing (Fararo, 1973: Ch. 8). Recursive state transformations take place "in the small" in the sense of a transition between $t$ and $t+1$, for any $t$; what the final equation shows is the "long-range" consequence and the dependence of the latter on the whole history of inputs.

As described and applied in Chapter 4, what $E$-state structuralism does is take this generic picture of the individual unit in a situation and embed it in a picture of a network of interacting units that are generating or regenerating social structure. To anticipate a discussion initiated in Chapter 2 and continued later in the book, it treats the $E$-state aspect as the methodological individualist element and makes the formal transition to the analytical object of interest: the social system of interaction, with a focus on its structural aspect. The *system* state, as contrasted with the actor's $E$-state, is a pattern of $E$-state relations (represented in a matrix or graph). The initial model implementing this idea treats a triad as the logically simplest model within the scope of the framework, illustrating rule 1.

In implementing these rules, it is to be remembered that in this book the effort is to work from existing subtraditions of general theoretical sociology. Problematic principles of representation loom large in this effort and, as it were, "delay" the passage to effective theoretical model building. This is one large problem of formalization in relation to extant theoretical ideas that, although important, are fuzzy or highly complex in character. These rules have been stated here to help the sociological reader see how distant the work of the following chapters is from what is really desirable in a theoretical science. As in all other such discussions in this chapter, we are stating cognitive ideals that together guide our work. Trade-offs among them are inevitable, with the result that one can never rest content with any given state of the process of theorizing.

## 1.5. The process worldview

In Section 1.2, general theoretical sociology was treated as a comprehensive research tradition. According to Laudan's (1977) model, which I am adapting to sociological theory, every research tradition has a worldview. The discussion of the worldview of general theoretical sociology was postponed in order to be able to relate it to the philosophical models of theory structure and theoretical explanation discussed in the two intervening sections. Two basic relations exist.

First, the worldview fits at the uppermost level of the meaning control system constituting a functional theoretical structure: It shapes the presuppositions of the theoretical frameworks of general theoretical sociology. In particular, it underlies the following fundamental principle of generative structuralism: *The interactive nexus of human organisms generates transformations in both the individual humans as such and the advancing nexus they constitute.*

Second, the worldview both elucidates and positively evaluates the realist conception of explanation as calling for generative mechanisms. At the same time, it is not unfriendly to the idea that a satisfying explanation invokes general principles that are instantiated in the construction of such generative models.

A process worldview is more appropriate to our current knowledge of the world than the two worldviews from which the classical phase of general theoretical sociology emerged. These were idealism and materialism. All attempts to fit the breakthroughs made by the classical theorists into one or another of these two philosophical molds fail. Their work, in its worldview aspect, rises above these received worldviews and articulates a more or less self-conscious process viewpoint.

The process worldview finds elements of truth in both antecedent worldviews but subordinates each to a more complete account of the nature of things and of the nature of human beings and societies. Within the classic tradition, it was spelled out more or less explicitly by Simmel and Mead. In the broader intellectual environment of general theoretical sociology, its most elaborate formulation is found in the works of Alfred North Whitehead (1925, 1927, 1929, 1933).[18]

What is the process world model? It is essentially a conceptual scheme, a set of interrelated highly general concepts, that can be used to characterize the world in general terms from a processual perspective. The process worldview posits that the ultimate actualities are not *enduring* things but activities described ultimately in terms of episodes of process in correlate states of the actual world. The reason for this postulate is that the model is intended to be satisfied in any past or future state of the world. This is required if the world model is to characterize the generativity of the universe in all generality. Thus, the process philosophical model posits that ultimate reality is comprised of units of process. The initial conditions of the process are given by whatever the process has generated in the past. Such process recursively generates the universe as an incomplete and incessantly changing nexus with hierarchical patterns of order contingently maintained amid process. So the point of view is one of *recursive generativity* in which the generic character of process is described in terms of events that implicate multiple actualities in relationship to each other.

The commonsense view that the world consists of things with properties is captured as an outcome of process. "Things with qualities" are emergent perceptions in process and are understood as conditionally stable states of a relational process. In science, this idea carries over into the dynamical systems point of view employed in the next chapter. Roughly speaking, an ordinary thing or object is a structurally stable state of a certain nexus of processes.[19]

How does the process worldview relate to the traditional world models? Idealism emphasizes perception and creativity. So does the process worldview but with a realist basis. The possibilities for any unit of process depend upon the given order already generated in the evolving world. The first phase of any instance of process is the reception of what has already been generated. Sense perception is one of the emergent outcomes, a high-level synthesis based on the reception of the world by the animal body. Creativity requires some enduring form of order. For instance, the novelty of the next utterance of a speaker is grounded in some embodied set of generative rules given for that speaking occasion. Such a structural feature is one of the emergent patterns of earlier episodes of process.

Materialism emphasizes physical bodies and constraints, especially those of the physico-organic environment. So does the process worldview. Any one actuality plays the role of some sort of object in the process constitutive of another actuality arising in a world including it. So the process worldview recognizes that any biophysical environment, although objectified for human perception as thinglike, is itself a subworld of process, of energetic transformations, of generativity. A rock, a leaf, a door, each is a nexus of actualities with some immanent patterned hierarchical structure that is objectified in human perception in such a way as to transmute the complex pattern of processes into one solid and silent thing. In this sense, human perception is a highly simplified edition of the actual world. It is not wrong, because *that* is what the organism accomplishes in its nexus with these environmental processes. But science, like investigative common experience, corrects the inference that things are only what they seem. The phenomenon, the transmuted thing observed, is a natural objectification of the structured generativity going on in that very same region where the phenomenon is located (except in illusory instances). So the process worldview opts for a realist world picture and for generativity as the way the world works.

The human world is not so different from its natural environment. Both are recursively generated through actual entities in the one universe of which they constitute components. Nor are these "worlds" concretely separate, although they are analytically separable. Thus, just as the real possibilities for a human act depend upon the material body and the entire social and natural environments at that junction of history, so too the real possibilities for social order depend upon the given biophysical conditions. It is true that human social reality involves definitions and institutional typifications (see Section 3.4), but these are aspects of the specific modes by which the human phase of a relational process is constituted. In a process perspective, *reality construction* is what is going on at any and all levels of the universe (Fararo, 1987a).

The relational processes among actualities are described in terms of forms of definiteness. These forms characterize objectified actualities and also the reaction to them in an actual entity. For instance, in the actual world a series of actual entities traces out a curve. The curve is a form of definiteness of the nexus of those actual entities. The curve is devoid of process itself, although it is a form that process takes under certain conditions. Again, in the actual world a series of actual entities takes on the appearance of green in the consciousness arising in another actual entity, some moment in the life history of a certain organism. The color green is a form of definiteness of the nexus of certain actual entities. Green is devoid of process itself, although it is a form that process takes under certain conditions. Again, an angry feeling arises. The feeling is processual and anger is a potentially recurrent subjective form of such emotion.

This very discussion indicates that forms of definiteness can become objects. Mathematics, for instance, includes the study of geometric forms in abstraction from the actualities that comprise their "contents" in certain occasions. Sociology, too, studies interaction forms in abstraction from the actualities that comprise their contents in certain occasions. In this sense, Simmel's fundamental axis of form and contents is one aspect of a process worldview.

In modern terms, one can interpret the ultimate units of process as including a cybernetic aspect. This means that there is some comparison process involving some transduced form of a received element of process. The generativity involves this comparison process and its outcome. In short, the ultimate unit of process is not just input–output: It is input, comparison, and output. The comparison is between the form of the input and the form of some reference signal (Powers, 1973) or "ideal" for that input. In a trivial occasion of empty space, this comparison process fades toward nonrealization, and the process is simply that of reception of a pattern of physical conditions that is then physically transmitted outward. But in a variety of natural processes, the more general cybernetic characterization holds. The reference signal need not be consciously entertained. For instance, when a mouse recognizes something as an item of food, what seems to happen is a rapid computation involving input signals the mouse records as distinctive odors that are neurologically compared with reference signals based on past experiences in its actual world. A ''match'' generates eating behavior.

Process epistemology presupposes the conceptual scheme of this general model and applies it to the characterization of the knowledge situation. Order is the endurance of some recurrent form of definiteness over occurrences. Organisms are instances of such order. In the nexus of an organism and other actualities in its world both are infused with such order, thus giving rise to the relations of observation. The occurrences in the region of the observed generate effects in their surroundings, transmitting elements or patterns to the body of the observer. In the body such elements become perceptions embedded in cybernetic control loops; and in a hierarchical patterning of such cybernetic processes, the higher levels have lower-level results as inputs.

Transmission has a vector character in the sense that information about the directionality of the source activity is preserved as it approaches the bodily boundary; then intrabodily transmutations and transmissions preserve this vector character. The ultimate percipient occurrence is then, in Whitehead's (1929) term, a complex ''prehension'' of the actual world: Recurrent elements such as colors and sounds are presented, and the vector character presents them as ''over there.'' This is a joint outcome of the causal powers of the enduring things in the region over there and the causal powers of the enduring bodily organs of the organism. All these enduring things – the body, its organs, the other things – are instances of structurally stable states of a relational process in the time frame of the faster processes of transmission. For instance, the enduring organism over there was so energetic vocally as to generate disturbances that propagated as waves to the enduring observing organism, which on that occasion generated a synthesis of those incoming waves into a particular presented form.

Such perception is by its nature ''significant'' in the sense of having a sign character Whitehead calls *symbolic reference:* The energetic units of process over there in the enduring things have led to the presentation of a form of definiteness over there for the organism here. The latter hears a sound over there with its ears. What is seen or what is heard or what is felt is a sign of actualities entering into the process of such hearing, seeing, and feeling as components of process. Such signs can be wrong, but natural selection has produced a world of organisms matched to a world of processes in such a way that the perceived is generally an effective sign of the actual.

In its specific Whiteheadian formulation, process philosophy has been influential at the uppermost levels of structures of theory in diverse subtraditions of general theoretical sociology.

1. Mead (1938) studied Whitehead's cosmological and epistemological works closely and seems to have based his conception of organisms and acts in part on such study. Mead's ''I'' and ''me'' distinction was ''in the air'' in speculative philosophy, and one generalized version of it was an important ingredient in Whitehead's process metaphysics. The foundations of social behaviorism in Mead's work take a process worldview as a highly general presupposition. Mead adds to Whitehead's discussion of symbolic reference processes the conditions in the nexus of interacting organisms that convert sign processes into *common symbolization.* Also, he points out how this common symbolization is associated with the rise of the self-concept in the conscious human organism.

In turn, this is in virtually complete agreement with Durkheim (1915), since the latter's depth sociology, as I called it earlier, insists on the social nature of the individual human organism, receiving the gift of language and other components of culture from an enduring social order that makes possible the symbolic communion of otherwise separate biophysical systems. But we must add the process worldview: The enduring social order is a contingent fact generated in the interaction process. In the recent interpretations of Durkheim, for instance by Bellah (1973) and Collins (1985), the older ''social mold'' interpretation (Homans, 1950:317) is replaced by a focus on what Bellah calls ''social creativity.'' The point is that with social creativity the focus shifts to how social interaction *recursively generates* the states of culture and social structure to which Durkheim pointed as aspects of human reality. Thus some sort of interactive generator defined over a network of human organisms with given biophysical properties, with special attention to states of sentiments, is required. This is the point of view in the next chapter.

2. The process worldview is part of the basis of Parsons's (1937) ''analytical realism.'' This is the idea that an analytical conceptual scheme involves elements that, in their interrelations, have values or instances that are realized in concrete actuality but do not exhaust that reality. Parsons cited Whitehead's (1925) fallacy of misplaced concreteness throughout his writings. His devotion to ''interpenetration'' as an interpretive construct also is Whiteheadian. As explained in Chapter 3, interpenetration can be conceived as a multilevel integration concept. Structural integration of a whole of parts is constituted by the overlap of subparts among the parts. In Whitehead's cosmology, the relevant whole is the actual

world with its actual entities as parts. But the actual entities are not discrete: Each is a complex prehension of others so that parts of the others become part of it. For Parsons, the structural integration constituting a social level of action is given through the interpenetration of actor–situation relational parts of the social whole.

3. Something similar to analytical realism, even in the same language of ''elements,'' was proposed by Homans (1950), whose preface cites Whitehead as one of a small number of major influences on him. Both tried to implement a process worldview in their sociological theories, as I discuss later in this book.

4. Systems philosophy (Laszlo, 1972), general systems thinking (Buckley, 1968), and such thinking in sociology (Buckley, 1967; Lilienfeld, 1978) all have roots partially in the Whiteheadian process world model. General living systems theory (Miller, 1970) also has roots in Whiteheadian thought.

5. Recent philosophical works have explored affinities between Whitehead and Hegel (Lucas, 1986) and between Whitehead and Marx (Kleinbach, 1982).

6. Schutz (1973) employs ideas from Whitehead when he suggests the significance of pre–scientific thought objects in arriving at a conception of the role of concepts in social reality and in theoretical social science. The Schutzian-inspired work of Garfinkel (1967) can be grounded in the process worldview. The fact that the concrete composition of any one actual entity is a relational–processual connectedness to the entire world of objectified actual entities implies we can never exhaust the descriptive characterization of an actual entity.

We may call this the *generalized indexicality principle,* following the terminology of Garfinkel (1967) and Collins (1975). The intuitive recognition of the principle is what people seem to rely upon in resisting efforts to ''make everything clear.'' The impossibility of doing without ''et cetera'' is an aspect of the principle. The significance of it for general theoretical sociology is discussed in Chapter 3. Also, according to the process worldview, general reality construction by interacting actualities has various levels and modes. Our obligation as social scientists is to understand the level and mode of reality construction in systems of human interaction, including interpretive procedures that maintain ''normal forms'' (as discussed in Chapter 3).

The methodological implications of the process worldview and of this generalized indexicality principle can be related to Parsons's analytical realism just mentioned. Using concepts, we can delineate forms of definiteness of actualities, and in this sense we have ''realism.'' But it is *analytical* rather than *concrete* realism, for the latter is impossible under a process worldview. But analytical realism is not necessarily put into the form of generative mechanisms, and so it only coincides or overlaps with the realist model of explanation if analytical elements are taken to define state variables of a dynamical system.[20] It is this interpretation of analytical action theory that is given in the first part of Chapter 3.

These strands of ideas that are linked to process philosophy relate to the point that this book treats general theoretical sociology as a single research tradition. With a process worldview, general theoretical sociology is seen to be more interconnected than it otherwise might appear. The various subtraditions of general theoretical sociology share component philosophical presuppositions, and to that extent there is one source of generalized conceptual connectedness.

Process philosophy provides general theoretical sociology with a conceptual basis for its ontology and epistemology. When this is done in detail – and I have only sketched the outlines of such a basis (also see Fararo, 1987a, and, for an earlier effort, Fararo, 1976) – we find that Mead, Durkheim, and other classical and contemporary theorists presuppose some basic elements of the world and draw upon them to formulate their ideas. The further discussion of the foundations of sociology on a process worldview basis should be undertaken by philosophically oriented social theorists as part of a great movement in the unification of theories and of subtraditions in general theoretical sociology in the current epoch.

## 1.6. Three issues

Readers may be expected to bring to this book a variety of images of past and present philosophical issues or debates that relate to the various philosophical models drawn upon here. It is time to look at three of these issues in order to make clear how they figure in the presuppositions of the theoretical work reported in this book.

### *1.6.1. The first issue: the natural science model*

One issue has to do with the *natural science model* for social science. In the simplest version of this debate, *positivists* are those who favor a natural science model, and *humanists* are those who do not. In this sense of positivism, I definitely take the natural science route. In an elaborated version of this dichotomy, Habermas (1971) proposes a third alternative in the form of critical theory with its interest in emancipation rather than analytical–empirical knowledge. In this trichotomy, the approach of this book makes no effort of contact with critical theory and hence is "positivistic" in Habermas's sense. According to the view expressed earlier in this chapter, *sociological theory* has three component modes of thought: general theoretical sociology, world-historical sociology, and normative social theory. The problem with Habermas's analysis is that his a priori philosophical arguments have led him to reject what I call general theoretical sociology even while he draws upon it to elucidate a complex combination of world-historical and normative theory.

Another version of the debate exists, however. In this version, positivists are those who propose a *particular model of natural science* that is then carried over to social science. Those who oppose the particular model can still accept a natural science model for social science *after first constructing an alternative model of natural science*. This is exactly the position of the realist philosophers of science.

From the point of view of realism, then, the positivist philosophy of science is based on two key ideas:

1. There is a methodological unity of natural and social science.
2. In natural science, the structure of theory is given by the hypothetico-deductive model, and the pattern of explanation is given by the covering law model.

The conclusion from these two premises is that ''real'' theory in sociology is hypothetico-deductive in structure and that real explanation in sociology must exhibit the covering law format.[21]

Realist philosophy of science is an alternative to the positivist philosophy of science that accepts the first premise but rejects the second. Since the first premise of positivism is accepted, the realist philosophy of science then proposes a new way of thinking about the unity of science.

The core of realism is the claim that models and especially models of generative mechanisms, as emphasized in Section 1.4.2, are central to modern science. But there are various wings of the realist history and philosophy of science. One wing, represented by Harré, stresses the role of analogy and downplays the role of formal mathematical models. A second wing, represented in books such as those edited by Leplin (1984) and Churchland and Hooker (1985), stresses formal mathematical models and does not make much of analogy.[22]

A representative realist in the second wing is Giere, who (writing in Churchland and Hooker, 1985:76) claims that an emerging consensus exists that not linguistic forms but models are central to science. He goes on to point out that even Suppes's advance within positivism in his treatment of models in terms of axioms framed within set theory is too constraining. Here the realist philosophy of science makes contact with the realist history of science (such as Kuhn, 1962; Laudan, 1977), which insists that reconstructed science should closely resemble what scientists actually do. In the history of even the most mathematical of sciences, theoretical physics, one finds very little explicit axiomatics but a veritable avalanche of models. So models are defined objects, combining mathematical concepts, empirical interpretations, idealizations, and approximations. The properties of these objects are derived and compared with those of real objects.

Where does my approach fit into the realist critique of positivism? With respect to the two premises, I accept the realist revision. General theoretical sociology is based on a conception of the unity of science under a revised understanding of natural science. This revised understanding is incorporated into my two integral philosophical models of theory structure and theoretical explanation. Namely, in both contexts, models as definite idealized objects play a critical role. They are the third level down in the meaning control hierarchy constituting a structure of theory, and they function in the explanation of phenomena by representing the generativity through which phenomena are produced.

Deductive hierarchy (positivist element) and models of generative mechanisms (realist element) are both real features in the structure and function of certain theories but are not always found together. To see a beautiful logical structure of theory is one thing. To see a beautiful account of the operation of an inner set of mechanisms that generates the observable phenomenon is another. Theory is involved in each instance, although one may be deficient in generativity and the other deficient in logical or mathematical organization. In certain cases, a theoretical system *combines* both of these properties, and we see a beautiful logical structure that, among other things, permits the construction of models of generative mechanisms. Both elements are features we strive for, without always attaining them, within a structure of theory given by a broader meaning control hierarchy.

### *1.6.2. The second issue: the cognitive status of theories*

Let us turn to the second issue. It concerns the cognitive status of theories in science. Essentially, it amounts to a realist critique of instrumentalism and a rejoinder. From Dewey and Wittgenstein to Toulmin, instrumentalists emphasized that, at their best, theories are maps and that we should not confuse the map with the territory mapped. But, says the realist, a theory *is* something that can be said to be true or in correspondence with the world. The critique of the instrumentalist view is not in regard to theory structure so much as in the interpretation of the successful theory: Just what has been shown? Does the actual world embody real structures corresponding to those in the model? If the answer is positive, then a realist position is taken. If the answer is negative, an instrumentalist[23] position has been adopted. To quote a recent explication of the two sides:

> Realism about theories says they aim at the truth, and sometimes get close to it. Realism about entities says that the objects mentioned in theories should really exist. Anti-realism

about theories says that our theories are not to be believed literally, and are at best useful, applicable and good at predicting. Anti-realism about entities says that the entities postulated by theories are at best useful intellectual fictions. (Hacking, 1983:x)

The same author notes that the realist position is part of a revival of metaphysics in the analysis of science. From this point of view, instrumentalists appear as "feet on the ground" practical types; realists appear as woolly metaphysicians. Instrumentalists ask us to remember that *we* are the authors of the modes of representation we invent to account for phenomena. They properly draw attention, as I have, to the importance of the idealization inherent in models. They warn of reification. Realists fail to see how science makes sense if there is a lack of continuity, in the relevant sense of matter–energy or symbolism, depending on the subject matter, between the "plain things in sight" and the postulated things that are supposed to produce or change them. The fiction view of theoretical entities is regarded as simply incoherent.

Where does my approach fit into this realist critique of instrumentalism? Here the worldview element of the philosophy of general theoretical sociology enters. According to the process worldview presented in the prior section, the epistemology of theoretical sociology is essentially realist. Phenomena are the way in which other actualities are presented to us through symbolic referential processes. These actualities are not random elements until we impose order on them. Indeed, such a view is essentially incoherent inasmuch as every moment of our lives is only possible against a background of layers of order characterizing the universe. Despite all the degrees of freedom in the idealizing and approximating processes involved in model building, ultimately we aim to understand various types of actualities in terms of the type of generativity and order characteristic of them. Because of normative elements, namely, cognitive operative ideals controlling scientific work, theories develop in the direction of conformity with patterns of process and order in the world.

Another argument in favor of realism is couched not in worldview terms but in terms of explanatory ideals. By including a focus on generative mechanisms within the meaning control hierarchy associated with a representational framework, I obtain a philosophical position in which the ultimate aim is one of constructing generative models that have derived properties that fit the phenomena. Because they are generative and because they fit, I am willing to say that they correspond to some real structure internal to the system being modeled. It is true that *regarding* a model structure as corresponding to something real is something additional to its formal structure and to its success in making predictions under given conditions. But it does not follow that we first have the model and later add a gratuitous realist interpretation. For we might never have defined the model if we had not been convinced that there was something there to be modeled.

Realism is an operative ideal in the production of models, not just in the interpretation of them after they exist.

### 1.6.3. The third issue: models

The third and final issue concerns a systematic ambiguity more than an issue. The problem is that the word *model* is used in quite different ways in various contexts. Rather different ideas and scientific practices may be involved. For instance, in sociology today we find the term used to characterize statistical analyses of data using regression equations, loglinear models, and the like. In one sense, such analyses do employ models. But they are not *social* theoretical in character despite the fact that the users have some background social theoretical concerns in mind in constructing the model. They are not direct instantiations of a mode of representation of the social phenomena of interest. Perhaps we can say that they are *statistical* theoretical models applying general statistical theory.

When a model is located quite directly within a meaning control hierarchy constituting a theory structure, ideally and often actually one can *derive* the model. This means that although specific assumptions are introduced in the setup, they are constrained by an overarching set of assumptions about *the entire category of such models*. The entire category refers to the whole domain of investigation taken as the subject matter of the research tradition building the theories. For instance, a certain specific set of equations is derived by applying a general form to a class of cases. Put in terms of a structure of theory, the category corresponds to all the possibilities for representation permitted and enabled by the mode of representation introduced through a representation principle defining a framework.

Among philosophers, Bunge (1973) has formulated what I take to be precisely this position. He also introduces a terminological distinction that is useful. The distinction is between model object and theoretical model. The *model object* is the defined conceptual entity intended to represent something in the world, its intended "referent" in Bunge's terms. A *theoretical model* is such a model object together with those specific assumptions about it that lead to derived testable properties of it. The theory aspect of the theoretical model resides in the possibility of being wrong, of deriving definite conclusions that, interpreted as expected observations, might be false. So one can have a model but not a theoretical model if none of the conditions taken to define the model are treated as open to possible rejection on empirical grounds. And note that for theoretical purposes we are always dealing with a "family" of model objects, and so a theoretical model is really about such a family in relation to the world. In the context of this book, not the empirical testing of models but work at the upper levels of theory structure is the prime contribution. Yet the sense of ultimate feedback control through empirical testing is also part of the tradition of general theoretical sociology, and its relevance is incorporated into the discussion at various points.

I shall sometimes use the term model object to emphasize that a prime task of a theorist is to define the conceptual and idealized entities that will be studied analytically. Such entities, such as a network, become the starting point of theory development, since specific mechanisms are ordinarily proposed relative to them. These specific mechanisms define theoretical models, converting what would be "mere" model objects – representations without empirical import in the sense of falsifiability – into genuine theoretical models. Hence, I will use the term theoretical model when I wish to draw attention to the theoretical element in model building.

Earlier, in Section 1.3, I used Bunge's term "comprehensive theory" to describe our aspiration of developing theories of wide scope that are simultaneously mathematical and substantive. Bunge uses this term to distinguish a "mere" theoretical model from such wide-scope theories that characterize fields such as theoretical physics.[24] As indicated in Section 1.3, the requirement for *initiating* such wide-scope theories within general theoretical sociology is the specification of a representation principle based on extant theory.

This book is based on the presupposition that general theoretical sociology needs formalization and unification, each conceived as ongoing efforts governed by ideals that may fail to be realized. The focus on representation principles means that one does not envision the task of a formal approach as one of translating empirical sentences into formal sentences. It most certainly is not one of contributing another listing of "propositions." Nor is it the ordering of such given propositions into some logical format. Any of these steps would miss entirely the role of the model objects, the conception of generativity, and the meaning hierarchy model of theory structure that are critical philosophical features of generative structuralism.

The three issues discussed in this section do not exhaust those discussed in this book that have a philosophical aspect. At various points, but especially in Section 2.10.2, causation is discussed. Methodological holism and methodological individualism are discussed in Section 2.11 and the latter again in Section 3.6.1. Issues related to social order, including voluntarism and constraint, objectivity and subjectivity, and the like, are discussed in Section 3.2.3. And these are only examples. Although this book does not attempt to lay out such issues and resolve them, an attempt *is* made to theorize in the spirit of unification, and such an enterprise is bound to arouse the suspicion that issues are simply not being faced. By referring to these and other conceptual and methodological problems that theorists legitimately define as topics within our purview, I hope to both work with and advance the tradition of general theoretical sociology.

## 1.7. Summary

This chapter has treated a number of preliminary questions, issues, and metatheoretical concepts that arise in doing general theoretical sociology.

Section 1.2 stated a viewpoint on general theoretical sociology as a single research tradition with a number of communicating subtraditions. In the next chapter, it will be shown that four key problems of general theoretical sociology can be framed within a dynamical systems framework. This framework instantiates, at the level of representation principle, a set of presuppositions that are claimed to constitute a comprehensive worldview of the tradition.

In Section 1.5, the existing worldviews were regarded as one-sided images that do not correspond to the perspective informing the work of the classical theorists, especially Mead, Simmel, and Durkheim. Instead, a process worldview can be sketched that formulates the most general presuppositions of general theoretical sociology as to the nature of reality and our knowledge of it. This process world model is not something new but rather an already existent ingredient in the historical lines of development of numerous subtraditions.

Certain philosophical questions and issues concerning theories and explanations were discussed to show how the approach taken here involves an integral philosophical model that draws upon and unifies elements of positivism, realism, and instrumentalism.

The first such question, posed and answered in Section 1.3, was, What form should theory take? One philosophical model, in the positivistic tradition, says that theory should be an interpreted axiomatic system. Another philosophical model, in the instrumentalist tradition, says that theory is a nondeductive meaning hierarchy. The distance between these two models, once one is committed to the adoption of a formal approach, is not as large as it seems. First, the mathematical axiomatic method involves the idea that the axiom set defines a category of models. The function of the theory is to study classes of such models. Their properties are reported as theorems. Empirical interpretations are supplemented with correspondence rules in the test of particular models. Second, the instrumentalist viewpoint can be implemented with more or less attention to the formal element in theory. When the formal element is properly recognized, then the nondeductive meaning hierarchy has a place for the mathematical axiomatics. The combination of these two models, as employed in this book, always involves some instrumentalist element of meaning hierarchy although not always the element of axiomatic theorizing. The instrumentalist element is also combined with a cybernetic viewpoint: There is a meaning control hierarchy. At the top are the general presuppositions followed in order by representation principles, models, and invariants. Ideally, such structures should exhibit development over time toward constituting comprehensive theories that are simultaneously formal–mathematical and substantive.

The next question, posed and answered in Section 1.4, was, What form should scientific explanation take? Again, two philosophical models were considered. In the positivistic tradition, explanation is explicated with the focus on deduction of certain statements from other and more general statements, employing the idea of covering laws. In the realist tradition, explanation is explicated by reference to models, namely, an explanatory model describes a generative mechanism. Again the distance between these two conceptions is reduced in my versions of these models. The traditional positivist does not give sufficient explicit consideration to the overwhelming importance of idealizing models. But the stress on generative mechanisms by realists is not always accompanied by a stress on formalism. Thus, when models are added to covering laws and formalism to generativity, the basically realist model of this book asserts that theoretical explanation involves formal generative models. To attain such objects, however, is difficult. In practice, as we may generally expect in the human situation, we find our operative ideals and our practice do not always coincide. This gives rise to incessant intellectual challenge and change.

Outlining these considerations, eventually we were led to consider some philosophical issues that relate to the task of general theoretical sociology. These were dealt with in Section 1.6, where three issues were stated and the direction of resolution adopted in the generative structuralist approach of this book was discussed. First, a natural science model for sociology is accepted but with natural science understood under a broader realist and instrumentalist conception than positivists employ. Second, a realist view of the cognitive status of theories was favored, primarily on the basis of worldview. Third, a distinction was drawn among model objects, theoretical models, and comprehensive theories. Comprehensive theories are understood in terms of the fundamental role of representation principles in the advance of theoretical science and constitute the ideal wide-scope formalized theoretical systems toward which our work is directed.

Our next task, initiated in the next chapter, is to consider the subject matter of general theoretical sociology as a whole. What is it about? What sort of model object should be constructed for purposes of theorizing about this domain? Can we state theoretical models so as to study their properties and report the results as theorems? What sorts of theorems? In answer to what problems? And what will comprehensive theory be like in relation to this subject matter? Is there really hope for a mathematically formulated comprehensive theory of our subject matter? On what basis? In addressing such questions, the next and subsequent chapters will employ component ideas staked out in this chapter: the primacy of process, model objects, generativity, theorems, and, as we move to definite problems in the theory of action systems and social structures, more definite theoretical procedures specific to the problems of general theoretical sociology.

# 2. Dynamical social systems and the key problems

## 2.1. Introduction

The main problems of general theoretical sociology are the problems of the emergence, maintenance, comparison, and transformation of social structures. The aim of this chapter is to show how these problems can be conceptually located within a general process-oriented analytical framework in which the system concept is fundamental. The method is that of the formal study of the properties of defined model objects. There may be (and indeed always are) difficulties in the way of implementing the "dynamical system" ideas to be developed, but their vital conceptual role at the center of general theoretical sociology is what this chapter is about. In short the statement that sets the theme for this chapter is the following:

> There are four interconnected fundamental problems of general theoretical sociology. Propositions answering to these problems are, *in principle,* all consequences of generators defining dynamical social systems.

The fundamental model object is called a *behavior manifold* defined over a complex network. It is a combination of the possibilities for process in a *state space* as controlled by the possibilities for variations of conditions in *parameter space*. The four structure problems are interpreted in terms of the analysis of the implications of theoretical models that specify social mechanisms on a behavior manifold. In brief, the analytical study of such a model proceeds by deductive elaboration to arrive at four types of theorems, each a theoretical answer to one of the four basic structure questions. To develop this framework, the dynamical system concept is linked to a subtradition of general theoretical sociology, namely, that running from Pareto and Durkheim to Homans and Simon. Among other things, the chapter retrieves the significance of the Paretan–Homans wing of systems thinking by showing how it helps us to understand social structures in process terms.

I begin in Section 2.2 with a general discussion of the systems idea in theoretical sociology, which provides a background for the conception of a dynamical system presented abstractly in Section 2.3. In Section 2.4, equilibration is framed within the wider context of dynamical systems, and in Section 2.5 four abstract types of theorems are defined. This will conclude the background and formal preparation for the construction of a general dynamical social system concept, which is begun in Sections 2.6 and 2.7 with discussions of Pareto and of Homans, respectively, the latter in terms of his early work. Then in Section 2.8, a formal concept of a general dynamical social system is set out that fuses the formal preparation and the theoretical discussion of the prior sections. The four abstract types of theorems become the core types of social structure theorems we should seek to derive in the study of theoretical models, as illustrated in Section 2.9. In Section 2.10, two additional topics are treated in terms of the dynamical social systems perspective: first, in Section 2.10.1, nonlinear theoretical analysis and, second, in Section 2.10.2, the concept of Durkheimian social generativity, which interprets Durkheim's social fact explanation account and integrates it with the generative mechanism conception governing the approach to explanation taken in this book. Also, in the latter section, a brief account of functional analysis is given in terms of the present framework. Finally, Section 2.11 undertakes a wide-ranging self-critique of the work of the chapter: It poses a number of methodological and conceptual problems that set the stage for some of the work in the next two chapters. A chapter summary is provided in Section 2.12.

## 2.2. The systems idea in theoretical sociology

Although there may never have been an epoch of sociology in which theoreticians agreed on the significance of the system idea in analyzing social life, there is a contrast between recent theorists and older theorists as to this issue. The notion that the system idea is central to any kind of rigorous analysis of a domain of interest seems to have gained its initial impetus in the works of Pareto via the influence of Henderson in the early 1930s on the then young sociologists Homans and Parsons. (See, for details, Parsons, 1977:Ch. 1, and Homans, 1984.) A correlate philosophical influence existed in the same Harvard environment in the 1930s in the person and writings of Alfred North Whitehead (for a further discussion, see Fararo, 1987a). Thus, the line of entry of the systems idea into theoretical sociology and into prominence during the 1950s is Pareto to Homans and Parsons via Henderson and Whitehead.

Recent and influential theorists not only seem to have abandoned any attempt to use the system idea but also have been highly critical of it, particularly Collins (1975, 1985) and Giddens (1984), although others could be mentioned. These recent theorists very much share the aspiration of developing some sort of general social theory. They simply believe, on the basis of what they regard as a barren path laid out by, in particular, Parsons, that the use of the system idea is simply of historical interest at this point.[1] I do not agree. Although Collins (1985) has done us a great service by distinguishing a second wing of what he calls the "Durkheimian tradition," one that is microsociological and focused on ritual solidarity, this tradition made its way into the systems tradition through the work of Homans (1950). One subsidiary aim of this chapter is to show that Durkheimian "depth sociology" (my name for the ritual solidarity wing Collins describes) corresponds to elements and processes in Homans's "internal system."

My general argument is that thinking in terms of systems and using a battery of concepts and analytical techniques developed in the modern epoch is an important element of theoretical sociology. Obviously, the theoretical frameworks launched under a system banner did not produce comprehensive theories unifying the field as a whole. However, this does not mean that I would join in the chorus of voices that claim that the associated theoretical ideas have no merit or that the entire systems framework should be repudiated. I would not even agree that the concept of function should be unconditionally abandoned, as suggested by Collins and Giddens. Moreover, other theoreticians who are attempting to organize ideas based on the classical theoretical heritage and our knowledge of the empirical social world seem to have little or no knowledge of the conceptual structure of dynamical systems theory. Admittedly, this apparatus cannot be simply "applied" as if it were a statistical algorithm. A mode of thought that failed to become institutionalized in sociology must be called upon. One must learn to think of *possibilities* formulated in terms of spaces and of mechanisms formulated in terms of abstract symbolic expressions. Model objects and idealizations must become second nature. We are a long way from this state in theoretical sociology. But this book aims to nudge colleagues in this direction. This is not to say that there are not also real-world constraints on what we are likely to achieve. As Duncan (1984) points out, social scientists do not have the measurement capabilities of physicists, and this is a genuine obstacle to fruitful theoretical utilization of the system idea. At the same time, however, there are purely qualitative uses that sociologists have not yet fully exploited. (See, e.g., Katzner, 1983.)

The conceptual task of the theoretician is to specify a class of systems in a particular domain in such a way that the problems of analysts of that domain can be treated by reference to this class of systems. In more formal terms, the task of the theoretician is to define appropriate categories of model objects and to specify mechanisms for the theoretical study of models with a view to proposing answers to questions of interest. Most importantly for the development of general theoretical sociology, the task is to work toward a comprehensive theory so that the constructed theoretical models are essentially specific theoretical applications of one set of definitions and assumptions.

The history of the use of the system idea in recent science shows that there are two overlapping ways of approaching systems thinking. In one approach, general systems thinking is the basic orientation. In the other approach, domain-specific systems are defined. The overlap occurs when, for instance, the domain-specific systems theorizing utilizes some mode of general systems thinking. The approach of this chapter will illustrate the latter overlapping category. Hence, I begin with a brief discussion of the modes of general systems thinking.

General systems thinking involves an interest in systems that are defined in ways that transcend or overlap empirical domains of scientific investigation and also an interest in the relationships among systems in distinct domains. Two general systems modes of thought seem to exist. One approach is mathematical and defines systems in terms that transcend empirical content; the focus is on the forms of the relationships that might be exhibited in a variety of types of systems. I term this general set of ideas *mathematical systems theory*. This viewpoint has been stressed by Anatol Rapoport. (See, e.g., Rapoport, 1968.) For example, a certain form of differential equation might describe a general growth process whatever the entities that exhibit the growth. A system of differential equations describes complex interdependencies among variables changing through time and may be interpreted in a variety of different empirical domains. Thus, in these and analogous cases, the general interpretation of the formalism or the category of model objects is given in abstract language so as to permit instantiation to an open-ended class of systems. Perhaps the most important idea in mathematical systems theory is the notion of a *dynamical system*. Many new and interesting developments are occurring in the general study of dynamical systems, especially the study of nonlinear dynamics generative of catastrophes and chaos. (See, for e.g., Hirsch and Smale, 1974; Zeeman, 1977; Abraham and Shaw, 1981; Thompson and Stewart, 1986.) It is intrinsic to the aim of this chapter to show how the elementary ideas of dynamical systems theory and some of the recent nonlinear mathematics have a strong bearing on general theoretical sociology.

The second approach to general systems thinking might be termed *comprehensive systems theory*. This sort of general systems thinking shares with mathematical systems theory the transcendence of particular empirical domains. But its aim is not to abstract from empirical content altogether but, rather, to synthesize diverse bodies of knowledge of systems in various domains, seeking higher generalities of concepts and principles. System taxonomies may be offered with the view that all systems in a given class have some interesting common property not shared with systems in another class.

Boulding (1956) offered an early effort in what became very common in later years, namely, a hierarchy of types of systems. His hierarchy starts with static structures such as crystals, moves ''up'' to ''clockworks'' such as solar systems, then to control mechanisms such as thermostats, then to open systems such as flames and cells, and so forth up to symbolic systems such as logic. Associated with this hierarchy is the idea that each level introduces some new type of phenomenon that can be the subject matter of a new type of scientific theory (e.g., cybernetics as the science of control mechanisms). Thus, the function of the comprehensive systems theory in this case is to conceptualize the hierarchy and to suggest the principles that might be the basis for the new types of theories.

Another and very ambitious effort in comprehensive systems theory is the living system theory of Miller (1978). Miller distinguishes three broad types of systems: concrete, conceptual, and abstracted systems. The components of concrete systems can be located as matter–energy in space–time regions; the parts of conceptual systems are symbols or terms; and the parts of abstracted systems are relationships selected from concrete systems. Living systems are a subset of the concrete systems. They form an inclusion hierarchy in nature: cell, organ, organism, group, organization, society, and supranational system. Cross-level generalizations, generic forms of subsystems (such as information-processing subsystems), and other such components are proposed as ingredients to be found in this hierarchy of living systems.

To summarize, the system concept has two more or less distinct contexts of deployment. One context is concerned with potential model objects, theoretical models, and comprehensive theories employing system ideas in a specified empirical domain. This yields domain-specific theories, such as ecological theory, economic theory, psychological theory, or sociological theory, insofar as these theoretical efforts conceptualize their domains in terms of systems. The second context of deployment of the system idea is general systems theory which, as indicated, has two forms: mathematical systems theory and comprehensive systems theory. Two obvious overlaps are, first, that in domain-specific systems theories, one may deploy mathematical systems thinking and, second, that in comprehensive systems theories, one may draw upon multiple domain-specific systems theories.

There is a sense in which Parsons was a comprehensive systems theorist relative to the wide domain of all living systems that produce conceptual systems. These he called action systems. And as is typical of comprehensive systems theorists, Parsons developed his own hierarchy conceptualization based on the AGIL scheme. In this hierarchy, we find social systems between cultural systems and personality systems. The comprehensive theory of social systems is a conceptual subsystem of action systems theory, which is a conceptual subsystem of living systems theory. Kuhn (1974), working very much within the tradition of general systems theory, tried to more specifically focus on the logic of social systems analysis. Thus, Kuhn and Parsons address approximately the same empirical domain. Further, each approaches it from the standpoint of applying general concepts of the type associated with the new domains discussed by Boulding, especially cybernetics as the science of control mechanisms. Homans (1950) used a different strategy. First, he followed a meaningful scientific strategy by restricting his scope to social systems in which interaction is possible between every pair of members. Second, he took the idea of systems of differential equations, as he saw it used in natural science, and abstracted from it certain procedures of thought. In doing so, he used a "system model" in a very self-conscious and adroit way to discuss group processes. Homans may be thought of as adopting the logic of mathematical systems theory to analyze groups but not as defining models or using formal procedures.

The upshot is that we can locate at least some of the substantial efforts to build social systems theory within a family of frameworks of general systems theory, as follows:

I. General systems theory

Domain: any system

Problems: develop language, concepts, principles, and models for the analysis of systems and attempt to generate cumulative knowledge of systems

Solutions proposed: (1) mathematical systems theory as a framework of interrelated modes of representation that yield models of forms of process that arise in a variety of empirical domains; (2) comprehensive systems theories as proposed frameworks for classifying and interrelating systems of all types whatsoever (e.g., Boulding; part of Miller's framework)

II. General living systems theory

Domain: any living system

Problems: develop language, concepts, principles, and models for the analysis of living systems and attempt to generate cumulative knowledge of such systems

Solutions proposed: hierarchy of living systems, process subsystems, cross-level generalizations (Miller)

III. General action systems theory

Domain: any living system that produces conceptual systems, that is, any action system

Problems: develop language, concepts, principles, and models for analysis of action systems and attempt to generate cumulative knowledge of such systems

Solutions proposed: AGIL framework of action system dimensions (in turn based on living system imperatives) with associated idea of functional differentiation (Parsons)

IV. General social systems theory

Domain: any system comprised of the interactions of two or more action systems

Problems: develop language, concepts, principles, and models for analysis of social systems and attempt to generate cumulative knowledge of such systems

Solutions proposed: (1) application of AGIL scheme to the social system as understood in terms of classical sociological convergence on the structure of social action (Parsons), (2) by a kind of analogy, apply the mode of thought used in mathematical systems thinking to groups conceived as dynamical systems, initially with certain sensible scope restrictions (Homans); (3) apply cybernetics to the conceptualization of the coupling of two or more human (action) systems with resulting focus on communication, transaction, and organization modes of analysis (Kuhn)

There may be a missing level in this listing: the general social systems theory for organisms with or *without* generated conceptual systems. This would involve the social biology frame of reference since studies of wolf packs, chimpanzee groups, and flocks of birds would be instances of the type of system of interest. In these social systems, there is interaction of living systems with some elements of social behavior present but not necessarily with production of and orientation to conceptual systems (although the discovery of these in other species cannot be ruled out a priori). Such social systems may not have much in the way of cultural traditions but may have much in the way of social structure. Miller's general living systems theory would be too general to capture the dynamics at this level, and neither Parsons nor Kuhn, among other social systems theorists, really grapple with the problem of social structural dynamics in groups of socially behaving animals. In fact, we might well wonder whether a good part of theoretical sociology is really about social systems in general and not just human-type social systems, that is, social systems in which orientation to concepts and symbols is so prominent.

My view is that the special focus of general theoretical sociology is the human-type social interaction system level with respect to problems of social structure. But we also ought to try to work more closely with social biologists to help develop the more general theory of social systems.[2] With regard to the more general levels of systems theorizing, my approach is instrumental. Dynamical systems theory – as the substantial contribution of mathematical systems theory – is a powerful set of formal ideas that we ought to learn to use, recognizing limitations but also resolving to try to overcome obstacles by innovative research. Comprehensive systems theory, at the general system level or Miller's near-general level of living systems, provides some sensitizing concepts and interesting ideas, but we should not worry about formally articulating our concepts to these higher levels of generality. We can let the comprehensive systems theorists do that (or we can do it by putting on a distinct role hat, so to speak, as has been done by Buckley, 1967).

Our task in general theoretical sociology is more specific relative to general systems thinking. We are oriented toward the empirical domain of human social systems and, even more specifically, to problems of social structure. Hence, for theoretical sociology the work of Parsons, Homans, Kuhn, and others is more directly relevant. In general, without trying to formalize directly entire received informal frameworks, we ought to try to transform their key ideas onto a formal basis. With the formal basis constructed, we then should attempt to generate theoretical models and, more generally, comprehensive theoretical frameworks that contain the received insights in the guise of equations or other formal but interpretable expressions of the theory. This is not to say that this book will attain that ultimate objective, but it is intended as a contribution in that direction.

The next section will provide a compact sketch of the elementary ideas of dynamical systems analysis as preparation for the later linking of it to general social systems concepts. The remainder of the chapter will focus on the concept of a dynamical social system with reference to both analytical procedures and content interests. It will not be my aim to teach the mathematics. Nevertheless, so far as possible, my aim is to speak to theoretical sociologists in general and not just to mathematical sociologists. The following remarks provide an overview that might be kept in mind in the perusal of the remainder of this chapter.

The main point is to set out a provisional concept of a general dynamical social system, drawing upon the early work of Homans (1950), and to use it to specify four types of sociological theorems it should be our aim to arrive at by theoretical analysis of models. The ideas are implemented by showing how Simon's formalization of Homans's framework, both in its linear and its nonlinear forms, constitutes the construction of a family of theoretical models concerning which we can prove theorems of the indicated types. These types of theorems deal with, respectively, the existence, stability, comparison, and change of social structures. In connection with this last problem, the idea of catastrophes is introduced, and the analysis shows how phenomena of both gradual and relatively abrupt social transformations are generated by the postulated mechanisms. The approach implements the process philosophical worldview by initiating a discussion of social structures from the perspective of a dynamical systems framework. Thus, as employed in this chapter, systems thinking is a mode of representation that facilitates the conceptualization and analysis of the most basic problems of general theoretical sociology. This does not mean that *only* dynamical systems ideas are sufficient. Later chapters will pursue other ideas and modes of representation, partly because of difficulties and problems I point out toward the end of this chapter. If I am successful, however, the reader will see a way to grasp the basic problems of the research tradition of general theoretical sociology as different aspects of one entity, the dynamical social system.

## 2.3. Dynamical systems: abstract sketch

The basic model object to be defined in this section is termed a *behavior manifold*. It presupposes some conception of a collection of units linked in some way so as to form a concrete system. These units and linkages are potentially in distinct *states* over time. This gives rise to a representation of the possible distinct states in terms of variables. For theory, we are interested in a generic set of states and corresponding variables that are utilized to describe the dynamics of any *such* system. Each such variable may be termed a *state variable*. The collection of such variables that are specified may be treated symbolically in terms of vector notation in which one boldface letter stands for a whole list of entities. This composite list of state variables will be termed the *state vector* or, sometimes, the vector variable. Each state variable ranges over a set of possible values. When all the possible ways of assigning a value to each of the variables is considered, we have a *state space,* the set of possible values of the state vector. A value of the state vector may be thought of as defining a point in state space, that point which in Cartesian coordinates has the values of the state variables for its components. The fact that the state variables assume different values through time means that the point is moving in state space either through a discrete set of points or through a continuous tracing out of a curve. Such a ‘‘motion’’ of the state vector is termed a trajectory.

For example, if two positive continuous variables are defined, the state space is the familiar positive quadrant of the $x$–$y$ plane. A point in this quadrant represents a value of the state vector, a possible system state. A curve in this quadrant with a directionality might represent a particular over-time tracing out of the changing state, a specific trajectory.

There are conditions of the configuration of units and their relations to each other or to the environment that either do not vary in time or are not taken to be states of the system of interest. Suppose a condition does not vary in time for a given system as it undergoes a series of changes of state. Nevertheless, the condition might have been different and might well be different at some later time. Also, another concrete system might be treated in terms of the same state vector but under different conditions. In short, we treat a family of systems in terms of the same state variables but regard them as in different conditions. Applying to these conditions the same logic as was applied to system states, we arrive at a number of variables whose values are aspects of the conditions. Each such variable is termed a *parameter*. Then we list all these parameters and denote the list by a boldface letter. This vector variable is termed the *parameter vector*. The set of all possible lists of values that the parameter vector can take is called the *parameter space*. Hence, the parameter space represents the various conditions of the system, either the same concrete system or different concrete systems considered to be in the same category for theoretical purposes. A particular value of the parameter vector defines a point in parameter space. It is important to note that the conditions may shift or change smoothly in the referent concrete system, so that parameter change is not ruled out in the study of dynamics by means of this model object. But at least in the initial study of a family of theoretical models, the parameter vector may be treated as fixed while the vector in state space traces out a trajectory. Then, at another phase in the analysis of the model, the element of parameter change is treated.

For example, if there is one parameter that may take any real number as a value, then a line labeled from minus to plus infinity is the parameter space. If we treat the parameter as fixed as the system changes state over time from some initial condition, then for any parameter value on the line, there is a corresponding motion or trajectory. Moreover, since the system might initially be in different states, for any given value of the parameter, a whole family of possible trajectories exists in state space.

A space is a set of possibilities for a system. Two spaces have been defined: the state space and the parameter space. The two taken together (formally, their Cartesian product) is called the *behavior manifold*. The basic model object of dynamical systems theory is the behavior manifold together with some representation of time in terms of some discrete or continuous space of possible time. For example, if the state variable consists of just one component and the parameter space consists of just one component and each must be positive, then the behavior manifold is the positive quadrant of the $x$–$y$ plane, with $x$ as the parameter and $y$ as the state variable. For each fixed value of $x$, the parameter, a motion of $y$ exists: It can be thought of as a motion on the vertical line above $x$. Hence, at each time, the system is in a certain state (in state space) under given conditions (in parameter space).

A theoretical model, given this model object, consists in some postulated or derived *generator* of changes of state. If the trajectories are considered as simply "given," we have no theoretical model. They must be derived. For theory, we require the generator to be applicable to any possible initial state and any possible set of conditions. Hence, the theoretical model recursively generates the over-time states of the system as a function of the initial state and the parameter. If the behavior manifold is considered to be associated with a discrete time process of change, then the generator will take the form of deriving the state at time $t+1$ from the state at $t$ for any discrete $t$ for any initial state for any value of the parameter. The appropriate mathematical form is a difference equation or system of such equations if the state space is multidimensional. If the behavior manifold is considered to be associated with a continuous-time process of change, then the generator will take the form of expressing the differential rate of change of each state variable in terms of the current state and the parameters. In either case, the deductive elaboration of the model consists in deriving the family of all possible trajectories, one per possible initial state and possible parameter vector.

A comprehensive theory intended to correspond to an entire subject matter domain of investigation from some distinct analytical viewpoint constrains the forms of model objects and theoretical models. By specification of the nature of the systems in the domain, the comprehensive theory yields some canonical forms of state description and constraints on the forms of specific generators. In practice, these constraints function as ''templates'' or abstract forms of process mechanisms that are filled in with more specific forms for the given cases under study.[3]

To illustrate this role of comprehensive theory in a dynamical systems context, consider general market equilibrium theory in economics (Arrow and Hahn, 1971). It specifies that a market is described in terms of quantities of commodities that firms may supply and that households may demand as a function of their prices at any time. This may be thought of as a standardized state description for the basic subject matter domain of the theory, the general competitive market. An excess-demand function is defined, which also depends on the price. The change in price depends on the excess-demand function. A small set of general assumptions about the excess demand is written down, sufficient for the general problem of interest to the theorists, namely, the determination of the equilibrium state at which a price exists that clears the market. This phase of the comprehensive competitive market theory may be thought of as constraining the form of any generator of market dynamics. A specific market theory, a theoretical model, would be defined by adding more specific assumptions to the general theory such that for given market conditions, a trajectory is generated in the state space of quantities of commodities and their prices.

A second illustration, from another domain, will serve to illustrate the setup of a theoretical model by specification of a generator. For this purpose, consider an ecological dynamical system. In particular, consider a pure predator–prey two-species system. Note how idealization enters into the very specification of the system. For theoretical purposes, whatever other interactions the real species have in some real ecological environment are neglected, and we pursue the analysis by considering the system in conceptual isolation. This is done by defining a model object. The basic model object is constructed by specification of the variables associated with the states of the two species and with their predator–prey relation. These states are taken to be their population sizes at any time. Since each population varies dynamically with the other, these states of the two species are intrinsically connected. The state space consists of the positive quadrant of the x–y plane, where $x$ and $y$ are the population of the prey and the population of the predator, respectively. It is shown in the literature (see, e.g., Kemeny and Snell, 1962) that this system can be represented in the form

$$dx/dt = ax - bxy$$
$$dy/dt = cxy - py$$

The reasoning leading to this pair of differential equations constituting the generator of the process is as follows. By idealizing assumption, the prey would grow without limit if there were no predators: If $y = 0$, then $x$ increases without limit in an exponential growth pattern with growth rate per individual given by parameter $a$. The term $xy$ represents the total possible interactions when there are $x$ prey and $y$ predators, and the coefficient $b$ relates to the probability of a kill. Such kills subtract from the growth of the prey, yielding the first equation. They add to the growth of the predators, as indicated by the first term of the second equation. On the other hand, if there were no prey, then the predators would die out: If $x = 0$, then $y$ undergoes exponential decay with parameter $p$.

The various parameters can be taken as time varying, but in this model they are defined as constants. They are nonnegative real numbers. Together, they constitute the four-dimensional parameter representing the possible conditions of the predator–prey system. The various birth and death rates are aspects of conditions in that they "condition" or "control" the dynamics of interdependent population change.

The state description in terms of populations and the use of birth and death rates as parameters is a feature of the comprehensive framework of ecological dynamics. In other words, in this instance, the general character of state description and of the mechanisms of change in population sizes prescribe the form of the model object (the behavior manifold). The specific form, as involving a four-dimensional parameter space, say, is a consequence of the conjunction of this determination of the general character and the particular decisions made in setting up the theoretical model. The same may be said of the generator. Its form is quite specific and is not dictated by any comprehensive theory. On the contrary, a number of other possible forms might have been introduced to define alternative theoretical models. For instance, the rate of growth of the prey in the absence of a predator population might have been represented in the terms of a logistic mechanism in which some carrying capacity (some upper limit to the prey in the given environment) is postulated. What remains invariant in all these possible models is that the logic of determining the change in population by counting births and subtracting deaths is an accounting identity. Thus, this accounting identity is a key feature of the framework level of theoretical ecology.[4]

Some important aspects of this dynamical system may be noted since they are features stressed in the sociological context to follow. First, it is a *coupling* of two differential equations, one for each component of the state of the system. The rate of change of each state variable depends on, among other things, the other state variable. This mutual dependency is the quantitative counterpart to the qualitative statement that the two species are interdependent.

Second, because of the product term, this is a nonlinear dynamical system. To test if a system is linear or nonlinear, check the right-hand side of each equation to see if it is a linear function of the state variables. Thus, the classification of a dynamical system as linear or nonlinear is a matter of the form of the generator and not the form of the generated trajectories.

Third, the notational conventions mentioned earlier may be illustrated here. The boldface convention and the grouping of state variables to define the state vector is indicated by writing $\mathbf{x}=(x, y)$. Similarly, with the convention of boldface notation, the parameter vector is $\mathbf{c}=(a, b, c, p)$. Since all these constants are nonnegative, $\mathbf{c}$ ranges over all possible lists of four nonnegative real numbers, and the set of all such values is the parameter space. When a particular set of numbers in the parameter space is assigned to $\mathbf{c}$, then a particular model in the model family – a particular version of the theoretical model – is specified with a definite implied behavior in state space. This behavior is discovered by applying appropriate mathematical techniques of dynamical systems theory to deduce the properties of the behavior of $\mathbf{x}$ as a function of time. Naturally, this is not done separately for each possible parameter value: It is done at one fell swoop by a general mathematical analysis. (See Kemeny and Snell, 1962.) On the other hand, in nonlinear systems we face the problem that such general solution procedures often are not available. In such cases, there is a separate computational analysis for each of a set of specific values of the vector of parameters. (An example is given in Section 4.8.)

In general, for any behavior manifold, a dynamical system may be represented in the form

$$d\mathbf{x}/dt=\mathbf{f}(\mathbf{x}, \mathbf{c}) \tag{2.3.1}$$

Here $d\mathbf{x}/dt$ is the derivative of $\mathbf{x}$ with respect to time, the time rate of change of the state vector, which stands for the list of time rates of change of each component variable.[5]

In the ecological example, we have the state vector $\mathbf{x}=(x, y)$ and the parameter vector $\mathbf{c}=(a, b, c, p)$. Then $\mathbf{f}(\mathbf{x}, \mathbf{c})$ is given by the pair of functions of the state variables and the parameters, as displayed on the right-hand side of the predator–prey dynamical system. The general form is totally flexible as to which of the state variables and which of the parameters actually influence any particular state variable's rate of change. In the case at hand, note that $\mathbf{f}$ simply refers to two functions. In general, there are as many functions in $\mathbf{f}$ as there are components of the state variable, and each component function is the right-hand side of one of the equations.

Given the general representation (2.3.1), an explication of some concepts of dynamical systems thinking as employed in this book can be undertaken.

1. The expression $\mathbf{f}(\mathbf{x}, \mathbf{c})$ will be said to specify the *generator* of the dynamics in state space by combining two or more mechanisms. For instance, in the ecological model we combined the intrinsic or natural rate of change of a population with the effects of its interactions with the other population.

2. A specified value of the state variable at a time conveniently taken to be time zero is denoted $\mathbf{x}_0$ and called the *initial state* of the system. The *initial condition* of the system is the initial state together with the values of the parameters.

3. Given the generator and the generic initial state $\mathbf{x}_0$, the process is *generated* by equation (2.3.1) in the sense that a solution of the latter is a trajectory of values of the state variable, denoted $\{\mathbf{x}(t)\}$. Since the specific *trajectory* or *behavior of the system* depends on the initial condition, we can write

$$\{\mathbf{x}(t)\}=\mathbf{g}(\mathbf{x}_0, \mathbf{c}) \tag{2.3.2}$$

For example, in the ecological model, provided $\mathbf{c}$ is in a particular subregion of parameter space (discovered by mathematical analysis of the implications of the dynamical system), $\{\mathbf{x}(t)\}$ is a closed curve that depends on the parameter value $\mathbf{c}$ but also on the initial state $\mathbf{x}_0$. Each initial state yields one member of the family of closed curves, corresponding to a particular value of $\mathbf{c}$. Each closed curve represents a pattern of interlocking cycles of the component population sizes $x$ and $y$.

It may not be apparent, but what is involved here is what was called *recursive generativity* in Chapter 1. A discrete-time version of (2.3.1) helps clarify this: Write $\mathbf{x}'=\mathbf{f}(\mathbf{x}, \mathbf{c})$, where $\mathbf{x}'$ is the next state generated from a given state and parameter value.[6] So any initial state $\mathbf{x}_0$ goes into $\mathbf{x}_0'$, which the generator then takes into $\mathbf{x}_0''=\mathbf{f}(\mathbf{x}_0', \mathbf{c})=\mathbf{f}[\mathbf{f}(\mathbf{x}_0, \mathbf{c}), \mathbf{c})]$ and so forth. This also shows clearly how the sequence of values of the state variable, the trajectory, is a function of the initial state and the parameter, as stated in (2.3.2) for the continuous-time case.

4. Consider an initial state such that the generator preserves it. The trajectory

consists merely of the point itself. But this means that the rate of change is zero for each state variable. This defines an *equilibrium state* of the dynamical system as any state of the process for which the generator takes the value zero. Thus, an equilibrium state $\mathbf{x}^E$ is any point in the state space that is a solution to the equation,

$$\mathbf{f}(\mathbf{x}, \mathbf{c}) = \mathbf{0} \tag{2.3.3}$$

If the functions in **f** are linear, ordinarily there cannot be more than one equilibrium solution; for nonlinear dynamical systems, the usual case is a number of distinct equilibrium states obtained as multiple solutions of this equation. Implicitly, such a collection of states, then, depends only on the parameter **c**, and in some cases we can solve (2.3.3) to find the solution set:

$$\{\mathbf{x}^E\} = \mathbf{g}(\mathbf{c}) \tag{2.3.4}$$

As an example, consider the ecological dynamical system. By putting $\mathbf{f}(\mathbf{x}, \mathbf{c}) = \mathbf{0} = (0, 0)$, we obtain as an instance of (2.3.3) the expressions

$$ax - bxy = 0$$
$$cxy - py = 0$$

We can solve this pair of simultaneous algebraic equations for all pairs of values of $x$ and $y$ that make it true. First note that the pair (0, 0) satisfies the pair of equations. Hence, the zero vector is an equilibrium state. If the initial state consists of no prey and no predator, there will never be any other state of the system. Using algebra, we obtain a second solution, the pair $(p/c, a/b)$. Thus there are two equilibrium states of this system:

$$\mathbf{x}^E(1) = \mathbf{0}$$
$$\mathbf{x}^E(2) = (p/c, a/b)$$

This pair of expressions is an example of the general form (2.3.4).

A point worth remembering is that when a theoretical model is under analysis, all statements are with reference to possibility, not actuality. The state space is a set of possibilities for actual state occupancy. The parameter space is a set of possibilities for parametric conditions. The equilibrium states are possible states of no motion, that is, states such that were the actual state at any time an equilibrium state, the system would remain in that state. To say that the system has two equilibrium states is not to say that these two states are ever occupied. They are special categories of possibilities as to the behavior of the system, as depending upon parameters.

A second point to note is that the analyst selects the state description that defines the meaning of equilibria. For instance, if the variables themselves refer to various rates, then the dynamical system is about the change of those rates and equilibria are time-invariant rates. For instance, if a rate of social interaction is a state variable, then in any equilibrium state of the system the rate of social interaction remains invariant under given parametric conditions.

A third point is that since the set of equilibrium states depends on the parameters, if parametric conditions change, so will the equilibrium states. Combining these last two points, the general caution emerges that equilibrium does not mean absence of change in any absolute sense. It is preferable to consider it a state of adjustment of the state variables to each other and to the parametric conditions, as will be illustrated in the next section.

A fourth point about equilibrium states needs to be made. Recall that the conceptual meaning of an equilibrium state of a system is not that the system *will be* found in such a state at any interval or point of time. Rather the general idea is that *if* the system is ever in a particular equilibrium state, *then* it will remain in that state under the given conditions (value of **c**). As was indicated earlier, a mathematical analysis would show that the behavior of the predator–prey model consists of a motion around a closed curve that, furthermore, is around the nonzero equilibrium state. This means that in this case the state of the system would not be expected to ever actually occupy the nonzero equilibrium state. Nevertheless, it plays a fundamental role as a point of reference for analysis, as will be seen in the next few paragraphs and throughout this chapter.[7]

5. Given any particular derived equilibrium state of a dynamical system, we can ask, Is this a stable equilibrium? The answer is given by *stability analysis* of an equilibrium state, which is based upon a study of the properties of the generator. By stability, in this context, one means that if the state of the system is initially near the particular equilibrium state being analytically investigated, then the state will stay near it. Such a state is an *attractor*. The behavior near the attractor may be one of approach to it asymptotically. Also, there might be an orbit around the equilibrium, as in the predator–prey case: There is no asymptotic approach to the equilibrium state but the system does not depart from a neighborhood of it which depends on the initial condition.[8]

There are well-known mathematical techniques for determining the stability of the equilibrium state of a linear dynamical system. In the cases of nonlinear systems exemplified by the product of $x$ and $y$ arising in the mechanism of the ecological system, a method of linear approximation may be useful. (See, e.g., Kemeny and Snell, 1962.) For my present conceptual purposes, it would be too lengthy a digression to go into such details. Suffice to say that the conceptual points I want to emphasize are:

i. We can have an equilibrium state that is unstable, so that starting a small distance from it, the distance becomes larger over time. Such a state is called a *repellor*. Since a dynamical system can have a multiplicity of equilibrium states, it can have equilibria that are unstable as well as equilibria that are stable: In a nonlinear dynamical system, there can be both attractors and repellors. In principle, for analytical purposes, repellors are as important as attractors, since the behavior of the system depends on what it is carried away from as well as what it is carried toward.

ii. The stability of an equilibrium state depends on the parameter **c.** Put in terms of the components of the latter, the values and the relationships among the component parameters matter. This point will be illustrated and amplified in later discussions.

iii. We study the model in terms of how the behavior of the system differs as a function of variations in the initial state and parameters. For example, in one region of parameter space, the mechanism may generate explosive growth in the state variable; in another region, it may generate decay or dissolution of the system; in a third region, it may produce a configuration of multiple equilibrium states, such as two attractors and a repellor. Other possibilities are cycles, as we saw in the ecological dynamical system. Thus there are varying forms of the behavior of the system, and these may vary with the region of parameter space. All these and other properties of the dynamical system are consequences of the postulation or derivation of the generator of the process.

6. The study of the way in which stable equilibrium states depend on the values of the parameters is called *comparative statics.* In general, this is the study of formula (2.3.4). For instance, in the ecological model, if the parameter $a$ increases, the equilibrium of the prey population increases, assuming other parameters remain the same. Thus, the basic mathematical operation is partial differentiation of the derived equation for an equilibrium state as a function of the parameters of the system. Recall that the parameters formally represent the conditions in which the system finds itself. Our empirical knowledge may inform us that these conditions depend on still other systems and their behavior. Thus, the stable equilibrium state of the system depends on the conditions, the parameters, which in turn may depend on the states of certain other systems in the environment of the system under analysis. So comparative statics is the theoretical correlate of *comparative analysis,* as understood in sociology. I shall say more about this later.

Concerning comparative statics note the *correspondence principle:* "The equations of comparative statics are a special case of general dynamic analysis" (Samuelson, 1964:262). This is obvious in the conceptual and formal description I have given, but as against the history of economic theory, it emerged in Samuelson's study as an important analytical discovery and tool of economic analysis.

7. Beyond comparative statics we have the problems of structural stability and

change, including *catastrophe analysis.* As previously mentioned, we try to draw a "portrait" of the dynamics of a system in state space as depending on the conditions of the system given in parameter space. Then there may be a derived partition of the parameter space such that in different regions of the space, we find that different *types* of outcomes arise in state space. If, now, a process is introduced into parameter space, the over-time change in the parameters may stay within a given region. If so, the same type of outcome arises in state space even though the particular outcome still depends on the value of the parameter. But the process may carry the now time-varying parameter into another region, in which case there has been "change," in the specific sense of change of type of outcome. For instance, from a region yielding a cyclic form of behavior in state space, the system passes over into a region yielding decay or dissolution. Also, this move into another region may entail crossing a boundary, and this may mean an abrupt shift from one type of system outcome to another. This latter shift is what is meant by a *catastrophe,* as in the case of a rapid movement to zero from a previous cyclic behavior.

8. Theoretical models may be extended to study the type of dynamics that arises when there is a feedback loop from the behavior in state space to the values of the parameters: The system changes its own conditions. This gives rise to incessant and sometimes dramatic changes. Roughly speaking, this is the sort of dynamics that Marx envisions: By virtue of assumed rational behavior of actors in their economic interactions (state space), a consequent tendency of technological advance exists. Considering technology as parametric, the economic interactions occurring within given forces of production tend to change those conditions. Idealizing the situation, the parametric conditions are shifted such that there is a competition between two modes of production, the old and the new, both corresponding, say, to distinct attractors in state space. The system dynamics may involve a catastrophe in the sense of the preceding paragraph.

In general, then, points 7 and 8 assert that structural stability and catastrophe analysis are concerned with what we might call a typology derived from the implications of the dynamical system and the study of the maintenance or change of types of systems either smoothly or with discontinuities. This implies two coupled dynamical systems, one of which controls the development of the other, since it provides the conditions under which the other experiences change of state. The main point here is that in addition to the analytical investigation of questions of the existence of equilibria, of stability of any particular equilibria, and of comparative statics, there are possibilities for the analytical investigation of questions related to even more complex dynamic aspects of a system.

*A note on types of process models.* Before concluding this section, it will be useful to provide the reader with a compact guide to some of the key choice sets involved in the construction of generative theoretical models. These remarks summarize some points made earlier and add some additional important considerations. There are four choice sets that should be kept in mind in terms of the possibilities for generative theoretical model building:

1. State space: discrete or continuous
2. Parameter space: discrete or continuous
3. Time domain: discrete or continuous
4. Generator: deterministic or stochastic

The term *dynamical system* is ordinarily used in the context of state and parameter spaces that are continuous and with a continuous time variable. It is ordinarily presupposed that the generator is deterministic (Hirsch and Smale, 1974:160; Thompson and Stewart, 1986:188). Without difficulty, however, the concept can be used more generally. The behavior manifold is defined when the state space and the parameter space are defined whatever the combination of choices made. The process viewpoint is incorporated into the specification of the time variable as continuous or discrete together with the postulation or derivation of the generator of the over-time process in state space as depending on the fixed or moving point in parameter space. And the generator may be stochastic or deterministic. It is in this wide sense that the concept of a dynamical system is used in this book; that is, it covers all meaningful combinations of the choices indicated in 1–4.

In a previous book (Fararo, 1973), the fundamental outlook was probabilistic. In the present book, this outlook is not repudiated, but the distinctive task here, as contrasted with that of the earlier work, has made it a matter of expediency to try to develop the ideas in a less complex context. In Section 3.6, however, the development of the ideas occurs within a stochastic framework. Also, the probabilistic outlook is employed throughout Chapter 4, culminating in a generative stochastic model in the last section of the book. For the purpose of putting into a wider perspective the deterministic approach employed later in this chapter and in the earlier parts of the next chapter, the following remarks about stochastic process models may be helpful.

There appear to be two major modes by which stochastic elements are introduced into the specification of generative models. The first mode yields a dynamical system in which the state variables are probabilities. To see what is involved, consider a one-dimensional state space. This state space provides what I have called an ''analytical ground'' (Fararo, 1973:Sect. 8.5) for a probabilistic dynamical system. The latter has a probability distribution over the analytical states as its state vector. Derived or postulated generators show how this probability vector is recursively transformed over time. This is the mode of defining stochastic generative models employed in Section 3.6. With a multidimensional analytical ground, the corresponding probabilistic models become very complex. In principle, however, they remain within the general conceptual framework of dynamical systems; they have the special character that the state of the system is described in terms of probability distributions over some analytical ground.

The second mode involves stochastic differential equations (Cobb, 1981). Again, to see what is involved, consider a one-dimensional state space. This type of system arises when one thinks of a process in the world as described by a systematic generator of the process in state space together with time varying random inputs. The state variable becomes a random variable in the sense of probability theory. In an important class of cases discussed by Cobb, the analyst postulates or aims to derive a quantity corresponding to an attractor of the process *without* the random inputs. Then the stochastic differential equation arises in the context of postulating how an *expected rate of change* of the random variable depends on the distance of the state from the attractor state and on the continuous random inputs. Cobb goes on to deal with stochastic catastrophes, showing how this important dynamical system idea can be coordinated to over-time data to perform a catastrophe data analysis. From the point of view of the conceptual sketch in this chapter, the easiest way to think about stochastic differential equations is that of adding to the right-hand side of equation (2.3.1) a term representing a time-varying random input. This way of putting it shows that for purposes of general theoretical sociology, we still need to solve the problem of learning how to derive the generators: the fundamental modes of transformation of social states. And it is this, rather than immediate applicability to data, that motivates the work of this chapter and the subsequent chapters. The remainder of this chapter, in particular, presupposes the context of the canonical combination defined by a continuous behavior manifold, continuous time variable, and deterministic generator.

## 2.4. Equilibrium and adjustment

The idea that equilibrium may be treated as an aspect of dynamical systems analysis is very important. In this section, I explicate what is meant by this idea by treating equilibration as adjustment of the state variables to each other and to the parametric conditions. I do so in a simple abstract model of a two-dimensional state space that will be given a sociological interpretation later.

The key to the whole paradigm is the dynamical system shown as expression (2.3.1). We can think of each of the equations of this system as describing how variables adjust to each other. Consider a system with two variables and one parameter. That is, $\mathbf{x} = (x, y)$ and $\mathbf{c} = c$. Later, the interpretations will introduce a greater number of parameters; it is the sheer logic of the abstract ideas that are of interest for the moment:

$$dx/dt = f_1(x, y; c) \tag{2.4.1a}$$
$$dy/dt = f_2(x, y; c) \tag{2.4.1b}$$

The variable $x$ adjusts to $y$ via the first equation, changing values unless $dx/dt = 0$. The equation determining the equilibria of variable $x$ is

$$f_1(x, y; c) = 0 \tag{2.4.2}$$

We can imagine this to describe a relation in the $x$–$y$ plane (with $c$ constant) and consider the simplest case where it is a function, so that Figure 2.1a obtains. This figure shows that we can use the equilibrium relation (2.4.2) to "read off" the adjusted value of $x$ for any given $y$. This adjusted value is the solution of (2.4.2) for $x$ in terms of $y$. Such a solution is denoted $x^E$. It is an equilibrium value, now seen to be a function of $y$. Similarly, equation (2.4.1b) yields

$$f_2(x, y; c) = 0 \tag{2.4.3}$$

Figure 2.1b shows that we can use this equation to find the adjusted value of $y$, denoted $y^E$, for any given value of $x$. This curve represents the solution of (2.4.3) for the equilibrium value $y^E$ as a function of $x$.

In Figures 2.1a and 2.1b the arrows show movements, in time, of the variables to their adjusted values. Our separation of the dynamics into two figures was purely an analytical tool to show that each variable adjusts to the other. But in the coupling of the two equations, given by (2.4.1), these two adjustment processes take place simultaneously. So Figure 2.1c synthesizes the two analyses: It shows that the dynamical system determining Figures 2.1a and 2.1b has two points where the curves cross. At these points, each of the variables is adjusted or equilibrated to the other, holding $c$ constant. There are, in this example, two equilibrium states. There is a pattern to the directions of the composite arrows showing the signs of the pair of $dx/dt$ and $dy/dt$ values as components of one vector whose direction varies with the region of the plane. The pattern shows that $E_1$ is unstable: It is a repellor. The process moves away from it. It also shows that $E_2$ is stable: It is an attractor, and the process moves toward it. This set of two curves and their superimposition to detect the system equilibrium states is for some unspecific but particular value of the parameter $c$. A very different diagram of the behavior of the system might emerge under different parametric conditions. But each and every one of these diagrams would be the outcome of the operation of the generator under varying parametric conditions.

This discussion relates to the way in which systems-oriented theoretical sociologists have used certain phrases. "Mutual dependence" (Homans, 1950) or

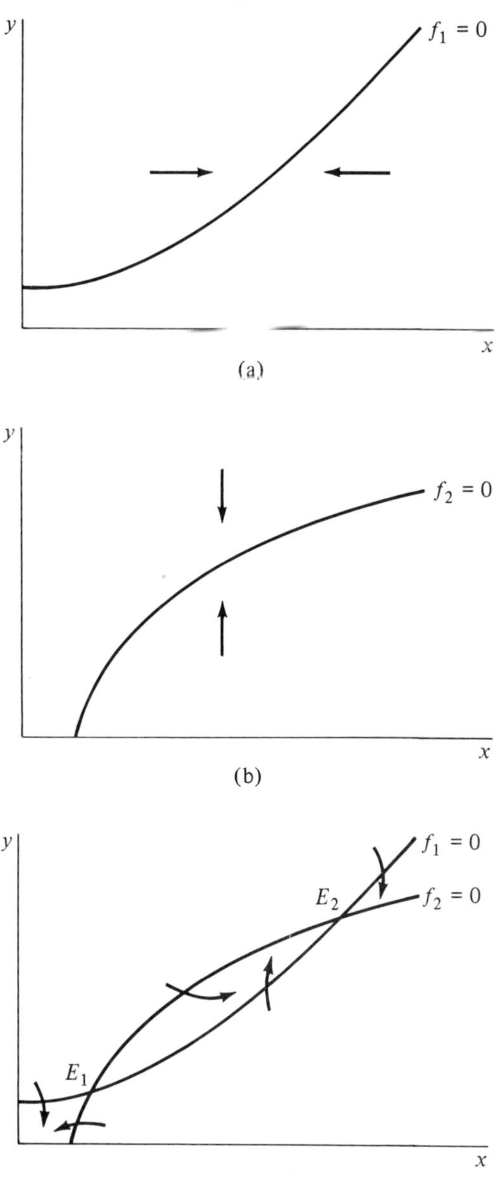


Figure 2.1. Equilibrium as adjustment

"analytical interdependence" (Parsons, 1937) is a type of relation between *variables* in a system. We could describe, in verbal terms, the $x$–$y$ mutual dependence in Figure 2.1 as follows: As $y$ increases, so does $x^E$ (Figure 2.1a); conversely, as $x$ increases, so does $y^E$ (Figure 2.1b). This means that as $y$ increases, the adjusted (equilibrium) value of $x$ increases, and as $x$ increases, the adjusted (equilibrium) value of $y$ increases. This is the mutual dependence statement.

The mutual dependence statement corresponds to two hypothetical experiments:

1. Select a value of $y$ and hold it constant over time while observing $x$ over time until $x$ stabilizes. (This corresponds to finding $x^E$ for a given $y$.) Change $y$ to a new fixed value. Observe over-time values of $x$ culminating in a new value of $x^E$. Vary $y$ to a new value. And so on. The result is a set of data points having a theoretical form given by $f_1(x, y; c)=0$, where $c$ is a relevant parameter held constant throughout the sequence of experiments wherein $y$ was set at successively different values to observe how $x$ adjusts to $y$ variations.
2. Do the same series of procedures, with $x$ and $y$ reversed in role. Plot the results. This corresponds to $f_2(x, y; c)=0$.

A third hypothetical experiment would be:

3. Select an initial pair of values for $(x, y)$ and then allow $x$ and $y$ to vary in time to arrive at a mutually adjusted state. Plot this final state as a point in the $(x, y)$ plane. Select a new initial pair of values of $(x, y)$ and observe them over time until they stabilize. Plot the result. Thus, one records a sequence of data points that are the *stabilized* pairs in the $x$–$y$ plane. With a correct model and under ideal conditions, these points should cluster around two points: zero and $E_2$, as in Figure 2.1c. The zero state can be regarded as a kind of *boundary equilibrium* that arises because the variables cannot be negative. One will *not* observe equilibrium $E_1$ because, as the arrows indicate, over-time values of the variables do not approach it or cycle around it. Its repellor character is shown by the fact that initial pairs of values chosen near it gravitate toward zero or $E_2$. Note that the parameter $c$ is held constant throughout this series of variations in the initial state.

Another data plotting would include all the data points indexed by *time observed* plotted for each of the preceding experiments. These plots correspond to over-time trajectories prior to arrival at values adjusted to the circumstances and would verify a prediction as to precise *path* to equilibrium.

These considerations play an important role in the interpretation of propositions about how two or more variables depend on each other. Consider an idea of the form "the greater the $x$, the greater the $y$," a type of statement frequently found in sociology. One formal interpretation of this statement is given by these dynamic considerations. We represent $dy/dt$ as depending on $x$ and perhaps other variables, with appropriate general or specific constraints to represent the direction of the relationship. If our intuition includes the idea that $x$ also depends on $y$, then the dynamical system interpretation would be that $dx/dt$ is a function of $y$ and perhaps other variables with constraints to cover the directionality of the relationship. If only one of two statements is the one we wish to stress as significant, then the relation is that between a dynamical variable and a variable to which it adjusts. The preceding arguments still apply except that we drop one of the two dynamical equations. For instance, if we drop the $dx/dt$ equation, then we are saying that $dy/dt$ depends on $x$ and on $c$ with $x$ in the role of time-varying parameter. In this analytical role, its change over time is externally generated: It is an input term or an *exogenous* variable. Thus, as $x$ changes over time, in regular or irregular ways, $y$ adjusts to it and $y^E$ is a function of $x$. So, for instance, if $x$ exhibits some periodic behavior, $y^E$ may mimic it and display periodic behavior. But this periodic behavior is still equilibrium behavior. To reiterate a point made in the prior section, the term *equilibrium* does not mean "no process"; rather, it means an attractor of process in the case of a stable equilibrium and a repellor of process in the case of unstable equilibrium.

So far we have imagined $c$ to be constant amid these variations and adjustments. If $c$ shifts in value, so does this trajectory of equilibrated values of $y$ as a function of $x$. We can think of $y$ as adjusting to $x$ in a fast process and to $c$ in a slow process if we have conceptualized $c$ as a parameter because its rate of change is ordinarily slower than that of $x$ and $y$ and so its values become conditions to which they adjust.

The theory in Homans (1950) illustrates such a situation. The following section examines this theory in greater detail, but let us use it now for an immediate example. Let $c$ be the magnitude of the authority that one person has over another, let $x$ be the strength of the positive sentiment that characterizes the relation between the pair, and let $y$ be their frequency of interaction. Homans posits that other things equal, the greater the frequency of interaction, the greater the strength of their positive sentiments toward each other (the more they like each other), and conversely, the more they like each other, the more frequently they interact. One of the important variables held constant is the magnitude of authority of one person over another, which I am interpreting as parameter $c$ in the two-variable system $x$–$y$ involving liking and interaction. From Homans's discussion and his explicit propositions, it is clear that the equilibrium of $y$ is a positive function of $x$ and the equilibrium of $x$ is a positive function of $y$. In other words, with little more by way of assumptions, we obtain an interpretation of Figure 2.1.

The parameter $c$, however, is in the background. For what values of $c$ is Figure

2.1 the form of the mutual dependence of $x$ and $y$? Although Homans provided only qualitative statements, enough is said to frame the following conjecture: If authority $c$ is sufficiently small, then Figure 2.1 holds; but if $c$ exceeds some (unknown) critical value, then Figure 2.1 does *not* hold: In particular, increases in interaction do not produce adjustments upward in liking, and increases in liking do not produce adjustments upward in interaction. The form of the mutual dependence between dynamic variables changes with changes in the parameter.

The complexity of such interrelationships allows a great deal of analytical flexibility so that Homans's theory is not locked into an empirical generalization to the effect that whenever and wherever two people start interacting more frequently, they also start liking each other more. But without more theoretical investigations of the complex interrelations, we have a fairly weak statement rather than a sharply stated theorem about the system.

It should be clear that this analytical conception of equilibration in a dynamical system must be discriminated from another usage promulgated by physical scientists, namely, equilibrium as associated with the laws of thermodynamics. Such laws show, for instance, that in a physically closed system, differentiation of parts tends to break down. The system moves toward a condition of macroscopic uniformity. This is illustrated by the everyday example of a system consisting of a cup of coffee in a given room. A cooling process occurs in which the temperature of the coffee adjusts to the temperature of the room, taken as a parameter of the process, to the point of matching it. Underlying this macroscopic equilibrium homogeneity is microscopic randomness of collisions of molecules in motion. Against the grain of this sort of dedifferentiation process is the empirical cosmological process of the birth as well as death of systems such as stars and organisms. Recent work with dissipative systems (see Babloyantz, 1986) tries to explain how such order can emerge in the far-from-equilibrium state. However, in this theoretical work ''equilibrium'' is in reference to the state variables of thermodynamics. This involves one particular general dynamical system given by the thermodynamic description of physical phenomena. Of course, the empirical social systems we treat in sociology are not immune from the laws of thermodynamics; each human organism, for instance, is in one aspect an open physical system to which a thermodynamic characterization applies. But this is the biophysical environment of the social system. As we shall see in Chapter 3, the possible social structures are functions of the biophysical parameters of the system, so nothing in theoretical sociology may violate the ultimate constraints of thermodynamics (or of genetics, or of mechanics, one might add). I do not mean, in these remarks, that far-from-equilibrium behavior is not significant in the case of the social state. The main point is that theoretical sociology should employ an abstract analytical conception of equilibrium in which this concept is in reference to certain states of the social system, not of the biophysical environment. Any special emergence of order-from-disorder phenomena in our field must be accounted for by the mechanisms of social interaction, not by a vague appeal to some thermodynamic situation.

## 2.5. Four types of theorems

The logic of studying a dynamical system specified in terms of a generator of changes in state culminates in my main point: This logic points the way toward a logic of social system theoretical investigations. I do not mean empirical research investigations. I mean analytical work that is initiated from within some theoretical framework that leads to the conceptualization of a class of model objects. Theoretical analysis of such a class then means specifying theoretical models and studying their properties. This will yield as deductions what Samuelson (1964) calls "operationally meaningful theorems."

What sorts of theorems should be aimed for? The logic of dynamical systems suggests the following:

> *Type 1 theorems.* These state the conditions (framed in terms of parameter space) under which equilibrium states exist.[9]
>
> *Type 2 theorems.* These inform us about the stability of the various equilibria: their classification as attractors or repellors.
>
> *Type 3 theorems.* These contain derived information about comparative statics: how a stable equilibrium varies with variation in parametric conditions.
>
> *Type 4 theorems.* These are about structural stability and catastrophes: the way in which the type of dynamic outcome varies with continuous change in the parametric conditions, including feedback to those conditions and both smooth and abrupt change.

These four types of theorems will receive an interpretation in terms of social structures in the remainder of this chapter and be referred to throughout this book. As preparation for this sociological interpretation, some further remarks on the nature of the abstract statements will be useful.

The dynamical system, when specified and analyzed, results in a complex portrait of *real dynamic possibilities*. Any actual systems that are in the empirical domain of some specified family of theoretical models will be characterized by only a few of these possibilities. Theory is concerned with the full manifold of all the really possible dynamic outcomes, as these depend on possible parametric conditions. Actual systems are characterized by initial conditions (parametric conditions plus the initial state), which reflect the way in which the historical actual world has shaped that system at that juncture of history. The real possibilities for any such system are then further restricted by these initial conditions. The theory may discover, by analysis, an array of possible attractors in state space. Yet, because some particular system is in a particular part of the state space to begin with – that is, at a particular time we call the initial time for analytical purposes – that system may not be able to reach most of these attractors. The really possible attractor states, in abstraction from initial conditions, become the really possible states without abstraction from initial conditions, and the latter are only a subset of the former. In the study of that actual system, then, real possibilities are eliminated. The *theoretician,* having supplied the generic manifold of real possibilities, now turns over the theoretical analysis to the empirical *model builder* concerned with that specific system. The model builder then imposes two constraints on the theoretical model that restrict real possibilities: the specification of the values of parameters and the specification of the initial state.[10]

In this way, dynamical systems thinking reflects and endorses Marx's point: History is always being made but under conditions established by the prior making of history. But the general function of the theoretician is to study the properties of the full manifold of real possibilities *without* restriction to particular parametric or initial conditions.[11]

The results of such theoretical studies are summarized in conditional statements. Type 1 theorems will be conditional statements linking equilibria to parametric conditions, stated in terms such as "*If* the system is in equilibrium state $E_1$, *then* the system is confined to a specified region of parameter space." Contrapositively, "*If* the parametric conditions are outside a specified region, then the system state is not $E_1$."

The following philosophical considerations apply not only to Type 1 theorems but to all types to be discussed. These conditional statements support what philosophers call counterfactual conditionals (Kaplan, 1964:91). The statements become counterfactual if one is thinking of some definite referent that is known *not* to be in equilibrium state $E_1$. Then the theoretical model implies: If the system *were* in equilibrium state $E_1$, then it *would be* confined to a certain region of parameter space. With this in mind and also to emphasize that theory deals with *possibilities,* it is often useful to frame derived statements in the subjunctive mood.

Kaplan (1964:Sect. 11) discusses how this property of supporting counterfactual conditionals relates to other properties of scientific statements that are shown by philosophical analysis to characterize laws. I am not equating theorems and laws however. My view is as follows. A law is not just a derived statement supportive of counterfactual conditionals. It also must be a sufficiently simple component of an empirically accepted theoretical model within the frame of reference of a representation principle and various presuppositions. These elements provide the esthetics and pragmatics of laws. As discussed in Chapter 1, a law is a type of discovered invariant. Some theorems might become laws because (1) what they state has an appealing simplicity, (2) the superordinate context of a theoretical system exists within which the model is constructed, and (3) the subordinate context of data gathered in accordance with the theoretical system provides empirical support for them. But even if some or all of these conditions fail for a class of theorems, they are still the key focus of the setup and study of theoretical models. On this view, laws are not the ultimate aim of a theoretical science. Answers to the problems of the field's tradition, with sufficient generality, are the aim. In the context of formalized theorizing, the answers are theorems. They need not possess the requisite simplicity of laws to count as answers, and to provoke our interest, they need not be known to be empirically correct. (We may even think they are wrong and yet value them as exemplars of possible answer forms.)

These philosophical remarks hold for all types of theorems. Let us return to the discussion of the types of theorems. An equilibrium that is not stable is not likely to be occupied in empirical realizations of the process, nor are we likely to be able to interpret the phenomena as orbits around it, which implies stability. Thus unstable equilibria function as repellors. Stable equilibria function as attractors for process. Understanding the dynamics of the behavior of a system will often mean understanding how the system is constituted by a number of possibly competing attractors and by one or more repellors. Type 2 theorems, on the stability classification of equilibria, will state the conditions on the parameters, usually in their relationships to each other, that are necessary or sufficient for stability of a given equilibrium. The theoretical task, once the theoretical model in the form of the dynamical system is derived or set up, is to analytically study the model to arrive at such characterizing theorems.

Type 3 theorems, about comparative statics, state the results of analytically studying how a stable equilibrium state depends on the parameters of the system. The aim is to see what happens under a conceptual shift in the value of a parameter. The conceptual shift corresponds to comparing social structures under two different cultural conditions, say. It is to be distinguished from studying the consequences of a continuous change in the parameter, which pertains to the last type of theorem.

Type 4 theorems are about the consequences in state space of continuous overtime variation in parameters. Of particular interest is a coupling of the dynamical system to a process in parameter space so that there is feedback from the dynamic outcomes to the conditions under which they occur. The focus is on such phenomena as the maintenance or change in the *type* of outcome of the dynamical system in state space. With smooth variation in parametric conditions, there may arise either smooth change or abrupt change of type. Catastrophe analysis presupposes a portrait of the system dynamics as a map over the parameter space and investigates boundary crossing phenomena in which a smoothly changing trajectory in parameter space produces a more or less rapid shift of form of behavior in state space through the crossing of a boundary in the portrait. Type 4 theorems will be illustrated later in the context of a dynamical social system.

Thus, according to this conceptualization of the role of the systems construct in theoretical sociology, it is associated with four aspects of the analytical investigation of a family of dynamical *social* systems specified by a theoretical model, yielding four corresponding types of general propositions. That is, theoretical sociology is concerned with an empirical domain treated in terms of dynamical systems. It will be our task in the remainder of this chapter to discuss the specific sociological interpretation of these abstract forms of theorems. But one can state the following attributes of the four types of theorems as interpreted in *any* such empirical domain:

> *They are derived rather than assumed:* Properties of a model object follow from a proposed generator defining a theoretical model.
> *They are idealizations rather than descriptions:* It is in the nature of theoretical analysis to introduce such idealizations to facilitate analysis.
> *They are empirical rather than a priori:* The theoretical model is our conjecture about the generative mechanism constitutive of the nature of the type of system under investigation; granted the idealization, the conjecture is still empirical in the sense of being subject to revision on the basis of a comparison of certain derived consequences with appropriate bodies of data.
> *They are general and conditional rather than particular and categorical:* Real possibilities are derived for conceptually varying parametric conditions, but further restrictions of real possibilities by specification of particular initial conditions holding for some actual system are applications or tests of the relevant theorems outside the scope of the theory proper.

## 2.6. Pareto and general theoretical sociology

In the past few sections, dynamical systems have been elucidated in terms of the nature of the basic forms of model objects as behavior manifolds and the way in which these are the basis for theoretical models and comprehensive theories. I now want to examine a subtradition of general theoretical sociology that approximates the logic of this type of approach to theory. The tradition starts with

Pareto. It intersects an environment at Harvard in the 1930s that included biologist Lawrence Henderson and philosopher Alfred North Whitehead.

Young George Homans entered this environment as a Harvard junior fellow and encountered Henderson's enthusiastic reception of Pareto's massive work (Pareto, 1935).[12] The fruits of this exposure were to be seen in 1950 with the publication of *The Human Group*. This book synthesized the nascent systems-theoretical subtradition with components of the Durkheimian tradition celebrated by Collins (1985): the focus on the emergent solidarity of the group, the component of ritual or noninstrumental exchange among members, the relationship of internal solidarity to external conflict, the processes of social control, the social character of the individual without an oversocialized conception of the human organism, and the critical but not dismissive attention to the work of the functionalist anthropologists. Thus, as will be seen in the next section, this book is a bridge between the ritual solidarity wing of the Durkheimian subtradition – what I call Durkheimian depth sociology – and the systems-theoretical tradition.

In 1952, shortly after Homans's 1950 book appeared, Herbert Simon created a formal theory based on it, one that treated the group as a dynamical system. (See, as the most convenience source, the collection of papers by him in Simon, 1957.) The paper by Simon remains the most impressive single piece of formal sociological theorizing we have. Along with other influences from the same Durkheimian tradition – such as the work of Lévi-Strauss and Radcliffe-Brown on kinship structures – this mathematical sociology development partially merged into the present-day social networks paradigm. Currently, the key problem of this paridigm is to get process and explanatory theory into model building. A comprehensive theoretical framework including both dynamical systems ideas and social network thinking is one way to do this. In short, this subtradition deserves to be part of our consciousness of components of general theoretical sociology that can be advanced and synthesized with other components. In this section, I discuss Pareto. Homans is treated in the following section. In each instance, the discussion will use the particular theorist as a point of departure for a discussion of aspects of general theoretical sociology.

Pareto's training and earlier work was in mathematics and physical science before he turned to economics and then, eventually, to sociology. Of all the classical theorists, he stands out as the most sophisticated with respect to the methodological presuppositions of theoretical analysis. In his 1896 work on political economy, he tabulated a kind of procedural analogy between classical mechanics and economics (see Finer, 1966:106–107). Contained in this tabulation (Table 2.1) is the conception of a pure or theoretical social science derived from a certain type of analogy to a pure or theoretical natural science.[13] The source Pareto uses is the procedure of analysis in classical mechanics. This source is transferred, by analogical reasoning, over into economics. The resulting procedures, as used in economics, have to be evaluated on their merits independently of their source in mechanics. What is good for mechanics may not be good for economics. But one would hardly suggest the analogy unless one believed the suggested directions of thinking in the subject matter discipline would be desirable. The point is that experience with the transferred mode of thought in its new habitat is what determines whether or not it is appropriate. Though not without its critics, today economic theory is massively mathematical and analytical in a sense that Pareto would have approved. If we separate the procedural from the substantive aspects of the critiques, however, we would find them to have differential merit. One can be an analytical economic theorist in Pareto's sense without being an advocate of some particular economic theory. Recent developments in analytical Marxism (Roemer, 1986) support this contention.

The analogy between a theoretical physical science and a theoretical social science found in Pareto's tabulation is restricted to the case of pure economics. Let me comment on this restricted analogy before remarking on the case of sociology.

Item 1 states the respective special subject matter of the physical science (mechanics) and the social science (economics or political economy). Note that in item 1a and 1b Pareto distinguishes between what we might call the theoretical science aspect and the empirical science aspect of each of the given sciences, respectively.

Item 1a introduces the theoretical procedure of defining model objects and appeals in each of the disciplinary contexts to some representation principle, that is, some formal and generalized way of representing the respective phenomena. Pure theory defines postulated sets of entities in abstract studies, says Pareto. These are the model objects, whereas the principles he cites pave the way toward theorizing with respect to these model objects. The important point is that the theoretical activity is with respect to idealized model objects, not directly with respect to the real world.

Item 1b supposes the theoretical models are now confronted with the problem of treating the real cases in the subject matter domain. The idealizations of theoretical models are supplemented by relevant considerations within that same domain that were omitted in the purely theoretical analysis. This is where friction appears in treating the real and humanly important case of the fall of a person in a parachute as contrasted with the classical idealized case of a freely falling body.

Where items 1a and 1b relate to idealization and to the procedure of treating real cases within the scope of a given science, respectively, items 2 and 3 point out that such real cases always have aspects outside the scope of any one science.

Table 2.1. *Pareto's procedural analogy*

| Mechanical phenomena | Economic phenomena |
|---|---|
| 1. Mechanics: the study of equilibrium and relative movement of a given number of material bodies, excluding other properties. | 1. Political economy: the study of production and exchange relationships among a given collection of human beings forming a society, any other properties excluded. |
| a. Pure mechanics: the study of a postulated set of material *points*, an abstract study of the equilibrium of forces and of motion. This employs D'Alembert's principle. | a. Pure political economy: the study of a postulated set of human beings each of whom is an *economic man*, an abstract study of economic phenomena arising under a maximization-of-utility principle. |
| b. Applied mechanics: brings into the explicit analysis such phenomena as elastic bodies, friction, and the like, omitted in the conception of material points in relative motion. Hence, this field more closely approximates real material bodies in the properties it considers relevant to motion. | b. Applied political economy: Human states, such as nonrational drives and beliefs, are brought into the analysis that was omitted in the conception of relations between economic men. Hence, this field more closely approximates real human beings in the properties it considers relevant to production and exchange. |
| 2. Real bodies have properties and relations that are not mechanical (e.g., optical, thermodynamical, electrical, chemical, biological). | 2. Real human beings have properties and relations that are not economic (e.g., legal, religious, ethical, intellectual, social organizational). |
| 3. Real bodies with only mechanical properties do not exist. | 3. Real people with only pure economic motivations do not exist. |
| 4. Two errors to be aware of: | 4. Two errors to be aware of: |
| a. Supposing a concrete phenomenon to be governed solely by mechanical forces. | a. Supposing a concrete phenomenon to be governed solely by economic motives. |
| b. Supposing a concrete physical phenomenon to be immune from the laws of pure mechanics. | b. Supposing a concrete social phenomenon to be immune from the laws of pure political economy. |

*Source:* Adapted, with permission, from S. E. Finer (ed.), *Vilfredo Pareto: Sociological Writings* (Praeger, 1966), pp. 106–107.

Real entities are not exhausted by their characterization in terms of models drawn from any one science, even in its ''applied'' (i.e., more empirical) phases. Consequently, Pareto notes in items 4a and 4b that one should be aware of two sorts of errors in relating theoretical work to the world. The referent is never merely a mirror image of the model. Only components of it instantiate the particular forms that are the focus of attention of any one theoretical framework. Later, Parsons called the viewpoint expressed in this epistemological principle ''analytical realism'' (Parsons, 1937). The units, relations, variables, and mechanisms dealt with in any one analytical theory correspond not to the referent entity or a concrete whole but to some systemic aspects of it isolated for analytical attention. This seems to me to be a sound principle, although one that introduces some substantial difficulty in implementation in the social sciences.

The discussion of the systematic extension of this analogy to sociology would be a project in its own right and a difficult one. My remarks will be brief. Consider the opening paragraph of Pareto's (1980:3) *Compendium:*

> Human society is the subject of many researches. Some of them constitute specialized disciplines: law, history, political economy, the history of religions, and the like; others have not yet been distinguished by special names. To the synthesis of them all, which aims at studying human society in general, we may give the name of *sociology*.

Is this compatible with a potential third column of Pareto's table in which sociology is treated as a science analogous to mechanics or economics? For one thing, sociology would have to somehow subsume economics within its ''synthesis of them all.'' For another, how could it synthesize such diverse fields and yet have a theoretical or pure aspect? How can a social science study ''human society in general'' and yet be as abstractly analytical as Pareto implies in his procedural analogy?

I suggest that *problems* concerning ''human society in general'' characterize sociology. In its various empirical studies, these problems translate in myriad ways into all sort of diverse concrete interests illustrating Pareto's list and much more. Yet there are generic problems corresponding to them.

The point of view in this book is that despite the enormous variety of interests within sociology, general theoretical sociology does have a core set of problems: *the theory of the emergence, maintenance, comparison, and transformation of social structures*. The subtraditions vary in their stress with respect to these problems. The microinteractionist tradition stresses emergence processes (symbolic interactionism) or the interpretive processes that go into the maintenance of existing structures (Goffman's interaction ritual, Garfinkel's indexicality, etc.). Functionalism, according to the dominant stereotype, concentrates on how structures are maintained, the problem of the stability of a social equilibrium. The conflict tradition treats social structures in historical comparative and transformative terms. According to the viewpoint to be developed later in this chapter, all four problems arise naturally whenever one considers the analysis of *any* theoretical model in the form of a dynamical social system. Note the one-sided character of many of these subtraditions from the standpoint of types of theorems on dynamical systems: emergence (Type 1), maintenance (Type 2), and comparison and transformation (Types 3 and 4). Surely, a construct that fuses all problems into the analysis of one type of general theoretical model has a role to play in the unification dynamic inherent in a theoretical science.

This does not clear away all the difficulties. It must be admitted, for example, that in taking this social structural route, the exact character of the properties and relations that are excluded is not easily specified. We cannot say economic relations are excluded, for instance. They are included under a certain analytical perspective, but the precise character of this perspective is elusive. We symbolize it by saying that our focus is social structure. Durkheim struggled to get the focus on this entity rather than the individual, even as the theory of the social individual took on special relevance in terms of the cult of the individual in modern social systems.[14] Today we can visualize our subject matter by reference to a social network as a model object. We know that we are interested in the dynamics and structure of *that* object and not the individual-in-an-environment frame of reference brought to sociology by almost every modern individual before encountering our point of view. It is possible that an even more carefully delineated but yet quite general scope for sociology might eventually become apparent around a properly understood concept of the integration dimension of social systems. In this book both the broader social structural focus and the narrower integrative focus are regarded as the core of our discipline's general theory.

So we discover our subject matter by a recursive process: We make some inroads on it in one generation, and this gives the next generation a somewhat different sense of what we are aiming to accomplish, a transformed sense of the subject matter. But this dynamical interpretation of the scope of the theory is not quite aligned to Pareto's more confident statements for the political economy case as he understood it.

A few words should be said about Pareto's general social theory (Pareto, 1935; Powers and Hanneman, 1983). It employs four analytical variables. These reflect his conception of sentiments as crucial to understanding the aspects of social life that economic theory has treated as elements of the applied area, as in Pareto's procedural point 1b for political economy. These are his famous residues and derivations. States of mind thought of as unobservable sentiments are manifested in observables at two levels: a relatively invariant level whose ideational content seems to recur in widely varying social circumstances in history and a more variable level that Pareto interprets as modes of justification of the invariant contents. The uniformities are the residues; the varying justifications are the derivations. For example, the unobservable sentiment of national solidarity, or patriotism, is manifested in residues that Pareto calls persistence of aggregates. A derivation might be ''my country, right or wrong.'' The residue is the observable index of the unobservable sentiment. Recently, Lopreato (1984) has suggested an interpretation of these sentiments as genetically based human nature. To these two nonrational elements Pareto appends two other variables. One he calls ''interests.'' This element corresponds, it appears, to the intuitive meaning of this term as used in the conflict subtradition of theoretical sociology. The fourth variable is the element of social heterogeneity and ''circulation'' or mobility, a pair of elements stressed in recent macrostructural theory (treated in Chapter 4).

Without constructing definite model objects, Pareto treats these four variables as mutually dependent in a verbal dynamical system with a state variable of four dimensions. He describes how changes in any one variable produce immediate effects on the other three variables as well as ''mediate'' effects. For instance, a change in residues produces an adjustment in derivations, in interests, and in heterogeneity, all in the sense of the interpretation of equilibration as adjustment set out in a previous section of this chapter. These three changes now produce immediate effects of their own. Among these are the three immediate effects on residues. But these three immediate effects combine to produce a further adjustive change in the residues over and above the originally postulated change. Then this new change has its further effects on the three other variables, its mediate effects on them. This process continues as long as the variables have not completely adjusted to each other. There is no actual mathematical model in Pareto's theoretical work. Rather the logic of the analysis of a system is carried over from the mathematical context to the verbal context. This procedure is the key to understanding how Homans (1950) elaborated upon the procedures and content of social theory stressed by Pareto. This is the topic of the next section.

## 2.7. Homans and the human group as a system

I am concerned here with the way that Homans implemented Pareto's recommended analytical procedures within sociology in his *The Human Group,* published in 1950. In one distinctive way, which reflected his greater sensitivity to the problem of rules of correspondence, Homans took a somewhat different starting point than Pareto. We can see this most distinctly in the difference in their conceptual frameworks.

A conceptual scheme is a set of concepts and any analytical relations among them that logically follow from definitions alone. It corresponds to the specification of a class of model objects appropriate to a domain. A theory adds principles from which derivations are obtained that are not true by definition. We can think of Homans's general framework as comprised of a conceptual scheme and a set of mechanisms that in a formal approach would comprise the means of defining generators of dynamical systems. One of Homans's key ideas was to ground the description of the mechanisms in a conceptual scheme rooted in concepts of "first-order." That is, such concepts involve relatively simple operations to arrive at observed instances, as compared with more complex, or "second-order," concepts.[15] It is likely that Homans took the centrality of the sentiment concept from Pareto. But he probably regarded the other concepts of Pareto's scheme as too far removed from observation to be taken as starting points for the specification of the basic mechanisms of social systems.

So Homans's own conceptual scheme includes the following concepts at the first-order abstraction level: activity, sentiment, and interaction. *Activity* refers to what specified persons are doing together in abstraction from the amount of interaction involved in that doing and from the sentiments involved. *Sentiment* refers to states of feeling. Homans notes that both participants and observers of social life use some sort of inferential procedure to label a person as in a certain state of sentiment. Thus, he implicitly accepts the Paretan distinction between residues (the observable clues) and sentiments (the underlying unobservable states). Just as Pareto often disregarded the distinction, so does Homans. Finally, *interaction* refers to the sheer contact between two or more persons in abstraction from their feelings and activities. Some sociologists may not like this way of using the word, but it would be an improper criticism to claim that interaction includes a lot more than such sheer contact. In Homans's conceptual scheme the content of interaction is abstracted from the sheer fact of interaction. But it is not omitted. It is analyzed via the other first-order social concepts, by cultural first-order concepts, and by second-order concepts.

In one aspect, this analytical abstraction of sheer interaction is analogous to the abstraction of sheer time in physics. For physics, an event is something going on in a region of space during a certain interval of time. The abstraction of the time interval from the complete event means that duration alone cannot tell us what is going on, only that something is going on. An interval of time is an aspect of any concrete event in its physical meaning. And what is going on is described in terms of other analytical physical elements, not the element of time. So too when persons interact, we know that something is going on: Some activities and some sentiments are implied but not *which* sentiments and activities.[16] In another aspect, there is a distribution of interactive episodes: For any pair of persons, interactive encounters are distributed in time and in various activity contexts, and for a set of persons during any time interval, there is a corresponding density of interaction in terms of aggregation over the set of all pairs.

To empirically identify first-order abstractions, we need a collection of people with sufficient interaction to prove of interest for analysis in terms of activities, interactions, and sentiments. What is needed is a clear indication of which people *are* and which *are not* in this system under analysis: Its degree of integration, its norms, the existence or nonexistence of differentiated status-roles – all are important but not essential for this purpose. These are variable properties of the system that will be accounted for by invoking the mechanisms that link the basic elements to each other. For instance, even a superficially structureless and transient thing such as a waiting line can be taken to be the system under analysis (Mann, 1969).

Homans suggests identifying the boundaries of such a system by isolating a subset of persons in a given larger set such that during a given period of time, they interact more frequently with each other than with others. This avoids assuming that they initially are members of a preconstituted group. They may be total strangers initially. The main import of this suggestion is: You specify a roster of *potential* members, the *persons,* such that their activities, sentiments, and interactions comprise the *social system* in an environment. The environment includes other such social systems as well as relevant cultural and physical systems.

Homans's conceptual scheme includes other concepts, although they are not his first-order abstractions. Of these, group *norm* is the most central. It is not first order because to identify a norm observationally, one must specify both a normative *idea* (about what ought to be the case) and a *mode of functioning* of this idea in the social system (so that it is not just an abstract ideal that is not taken seriously). The orientation to a normative idea (such as: One ought to repay debts) might be classified as a normative sentiment (Parsons, 1937:75). What makes this type of idea a group norm in this context is that, first, it is an aspect of a generated outcome of the interactions of certain persons[17]; second, it is one term in ongoing comparison processes in which the other term consists of some aspect of actual interactions, activities, and sentiments; and, third, such comparisons lead to tendencies in the relevant state to change in a direction conformable with the normative sentiment. Such comparisons and tendencies are aspects of the interactions.

At this point, then, we see that Homans's conceptual scheme includes interaction as a contentless element and content elements of activities and sentiments, including normative sentiments. A model object representing the social system, so understood, requires representations corresponding to the elements of this conceptual scheme, especially (1) a set of persons; (2) a set of types of activities;

(3) one or more relations among the activities, such as input–output relations; (4) a matrix of differential participation of persons in activities; (5) a matrix of sentiments of persons toward the activities, including normative sentiments; (6) matrices of sentiments of the persons toward each other, including normative sentiments; and (7) matrices of interaction rates between all pairs of persons.

Abstractly, we see that all this is readily represented in terms of matrices corresponding to the multiple network of relations among persons, their sentiments, activities, and interaction states. For the purpose of this chapter, however, the basic model object will presuppose this complex network model and concentrate on process. Namely, the behavior manifold will be the model object. The pursuit of the latter takes us more directly into the problem of constructing theoretical models of the dynamical systems type. I presuppose that the behavior manifold is constructed relative to the complex picture that a network model would provide were we to define it in formal detail. Put another way, the general form of the model object is that of a state space whose elements are vector and matrix variables, for example, states of a multiple network of persons. It would be counterproductive to introduce such a complex apparatus to make a basically conceptual contribution in this chapter, one that will have to be qualified later as well. I shall return to the underlying network by way of criticism of the particular dynamical system studied in what follows.

Just as Homans's conceptual scheme corresponds to the problem of specification of a model object, his conception of the processes of the social system corresponds to the construction of theoretical models within a comprehensive framework. The system is treated as in an environment with respect to which it must adjust or adapt. So there is a general dimension of adaptation. Internally, the relevant general dimension is integration. Adaptation and integration are linked to each other: The outcome of interpersonal processes over and beyond those called for in relation to the environment has an effect upon the mode and level of adaptation to that environment. Also, changes in the environment that lead to adaptive changes may affect interpersonal relations, the integration dimension.

Adaptation is associated with the organization of instrumental activities, such as their input–output relations, and with the division of labor. Homans also mentions the empirical tendency for some chain of command to form.

The integration dimension, as noted, is associated with interpersonal sentiment relations, with the emergence of group norms, and with the consequences of these in terms of the buildup, maintenance, or change of social relations, including social control.

In developing these ideas, Homans can be seen to focus especially on three types of outcomes in social system dynamics, usefully distinguished in terms of the initial condition of the system and consequent process outcome:

1. In the initial condition, there is no actual group, only a set of persons with some initial, perhaps very small density of interactions. What the dynamics may do is generate a group and its correlate set of members, so we call this *buildup*. With this generated member–group relation, there are elements of *standardization* and *differentiation:* activities, sentiments, interactions, and norms become standardized and persons become differentiated in terms of (a) the patterning of their relations to each other in terms of these states including (b) the emergence of subgroups with their patterns of potential or actual antagonism in some respects and cooperation in other respects.

As a matter of conceptualization and terminology, here and throughout this book the terms *member* and *group* will be used to refer to two aspects of what is generated (under some conditions) by the mechanisms of a dynamical social system. Adopting a phrase from Cooley, we can say that member and group are *twin-born*. One concept refers to the persons individually in relation to the whole they then constitute, whereas the other concept refers to them collectively, as that specific generated whole.[18]

2. The initial condition involves a recognizable group in an environment to which it is adapted, but some change in the environment produces adjustments that lead to a gradual or sudden decay of the structure, so that we may call this "build-down" or *decay:* This reverses the standardization achieved in some prior buildup. In the limit, it can yield the end of the specific group's existence, although it may not imply the dissolution of all subgroups.

3. The initial state is some fixed or moving stable equilibrium, and the dynamics maintain this state, an outcome called *steady state:* It is not that nothing is going on but that the buildup, under given conditions, has gone as far as it can go. Steady states include cyclic behavior of the states of the elements, since part of the definition includes the variation from "normal" (attractor state) with such departures tending to be restored (by the assumed stability).

For visualization of these three modes of behavior in state space, imagine a graph of each in the $t$–$x$ plane, where $x$ is a way of picturing the actual complex state and $t$ is time. One may think of the first outcome as a logistic growth curve. The second outcome is best thought of as an exponential decay curve. Finally the third outcome is best pictured not as a straight line of constancy but as a moving cycle with an average straight line running through it.

Note that buildup and decay are both terms that point to the integration significance of the events constituting the processes in the system. They are dramatically distinct as outcomes. Yet each outcome points to the same conceptual dimension of social life, having to do with what Durkheim called solidarity. Thus, we must sharply distinguish the generic integration *dimension* that orients much of our analysis of social systems from the specifically integrative (buildup) or disintegrative (decay) outcomes that the processes generate. To the extent that a clear analytical distinction can be maintained between adaptation and integration, the same remarks apply: The adaptation dimension of process may generate a range of possible outcomes or states of adaptation to the environment.

In Homans's case studies, the Bank Wiring Room Group and the Norton Street Gang (Homans, 1950:Chs. 1–8) exemplify the first outcome, buildup. In the Bank Wiring Room case, we can idealize the situation as one in which the members did not at first known each other well and certainly did not constitute a specific group. Over time, a group was generated whose structure is depicted by Homans in terms of network diagrams drawing upon data of the original study. Similarly, the young men of Norton Street may be pictured, as an initial condition, as simply in some proximity, "thrown together" within the environment. The gang is the emergent unity, with its internal differentiated structure, adapted to that environment.

Hilltown (Homans, 1950:Ch. 13) exemplifies the second outcome, build-down or decay. Using historical data, Homans shows how the complex internal social structure of the town gradually declined when a significant technological change occurred in its environment. The adaptation, in this instance, led to integration consequences that amounted to a near dissolution of the group, since the normative ideas no longer functioned as norms and the amount of activity and density of interaction among residents severely declined.

The third type of outcome, steady state, is probably best represented by Homans's (1950:Chs. 9 and 10) discussion of Tikopia. Not only have interpersonal relations stabilized, but also their form has been perpetuated through a complex kinship system linked to patterns of authority in an ongoing pattern that endures despite the turnover of the concrete persons in membership relation to the group. Here we have Parsons's latent pattern maintenance dimension of social dynamics, or in other words, a social reproduction dimension.[19]

Homans's "external" and "internal" systems are dynamical subsystems of the system since they do not correspond to subgroups but to analytically defined aspects of the system. They correspond to the adaptation dimension and the integration dimension. In turn, the integration dimension has strong roots in the Durkheimian tradition, which fed into Homans's work, as we see in his citations to Mayo and Warner, as well as to Durkheim, Parsons, Malinowski, and Radcliffe-Brown. This tradition gave birth to the idea that social organization involves exchange and a norm of reciprocity (Homans, 1950:284–288) as in the exchange of favors in a group and the way in which the leader gets some of his or her power from such an exchange network. Ceremonial or ritual exchange is distinguished from the external system. That is, the integration dimension is associated with ritual solidarity, with expressive behavior, (i.e., activity in symbolic relation to sentiments such as those of common belonging to a group (Homans, 1950:137). The "ritual disequilibrium" that Goffman (1967) finds in the details of interaction is the same Durkheimian idea we find in Homans's (1950:Ch. 11) discussion of social control. The adaptation dimension is the contrast required to bring out the meaning of the integration forces in the group: Instrumental behavior in the division of labor is the primary component of adaptation. So the social dynamics has two faces, one pointing toward the environment and calling out the rational–instrumental side of action, the other pointing inward and calling out the nonrational–expressive side of action. This is true under all conditions, but the processes do not always lead to the same result: There can be a buildup of a group, a decay, or a steady state.

How are these three types of outcome generated? Homans provides a rather extensive set of helpful statements he calls *analytical hypotheses*. These are modes of general relationship among the elements. They include, for instance, the interaction–sentiment relationship referred to earlier (in Section 2.4) to illustrate the concept of equilibration. (See also Table 2.2 in the following section.) We can think of such *pair relationships* between analytical elements as Homans's attempt to get a dynamical system perspective into his analysis, albeit without the mathematics. Interpreted in process terms, each such pair relationship may define a mechanism qualified in what it produces by the simultaneous action of all the other relevant mechanisms in the total generative process. But the necessary synthesis of these mechanisms to define a generator and hence a dynamical social system cannot be accomplished by words. The task of general theoretical sociology is indeed formidable, more formidable than most theorists even realize and yet full of the excitement of work to be done.

## 2.8. General dynamical social systems and types of social structure theorems

Two strands of thought have been introduced in this chapter. In one strand, the ideas were formal: behavior manifold, dynamical system, four types of theorems. In the other strand, the ideas were methodological and sociological: Pareto's procedural analogy and Homans's sociological use of the systems idea to describe groups as social systems. The next step is the joining of these strands into a conceptual knot that simultaneously specifies a concept of a general dynamical social system, a set of four key problems of social structure, and a set of four corresponding types of social structure theorems.

It is not that this is a final product. Far from it. It is that at least we will have one definite entity on display that converts the abstract dynamical system into an interpretable dynamical social system. The model object will remain fairly abstract, and the total mechanism, in the form of a system of equations, will not be specified. Only when we reduce the complexity of the general dynamical social system do we arrive at definite equations and definite theorems. But the general form is important for the purposes of this book, since it corresponds to the aspired level of comprehensive theory at which most discussion in sociological theory is couched.

By a general dynamical social system I mean the general form of a model object that is intended as a flexible basis for reference to any one of an indefinitely large set of social systems. Among other things, the term *general* means that the number of persons or other social actors is not specified. In principle, the ideas should specialize to a dyad or to a triad and still describe a sensible conception of social process and social structure. Similarly, the conceptual structure should have an intelligible meaning for large-scale systems.[30] Also, the term *general* means that there are no social systems in the class of all such systems that are such that the concepts are too restricted to apply to them. However, for more specialized analyses, additional concepts and propositions may be appended. I also should mention that the discussion of such a general dynamical social system continues in the next two chapters.

I shall introduce certain notations, parallel to the general format, to elucidate the system, following closely the scheme proposed by Homans. Whereas Homans writes of an external system and an internal system, I shall write of an adaptation system and an integration system as two subsystems of the general dynamical social system.

The social system exists in an environment. The states of its activities, interactions, and sentiments that relate to dynamic adjustments to the environment will be termed the *adaptation system.* In addition, the social system is not confined to these adaptation states but generates other states of activity, interaction, and sentiment. These states make up the *integration system.* A basic concept is framed in these terms: The two *subsystems* are mutually dependent.

Let us use the formal trick of a boldface letter to stand for a whole array of variables. Then the state vector $\mathbf{x}$ of the abstract dynamical system has two major sets of components in this model. Namely, $\mathbf{x} = (\mathbf{A}, \mathbf{I})$, where $\mathbf{A}$ represents a vector of adaptation system variables and $\mathbf{I}$ represents a vector of integration system variables. Hence $d\mathbf{x}/dt = (d\mathbf{A}/dt, d\mathbf{I}/dt)$. The abstract form of the general dynamical social system is:

$$d\mathbf{A}/dt = \mathbf{f}_1(\mathbf{A}, \mathbf{I}; \mathbf{c}) \qquad (2.8.1a)$$
$$d\mathbf{I}/dt = \mathbf{f}_2(\mathbf{A}, \mathbf{I}; \mathbf{c}) \qquad (2.8.1b)$$

The interpretation is that the state of the system is comprised of pair $(\mathbf{A}, \mathbf{I})$, where $\mathbf{A}$ and $\mathbf{I}$ refer to lists of variables of the adaptation and integration system, respectively, and where $\mathbf{c}$ is a list of parameters.

We can interpret $\mathbf{A}$ and $\mathbf{I}$ in terms of the concepts of Homans's conceptual scheme. It is convenient to refer to each as a list or vector of activity variables, interaction variables, and sentiment variables. At this point we need to refer to the underlying (unconstructed) model object corresponding to this conceptual scheme. In this model object, each of these state variables has a vector or matrix form.[21] For instance, the integration sentiment variable is a matrix of interpersonal sentiment state descriptions in some quantitative form. As another example, in the Bank Wiring Room, the work activity has an associated division of labor that one could treat as an adaptation state described by a matrix of assignments of persons to types of work tasks; it also has state descriptions in terms of who helps whom, the amount of help the workers give each other, which one could treat as an integration state variable. In linkage to Homans, whatever he treats as the external system is an adaptation state in this terminology, and whatever he treats as the internal system is an integration state. As mentioned earlier, explicit network representations are not given here since the analysis to follow concentrates on the logic of dynamical systems analysis. But conceptually they are very important. The use of boldface letters throughout serves as a formal reminder of the inner complexity of any particular variable. Thus:

$$\mathbf{A} = (\mathbf{a}_A, \mathbf{i}_A, \mathbf{s}_A) \tag{2.8.2a}$$
$$\mathbf{I} = (\mathbf{a}_I, \mathbf{i}_I, \mathbf{s}_I) \tag{2.8.2b}$$

where the states pertain to

$\mathbf{a}_A$: activities adapting to environment
$\mathbf{i}_A$: interaction coordinating these activities
$\mathbf{s}_A$: motivation for these activities
$\mathbf{a}_I$: emergent social activities
$\mathbf{i}_I$: interactions in these emergent activities
$\mathbf{s}_I$: emergent social sentiments
$\mathbf{c}$: parameters

The term *emergent* is used here because it best conveys the intuitive idea in the case of buildup of group structure. But is should be thought of in terms of an important conceptual heritage. One might write, instead, "expressive activity," "ceremonial activity," or even "ritual activity." This would make plain the connection to Goffman (1967:55) when he writes, "The important point is that ceremonial activity, like substantive activity, is an analytical element referring to a component or function of activity, not to concrete empirical action itself." Indeed, in a footnote, Goffman (1967:53) explicitly states that the distinction is taken from Durkheim and notes the equivalence to Parsons's (1937) distinction between intrinsic or instrumental and expressive or symbolic elements. So the *elements* or state variables of activity entering into $\mathbf{a}_A$ and $\mathbf{a}_I$, respectively, correspond to a conceptual distinction with strong roots in the Durkheimian tradition. The corresponding element interpretation applies as well to the interaction and sentiment states.

With somewhat greater formal definiteness, the complexity of the state variables is indicated by the following incomplete sketch of interpretations:

$\mathbf{a}_A$, $\mathbf{a}_I$: matrices of persons by activities, where the typical entry records some state of participation of a given person in a given activity

$\mathbf{i}_A$, $\mathbf{i}_I$: matrices of persons by persons, where the typical entry records some state of contact, such as frequency of interactions of certain sorts

$\mathbf{s}_A$, $\mathbf{s}_I$: matrices of persons by activities (to represent motivational states in relation to various activities and normative sentiments toward the activities) and of persons by persons (to represent interpersonal sentiments, including those defining emergent status orders, etc.)

Each of these matrices corresponds to a network in which the nodes are of one or more types (persons, activities) and weighted lines represent the existence and magnitudes of the relationships the various components of the complex state variable **(A, I)** include. Each entry in each matrix is a function of time. The rate of change of any particular substate (such as the sentiments connecting two persons at a given time) depends on the state of the whole network so far as the general system is concerned, although in definite models one would expect only states of some of the parts of the system to "matter" in the change of state of any one part in a small time interval.

For analytical investigation of particular types of systems, certain of the matrices may be treated as constants. For instance, the division of labor may be treated as given while other elements, such as an emergent expressive activity matrix with a corresponding interpersonal sentiment matrix, are conceived as time varying.

As examples of other types of special cases, consider the initial state given by $\mathbf{A} = \mathbf{A}_0$ and $\mathbf{I} = \mathbf{0}$. This is a case in which initially there is no group but only some "seeding" of the dynamics through some initial small level of instrumental interaction. Another special case would take the form $\mathbf{A} = \mathbf{0}$ and $\mathbf{I} = \mathbf{I}_0$. This is a case of an initially pure expressive system of interaction the dynamics potentially would carry into some state involving adaptation to the environment. Another whole family of special cases would involve the size parameter, the number of persons in the network.

Two other points about the general system relate to some remarks made by Homans (1950:109). First, he tells us that the term "internal system" was adopted to suggest aspects of the social system not directly conditioned by the environment. This would suggest that in equations (2.8.1), the total set of parameters could be partitioned in such a way that those describing the environment would appear only in the first equation. For simplicity, however, I do not indicate this formally. Second, he notes that "social life is never wholly utilitarian: it elaborates itself, complicates itself, beyond the demands of the original situation." This statement confounds two distinct items, namely, the utilitarian element and the initial conditions ("original situation"). The former refers to aspects of the adaptation subsystem. Thinking of the emergence aspect, Homans seems to be presupposing the initial condition in which $\mathbf{I}=\mathbf{0}$. This resembles the Marxian strategy of taking the mode of production as the fundamental basis of social life, yet adding that its concrete character can be modified by the emergent social structure based on it. Durkheim (1964), however, would argue that the presupposed original situation of a division of labor without a prior state of integration is fictional. It may be valid for a work group or some other group in a societal environment, but it could not be valid for a group that constitutes a society, because communicative interaction generative and regenerative of social bonds would be presupposed. This may be a case of theoretical dispute resting on a confusion of initial conditions and generative mechanisms. The context here shifts the focus to the mechanisms, not the initial conditions. Also, an important feature of (2.8.1) should be noted. One could have interpreted Homans to be focused entirely on the integration system, with the "external system," to use his phrase, as a complex parameter **A** for the integration process. (Indeed, it will be argued in Chapter 3 that his later work has precisely this internal system focus.) It is quite clear, however, that Homans is proposing a feedback effect of integration on adaptation. The elaboration of the group's internal system acts back upon the external system. This is why the more complex coupling of two dynamic subsystems has been taken as the general form of the model object. The various possibilities for initial conditions, as indicated, frame a huge space of analytical special cases.

The system (2.8.1) together with (2.8.2) with this general conceptual interpretation will be termed the *general dynamical social system.* All the special cases of the general system as treated from the abstract theoretical viewpoint must be distinguished from *instantiations* or *applications* to concrete categories of groups. The problems of general theoretical sociology and the sorts of theoretical knowledge to which it aspires require it to retain a level of abstraction higher than might be employed if we were interested in, say, a theory of work groups, a theory of gangs, or a theory of families.

The next conceptual task is to make the remainder of the transition from the abstract dynamical systems framework to the general dynamical social systems framework. This means stating the types of theorems we should aim to demonstrate for families of theoretical models in terms of the social system case. To begin with, the following correspondence is postulated between sociological terms and entities in the general dynamical social system:

1. *Social mechanisms:* The question is, What drives the process in the system whose state is described by the state variables? The social mechanisms are the basis of the generator of the adaptive and integration processes, that is, of over-time change in **A** or **I** as generated by equations (2.8.1). Each family of theoretical models will draw upon our knowledge of social processes to conjecture a definite generator in this sense.

2. *Social structure:* The question is, What, if any, potentially enduring forms of social interaction are possible under given parametric conditions, and what do they look like? Then a social structure is any equilibrium state of both **A** and **I** – that is, an equilibrium state of the dynamical social system. A social structure is a state of definite adjusted values of all the variables under a definite set of parametric conditions. In interpreting this statement, recall that the variables entering into **A** and **I** are matrix variables referring to state descriptions of activities, sentiments, and interactions connecting all pairs of members.

A narrower meaning of social structure would refer specifically to the equilibria of **I** only. Classically, the division of labor has been considered a central component of social structure, and in the present framework, this fits under **A** rather than **I**. But the "core" of social structure as consisting of states of specific *integration substructures* also has been stressed in sociological theory. This is just one example of the dual focus of general theoretical sociology on the problems of social structure in the wide sense and on the problems of the integration process and its outcomes, which I identify with the **I** dimension. In other words, state (**A**, **I**) is the wide scope of general theoretical sociology, whereas **I** is the narrow. In the latter case, **A** formally becomes a basic parameter of the integration process.

3. *Social control:* The question is, Is some particular social structure the sort of structure that will survive the inevitable disturbances or departures from it? That is, will the mechanisms of the system tend to keep the state of the system near the social structure? (Recall that the equilibrium need not be an occupied state; it can be a point around which an orbital trajectory is generated.) *So social control refers to the process of adjustment itself, given a reference social structure.* In a stable case, the "arrows" (as in Figure 2.1c) bring the system back toward an equilibrium state, a social structure, assuming some real or hypothetical departure from it. If there are two or more equilibria compatible with environmental conditions, that is, two or more possible social structures for a fixed parameter level, then disturbances introduced into one social structure may produce an initial condition wherein the social dynamics carries the state to another

social structure without any environmental change. Hence, except in certain cases (where there is a unique stable equilibrium), social control may not be "successful." We can envision "disturbances" as events that are produced in the group that are not generated by the analytically pure social system mechanisms incorporated into the general social system equations.

4. *Comparative social statics:* The question is, Why and how does social structure vary from one social system to another? The comparison involves showing how social structural features vary with respect to variation in the parameters of the dynamical social system.

5. *Social change:* The question is, Why and how does the type of social structure change? The various possible social structures generated under the given parametric conditions may yield a typology: In various regions of parameter space, different forms of social structures arise. Change means passage to another region of parameter space because this means another form or type of social structure. One way this can occur is through exogenous change in the parametric conditions, perhaps slowly, which may nevertheless produce a relatively rapid change of structure (catastrophe). Another way this can occur is through a feedback loop from the process in state space to a process in parameter space so that the generated outcomes of the social mechanism act back on the conditions under which the social structure was generated. This can change these conditions and thereby change the social structure to another type. Initial states of the system are also involved here because, with multiple possible social structures, the nearness to a previous *one* of the possibilities implies some set of initial distances to the newly relevant set of social structures. Therefore, among the attractors in the latter set, some are more likely than others to be selected as the realized structure. In this way, abstractly represented givens, corresponding to the cumulative effects of history up to the initial time, exercise their required constraint on the possibilities for structural transformation.

As an example of a classical social change theory under these rubrics and procedures, consider once again the Marxian component of the tradition of general theoretical sociology with regard to structural change. As before, regard technology in terms of a set of parameters of the social system. Certain rational instrumental interactions in given social relations of production (component of an equilibrated **A**-state) tend to generate technological innovations (parameter change). This is feedback from social process outcomes to the conditions under which the process is taking place. But this can change the social structure because the dynamical system now produces an adjustment to the new technological conditions.

Based on these conceptual correspondences between the ideas of sociology and the components and aspects of the defined general dynamical social system, we can now state the four types of theorems that theoretical sociology should aim to derive in the study of theoretical models. These arise from interpreting the four abstract types of theorems set out in Section 2.5 in terms of the preceding general correspondence. They are defined here, and they will be referred to frequently throughout this book:

*Type 1 theorem – existence and forms of social structures:* The formal problem of investigating the conditions for the existence of equilibrium states becomes a tool for addressing a key problem of general theoretical sociology: What social structures are possible, if any, under varying conditions? The question is, What does the generator imply in terms of the existence and form of social structures under given parametric conditions? Note that the matrix forms of the components of the state variables imply that such equilibria will have the form of multiple networks.

*Type 2 theorem – stability of social structures:* A key problem of general theoretical sociology concerns the endurance of structures of social relations. But endurance, in the sense of over-time invariance, is a consequence of the dynamic property of social control. (More broadly, social reproduction is involved, to be discussed in the next chapter.) So the question is, For each of the derived possible social structures, is it an attractor for process or a repellor? Put another way, will social control be successful or not?

*Type 3 theorem – comparative statics of social structures:* Many empirical problems of sociology involve comparison of social structures under varying conditions. A key problem of general theoretical sociology concerns how stable social structures vary as their conditions vary. The question is, How do the properties of the stable social structure depend on parametric conditions? If one or more cultural parameters shift, for instance, how will the stable social structure shift?

*Type 4 theorem – change of social structures:* A classical interest in sociology is to describe and account for various forms of social change, defined as change in type of social structure. A key problem of general theoretical sociology concerns the path and modes of structural change as these are generated dynamically. The question is, Why and how do social structures change? More explicitly, why do they change type? One formal procedure is to try to generate a typology of structures associated with regions of parameter space; introduce a process on parameter space and possibly a feedback loop from state space to parameter space; investigate how the social structure changes as the parameter changes over time.

Structural representations come into their own when we try to analyze the generated attractor state of a complex social network process. Three types of

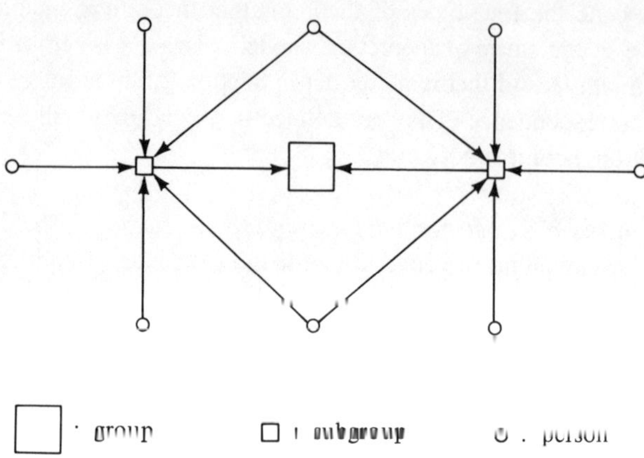

Figure 2.2. Structure of inclusion relations

network representations are useful in highlighting corresponding aspects of social structures.

The first structural representation has to do with the configuration of groups comprising a structure. First, the attractor state need not imply that the whole system of interaction is a group. What might exist could be a social formation lacking any generated membership sentiments and activities with respect to the whole network as contrasted with more local clusterings. Second, we need some way of formally representing the configuration of groups generated. This configuration will feature membership of persons in groups, inclusion of groups in other groups, and overlapping of groups through shared membership.

Figure 2.2 illustrates the type of network representation that one can use for representing this configuration. In the illustration, there are three types of nodes to represent members, subgroups, and groups, respectively. The ties between nodes represent the inclusion relation, including membership as the case of a person tied to a subgroup. The diagram can be interpreted as transitive: When person *a* is a member of subgroup *g* included in group *G*, then *a* is also a member of *G*. Nontransitive configurations also make sense. (For details on this and related aspects of this mode of representation, see Fararo and Doreian, 1984.) This configuration is a special case of the general phenomenon of interpenetration discussed in the next chapter.

The second structural representation has to do with the element of stable forms of social activity, whether instrumental–substantive or expressive–ceremonial. For instance, consider the scheme of possible sequential work flows in the Bank Wiring Room. This is shown both as a graph and as a binary matrix in Figure

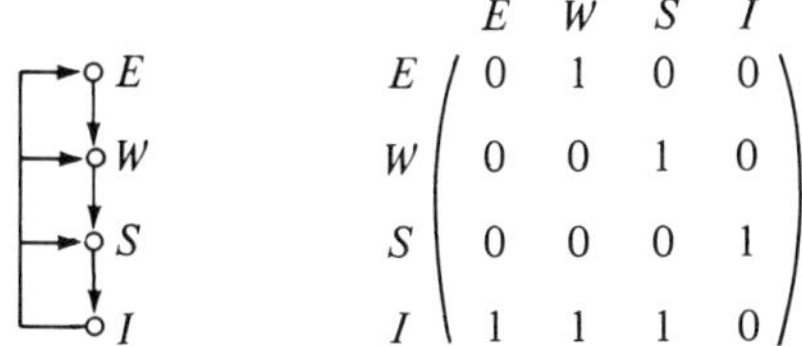

Figure 2.3. Structure of action relations

2.3. There are three connected subactivities of the work activity (*W*, wiring; *S*, soldering; *I*, inspecting) and one environmental node (*E*). The standard flow is from *E* to *W* to *S* to *I* and back to *E*. But node *I* can result in a test failure of an item with its return to *S* or to *W*. Thus the network implies such possible sequences (with arrows omitted) as *EWSIE* (standard), *EWSISIE*, *EWSISISIE*, *EWSIWSIE*, *EWSIWSISIE*, and so forth. Some of these will never be realized, of course, but they are a kind of infinite set of action possibilities generated by an *action structure*. In general, then, the nodes represent types of action or activity as they are linked in a structure of possibilities for realization. Such activity or action structures are part of the background for the next chapter, where the language analogy informs *structural–generative action theory*. Recurrent social practices, such as institutions, can be thought of as stable action structures. They are associated with still another aspect of social structures that is not shown: the assignment of persons to instrumental activity nodes, each such possible assignment defining a possible division of labor. In the attractor state, some stable division of labor exists and is adjusted to the other aspects of the complete social structure.

These first two aspects of social structure seem to be closely related to the distinction made by Burt (1987) between cohesion and structural equivalence. *Cohesion* relates to the membership relation as a generated outcome of the interaction process and so to the configuration of groups. *Equivalence* relates to occupancy of the same position. Two persons who occupy the same position in the division of labor are structurally equivalent[22] but do not, as such, form a group. Marx's famous class mobilization problem, with a generalized form in Dahrendorf (1959), deals with the conditions under which structurally equivalent actors in the control of a work process come to constitute a set of groups in conflictual interaction.

The third type of structural representation relates to the differentiated character of relations among the persons. Concrete relations between persons are made up of patterns of interaction in activities and of sentiments, including normative sentiments. But according to the general dynamical social system framework, the two-dimensional character of the general social structure implies that con-

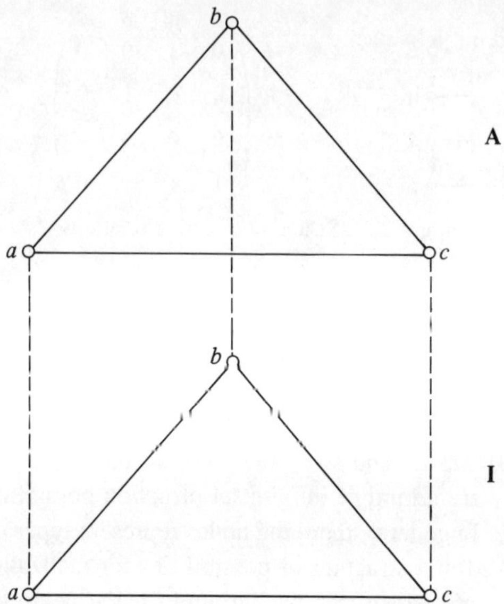


Figure 2.4. Structure of social relations

crete social relations can be regarded as composed of two analytical component relations. To show this ''multiplex'' character of social relations, a type of network representation can be adapted from Bates and Harvey (1975). An an illustration, consider a three-person system and the structure shown in Figure 2.4. The relational structure consists of an **A** substructure and a linked **I** substructure. The link consists of ''reflexive'' ties: The same persons who stand in **A** relational states also stand in **I** relational states, as shown in Figure 2.4.

For instance, if *a, b,* and *c* in Figure 2.4 are three members comprising a work group, then the overall social structure of the group consists of an adaptation substructure where they occupy positions in the division of labor and an integration substructure where their relations are expressive–symbolic. One thinks of the concrete persons as switching from one substructure or role relation to another with changing situational conditions. For instance, people in a conversation in a hospital corridor may switch from nurse–nurse to friend–friend and back again in the course of a single encounter. Institutionally, we would say that nurses are interacting, but a certain proportion of this interaction is in one relation and the complementary proportion in the other relation. This type of network diagram will be very important in the next chapter.

The attractor states also include generated group norms, both of local subgroups and of the whole group if the latter is a generated feature of the structure. Obviously, the attractor state or social structure is the whole complex of states of all the elements and not just a set of group norms. In fact, Homans (1950) makes it quite clear that, in my terms, the attractor state may be expected to involve systematic differences between the actual states of relevant activities, sentiments, and interaction and the group norms applying to those states. It is movement away from the customary level of compliance with norms on the part of a member or subset of members that constitutes a "disturbance" or "departure" event that calls forth the social control processes that tend to restore that level of compliance in the attractor state.

The conception of social structures as attractor states of dynamical social systems with the two dimensions of adaptation to environment and internal integration can be related to the distinction made by Lockwood (1964) between system integration and social integration. Social integration, as a dimension of dynamic analysis, is indicated by state variable **I.** System integration refers to the mutual compatibility of various components of the system taken as a whole. The possible **A** substructures depend on **I** as **A** adjusts to **I**. But since **I,** in turn, adjusts to **A,** there is a subset of possible **I** substructures compatible with a given state of adaptation. Taken together, they mutually determine a subset of joint states that are the really possible social structures with substructural **A** and **I** components under given conditions. So we are studying *system* "integration" when we are studying the dynamics of the whole with special attention to really possible social structures, and we are studying *social* integration when we attend especially to the **I** dynamical subsystem.

Consider Durkheim's (1915) description of the clan recurrently gathering to engage in ceremonial activity and then dispersing to go about its mundane instrumental activity. We can give this an interpretation as a process of selecting a substructure from the multiplex structure: in Figure 2.4 from the upper **A** substructure to the lower **I** substructure and back again later (in the upper substructure, the density of interaction among nodes may be reduced because of dispersal). This relational switching process itself calls for an explanation: What is the micromechanism by which the substructures are recurrently activated and then deactivated? What we require is action responsive to situational conditions. The next chapter, especially in terms of what I call structural–generative theory, treats this problem.

An alternative way of explaining the Durkheimian cycle in the two-dimensional framework of social structures is to extend the idea of attractor to stable cycles. The primary meaning of *attractor* and so stable or really possible *social structure* is a certain state of the system, as indicated thus far. But a generalized meaning, briefly discussed earlier (in note 8), exists. Here cycles are the entities that exhibit the requisite stability: Departure from the cycle tends to restore that cycle.

If both dimensions were simple one-dimensional scalar states, we could think of this as a negatively sloped ellipse in the state space with the temporal movement as an orbit. In the ongoing group, the gradual lowering of **I** that accompanies the increase in **A** is followed by a restoration of **I** to higher levels in the ceremonial gathering with a corresponding lowering of **A.** But as this is followed by an increase in **A,** the **I**-state recedes again as the group disperses to go about its mundane activity in the environment. Here social structure denotes a recurrent pattern of alternating modes of activity, taking a slab of time for realization. From a process worldview standpoint, this is an appealing element of this interpretation of Durkheimian cycles.

These conceptions of dynamics in state space, of relational switching, and of cycle attractors are based on the fundamental idea of equating stable social structure with *attractor of social network dynamics*. And, as just indicated, we have two meanings of attractor: attractor states and attractor cycles. For completeness, let me add that as mentioned earlier (note 8), the concept of chaos can be kept in mind as a third meaning of attractor. Such attractors arise under certain parametric conditions in some nonlinear models. These are the so-called strange attractors characterized by a kind of bounded wildness of behavior in state space. Potentially, then, there are strange social structures to be considered in the future of general theoretical sociology. The important thing to note, in this regard, is that like catastrophes, strange attractors arise in a context of a theoretical model with a continuum of parametric conditions in which certain values of the parameters are critical. The problem for the theorist is *not* to posit some all-embracing catastrophe or chaos approach to social dynamics but to show how any definite theoretical model yields different types of outcomes under different parametric conditions. To say it another way, both catastrophe analysis and chaos analysis are two tasks that can be undertaken in the broader context of the formal analysis of any nonlinear dynamical social system model. A catastrophe analysis is illustrated later, but I do not attempt any search for chaotic attractors in this book.

With appropriate reinterpretations of the state variables, the underlying model object may be made to refer not to the ultimate level of analysis in which we deal with "real individuals, their activity and the material conditions" (Marx and Engels, 1972:6) but to other levels of analysis and to multilevel analysis. The following remarks illustrate this point.

First, we can treat the emergence of other levels of structure. Homans (1950:Ch. 13) provides an example in his own work. Families become the primitive social units. He sets up what amounts to a threefold analogy: Family is to person as class is to subgroup as community is to group. The families replace the persons as the units of the model object, and it is their interactions, activities, and sentiments that are analyzed. The generator and the corresponding theorems then treat the problems of the emergence of social structures connecting families, the maintenance of such structures, their comparison, and their change. Social classes are aspects of the differentiation process, starting from an activity matrix in which families participate in both instrumental activities (e.g., work) and in emergent expressive activities (e.g., visiting, picnicking, and so forth). Just as subgroups of persons emerge as parts of the emergent structure of a dynamical system of interactions among persons, so social classes (with families as members) emerge as parts of the emergent structure of a dynamical system of interactions among families. Note that the emergent membership relation is now based on a shared feeling of family members of belonging to a certain class of families.

Second, we can treat multilevel phenomena. For general theoretical sociology, the primary and ultimate case of this category of analysis is the treatment of the individual as a social being. This means, among other things, that the constitutive structure of the individual as a person and the social structure of the widest collectivity to which that person is referred as a member are not independent. Thus, "the real individuals" in Marx's sense are his "species-beings" (Ollman, 1976) who acquire constitutive structure in social interaction and who employ it in further interaction. The process of constituting a person from a human organism presupposes a socially structured collectivity, whereas the emergence of new collectivities presupposes persons. In principle, these various processes and structures can be treated, and the topic is discussed again in Chapter 3.

This discussion has set out the contours of the main problems of general theoretical sociology within a dynamical systems framework. The key presupposition is a process worldview in which any structure is a contingent and probably not a uniquely possible outcome of process. The key principle is that all networks of social interaction involving people – whether readily recognized groups or more amorphous forms, whether transient or enduring, whether tiny or huge – are dynamical social systems. All are in some environment and all can be analyzed in terms of what their interactions bring forth by way of the states of their constitutive interactions. Theoretical models are specifications of the general dynamical social system to particular categories or levels of social phenomena. The four types of theorems are answers to four interconnected questions about any such dynamical social system.

This is a grounded beginning, not an ending. By a "grounded" beginning, I mean a conceptual and formal starting point that emerges not as a mathematical exercise but as rooted in an important subtradition of general theoretical sociology. This subtradition began with Pareto and continued in the early work of Homans. As I have presented the model object and the comprehensive framework, this subtradition is not isolated from other subtraditions. It shares with the Marxian subtradition an attempt to initiate social theory from a material foundation reflected in the state variables representing aspects of the activities and sentiments related to the environment. These components of the state of the system, denoted **A**, concern the scheme of instrumental activity or "mode of production" in the Marxian interpretation. The subtradition also overlaps the Durkheimian subtradition, especially in its **I** state vector, which represents emergent sentiments and activities that relate closely to ritual forms that enter into the production and expression of a sense of membership and of collective identity. Thus, both a Marxian material basis (**A**) and the core of Durkheimian "depth sociology" (**I**) are component aspects of the complete state of the system. But on the one hand, Durkheim also dealt with the causes and solidarity consequences of the division of labor. And on the other hand, Marxian classes that come to be constituted as actors do so through emergent internal social relations (**I**) grounded in structured material interest differences and the conflicts to which they give rise. Thus the mutual dependence of **I** and **A**, these remarks show, were central to the analyses of both Marx and Durkheim.

In terms of the four-level meaning control hierarchy of Chapter 1, we can indicate a few elements without striving for completeness[23]:

I. Presuppositions: process philosophical worldview
II. Framework: general dynamical social system
    Types of social structure theorems
III. Theoretical models
    Social structure theorems
IV. Invariants

At level I, one could also add some of Pareto's procedural points. The main discussion of this section has been couched at level II of theory structure. What is the representation principle? In one sense, it is simply that a human group is a dynamical social system. But in several ways the preceding discussion is more specific than this statement would indicate.

First, it is not intended that the principle merely provide a way to describe networks that form unitary groups. Under some conditions, the network processes may generate a configuration of groups that are not all included in one superordinate group. Second, drawing upon Homans's conceptual scheme, the form of the dynamical social system has been constrained to some extent: it comprises two fundamental coupled subsystems based on the dimensions of adaptation and integration. Third, the conceptual correspondence between the analytical aspects of abstract dynamical systems and sociological ideas has involved an important interpretation of social structure. This mode of interpretation may be treated as a more specific though highly generalized representation principle. To state it, let us define a *social order* as a stable social structure.

*Social order representation principle:* A social order is an attractor state or class of states of a dynamical social system.

Given that the dynamical social system is represented in terms of a coupling of adaptation and integration subsystems, a social order will be analyzable as comprising multiplex social relations involving instrumental–substantive and expressive–ceremonial strands of relatedness.

The *types* of theorems are not themselves items of theoretical knowledge, although they perform an important function in the framework as providing theoretical analysis with some objectives that relate to the entire tradition of general theoretical sociology. At level III, actual social structure theorems are to be obtained by analysis of constructed theoretical models. At this level, the four rules of process model construction set out in Section 1.4.3 apply. The history of sociological theory includes much thought that can be put into the form of *conjectured theorems.* A key example is Parsons (1937), whose conception of a common value system as a necessary condition for social order is a conjectured theorem. This is the point of view taken toward Parsons's work in the next chapter. Finally, the concept of invariants, as defined earlier, is not purely theoretical. A simple formula derived within a model may be a potential invariant (law), and a parameter appearing in it would then function as another invariant. But for this to be so, something more is needed than formal derivation: Under suitable empirical conditions, the derived properties of the model agree sufficiently well with the relevant properties of appropriate data. Thus, invariants represent a blend of theory and empirical fact.

Theory is concerned with delineation of real possibilities from conceptualized spaces representing all the logically possible states of a system. The really possible social systems are constrained: Theorems state, for instance, necessary conditions for social structures to be generated and maintained. Thus, our general theoretical interests are those corresponding to a comprehensive theory of social systems that will contain theorems about classes of theoretical models, theorems reviewed above: existence and forms of social structures, stability classification of such structures, comparative statics of social structures, and social structural change, including catastrophes.

But how does one go about constructing such a comprehensive theory? Clearly, there are no theorems without some sort of conjectured mechanisms. For everything depends on the form of the generator. A comprehensive theory cannot specify some particular generator. All it could possibly do is set down some very general template (such as $F = ma$ or what was earlier called an ecological accounting identity with regard to births and deaths) that constrains the form of any theoretical model. Not the template but the theoretical model is the entity – the model object and the theoretical assumptions about it – from which we can derive consequences. Such a template should arise from the consideration of basic principles and from experience with models constructed within the framework. This presupposes a dynamics of science: The state of the framework changes as a result of experience with models even as models are more or less controlled by the framework at any given time. At this time in the history of general theoretical sociology we do not really know how to set out such a template. And we cannot be sure of how to arrive at it.

Homans, approaching the problem from his own perhaps more empirical point of view, sought to frame hypotheses. From the present point of view, these hypotheses are not ideal ways of specifying mechanisms that combine to form a generator. The problem is that most of them are of the form that suggests they might better be regarded as statements we would want to explain from a more fundamental generative process. Table 2.2 lists some of these hypotheses along with the variables of the general dynamical social system to which they relate.

I do not want to claim that these hypotheses describe mechanisms that combine into one master mechanism, a generator. Their standing is much more analogous to the consensus-liking proposition taken to require generative explanation in Section 1.4. The coupling of $p$-centric balance processes would play the role of providing a social generator of such a statement, regarded as an aspect of certain attractor states. Note that the first proposition in the table is essentially a special case of the success proposition stated in Section 1.3.1. It is a general principle of action in situations. I shall return to the problem of deriving the social generator from assumptions about actors in situations in Section 2.11. Even if some of these statements describe mechanisms, the general case is far too complex to expect it to yield an analyzable theoretical model, as previously pointed out. Nevertheless, the table shows that we are one step beyond merely listing general ideas about the component states of the system. Insofar as these hypotheses emerge out of a heritage of empirical social science studies, they represent some knowledge about how the various elements are connected. They add substance to the framework while not solving the complexity problem.

The wisdom of scientific tradition says, when a problem is too complex, replace it with a simpler problem, trying to preserve as much as possible of the original substance. It will be seen in this book that using a strategy that begins with ideas that are both simple and formal couched within a more comprehensive framework, some problems just do not go away.[24] Nonlinearity reappears at every turn, even where we begin with some simple linear operators (as in the adaptive rationality model to be defined and studied in Chapter 3), and nonlinear systems have an interesting dual property. Conceptually, they are very attractive because so much in the way of variant forms of dynamic behavior in state space

Table 2.2. *Homans's hypotheses: examples*

| Pair | Propositions and remarks |
|---|---|
| $s_A$, $a_A$ | Motivation for an instrumental activity is continuously regenerated to the extent that the activity outcomes satisfy the motive (reinforcement), and if either element changes, so will the other. |
| $a_A$, $i_A$ | The scheme of activity (division of labor) is mutually dependent with the scheme of interaction that coordinates the partial activities of members: If either changes, so will the other. In the special case of supervisory activity, the interactive coordination takes the invariant form of a chain of command with each person having a limited span of control. |
| $i_I$, $s_I$ | The more frequently persons interact, the greater their degree of liking and conversely. See Section 2.4 for the proper interpretation. The greater the frequency of interaction, the greater the similarity of norms, and once established, norms change more slowly than actual activities. The more nearly equal in social rank persons are, the more frequently they will interact with one another (and conversely). |
| $s_I$, $a_I$ | The higher the rank of a person within a group, the more nearly the activities of that person conform to the norms and values of the group, and conversely. Persons who feel sentiments of liking for one another express these sentiments in activities over and above external system activities, which may further strengthen the sentiments of liking. |
| $i_I$, $a_I$; $i_I$, $s_I$ | Persons who interact with one another frequently are more similar to one another in their activities and sentiments than they are to other persons with whom they interact less frequently: The greater the frequency of interaction, the more similar the activities. |

may be implied. This gives the sociological imagination much with which to work. On the other hand, the analysis of such systems usually is very difficult. As we shall see, I shall end up advising computer-based thought experiments where the analytical method breaks down. Other tactics will be employed at various points, including probabilistic state descriptions and discrete- rather than continuous-time representations. In all such cases, my point of view will be that although these are technically important variants, conceptually they remain within the framework of approaching social structure from the point of view of dynamical systems.

The Pareto–Homans systems-theoretical subtradition went a step farther with an important contribution by Simon. And Simon made an essential simplification that permitted formal theory to proceed. This is the starting point of the next section, as we pass from the framework level to the study of some definite theoretical models.

## 2.9. Example: four social structure theorems

The line of analytical theory from Pareto to Homans, as of 1950, led to a mathematical theory almost immediately. Pareto, trained in how natural scientists and engineers treated systems, had provided the methodological groundwork and some of the substantive ideas. Homans, as I have interpreted him, carried these ideas forward in many ways. Yet he employed not a bit of mathematics or formal analysis. A mathematician or a mathematically trained analyst reading Homans's work, however, could not fail to see the signposts along the way: Homans (1950:Ch. 11) tells us in no uncertain terms that his verbal propositions and accounts emerge by an "as if" process of thinking of groups in terms of differential equations (without writing down any formulas).[25] Thus, when Herbert Simon encountered Homans, he was led to an effort to bring the equations into the open, to formalize Homans's theory. In this section, I reanalyze Simon's formalization. The aim is to illustrate the general framework of dynamical social systems theory and to demonstrate that with judicious simplifications and idealizations, definite theorems can be obtained. In fact, four theorems, corresponding to the four general types, will be stated. I reserve criticism of the model and of the entire approach until Section 2.11.

Simon's 1952 article reprinted in Simon (1957), defined the following variables:

$A$ = amount of activity
$I$ = intensity of interaction
$F$ = level of friendliness
$E$ = amount of imposed activity

These are intended as aggregated terms, the consequences of which will be discussed in a later section. The $I$ variable can be measured in terms of the amount of time the average pair interacts or in terms of the average frequency of interaction per pair. Variable $A$ also could be measured in terms of time spent in activities of the group per unit time per member. Activity $E$ would be in the same units. The sentiment variable $F$ might be thought of measured by some sociometric procedure. There are really two possibilities for $F$: as a nonnegative variable or as a variable that might be negative (e.g., hostility in interpersonal relations). In Simon's formal theory, all the variables are assumed to be positive, as are all the constants introduced in defining mechanisms.

Let us see how Simon represents the various mechanisms and combines them into a generator.

A level of friendliness among a set of interacting persons yields a certain intensity of interaction. The general "translation" of sentiment into interaction may be denoted

$$I = a_1 F$$

We see that the coefficient $a_1$ measures a kind of expressive immediacy, the extent to which positive sentiments translate into interaction. Thus, we may think of its reciprocal, $1/a_1$, as a *coefficient of affective neutrality*. For instance, friendly feelings among a group of peers will have a lower affective neutrality than the same feelings among persons characterized by differences in authority. The authority difference appears to neutralize the sentiments so far as their translation into intensity of interaction is concerned.

A scheme of activity implies a certain amount of interaction. Each scheme can be characterized in terms of how it "translates" $A$ into $I$. For instance, a row of workers each independently assembling parts of a device do not require much, if any, interaction. By contrast, the required interaction is considerable among workers who coordinate their activities to produce a joint activity, such as conducting exchanges in a stock market. The general translation formula can be written

$$I = a_2 A.$$

The term $a_2$ may be called the *coefficient of interdependence,* following Simon's own usage.

Simon's theoretical model treats the intensity of interaction as a joint outcome of both of these translations, combining them additively:

$$I = a_1 F + a_2 A \qquad (2.9.1a)$$

Hence, the lower the affective neutrality and the greater the interdependence of the activities, the greater the intensity of interaction. This equation is not dynamic: interaction is an algebraic sum of two components, which represents an immediate translation of activity and sentiment into a certain level of interaction. The next two equations are dynamic.

First, friendship adjusts to interaction, so that corresponding to a certain amount of interaction, sentiments equilibrate to a level adjusted to that amount: The greater the interaction, the greater the adjusted level of friendship. Simon proposes the form:

$$dF/dt = b(I - \beta F) \tag{2.9.1b}$$

Second, activity equilibrates to the level of friendship: for a given level of friendship, the amount of activity adjusts to it; the greater the friendship, the greater the adjusted level of activity. Also and independently, activity equilibrates to the demand for activity given from the environment: The greater the demand, the greater the adjusted level of activity. Simon assumes these two mechanisms combine additively:

$$dA/dt = c_1(F - \delta A) + c_2(E - A) \tag{2.9.1c}$$

Some further terminology may be introduced to name the constants, appropriate to the nature of the mechanisms. We have seen that (2.9.1b) says that friendship adjusts to interaction. If we put $dF/dt = 0$, then the equilibrium relation is

$$F_{\text{eq}} = (1/\beta)I \tag{2.9.2}$$

The greater the coefficient, the greater the equilibrated level of friendship for any given intensity of interaction. Thus Simon calls $1/\beta$ the *congeniality* coefficient.

Consider again (2.9.1c). In this adjustment process, $A$ *would* equal $E$ if $c_1$ were zero. On the other hand, suppose $c_2 = 0$. Then $A_{\text{eq}}$ would be given by $(1/\delta)F$. That is, for any given level of friendship, the generated (expressive) activity would equilibrate at the level determined by the coefficient $1/\delta$. Hence Simon calls this the *spontaneity* constant. Recall that activity is called expressive if it is generated by interpersonal sentiments rather than by the motives for task-oriented activity. Thus this constant is a rather important property of the integration system.

From the standpoint of dynamical systems ideas, the dynamic variables in equations (2.9.1a)–(2.9.1c) are $F$ and $A$. We can treat $E$ as an input or exogenous variable and for convenience treat it as a parameter. But note that $I$ is a function of $F$ and $A$. If we replace $I$ in equation (2.9.1b) with the linear combination of the state variables given in equation (2.9.1a), then we have the dynamical system given by

$$\mathrm{d}F/dt = b[a_2 A - (\beta - a_1)F] \tag{2.9.3a}$$

$$\mathrm{d}A/dt = c_1(F - \delta A) + c_2(E - A) \tag{2.9.3b}$$

With two state variables, the state space becomes the positive quadrant of the $x$–$y$ plane, with $x = A$ and $y = F$. I term the dynamical system (2.9.3) the *Simon–Homans linear model.* Although it does not directly instantiate the form of the general system in (2.8.1), it may be considered as a theoretical model within the theory structure associated with the representation principle that human groups are dynamical social systems. Recall that when a definite theoretical model is specified, analytical investigations leading to four types of theorems can be undertaken corresponding to the existence and form of social structures, their social control aspect, their comparative statics aspect, and their social change aspect. The advantage of Simon's simplification is that we can attain definite theorems of these types. They are of interest in their own right and also serve to illustrate the ideas presented about the general dynamical social system. This will be the focus of the following treatment of the model.

*Problem 1: social equilibrium — the conditions for the existence of social structures.* Given the dynamical system (2.9.3), the first problem has the mathematical form of solving for the equilibrium solutions. This is a linear system, so there is at most one equilibrium state for any given set of values of all the parameters. The theorem we seek informs us of the parametric conditions under which the social mechanisms defining the generator of the process imply the existence of such an equilibrium.

We obtain a pair of equations for the social structure by setting $dF/dt=0$ and $dA/dt=0$ in (2.9.3). (With regard to the following discussion, see Figure 2.5.) We obtain

$$\text{Line 1 } (dF/dt=0): \quad F=[a_2/(\beta-a_1)]A \qquad (2.9.4a)$$

$$\text{Line 2 } (dA/dt=0): \quad F=[\delta+c_2/c_1]A-(c_2/c_1)E \qquad (2.9.4b)$$

Recall that $F$ and $A$ are positive. Note that line 1 passes through the origin, and because $F$ must not be negative and the constants are positive, we require that $\beta>a_1$. So we have a straight line with positive slope through the origin. The slope is given by the expression in brackets, which is a function of the constants. Similarly, line 2 is a straight line. It has a negative intercept that depends on $E$ and the ratio of the $c$ constants. Its slope is the expression shown in brackets, the coefficient of $A$.

There are two cases with regard to the lines, given that the condition $\beta>a_1$ (or, equivalently, $1/a_1>1/\beta$) holds:

Case 1. Slope(line 1) > slope(line 2) (Figure 2.5a). In this case, the lines do not intersect in the state space. Hence there is no equilibrium state. No social structure is possible under these conditions.

Case 2. Slope(line 1) < slope(line 2) (Figure 2.5b). In this case, the lines do intersect and a social structure is possible. The comparative slope condition means that

$$\delta+c_2/c_1>a_2/(\beta-a_1)$$

It will be convenient to write this condition in the form

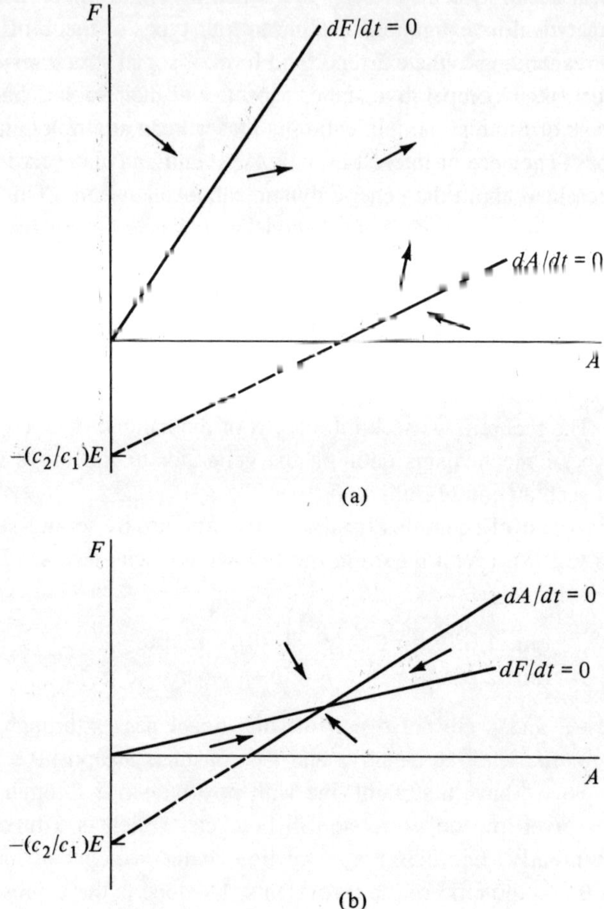


Figure 2.5. Dynamic outcomes for linear model

$$K > 0 \tag{2.9.5}$$

where $K = (\beta - a_1)(c_1\delta + c_2) - a_2c_1$.

Hence, we obtain the following preliminary result:

> For the linear Simon–Homans theoretical model, a social structure is possible if and only if affective neutrality is not too small and condition (2.9.5) holds.

The affective neutrality condition comes from the necessary condition that $\beta > a_1$. This is the same as saying that $1/a_1 > 1/\beta$, which says that the coefficient of affective neutrality must be greater than the congeniality constant characterizing the group's interactions. Affective neutrality is "too small" is a way of saying that this required inequality fails to hold. An equivalent way of framing this condition would be: "Congeniality must not be too great." Sometimes, in the study of a theoretical model, for some reason a necessary condition can be discovered but not sufficient conditions. Also, even if, as in the current case, we can find necessary and sufficient conditions, it may be useful to state an important necessary condition on its own. Particularly because the condition in (2.9.5) has not received any interesting sociological interpretation, I shall focus theoretical attention on the affective neutrality result because of its obvious link to Parsons's (1951) framework. Thus, the following will be regarded as an interpretable theoretical answer to the first problem:

> *Theorem 1:* For the linear Simon–Homans theoretical model, a necessary condition for the existence of a social structure is that affective neutrality is not too small.

Note the form of the theorem. Each theorem is a statement of a property of a theoretical model. As stated, the theorem cannot be false. But a class of groups whose social dynamics we regard as within the scope of the theoretical model may have state descriptions that in some sense fail to exhibit the deduced properties of the model. The opening clause, "for the linear Simon–Homans theoretical model," essentially stands for the complete set of assumptions that define the theoretical model, whereas the remainder of the sentence is a logically derived statement holding for this model. This is typical (but not necessary) of formal theoretical analysis, and often one simply reports the derived properties as theorems without the opening clause. In such a form a theorem is empirically meaningful in the sense of being refutable, and its refutation calls into question one or more of the assumptions from which it was deduced. Put in model terms, such a refutation calls into question the conjectured mechanisms imposed on a model object referent to entities in a specified empirical domain.

*Problem 2: stability of the structure – social control.* The general question now is as follows. Suppose the system is in a state near one of the possible social structures. Will the social dynamics keep the state of the system near this structure or not? If so, the departures from the social equilibrium are being held in check, and thus, by definition, successful social control exists. If not, social control – which is just social dynamics analyzed with respect to the stability analysis of a particular social structure – is ineffective; and the process will carry the system toward some alternative social structure if one exists.

For the Simon–Homans linear model, this question is already answered by the result that, for this model, if a social structure exists, it is stable. To see this, consider the four regions of state space demarcated by the intersection of lines 1 and 2 in Figure 2.5b. The reader can verify that $dA/dt$ and $dF/dt$ have the pattern of signs that justifies drawing the vector of movement out of a state in a given region in the direction shown. All four arrows point to the equilibrium state. Hence, that state is stable. No additional conditions were needed in this case. Since this is the only possible social structure under the given conditions, we are done.

> *Theorem 2.* For the Simon–Homans linear system, if a social structure exists, then it is an attractor of social process: There is effective social control in that the social structure is a *stable* equilibrium state of the system.

*Problem 3: comparative social statics.* We now focus on the theoretical question, How do stable social structures vary with parametric conditions?

This is a comparative statics problem, where we express a stable social structural state as a function of parameters. Then we differentiate to see how the structure shifts with a shift in some parameter of interest. In this model, the parametric conditions are the various constants together with the input variable $E$. Since $E$ has the interesting interpretation as the activity required by the environment, it is natural to consider how the stable social structure varies as E varies. What we require are the expressions for equilibrium values of $A$ and $F$ in terms of the parameters. From the equilibrium equations, we derive

$$A_{eq} = [c_2(\beta - a_1)/K]E \qquad (2.9.6a)$$
$$F_{eq} = [c_2 a_2/K]E \qquad (2.9.6b)$$

These expressions have been written to make it obvious that we are expressing the stable equilibrium state of the system – the pair ($A_{eq}$, $F_{eq}$) – as functions of $E$. Differentiating with respect to $E$ to see how the social structure changes with changes in the environmental demands, yields the bracketed expressions, respectively, for the two components of activity and friendship. Since these are stable equilibrium states we are investigating, we know that the coefficients in (2.9.6) are positive: $K > 0$ was condition (2.9.5) and our necessary condition $\beta > a_1$ is used here too. Thus an upward shift in $E$ produces, after the dynamics adjusts the state to the new conditions, a higher level of both activity and friendship. Since interaction is a positive linear combination of these two states, the total amount of interaction will also increase. Hence, we have an example of the third type of theorem:

*Theorem 3:* For the Simon–Homans linear theoretical model, a shift in the environmental demand produces a shift in the same direction in the stable social structure of the system.

In this context, Simon (1957:106) produces a very interesting theoretical result. This result illustrates that although the paradigm of four theorem types is important and useful, it should not be construed as a ritual form intolerant of creative departures from its suggested procedural format. Simon asks how large the equilibrium value of $A$ will be as compared with $E$. The equations of the model allow a social structure to be possible even if the amount of activity is less than that required by the environment. In fact, Simon shows that $A_{eq} > E$ if and only if the following relationship holds:

$$\delta(\beta - a_1) > a_2 \tag{2.9.7}$$

Asking what relationships among parameters tend to favor this condition, Simon finds results such as the following two:

(i) $a_2$ large (high interdependence of activities)
(ii) $1/\delta$ large (high spontaneity)

Drawing on Durkheim at this point, Simon interprets $A_{eq} < E$ as a condition of anomie and notes that condition (i) implies that little interdependence of activities is conducive to anomie.

*Problem 4: social change.* The problem now is that the parameter is viewed as undergoing continuous change over time and we wish to analytically investigate how the social structure changes. There is now a joint examination of both the parameter space and the state space phenomena over time. Catastrophe analysis is relevant (Fararo, 1978).

In the Simon–Homans linear model, we know that the relative slopes of the two equilibrium lines separate two sorts of systems: those that have a stable social structure and those that undergo explosive growth in the state, which so far as the model is unconcerned is unchecked. (Any real group state cannot go unchecked, but what happens in this case is outside the scope of the linear model.) Hence, the relationship that formulates the boundary between these two types of systems is

$$\delta + (c_2/c_1) = a_2/(\beta - a_1) \tag{2.9.8}$$

Hence, if any of these terms is envisioned as varying in time, then the over-time behavior may lead to a crossing of this boundary line. This is a catastrophe: a shift from a stable social structure to one characterized by unlimited and eventually nonviable growth of activity and friendship or the reverse shift. I adopt the term *structuration* from Giddens (1984) to denote the catastrophe of moving from a system without a stable structure to a system with a stable structure.[26] Naturally, destructuration is the reverse catastrophe.

> *Theorem 4:* For the Simon–Homans linear model, both a structuration catastrophe and a destructuration catastrophe are possible. They occur if the boundary (2.9.8) is crossed through over-time changes in the values of the constants.

An important general point about explanation in theoretical sociology can be made by reference to this model. In a dynamical systems context, the primary exemplification of explanation is the passage from the mechanisms that define the model to their implied recursively generated consequences in the form of possible social structures and their stability, comparative statics, and dynamic change. But an important secondary meaning of explanation exists. This is illustrated in the context of Theorem 4. If a destructuration catastrophe occurs, our immediate explanation will be not by appeal to the generic mechanisms but by reference to a change in the relevant parameter. In a quite legitimate sense, it is the change in this parameter that produces the destructuration. As such it is a *control parameter,* to use the language of catastrophe theorists (Zeeman, 1977). It is one interpretation of the difficult concept of *causation:* Change in the control parameter causes the change in the state. We can even take the intervention point of view that is probably the social origin of the concept of causation: If we *make* the control parameter change in a certain way, then (with other parameters fixed) the state will change in a specified way. If explanation means "providing a cause," then the relation of the control parameter to a state that adjusts to it is a causal-explanatory relation. If we ask *why* this causal relation holds, however, then the generative mechanism provides the answer. The point of view of this book is that specifying generative mechanisms is the more fundamental mode of explanation. But it also shows the legitimacy and significance of causal accounts that relate variables to variables: The causal variable should be interpreted as a control parameter; the caused variable, as a state variable; and the causal relation, as itself requiring explanation by reference to the construction of an appropriate dynamical system model. These remarks relate to the earlier discussion in Chapter 1 and to an upcoming summing up on causation in a dynamical systems perspective (in Section 2.10.2).

The four theorems stated in this section were intended to be of interest in their own right and also to illustrate the general ideas outlined earlier concerning the analysis of the general dynamical social system. The linear character of the theoretical model, however, restricts the possibilities for social dynamics and social structure. For instance, because of linearity, only one (if any) social structure is really possible given the environmental parameters. More interesting phenomena can be generated if we pass to the domain of nonlinear models. This is the topic of the next section.

## 2.10. Nonlinear dynamics, causal explanation, and functional analysis

This section expands on several topics that have been mentioned earlier: the character and importance of nonlinear theoretical models, the way in which Durkheimian causal explanation relates to the realist philosophical generative model adopted in this book, and finally, how functional analysis can be interpreted in this conceptual setting.

### *2.10.1. Nonlinear social dynamics*

Nonlinear dynamics is one of the most important areas of contemporary applied mathematical research. In the 1970s, the big idea was catastrophe, which only came into sharp focus with nonlinear dynamics. The catastrophe ideas were developed earlier by Thom and then summarized by him in a book translated into English in the mid-1970s (Thom, 1975). At about the same time, an English mathematician led a virtual intellectual movement to create a new basis for social science through the construction of catastrophe models (Zeeman, 1976, 1977). There was a faddish quality to this movement, and it has died down. But the ideas do have extensive relevance to social science if not made into *the* mathematical method for our use (Fararo, 1978). In the late 1980s, the big idea was chaos, which again only became visible in studying the implications of nonlinear generators. Concentrating on "strange" attractors in dynamical systems, chaos analysis is adding to our battery of concepts and techniques for setting up theoretical models and studying them on the basis of a dynamical systems standpoint (Thompson and Stewart, 1986). In this section, only the catastrophe component of these two recent developments in nonlinear analysis will make an appearance.[27]

I shall examine and develop a little further the nonlinear version of the Simon–Homans theoretical model. From this standpoint, the linear model is thought of as an approximation in the neighborhood of an equilibrium state of the more general nonlinear formulation. To repeat, nonlinearity introduces additional real possibilities for social dynamics that are excluded if we remain in the framework of linear models. In particular, as mentioned earlier, to any given set of values of the constants and the input $E$, there may be a multiplicity of possible social structures, that is, equilibria.

The basic idea is to generalize the linear form of the mechanisms in (2.9.1). The amount of interaction will be some monotone increasing function of $F$ and $A$ with linearity as a special case. When this generalized expression is substituted in the second equation of (2.9.1), that equation becomes nonlinear. Similarly, the third equation is generalized. The dynamical system (2.9.3) becomes the general nonlinear system specified by

$$dF/dt = f_1(A, F) \qquad (2.10.1a)$$
$$dA/dt = f_2(A, F; E) \qquad (2.10.1b)$$

The equilibrium equations may be written in the form

$$\text{Curve 1 } (dF/dt=0): \quad f_1(A, F)=0 \qquad (2.10.2a)$$
$$\text{Curve 2 } (dA/dt=0): \quad f_2(A, F)=0 \qquad (2.10.2b)$$

These are curves in the state space, the positive quadrant of the $A$–$F$ plane, generalizing the two straight lines given by (2.9.4). The shapes of the curves determine the qualitative properties of the system (e.g., the number of equilibria and the stability or not of each). In terms of curve 1, $F$ dynamically adjusts to given values of $A$. In terms of curve 2, $A$ dynamically adjusts to given values of $F$. As in the linear model, the points where the two curves intersect define the system equilibrium states where each state variable is adjusted to the other, given a value of the input parameter $E$.

The interpretation of equilibration as the adjustment of the state variables to each other and to the parameter $E$ leads to the following postulates that yield the qualitative properties of the system:

1. Variable $F$ adjusts to $A$ in such a way that greater activity will produce greater equilibrated friendship. Thus, curve 1 is monotone increasing.
2. As $A$ increases, $F$ increases at a declining rate.
3. Below some level of activity, call it $A^*$, there is no friendship.
4. Variable $A$ adjusts to $F$ in such a way that greater friendship will produce greater equilibrated levels of activity. Thus, curve 2 is monotone increasing (with the functional relation from $F$ to $A$).
5. As $F$ increases, $A$ increases at a declining rate.
6. When $F=0$, the equilibrated value of $A$ will be nonzero (which really is a statement that input parameter $E$ guarantees some activity). Call this value $M$.
7. As $E$ increases, at any given level of $F$, the level of $A$ increases.

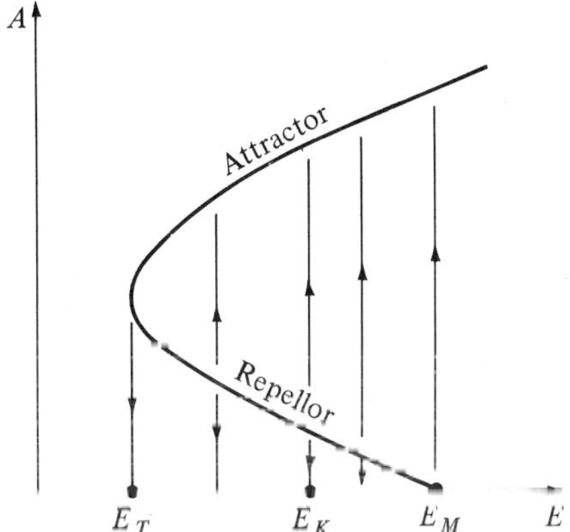


Figure 2.6. Nonlinear dynamics in behavior manifold

A number of theorems that relate to comparative statics and catastrophe analysis follow from these postulates defining the nonlinear model, as shown in detail elsewhere (Fararo, 1984b).

> *Theorem 1* (comparative statics): If E decreases, then if a stable social structure exists before and after the adjustment, it will be characterized by a lower set of values of both $A$ and $F$.

Note that this result generalizes Theorem 3 of the linear model, the comparative statics theorem. The logic of such a theorem is to ask how any stable equilibrium state of a dynamical system varies with variations in the parameters of the system.

The next result is a theorem of Type 4, that is, relating to social change. The initial step is to treat the state of the system in terms of $A$ alone. The simplification is justified for the scope of the analysis involved, since when parameter $E$ changes, it changes $F$ via the change in $A$ and in the same direction. Thus $E$ will be our parameter for this analysis. Its range of variation is parameter space, the nonnegative portion of the real line. The analysis is easiest to follow in terms of the behavior manifold: the set-theoretical (Cartesian) product of the parameter space and the state space. With one-dimensional spaces, such a product is simply the familiar $x$–$y$ plane, with the $x$ axis labeled by the parameter and the $y$ axis labeled by the state variable. Thus, our treatment involves the positive quadrant of the $E$–$A$ plane. We postulate that $E$ changes more slowly than $A$. As $E$ continuously changes over time, at this slower rate, the nonlinear social dynamics adjusts $A$ to $E$. We have the situation shown in Figure 2.6.

For a certain region of the parameter space, the values of $E$ are such that we have two equilibria. The smaller of the two equilibrium values is the unstable one. Hence the lower branch of the curve depicting the two possible equilibria is the repellor branch; the upper is the attractor branch. For a fixed value of $E$ in this region, the dynamics are arrows up or down, as shown, that adjust $A$ to $E$. But the curve also has a tangent point above $E_T$. If $E$ were decreasing from an initial condition $E_K$ with a corresponding stable equilibrium on the upper branch, then the activity state would track it by adjusting along the upper branch. So $A$ would dynamically adjust to successively lower equilibrated values. Then as $E$ crossed the point $E_T$, the dynamics would carry $A$ toward zero. But this implies, since $A < A^*$, that $F$ also goes to zero. Thus a small change in $E$ produces a rapid and large change in the social structure, in fact dissolving the group. This is the *destructuration catastrophe* implied by the nonlinear model.

> *Theorem 2* (catastrophes): For the nonlinear Simon–Homans theoretical model, a destructuration catastrophe is possible, and it occurs when $E$ decreases below some threshold value $E_T$.

Suppose now we envision a process of bringing a group into existence, that is, establishing a stable social structure from certain initial conditions where it does not exist. Let these initial conditions be such that $E$ will increase from below $E_T$ with activity and friendship each at zero. Then the dynamic on the parameter space carries $E$ across $E_T$ toward and then past $E_K$ with still no activity until $E$ crosses $E_M$, when the nonlinear dynamical system for $A$ and $F$ will quickly (relative to the rate of change of $E$) carry the system to a state on the upper branch. Thus, a stable social structure will rather quickly be formed when the threshold $E_M$ is crossed. The existence of this threshold follows from the postulates: It is that value of $E$ corresponding to point $M$ of postulate 6. This is the *structuration catastrophe* implied for the nonlinear model.

> *Theorem 3* (catastrophes): For the nonlinear Simon–Homans theoretical model, a structuration catastrophe is possible, and it occurs when with zero levels of $A$ and $F$ the parameter $E$ increases and crosses a threshold point $E_M$.

This concludes my examination of the Simon–Homans theoretical model in its linear and nonlinear forms. My central focus has been on the way in which the analysis of the dynamical systems specified by the linear and nonlinear models illustrate my general discussion of the general dynamical social system. Contrary to the argument in Buckley (1967), the examination shows that the model allows a treatment of *morphogenesis*. Once social structure is identified with the equilibrium solutions of the dynamical social system – as a contingent outcome of dynamic process rather than a given state of affairs – and once we treat these structures as multiple possibilities that dynamically adjust to time-varying inputs or parameters, we obtain a direct representation of the breakdown and formation of social structures. In general, as the parameter space is envisioned as a scene of its own dynamics – either explicitly represented by some mechanisms or merely taken as unexplained over-time variation – the transformation of social structure over time logically follows. The present analysis thereby illustrates catastrophes in nonlinear dynamics. As mentioned at the start of this section, this does not exhaust the possibilities for rich results through nonlinear dynamical systems analysis. Chaos is one key idea that will play a role in the future. Both catastrophes and chaos imply the existence of threshold phenomena, which do make their appearance in social phenomena. The potentialities for very interesting studies in the study of threshold phenomena are just beginning to be explored in sociology. See, especially, Granovetter (1978) and Granovetter and Soong (1983).

### 2.10.2. *On explanation and functional analysis*

Two meanings of explanation in theoretical sociology can be specified and related, as mentioned in Chapter 1. First, we have Durkheimian causal explanation in the sense that what requires explanation is a social fact and what is invoked to explain it is another social fact. In the present context, a social fact is a social state or a sociocultural condition (represented as a parameter value) of a dynamical social system over a social network. It may also be some function of such a state and conditions (e.g., suicide rates). I first shall treat the conceptually simplest situation in which we try to explain some state or substate of a system. Two more specific meanings that might be assigned to explicate such Durkheimian causal explanation can be symbolized as follows:

1. Parameter $\rightarrow$ outcome in state space
2. Initial state $\rightarrow$ state at time $t$ (under given conditions)

We saw an example of the first type in the catastrophe discussion of Theorem 4 of the linear model, which would also apply to the theorems of the nonlinear model. Another important class of cases under the first type involves comparative statics: The outcome is some attractor. To explain a given enduring social state, we interpret it dynamically as an attractor and then explain it by showing that it is to be expected under the given parametric conditions. If these conditions vary, so does the attractor. The asymmetry required for a causal relation between variables holds provided that any feedback loop from state space to parameter space is such that the parameter changes at a much slower rate. In the latter case, the feedback can be represented in terms of a recursive process in which to each value of the parameter there is a fast dynamics in state space that yields an outcome that results in an updated value of the parameter. Otherwise, we would have an analytical relationship that is only one side of a mutual dependence relation, as discussed in Section 2.4.

The second meaning says that to explain any state of the system, whether an attractor or not, one invokes the initial state of the system. According to D'Abro (1951:Vol. I, Ch. 7), this is the primary meaning of causality in physics. Asymmetry holds through the directionality of time: A later state cannot cause an earlier state. A generalization of this idea was seen in Section 1.4.3; namely, the state at time $t$ is explained by the initial state and the history of inputs since that time.

These two meanings of Durkheimian causal explanation have one major element in common: They are ultimately justified in theoretical terms as consequences of some generative mechanism defining a dynamical system. The first type of Durkheimian causal explanation is justified by a theorem. This is what makes the connection more than just an observed empirical correlation between two social facts: We know that the generator, operating under varying social conditions, will yield distinct social structural facts. Given any present enduring state, if those conditions were different, then the enduring state would be different. This counterfactual conditional aspect of the theorem was pointed out earlier in Section 2.5. The special case of law corresponds closely to Durkheim's context. However, where he thinks of the law as inductively emerging from empirical investigation, I think of the law as deductively emerging from theoretical investigation but supported by data that, in the whole context, support the theoretical model within which it is logically derived. Still, as in the case of the liking-consensus example of Chapter 1, we can begin with an empirical law or regularity and only later find a way to represent the phenomena to which it refers in such a way as to derive its form within a theoretical model. The history of science shows many examples of this sort of development.

The second type of Durkheimian causal explanation also receives its theoretical justification from the generator: It carries the specified initial state into the state being explained, so that the connection between the two social facts is again more than just an over-time correlation.

Durkheimian causal explanation that is theoretically justified by a social generative mechanism I call *Durkheimian social generativity*. That is, some combination of social interactive mechanisms logically implies the two types of Durkheimian causal explanations of social facts. Durkheimian generativity is in the spirit of unification. Positivistic *causal models* relate variables and miss the generativity. Realists emphasize generative mechanisms and denigrate the search for causal relations among variables. Durkheimian generativity subordinates the positivist search for causal relations to a realist primacy of process but finds a place for social facts explaining social facts *via* the mechanism. Moreover, as understood here, Durkheimian social generativity requires a further "structuralist" element; namely, it applies to a state description of a social network.

Let us turn now to another version of the Durkheimian idea of social facts invoked to explain social facts. The facts to be explained are social but not constitutive of a defined social structure that enters into the explanation. These facts may be properties of culture, or they may be aggregated rates of individual states or acts – just to mention the two most prominent species of such facts. In the typical form, the facts may be interpreted as corresponding to comparative statics of the relevant process, so that variations in these social facts are conditioned by variations in social structural facts.

A partial and informal sketch of a theoretical model may serve as an illustration of what is meant. This sketch then will lead into a very general idea about the theoretical meaning of the sociology of some phenomenon. The sketch will be based on an interpretation of some of the mathematical ideas introduced by Coleman (1964) in the analysis of "networks of social influence" as described in detail elsewhere (Fararo, 1973:Sect. 13.2). The relevant type of model object involves a stochastic process with two levels of state description, individual and aggregate, *given* a stable social structure.

Consider the social fact that in a population of groups, the suicide rate varies in the way that led Durkheim (1951) to propose his law of suicide. The intuitive idea is that the probability of suicide relates to the individual's social integration. In this context Durkheim uses at least two subordinate meanings of *integration*, but a primary reference is to the extent of enduring social ties surrounding an individual. Treating only this element, a version of the law may be put in the form: The greater the cohesion of a group, the lower its suicide rate. The comparative statics aspect is clear: Such a rate varies in time but adjusts, in the equilibration sense, to a social structural state (functioning here in a parametric role) in the way that the proposition states. If this form of the law is accepted, then when two particular groups are compared with respect to their suicide rates, the difference is explained by pointing out the differences in their cohesion. But granting its invariant character for the sake of this discussion, what explains the law of suicide itself?

The network analysis begins with a translation of the group-level concept of cohesion so that it is constituted by a fact about the social structure in the sense of some attractor state of a social network. The translation may be put in the form: Cohesion is the density of positive interpersonal sentiments among members. The suicide rate is clearly a very different type of social fact. It is not, as such, social structural but an aggregation over individual-level acts. A model object is involved here: a social network of positive interpersonal ties, with each node in one of two states. These states of nodes vary in time. They represent the perhaps transient goal state or disposition toward suicidal or nonsuicidal action. We can posit that in any small time interval the transition between such states depends on some environmental events and on the influences of other nodes in the network. In particular, we can assume that each node has a chance of transition from one dispositional state to another with a rate that depends on the number of nodes to which it is linked that are in each such state.

The formal specification of this influence assumption defines a generative theoretical model. In the formal study of the various possible outcomes it generates, we would expect one such outcome to capture Durkheim's law. Another outcome that might arise is a Jonestown-type mass suicide. Such different types of outcomes probably depend on the particulars of the mechanisms of influence, on the relative magnitudes of parameters of the influence process, and on the group size. We can think of labeling the ties in the network by influence parameters proportional to the presumed strength of ties. Also, some assumption is needed about how the suicidal act depends on the suicidal state. The upshot of this admitted mere sketch is that Durkheim's law would be derived *under certain social conditions* in addition to those formulated in terms of cohesion. It would be an instance of starting from what was called an invariant in Chapter 1 and then interpreting it in terms of a theoretical model in such a way as to make clearer the conditions under which it is expected to hold. So Durkheim's law would be explained but also qualified, a quite common practice in theoretical sciences.

A key point in this type of explanation is that an attractor state of the social network is presupposed. To employ the explanatory procedure, we invoke social order in the sense of a set of conditions that shapes the form of a social process that itself is not definitive of that social order. The explanation occurs through a postulated generative process model that shows, at the level of derived results, how variations in the social structural fact produce variations in the other social fact. When there is a focus on such explanations of nonconstitutive social facts (types of collective-level facts about human action) via social structural facts, theoretical sociology shifts in focus from the four key problems framed in this chapter to another and closely related focus. Tentatively, it is suggested that this provides a distinction between general theoretical sociology and related theoretical work in sociology. It cannot be claimed that this distinction is without any ambiguities, but it serves a useful function in helping to delineate further general theoretical sociology as having interests that do not exhaust all possible theoretical interests in sociology. Many of these interests can be encompassed with the following summary statement cast in the form of a definition:

> By the *theoretical sociology of X* is meant the construction and analysis of generative theoretical models such that the dynamics and attractor states of $X$ are shown to depend on social structural conditions.

So, in the theoretical sociology of $X$, social structural properties are variable conditions in the parameter space, and the variable properties of $X$ constitute the definition of the state space in formulating the behavior manifold. By contrast, in general theoretical sociology, the role of social structure in relation to the behavior manifold is reversed: A social structure is a contingent possibility of the forms of interaction conceptualized in state space, and other elements take the role of defining the parameter space. Since $X$ can be any aspect of human activity, as $X$ varies, an infinite family of Durkheimian social facts exists. Each type of such fact is treated in terms of how its dynamics and adjusted states are conditioned by social structure.

The distinction suggested is analytical and flexible. For instance, when $X$ is some state of culture, the production of $X$ can be treated in terms of the theoretical sociology of $X$. In the actual world, however, changes in $X$ may produce changes in the very social structure that is the ground for the production of $X$. An example is the production of science in academic settings and the invention of new academic roles for research and teaching of new sciences. This suggests an analytical perspective not antithetical to the theoretical sociology of $X$ in which $X$ is treated as endogenous in a dynamical system that is sociocultural. In other words, $X$ and the relevant social states are treated as mutually dependent state variables. The attractors of the sociocultural dynamical system then comprise social structures together with certain cultural structures (cultural states adjusted to social states and to the defined parameters of the relevant sociocultural process). The distinctive focus of general theoretical sociology remains the formation and transformation of social structures, but this focus can be embedded within a broader sociocultural dynamical focus.

Let us turn now to functional analysis in the context of dynamical social systems and Durkheimian social generativity. Functional analysis rests on three presuppositions: (1) For a given type of system, we know that certain conditions are necessary for an attractor state to exist; (2) we suppose that a specific attractor state does exist in some system of the given type; and (3) we want to theoretically show how the necessary conditions are generated or regenerated so as to maintain the attractor state.

Clearly, the first presupposition is met if we have derived a combination Type 1 and Type 2 theorem, assuming the theorem formulates some necessary conditions. The second presupposition can be general and hypothetical or it can be specific and factual about an instance of the type of system within the scope of the theoretical model. Then the third presupposition formulates the functional analysis problem.

For example, suppose that a system of interaction is interpreted in terms of the Simon–Homans linear system and is assumed to be in an attractor state. Thus, according to one of the theorems, it must be the case that affective neutrality is not too small. How does that happen to be the case? Then we are asking how a normative cultural condition required for social order is generated.

We get some sense of how this explanation might proceed from work in applied catastrophe theory (Thom, 1975; Zeeman, 1977). In this context, the state space is called the *substrate* by contrast with the *control* space, where parametric conditions are envisioned as themselves changing over time. We couple two levels of process with feedback from the social dynamics to the controlling normative conditions. The feedback can be represented in terms of a recursive process in which to each value of the normative parameter there is a fast dynamics in social state space that yields an outcome that results in an updated normative parameter. Hence, the necessary degree of affective neutrality could be accounted for in terms of Durkheimian social generativity in state space.

Is this embedding of functional analysis within the framework of the general dynamical social system close to functional *explanation?* Much depends on how the idea is defined. Careful analyses by several authors (Stinchcombe, 1968; van Parijs, 1981; Faia, 1986) show that the conceptual setting of dynamical social systems is *essential* to explicate the meaning of functional explanation and to realize its potentialities for social science. Stinchcombe links this form of explanation to cybernetic conceptions as well as evolutionary processes. Philosopher van Parijs aims to show that there is a sound foundation to the idea of latent functional explanation. He links such explanation to the logic of gradient dynamical systems (Fararo, 1978) used in applied catastrophe theory, featuring a kind of dynamic ''satisficing'' process as one form of evolutionary model that differs from the standard natural selection type. Sociologist Faia seems to be building on Stinchcombe's analysis, aiming to show that in a proper dynamic context we now have the data-analytical models that make functional thought viable and important.

This concludes a brief indication of how causal explanation and functional analysis can be embedded within a dynamical social systems framework stressing the importance of generativity. But despite the positive elements I have stressed, there are some serious conceptual problems in this framework from the standpoint of the emerging do's and don'ts of the general theoretical sociology research tradition. As described in Chapter 1, this tradition is beginning to pull together certain normatively expressed desiderata for good theoretical models.

When these are applied to the theoretical model just outlined, we arrive at disparities that constitute conceptual problems. Some problems arise because of intrinsic difficulties in exploiting the potentialities of the concept of a general dynamical social system. I turn to these conceptual and procedural problems in the next section.

## 2.11. Complexity, action theory, and structuralism

When the general dynamical social system model was defined in Section 2.8, it was noted that the two-component state variable (**A**, **I**) is very complex. Both components, when represented formally, involve sets of matrices relating to activities, sentiments, and interactions. A typical dimension of such a matrix corresponds to the number of social units, which so far have been taken as persons. Even for a small group, this is still considerable complexity. Thus, the main problem with generating the advance of theoretical knowledge by direct reference to models of this form is that except when the number of such social units is very small, we have to find a way to grapple with the sheer dimensionality problem. When the number of given parts is small, attention naturally focuses directly on the dynamical system associated with the state variable formulation. But when the number of such parts of the system is even moderate, much less large, formal theoretical analysis begins to break down. Apart from dimensionality, there may be very incomplete knowledge of all but a few of the mechanisms linking the variables, introducing arbitrary elements into the conjectured generator of process. Even with full knowledge or at least a complete conjectured mechanism in the sense defined earlier, the system is likely to be nonlinear. Of course, passage to probabilistic theoretical models is an important strategy in coping with these problems. But stochastic processes are themselves likely to be quite complex and also lead to nonlinear dynamics in many cases.

Thus, the analytical difficulties multiply. Scientists often pass to simulation studies under such conditions, provided enough is known or can plausibly be conjectured about the mechanism. The question is the overall outcome in terms of what the total mechanism, what I have called the generator, implies about the behavior of the system over time and about the possible equilibria and their stability. We have a busy future ahead of us in the conduct of such simulation studies even if the methodology of simulation may make the statement of general results, theorems, illusive. (For a more extended discussion, see Section 3.6.) The problem is that the output of computer studies resembles the output of an enormous number of actual processes that we were fortunate enough to observe in detail. Such an output is more like a data record than anything else, except that we know the "data" were generated by our theoretical model under known initial conditions. But for theory, it is not such generated records we want but general answers to general questions. So, although theoretical sociologists will more and more be involved in conducting high-speed, high-volume computerized simulations of nonlinear dynamics, there still will be a need for additional tools and methods.

Another way such analytical complexity is approached is through explicit reduction in complexity. One value of Simon's formalization is to show that such a method can yield interesting theorems of the type that general theoretical sociology should take as the core of the discipline's knowledge [illegible]. But, also, this particular mode of reduction in complexity reveals some drawbacks that suggest the need for other strategies of reduction. The state of the system has been described in the Simon–Homans models by aggregation, as indicated earlier. Various types of activity, interactions, and sentiments have been aggregated. In this aggregation, the matrix or network format has been reduced to a scalar property of the whole along each of the theoretical dimensions. There is no way, at such an aggregated level, to describe the forms of possible social structures that might arise under varying parametric conditions, at least in any considerably differentiated terms. We want to show that the generator can transform the initial multiple network into another such network, the latter equilibrated to its environment in the stable case. But the Simon–Homans aggregated version of the dynamics leads us to characterize the social structure in terms of global summary properties (such as total amount of activity and average friendliness) rather than in terms of a differentiation of the persons and their activities and sentiments, including such emergent substructures as groups, strata, positions, and roles. As network analysts have emphasized, such social differentiation is mapped through taking into account both direct and indirect ties in the structure.

In sum, the theoretical model violates an emerging "do" among the do's and don'ts of the general theoretical sociology research tradition: *Do* represent social structure in terms of networks in order to study differentiation as an emergent feature of social interaction.[28]

Let us consider an example of this problem. If we reconstruct Homans's reanalysis of Whyte's data on the Norton Street Gang (Whyte, 1943; Homans, 1950:Ch. 8), we notice that Homans treats "the position of the leader" as an aspect of the equilibrium state of the system, its social structure in the disaggregated sense. That is, the states refer to elements of direct and indirect relationships among persons, not to scalar properties of the group as a whole. The equilibrium state of the system has an aspect called *position of leadership* if and only if there exists a person $p$ such that the state of the system includes:

$p$ gives most direction to others
$p$ conforms most to the group norms
$p$ has the highest rank in the emergent status hierarchy
$p$ is most central in the communications network of the group

Note that these relationally induced properties of person $p$ arise from the basic first-order concepts of activity, sentiments, and interaction together with the emergent group norms.

This reconstruction of Homans's discussion of the position of the leader says that there exists a person $p$ such that with respect to a certain subset of the complete set of values of the state variables, $p$ is at a simultaneous relative maximum with respect to each such variable relative to the equilibrated values of all the other group members with respect to those same variables. Very importantly, we see that a *position* in (or, in a more ambiguous sense, a part of) a social structure is a one-sided aspect of a pattern of relations. The part illustrated here is that of *leader*.[29]

In further reference to the leadership example, let each person have an equilibrium state description in terms of activities, sentiments, and interactions *in terms of the state of the network*. Thus, typical person $p$'s state might be: gives direction to specified others in the group; conforms to norm $A$ but deviates from norm $B$ by a certain amount; has a certain rank, in the sense of honorific status, in the group; and has a certain centrality measure in the communication network of the group. We have a number of ways of defining all these elements in a fairly precise way that depends on the relevant matrix and so on the full pattern of direct and indirect ties. See, for instance, Doreian (1986), Freeman (1979), and Bonacich (1987), respectively, for status, centrality, and power in relation to centrality. This equilibrium state description as defined for a person in the group would constitute that person's position in the group with respect to the state variables specified. Thus, every person has a position in equilibrium in the social structure. The leader position is defined by its relation to all other positions in that structure.[30]

It is such a differentiated sense of social structure that constitutes the root meaning formalized in the context of the general dynamical social system. And it is this root meaning that was lost in the mode of complexity reduction inherent in the Simon–Homans linear and nonlinear models. Quite apart from problems of other kinds – such as missing some of the relationships in Table 2.2 suggested by Homans – this is a serious problem in the theoretical model from the standpoint of its contribution to theoretical sociology: It does not allow us to characterize the attractor states of social process, the social structures, as networks of social relations with various analytically discerned emergent substructures.

A further difficulty in this respect is the carryover into the other three types of theorems. Aggregation implies that the relevant stability analysis overlooks shifts in the network that are within the same aggregated class in terms of the values of the aggregated variables. Also, comparative statics cannot reveal how the social network shifts with shifts in external parameters. Finally, the possibilities of catastrophes that involve shifts in the structural type of the social network is outside the scope of the model.

In brief, the problem with the Simon–Homans theoretical model from the standpoint of general theoretical sociology is that its state description obscures the social structure and structural transformation. If we believe that the central results of theoretical sociology are associated with the derivation of the types of theorems indicated earlier, all of which center on the concept of social structure, then the dynamic models must retain the general dynamical social system's underlying model object, the social network.

Yet the reader may well wonder how one can preserve a focus on the social network in the case of large-scale systems. The biased network approach introduced in Chapter 4 is responsive to this question. It also responds to the query that might be put by a macrostructuralist such as Blau (1977): Is not network analysis essentially a microanalytical tool, and is not macrosociology in need of a distinctive concept of social structure? In brief, the reply given in Chapter 4 is to formalize *both* certain key ideas of microsociology (in its network form) and of macrosociology (in its Blau-type macrostructural form) within a single framework given by a representation principle and its presuppositions.

There is a further important point that relates to processes and networks. To lead up to it, let us interpret equations (2.9.3) as describing a linear dynamical system for a *pair* of persons. For a whole network, which can be thought of as a set of pairs, imagine that we have a set of such dynamical systems, one per pair. By summing over all equations representing pairs and using linearity, we obtain the aggregate system. Dividing this result by the number of pairs, we arrive at a single system with the same form as (2.9.3). In fact, we can regard this as the meaning of aggregation for the linear relational process in which a pair of persons is described in terms of the strength of their tie at a particular time (the $F$ term) and their amount of joint activity (the $A$ term).

This apparently straightforward aggregation, however, assumes that the dynamics of one pair in *uncoupled* to that of any other pair. We simply treated the whole process as a collection of independent pair processes. Now consider one important mechanism that we have learned about in the study of interaction systems and that was treated in Chapter 1: interpersonal balance. For this purpose, we let $F$ take negative as well as positive values. Then, for instance, the dynamics of pair (1, 2) will depend on the current state of pairs (1, 3) and (2, 3). We could represent this as an added term in the sentiment equation for the change of $F_{12}$, namely, a term proportional to the product $F_{13}F_{23}$. In other words, when $A$ and $B$ both like $C$ or when they both dislike $C$, this contributes to increasing their positive sentiments toward each other, whereas if they have dissimilar feelings about $C$, this tends to reduce their favorable sentiments toward each other. So in this dynamical social system the *relational processes are coupled to each other*. The rate of change in the state for one pair depends on the state of other pairs as well as that of the pair itself. I express this general idea by also saying that relation *interlock* exists.

The concept of interlock, the idea that the state of any one relation depends on the state of other relations in a *network* of relations, is a keynote idea of the network research tradition. The conceptual development of this idea was the major contribution of anthropologist Nadel (1957), whose work influenced sociologists such as Harrison White who were influential in initiating structuralist research programs (Lorrain and White, 1971; White, Boorman, and Breiger, 1976). The main point is that any consideration of mechanisms that characterize real social interaction leads to (1) interlock and, therefore, (2) nonlinear dynamical systems.

Although headway on the nonlinear social dynamics of interlock is difficult to make, the important point for theoretical sociologists is to see what the problem is, how difficult it is, and yet how significantly central it is to our enterprise.

This discussion has made use of one of the emerging small number of do's and don'ts of the research tradition of general theoretical sociology that are comimg into focus at this time: the conception of representing social structure in terms of networks. The present discussion of the Simon–Homans theoretical models was critical of them on the grounds provided by this conception. It points in a ''structuralist'' direction in that it requires that the dynamic models reflect the basic element of interlock.

Drawing upon the same emerging sense of what social theory requires, we are led to another problem that points in another but not antithetical direction. It is very important to note that this problem exists and that it is in no way opposed to the structuralist viewpoint. The problem is that there is really no general dynamical social system without the generator. But the generator is a representation of a compounding of a number of specific mechanisms drawn together to show how they generate possible social structures and transformations of social structures. It is true that Homans went a good distance in informing us about the elements that must enter into these mechanisms, as shown in Table 2.2. However, even if these are represented as relations among state variables, as anticipated in general terms earlier in this chapter and illustrated in the Simon–Homans models, this is not sufficient for general theoretical sociology. Here we apply the second of the emerging convergent elements of the research tradition of general theoretical sociology: It must be grounded in a theory of action. For some examples of statements of this idea, see Boudon (1974, 1981), Harré and Secord (1973), and Abell (1984). These authors all take the static regression model as the typical "variable" approach to be criticized. But even with the far superior dynamical systems conception, state variables are the key entities, and the critical points made apply. A change in one variable that produces a change in another variable is not an *intelligible* explanation until derived from a theoretical model of interaction. This is the Weberian element in general theoretical sociology.

The argument has two steps.

First, as discussed earlier, the causal relation between control parameters and state variables is explained by the generator. Hence, any conception of sociology requiring us to show how certain social structural phenomena are caused is reduced to the explication and representation of generative mechanisms.

Second, the generator is a combination of mechanisms that carry a state of socially interactive activities and sentiments (including normative sentiments) into a new state. But social interaction, by definition, is a coupling of two or more action processes of distinct actors. Hence, the more nearly ultimate level of explanation involves generating acts by actors in situations.

Fundamental principles about action, then, should imply certain forms of interaction or, at least, constraints on such forms via the "coupling" of models representing actors in situations.

This leads to a *theoretical procedure* to be applied in the following chapter. It is straightforward in conception but difficult in practice. It consists of three steps:

1. Define a general actor–situation dynamic model.
2. "Couple" two or more such models to derive a dynamical social system model.
3. Study this social system model to derive interpretable social structure theorems of the four types.

The new element, relative to the Simon–Homans models, is the derivation of the equations of the dynamical social system from postulates defining actor–situation models. If actor $A$ is described by model $M(A)$ and actor $B$ by model $M(B)$, then the generator of the dynamical social system based on these two actors is some coupling of $M(A)$ and $M(B)$. In turn, this new element relates to the point mentioned earlier that the general framework level requires some sort of template, something that functions like the birth and death accounting identity in ecology and demography or the $F = ma$ form in classical mechanics. For instance, our template may be based on some simple principles of action along with some acquired experience in how to derive dynamical social system models from them.

In Section 1.4, this theoretical procedure was anticipated in the example given concerning the use of the structural balance idea to account for the consensus-liking and dissensus-disliking patterns. These patterns were interpreted as different forms of the possible stable states satisfying the structural balance definition. It was argued, however, that what was needed for a stronger explanation was generativity. Newcomb's communication link between $p$-centric systems is precisely a coupling device linking actor models to account for a collective system property in stable equilibrium. What was needed, it was pointed out, was a formal representation of communication and balancing mechanisms operating through time, a mode of generating the equilibrium cases under specified conditions. In short, the discussion anticipated the idea being discussed here.

Although in the next chapter a number of principles of action are stated, I reserve treatment of the coupling procedure and its consequences to one model in which the principle is that action is an adaptively rational process. The coupling of such adaptively rational actors then generates social interaction in the sense of a recursive process with possible stable states that, in the case of a pair, correspond to an elementary form of social structure called a social relation.

It is essential to realize that in this procedure an actor–situation model is not of interest in its own right, at least in this understanding of the key problems of general theoretical sociology. Rather, certain principles about action in situations, when applied to each acting unit, *generate* social interaction. That is, the fundamental mechanism of the social system becomes such explicated interaction of actors who behave in accordance with certain principles.

In another sense, however, the actor–situation starting point has enormous ramifications for the specification of dynamical social system models. A research tradition involves ontological as well as methodological commitments. When an actor–situation tradition of thought is invoked, the ontology of its theories features entities that shape the definition of the state space for social dynamics. In the Parsonian analytical branch of action theory, for instance, what are termed operative ideals in Chapter 3 become the dominant entities. Action is generated under normative control, and dynamical social systems have states that are constituted through the coupling of models of actors described in terms of normative hierarchies of control. Other branches of action theory pose somewhat different fundamental entities. The result is that the unification process that ought to accompany or follow formalization is difficult to implement, as will be seen in Chapter 3. This is not the same as saying that there are permanent barriers between theories with distinct entities because one thing that formalization can bring out is the way that two formally specified classes of models can be articulated. An interesting aspect of this process is that the ideal of simplicity moves theories in the direction of postulating highly ''abstract'' constructs that are only very indirectly related to observables. This point is taken up again and illustrated in detail in the elaboration of *E*-state structuralism in Section 4.9.

Summing up this discussion so far, we note that among the elements of the research tradition of general theoretical sociology, two ideas are coming into focus as do's and don'ts. They are normative ideas, ideals that guide our work. First, to really answer structural questions requires state descriptions in terms of networks and attendance to the critical property of interlock of relations. Second, to really have an intelligible explanation of social structural phenomena, the generator of any dynamical social system should be derived through a procedure of coupling models based on principles of action in situations. The first result orients us to structuralism. The second result orients us to action principles.

These ideas relate very much to current concerns with the so-called micro–macro problem, as indicated by *The Micro–Macro Link* (Alexander et al., 1987). In turn, this problem relates to the underlying philosophical problem of methodological holism versus methodological individualism (Lukes, 1977:Pt. 3).

Concerning holism and individualism in methodology, the generative structuralist approach taken in this book is integrative in spirit. First, methodological holism is indicated by the analytical focus on the dynamical social system and its emergent structural properties. Second, methodological individualism is indicated by the demand for grounding social generativity on principles of action of individual human beings. Collectivities are states of social structure: Membership sentiments arise in social interaction and are not ultimate givens for theoretical sociology. A commitment to methodological individualism in this sense should not be confused with any sort of denial of the social nature of the human individual. It is a commitment to treating interaction (or, more generally, interdependence)[31] through a particular theoretical procedure for the sake of explanation.

Put in this form, the approach taken here is consistent with that of many of the contributors to *The Micro–Macro Link*. In short, it is one more contribution to implementing a third ''do'' among the emerging norms of general theoretical sociology: Do try to link micro and macro levels. But my approach is intentionally quite general and abstract in its focus compared with some alternatives. For instance, it does not start from some empirical fact about a particular society and attempt to explain it in terms of principles about action. It starts, instead, with the conception of a network of interacting human beings and the conception of a behavior manifold for the dynamic description of this entity. It moves from there to the generic problems of theory, presupposing that there is a need to specify these problems formally and to show how they can be addressed in terms of various theoretical procedures. This has been the aim of setting out and illustrating the four theorem types and of the present self-critique of that work in terms of the idea of deriving the social generator through the coupling of actor models. So the joint commitment to both action theory and structuralism is the difficult but derived commitment I obtain.

There is another criticism of the framework employed in this chapter that should be mentioned. Generativity has another aspect in the context of dynamical systems. This aspect is both empirical and conceptual. That is, the concept *state* should be distinguished from *observables* in the form: Given the state of the system and the pattern of arrival of stimulation or inputs, the observables are manifested or generated. In other words, in conformity with the realist model of explanation, the conception of generativity is closely tied conceptually to a hypothetical model of the "inner" mechanisms that account for the observables. This conceptual point receives its vindication when process models are empirically tested. As in the case of Markov chains with observable states, the absence of any historical effects condemns such models to a purely baseline role without much explanatory significance. But if one constructs a model with a hypothetical set of events and mechanisms at the state level with the observables as (mathematical) *functions* of the state, such models are restored to empirical significance while simultaneously satisfying realist philosophical presuppositions. I call this the *state space approach* to dynamical systems thinking (Fararo, 1973:Sects. 8.8 and 8.9). For a more recent discussion, see Fararo (1987b).

Note that Homans (1950) avoided a concept such as *expectation* in his social system model, whereas Parsons (1951) made it central. According to the point being made, Parsons is nearer the correct rendition of the state space representation: Behavioral events will be displayed as functions of expectation states that are not themselves observable. *Theories* invent models of expectation processes and their coupling to account for the observables of social interaction. The next chapter treats Parsonian expectations in the context of dynamical systems, distinguishing normative and nonnormative elements in them.

The state space approach is also central to the research program of expectation states theory (Berger, Wagner, and Zelditch, 1985). It seems to be no accident that the most senior researchers in this program were trained at Harvard by, among others, Parsons. A further discussion of the logic of expectation states theory and of the procedure of constructing theories satisfying the state space approach occurs in Section 4.9.

Ideally, the remainder of this book should consist of the working out of the implications of the theoretical procedure of defining and coupling actor–situation models in the context of interlock dynamics of multiple actors and a state space approach. Although the next chapter does focus on action theory and the fourth chapter on structuralism, what actually occurs in these chapters departs from this ideal. Stated most simply, the four chapters of this book represent mutually interdependent developments that have been occurring in my formal thought about the problems of theoretical sociology. It would be a false record of the facts to say that first one thought out the philosophy of general theoretical sociology, then one formalized its fundamental problems within a dynamical systems framework, then one turned to action theory to derive interactive models, and finally one turned to structuralism to treat interlock properly. The actual story is that all four developments occurred together. They are four component states of a single process of formalization in relation to general theoretical sociology.

Thus, other considerations have entered into the remainder of this book apart from those suggested by the coupling procedure, the treatment of interlock, and the state space approach. Other subtraditions of general theoretical sociology are called upon in formulating principles of action. Some of these lead to distinct modes of formalization not directly related to the ideas of social networks and state variables. An example is the concept of an interpretive procedure as used in ethnomethodology when it analyzes the activities of actors in social situations. Others are related to the dynamical system conceptions but have focused on problems at a level that corresponds to embedding the general dynamical social system in a wider system. An example is the concept of internalization of normative culture in the Durkheimian–Parsonian perspective on the problem of social order.

These remarks relate to the idea of general theoretical sociology as a single research tradition. This book argues not that general theoretical sociology *is* unified at the level of general theory but that a unification dynamic is increasingly recognized as a major "do" of the do's and don'ts of the research tradition. With a variety of extant theoretical frameworks and a variety of definite models given in the various subtraditions of the field, this book addresses not only formalization but also potential and actual opportunities for unification. A unification dynamic is a recursive operation in which the results of any one integrative episode become theoretical materials for another episode. When Merton (1968:Ch. 2) presented his argument for sociological theories of the middle range, he accompanied it with a conception of a unification dynamic using the phrase "consolidation of theories." More recently, Wagner and Berger (1985) stressed that *proliferation* of specific theories within a research program should be accompanied by *integration* of such theories. These authors embedded Merton's consolidation directive within a broader set of guidelines for cumulative theorizing. In terms of the model of theory structures used in this book, their proliferation–integration dynamic occurs at the level of theoretical models and is governed by certain presuppositions and representation principles. By contrast, in this book, these upper levels are the focus. In particular, I treat two vexing issues confronting general theoretical sociology that are not solved by the middle-range approach. First, the key general problems of the field need formulation. Middle-range theorizing does not tell us which problems are most significant or how they relate to one another. It leads to cumulation within the particularistic boundaries of a specific research program. Second, proliferation of variant presuppositions and principles through many research subtraditions has not been accompanied by sufficient integrative effort. Again, particularistic boundaries between perspectives have prevented cumulative general theorizing from taking on a dynamic of its own. Defining our key general problems, specifying types of theorems, proposing representation principles, and engaging in unification of otherwise separate research programs – these are the core commitments of this book.

Finally, the "curse of dimensionality" (Bellman, 1961) warns us that large-scale systems may require special treatment. Macro-level theoretical frameworks and models acquire a coherent logic of their own and, in origin, are not simply derived from the action basis. Furthermore, these models often take the form of purely static model objects supplemented with reasonable principles. The results are interesting properties of macrostructures but are not derived from any dynamical system at all. In such cases, it remains an item on the research agenda to work from macrostructural knowledge of this sort back toward dynamical social systems, even as the action approach works from actor–situation toward the dynamical social system. So a more accurate image of the process carried out in this book is that of hovering around the dynamical social system, approaching now from the action side, now from the static macrostructural side, now from the generative rule side, and so forth.

One further element of the action and the structuralist directions of development of the ideas encountered in this chapter deserves mention. This relates to the two directions of orientation called for, the action direction and the structuralist direction.

Consider first the action direction. The focus on the coupling of the action processes of actors has a certain logic that keeps its structural focus at an elementary level: To demonstrate that one can generate interaction or show how interaction is enabled by a preexisting structure, one can begin with the logically simplest case, the dyad. There is no particular reason to attempt analysis of groups of more than two persons if one cannot even work out the basic logic of formulating an action principle and then coupling actor models to generate the consequences of interaction between two persons. To illustrate, consider once again the *ABX* model, as described in Chapter 1, with *X* as a noninteractant and *A* and *B* as actors. The *p*-centric balance principle plays the role of the action principle. As already noted, the aim to derive the consensus-liking and dissensus-disliking configurations as characteristic of the generated social structure illustrates the method of starting from action, coupling actor models, and then deriving social structure theorems. Yet, the process was not formalized even for two actors. To actually derive the generator, to literally generate the process and show, formally, that the resulting equilibria have certain forms – that is on the agenda of theoretical sociology. Meanwhile, the basic *ABX* model has $n=2$ and it is not a social network, but a single tie, whose dynamics are represented and studied.

Consider now the structuralist orientation. There is no interesting social network if the "network" is reduced to a pair of nodes. Networks are model objects for which the corresponding dynamics must [illegible] coupled pairs of actors, that is, interlock. This is a second level of coupling that introduces fresh problems. That is, the action direction orients the theoretician to the analytical problems connected with coupling distinct actors to generate interaction. The structuralist direction orients the theoretician to the analytical problems connected with coupling distinct pairs of actors. In principle, the triad is the minimal unit of interest from a structuralist standpoint.[32]

Thus, these considerations, added to earlier reasons for not expecting a "straightforward" construction by the steps leading from action principles to social structure theorems, create a further gap between action-theoretical research and structuralist research. It is true that a perfected action approach would in principle write down the model of the interlock and capture structural analysis within its frame of reference. But we are nowhere near such a viable general unification of theoretical sociology. We must expect gaps, disjunctions among levels of analysis, even as we work toward various modes of integration of theory in sociology. General theoretical sociology is still unitary as a research tradition as long as we continue to communicate across subtraditional contexts and are responsive to good ideas from whatever corner of the field they come.

## 2.12. Summary

The system idea is employed in two contexts in theoretical science. On the one hand, there are domain-specific systems theories intended to apply to particular empirical domains, such as ecological systems. On the other hand, there is general systems theorizing. As interpreted here, the latter entails two quite different activities. In one form, it involves the construction of comprehensive systems theories; in another, it involves the activity and results of mathematical systems theory. The latter includes the especially important field of mathematics focused on dynamical systems. These types of systems inquiry overlap. In particular, in formulating theory using the concept of system, general theoretical sociology can draw upon both types of general systems thinking to formulate its domain-specific body of theory.

The construction of a dynamical system begins with the specification of a model object called a behavior manifold, the space of possible states and parametric conditions. Given the behavior manifold, the dynamical system is specified through a generator of process, that is, change of state over time. Concepts such as initial state, initial condition, behavior of the system, equilibrium state, stability, attractor state, repellor state, catastrophe, and still others are all defined in terms of the behavior manifold and the generator. In particular, equilibration as adjustment of state variables to each other and to the parametric conditions can be elucidated within a dynamical systems framework. More generally, when and if a dynamical system can be analyzed in complete detail, it yields a complex portrait of all the real dynamical possibilities. Of particular interest are the attractors. A system that is adjusted to its conditions will stay near an attractor. If the circumstances are exogenously changing over time, then the behavior of the system may stay near an incessantly changing attractor state. Finally, there are a number of generic types of analysis that lead to generic types of theorems when one studies a constructed dynamical system.

In this chapter, these ideas have been coordinated to general theoretical sociology by drawing upon the subtradition that runs from Pareto through Homans to Simon. In Pareto we find a sophisticated statement of the analytical viewpoint in sociological theory and attention to the role of sentiments in human action. Homans, in his 1950 work, developed an important model of the human group using a systems mode of thought in verbal form. In particular, the simultaneous treatment of adaptation and integration processes of groups is to be noted as well as the treatment of dynamical possibilities, such as buildup and dissolution as well as steady states.

When we coordinate the dynamical systems framework and the Homans framework for a process-oriented treatment of groups as evolving social networks, we obtain the concept of a general dynamical social system. This system has two dynamical subsystems, here called the adaptation and the integration systems (corresponding to Homans's external and internal systems). Very importantly, the specification of the integration subsystem is close in spirit to the Durkheimian tradition of general theoretical sociology. Durkheim's consideration of changes in division of labor, interpreted in terms of the instrumental context, is represented in the adaptation subsystem and the fact that the integration subsystem adjusts to it. Control parameters such as population size are in causal relation to changes in the division of labor and hence the state of integration, but the deeper explanation of these causal relations is in terms of the generative mechanisms of the dynamical social system itself. Because the behavior of the system depends on the parameters and the parameters may be subject to exogenous and irregular changes, no one necessary over-time form of behavior – whether cyclic or anything else – is necessitated in empirical reality. Theoretical analysis does not aim for absolute statements about such consequences but conditional propositions that relate the system dynamics and structural possibilities to the parametric properties of the conditions in which the system exists.

Applying the conception of four types of analytical problems to the general dynamical social system, we arrive at a roster of four theorem types that, ideally, we should aim to demonstrate in the process of setting up and studying models. These theorems are formalized theoretical versions of empirical problems of the emergence, stability, comparison, and change of social structures. A social structure is a special state of the dynamical social system, one in which the network is adjusted to its conditions. A really possible social structure or social order has the additional property of stability so that it is an attractor of social process. The aims of theory are to derive the conditions for the existence of such social orders and to answer related general questions pertaining to the comparison and change of social orders with conceptual shift or dynamic change in conditions, respectively.

As a matter of interest in its own right and as an illustration of the abstract ideas, the Simon-formalized studies of Homans's theory were reanalyzed from the current standpoint. First, the linear model was shown to imply specific instances of the four theorem types. Second, the nonlinear model was analyzed in terms of catastrophe analysis to show how recent developments in nonlinear analysis can be applied to social systems. Interesting results are obtained in terms of the existence of what were called structuration and destructuration catastrophes. Third, a conceptual analysis of the general dynamical social system and the Simon–Homans models led to the statement of two guidelines for further investigations. On the one hand, we require principles of action; on the other hand, we require an approach that is structuralist in the specific sense of preserving the focus on network in deriving dynamical system models.

In the next chapter, the focus is on action principles in general theoretical sociology, whereas the chapter after that develops one strand of principles and models within structuralism.

# 3. Action theory and social order

## 3.1. Introduction

The first chapter of this book interpreted general theoretical sociology as a comprehensive research tradition with a number of important subtraditions. This research tradition, it was maintained, is based on a process worldview. Both individuals and societies are enduring forms of order. And endurance is problematic. Structure is not an ultimate given but a conditional attainment. Yet, for our purposes, not all instances of endurance present problems for theory. It is *social* structures that are the conditional attainments requiring our explanatory efforts. Under what conditions does interaction yield or reproduce stable social structures? How do we compare such structures? How do such structures change as to type?

Such questions show that the process worldview leads directly into dynamical social systems, treated in the second chapter. The tradition of general theoretical sociology was drawn upon to state formally four key problems and a corresponding set of four types of theorems about social structure. These are at the core of the knowledge quest of the comprehensive tradition. The four types of theorems, arrived at through the study of the properties of definite model objects, pertain to the emergence, maintenance, comparison, and change of social structures.

However, in exhibiting the logic of these ideas in the study of theoretical models, two conceptual problems were located and discussed at the end of Chapter 2. These problems arose by comparison of the theoretical logic of the models with the emerging consensual do's and don'ts of the comprehensive tradition.

First, it was argued that the elimination of the network aspect, featuring the inclusion of indirect as well as direct ties, leads to models that are deficient in terms of how they represent structural phenomena.

Second, it was argued that in the absence of a more explicit treatment of action, the models would be deficient in explanatory significance. It is not that actors are fully formed independent of social structures and then produce these structures. It is really that the interactions are primary and the structures are more or less conditionally enduring forms immanent in the interactive nexus. In turn this implies that *for the purpose of addressing problems of social structure, we should start with some principles and models of action in social situations. Action theory* is based on this presupposition and is the subject of this chapter. Various subtraditions adopt distinct principles of action, however, based on more specific presuppositions about the significance of various aspects of action.

Probably the best-known action point of view toward social analysis is found in the works of Weber (1978) and Parsons (1937). Both authors regard an action frame of reference as a way to bridge naturalistic and interpretive approaches to social theory. An act is an event, a *process* in the world, on the one hand, that has meaning, on the other. Contemporary action theories implement this broad metatheoretical conception of the bridge role of the idea of action in various models.

One way to envision the process emphasis is to map observable action into a network as a model object in which the nodes are process units representing *unit acts,* units that are acts and hence processes. Then the linkages in the network are relationships among such unit acts, such as the product of one act becoming a resource or input for another act. This point of view characterizes what is called structural–generative action theory in Section 3.4, but the image can function in other theoretical contexts as an aid to the imagination. A recurrent unit act is any node in an action structure, an enduring action network. There is an essential methodological point to appreciate here, simple as it is. The unit acts are definitely not the ultimately smallest bits of behavior with meaning in any model-free sense. They are the primitive acts of which actions, as represented in the model, are composed. They have the same status as particles in mechanics: For some purposes a complex physical body is taken as simply a particle; for other purposes it is represented as a system of particles. Similarly, an observable action in the world may be represented by a path of unit acts or by an entire action structure or substructure, or it may be represented as a node in such a structure – a *unit,* or part, of a wider action structure.

Another way to envision the process emphasis will be presented in this chapter. We map action into a model object in which actors are represented as dynamical normative control systems. They generate meaningful action through internal subnodes representing functions in the control process. So the single actor is such an action system, and the coupling of such actors is an action system. An action structure is conceptualized as an attractor state of a network of coupled single-actor systems. This is the point of view in Sections 3.2 and 3.3.

Taking into account that the actor of an act may be a collectivity, we have the following possibilities for the representation of action in the world:

I. Unit act
  A. Individual actor
  B. Collective actor
II. Action system
  A. Single-actor model
    1. Individual actor
    2. Collective actor
  B. Interaction model: at least two distinct actors
    1. Multiple individual actors
    2. Multiple collective actors
    3. Individual actors and collective actors

An example illustrates analytical flexibility. We can treat a particular domain of action in the world, such as the Supreme Court of the United States, in several ways, each capturing aspects of the court. "Supreme Court decision process" might be a node in some wider action structure for some purposes. This would be a type IB representation. The wider action structure might be of type IIA2. This sort of action system model treats the court as a single collective actor that engages in a series of action processes, such as "agreeing to hear a case," as well as "deciding a case." Another representation might employ a model of type IIB1, a process in which the member judges interactively formulate their opinions on cases before the court. A model of types IIB2 or IIB3 might be based on treating the court as one actor in a system of interaction involving individual and collective actors representing interested parties.

One other terminological point is necessary. The phrase *social action system* or *system of social action* is frequently used in sociological theory. I shall mean by a social action system any action system comprehended under an interaction model or a single collective actor model.

Weber distinguishes between direct observational understanding and explanatory understanding. The former is a *representation* made by an actor (participant or observer) of a behavioral event as constituting an instance of an act of a given type, such as voting. It is *what* is occurring as a motivated behavior. As performed by the analyst, observational understanding is a mapping of behavioral events into some action structure. Explanatory understanding is an actor's representation of the actor's reason for that observationally understood act. Weber emphasizes the perceptual or interpretive standpoint toward action. There is also a *generative* standpoint. Here the focus is on the production of forms of action, and this is the point of view emphasized at various places in this chapter.

The reader may wish to look again at Figure 2.3. In the present language, wiring (*W*), soldering (*S*), and inspecting (*I*) are unit acts of an action structure that includes an environmental node. The possibilities of product flow from *I* show that the action structure yields not a unique form of interaction but a potentially infinite set of possible forms of interaction, as described for Figure 2.3. This reference back to an example from Homans reminds us that we must not make the error of thinking that a theoretical analysis is outside the action frame of reference simply because the word *activity* is used rather than the word *action*.

In the Bank Wiring Room case the obvious action system model being employed is the interaction type. Also, there are sentiments motivating the work acts. The original motives brought to the group from the environment included the ''need'' to work not only for an income but also in order to be a man in the way in which men are defined in that environment. Thus, in this context, the category of sentiment corresponds to Weber's subjective meaning complex in providing actors (observers or participants) with an understanding of an actor's reasons for engaging in certain acts in the action system under analysis.

Given these orientation remarks, in the following sections three developments within action theory will be treated: analytical action theory, structural–generative action theory, and adaptively rational action theory. They can be thought of as contributions linked to three subtraditions of general theoretical sociology. In the present context, these subtraditions are viewed as three ''branches'' of action theory. In each case, a representation principle is the key focus of attention, and it is important to keep in mind that these are, in the terminology of Section 1.3.3, *problematic* rather than *established* principles.

The first branch, *analytical action theory,* is associated with the work of Talcott Parsons. One can think of his work as a partially successful effort to unify strands of theory and method derived from the classics, especially from Durkheim, Weber, and Pareto. This is action theory in a narrow sense, which some sociologists think of as *the* general theory of action within sociology.

My contribution to the further development of analytical action theory will be twofold. Both developments are largely conceptual and representational.

First, I shall interpret this subtradition as strongly focused on an intuitive conception of normative control. Formally, this leads to the statement of a general principle of action that has the potential to function in the instrumentalist mode in defining a framework within which theoretical models can be constructed and studied. The principle states that the actor–situation system is a dynamical normative control system. This links an empirical domain, that of human action, to a formal mode of representation of the cybernetic type. Having stated and discussed the principle, the remainder of the section elaborates and builds upon it. In one context, the principle helps illuminate the metatheory of analytical action theory by showing how such binary oppositions as ideal versus material and subjective versus objective are two sides of one relational whole. In another context, the principle is applied to the formal problem of representing cybernetic hierarchy as a process through which action is generated as an event with normative meaning. In turn, this leads to an image of a social system as a network of coupled normative control systems. This image sharply pinpoints that the "expected" product of autonomous normative control systems in interaction is conflict and coercion. Hence, social order emerges as the key problem in analytical action theory. Formally, the control principle defines a general template for a social generator, one of the objectives of any general theory of action, and so is responsive to the conceptual problems discussed at the end of Chapter 2.

Second, I shall interpret analytical action theory in terms of dynamical systems. The AGIL scheme receives a process-oriented interpretation. It turns out that one can construe Parsons as attempting to conjecture the general *content* of social order theorems, those about necessary conditions for a social attractor state. Such a conjecture is related to the control principle of action via the specification of the nature of the parametric conditions in terms of states of pattern variables that characterize values. This section also includes a discussion of interpenetration as a key idea in analytical action theory.[1]

The second development in this chapter relates especially to interpretive sociology. I term it *structural–generative action theory*. The theory starts from a combination of a sociological component, a philosophical component, and a formal component. The sociological component reflects the current state of the interpretive subtradition of general theoretical sociology: Tacit social knowledge is the key idea. The philosophical component is realist: Explanation involves structural generativity. When the interpretive conceptions and the structural generativity conception are combined, we are led to the formal component, modules of procedural rules represented formally as production systems. Thus, where a purely positivist position as to theoretical sociology might denigrate this type of theory, it fits naturally into the philosophical framework of the approach adopted in this book.

But structural–generative action theory also attempts to articulate interpretive sociology and analytical action theory in the spirit of unification. First, the production formalism can be employed to treat the structure of social action systems as understood in analytical action theory. Second, the joint deployment of production rules in the two theoretical contexts encourages possible unifying efforts. But here, as everywhere in this book, such possibilities are not yet fully exploited. They are items on the agenda of a theoretical sociology pursued in the spirit of unification.

The third branch of action theory treated in this chapter is called the *theory of adaptively rational action,* since the key principle is that the action of an actor in a recurrent situation is an adaptively rational process. A number of developments are presented. The theory relates most strongly to what is sometimes called *exchange theory*. The works of Homans (1974), Emerson (1981), and Coleman (1986) are illustrative of this subtradition of general theoretical sociology. In the context of first discussing a number of topics concerned with methodological individualism and adaptive rationality, two types of theories are specified. One is a dynamic version of rational choice theory, and the other is a behavioral theory. Although the first type is illustrated and its importance is stressed, the main efforts here are with respect to formalization of the foundations of the Homans–Emerson approach through behavioral theory.

In treating adaptive action from this standpoint, I begin with a general representation of the actor–situation system as adaptively rational. A dynamical system of the probabilistic type is employed as the model object. Second, to derive an interaction system, two actors are treated as units in each other's situations. The theoretical procedure of coupling single-actor models to derive interaction models is then employed. The adaptive equations for each actor recursively generate the joint events constituting the successive interactive episodes. Hence, a dynamical social interaction system is derived from the coupling of the adaptively rational models, one for each actor. Using the iterated Prisoner's Dilemma situation studied by Axelrod (1984), a series of numerical simulations are the basis of the analysis in which the system model is studied from the standpoint of its generated equilibria and stability features as dependent on parametric conditions. The simulation analysis illustrates the important point that general theoretical sociology must learn to use computers for the conduct of theoretical analysis. In this way, the context of this third branch of action theory provides an opportunity to explicate two theoretical procedures of general interest: coupling actor models to derive a dynamical social interactive system and studying derived theoretical models by use of computer simulation. That is, the role of comprehensive theory becomes that of providing the generalized template that is the basis for derivation of models too complex to study analytically but sufficiently specific to allow computer analysis.

This chapter contains various discussions at the presuppositional level of theory structure. Alexander (1982) suggests that sociological theory has two fundamental presuppositional problems. These relate to action and to social order, respectively. The presuppositional problem of action concerns the role of rationality in social theory. Classic sociological contributions, such as those of Pareto and Durkheim, stressed the role of nonrational elements in understanding social life. This has tilted sociological theory in one direction and created difficulties in terms of how rational action is to be understood and placed within a structure of theory. The presuppositional problem of order concerns how such order is to be explained. Alexander frames this as an issue dividing individualistic and collectivisitic approaches. This chapter is not structured to reflect Alexander's mapping of sociological theory directly. But these two presuppositional problems do arise and are treated at a number of points. The two problems strongly intersect in the development of the comprehensive tradition of general theoretical sociology. The important combination of the two issues comes into focus when the theory of adaptively rational action is treated in relation to Durkheimian depth sociology in Section 3.5.

The chapter concludes with a discussion of the nexus of these three branches of action theory from the standpoint of a formalization and unification orientation.

## 3.2. Analytical action theory: the control principle of action

By analytical action theory I primarily mean the conceptual schemes and principles of Talcott Parsons and his collaborators. My view on this branch of action theory is largely shaped by a reading of it in terms of dynamical systems. This interpretation is compatible with Parsons's own approach, especially in his mid-period. (See, e.g., Parsons, 1954:Ch. 11.) Before initiating formal work addressed to two key features of the theory in this and the next section, a brief set of remarks on two of his early works will serve to introduce my orientation to the contributions of Parsons to general theoretical sociology.

### 3.2.1. *Interpreting Parsons dynamically*

My interpretation is in terms of networks and dynamical systems.

1. *The Structure of Social Action* (Parsons, 1937): A network image of the structure of action systems is suggested in this book. The nodes are types of unit acts. There are two types of links representing two key relations, which we can think of as two types of directed lines (say, solid and dotted): an intrinsic means–end relation and a symbolic–expressive means–end relation. The terminal point of any directed line is called an end, the initial point a means.[2] This picture is an anticipation of the later focus on cybernetic hierarchy: There are nodes that are ultimate in the sense of constituting only ends, not means; there are nodes that are ultimate in the sense of constituting only means, not ends; and there is an intermediate sector of the network in which each node is both a means and an end. Parsons identifies the intermediate sector as the structural model of political economy, and he suggests that a theory richer than economic theory will have to deal with the part of the structure that is characterized by ultimate ends. In the symbolic–expressive case, the ultimate nodes are acts that express vague "value-

attitudes,'' such as a sense of the sacred expressed in ritual acts. Amid this complex reconstruction of Pareto, Durkheim, and Weber in terms of such a means–end action structure, Parsons also employs a more dynamic idea. Here he looks for the theoretical significance of the ultimate nodes in the overall process of action. The key idea is called the ''sociologistic theorem.'' In the context of a dynamical systems framework we may state it in the form:

> *Sociologistic theorem* [conjecture] (Parsons, 1937). A necessary cultural condition for the existence of a stable social equilibrium state is a common moral value system.

The further idea is that such values are implemented in institutional norms that control the ''bombardments of interests'' in the intermediate means–end sector. So this statement has the form of stating a necessary parametric condition if a dynamical social system is to have an attractor state, a stable equilibrium. In other words, in this interpretation, the ''problem of social order'' is the problem of the conditions needed for the existence of stable social structures. The conjectured theorem points in a cultural direction to values that are controlling, but not alone determining, the form that institutions take.

2. *The Social System* (Parsons, 1951): In this book, Parsons sketches a logic that approximates the idea of deriving the conditions required for stable states of interaction through the coupling of actor–situation models with their defininig properties. The work leads him to the ''fundamental dynamic theorem of sociology'' (Parsons, 1951:42). To state it as a theorem conjecture, two points need to be made. First, at this stage Parsons defines three types of institutions: relational (which constitute the definitions of status-role bundles), regulative (which introduce further normative control in the context of given relational institutions), and cultural (which do not directly relate to the definition of status-roles or to the regulation of interpersonal conduct in roles). Second, Parsons can be interpreted to employ at this stage a triad of interrelated dynamical subsystems corresponding to social, personality, and cultural elements. The social system is characterized by expectation states (concerning self–other behavior and attitudes). The personality system is characterized by need-disposition motivational states and the cultural system by moral value states (as distinguished from states of cognitive or other sorts of values). An approximate statement of it is then:

> *Fundamental dynamic theorem of sociology* [conjecture] (Parsons, 1951). A necessary condition for a stable equilibrium state of a social interaction system is that an internalization relation exists between need-disposition states and moral value states.

Intuitively, the necessary condition is that the actors have ''introjected'' moral values. Ideally, this would be a genuine theorem about a theoretical model, and the requisite level of such introjection would be described in terms of some inequality, as in the instance of the linear Simon–Homans model described in Chapter 2.

The conjecture says that internalization is necessary for relational institutions to exist since the context appears to be that of trying to account for emergent enduring structures. In fact, there is little focus on generativity in the sense of the prior chapters, although there is a definite sense of operating within a process worldview. As mapped into the idea of substrates and control spaces (Section 2.8), the image one gets of the appropriate model object is of a three-level stack of behavior manifolds (possible states with possible parametric conditions). A dynamic state in one space is an element of the parameter space for the next level down. The expectations are states relative to value parameters and are themselves parameters relative to need-disposition states. The lowest and fastest-changing dynamics are those of need dispositions that adjust to (are shaped by) social structures of expectation states in socialization. The highest and slowest-changing dynamics are those of moral values that are institutionalized as social expectation states adjust to (are shaped by) them.

During and after the 1950s, Parsons developed the AGIL scheme and also drew upon the emerging discussion of cybernetics to develop his analytical action theory. The remainder of this section is focused on a model of dynamic normative control drawn from cybernetics, whereas the following section is focused on the AGIL scheme.

### *3.2.2. A dynamical normative control system model*

Consider the following statement by Parsons (1937):

> A normative orientation is fundamental to the schema of action in the same sense that space is fundamental to that of the classical mechanics; in terms of the given conceptual scheme *there is no such thing as action except as effort to conform with norms* [my emphasis] just as there is no such thing as motion except as change of location in space. (Parsons, 1937:76–77)

One way of stating an objective of this entire section is: If I am successful in my efforts, the reader will be persuaded that the preceding statement is literally correct and exactly interpreted in terms of a *cybernetic* (Wiener, 1948) or control system model. I begin by briefly reviewing some formulations of the basic concept of cybernetic control, both abstractly and in terms of its interpretation. Then I adopt it as a way of formalizing the idea of a normative orientation of action. Since it is relevant, the relation of the control principle of action to current metatheoretical debate also will be discussed in terms of polarities such as subjective–objective and voluntary–constraining. Thereafter, I define a formal model object in mathematical terms and show how one can interpret the consequences of this model in the action domain.

The control principle of action (to be formally stated in what follows) treats action as a cybernetic process. There are a number of conceptual structures put forward in the history of social and behavioral science that have employed such a principle.

1. *The TOTE unit* (Miller, Galanter, and Pribram, 1960): In a pioneering conceptual and theoretical study of the logic of action as a control process, these authors proposed a test–operate–test (TOTE) unit to replace a purely behavioristic unit such as a reflex arc or a stimulus–response connection. A TOTE unit is a formal representation of a plan for behavior activated under certain conditions. The fundamental idea is that every action has a test phase and an operational phase. The latter can have embedded subtests and suboperations to form hierarchies of control. Activation of a plan means that the process of behavioral control enters the test phase of a TOTE unit in which some specified situational condition is tested for.

Then there are two possibilities. In one type of TOTE unit, if comparison shows the test condition does not hold, some operation occurs that acts in the direction of changing the situation toward it and the test is executed once again. Calling the condition tested for in the test phase the *end* and the operational phase the *means* coordinates this model to the language used by Parsons (1937). The test phase involves a comparison of the end with knowledge of the situation. Recursively, the cycle continues until either the test is passed, in which case the end is realized, or some higher-order control aborts the plan. Through the loop of testing and operating, unless the plan is aborted, the situation is gradually brought into concordance with the plan's test condition, the end or goal. At this point, the process exits the particular TOTE unit and the control process continues with some other unit.

In a second type of TOTE unit, if the condition being tested for exists, then an operation is performed; if not, the control process shifts to some other TOTE unit based on the overall hierarchical organization. It is useful to coordinate this type of TOTE unit to the idea of a *production system,* which is employed in the modern computational model of mind discussed briefly in Chapter 1 (Newell and Simon, 1972) and to be employed later in this chapter. A production system is a list of rules, which in TOTE unit terms may be written as

$$\begin{array}{c} \text{TEST}_1 \rightarrow \text{OPERATE}_1 \\ \text{TEST}_2 \rightarrow \text{OPERATE}_2 \\ \vdots \quad\quad \vdots \end{array}$$

If the comparison process between the test condition and situation knowledge has the outcome that $TEST_1$ passes, then $OPERATE_1$ is activated. If not, the process shifts to $TEST_2$. Embedding and recursion occur here too. Any OPERATE can have an internal structure of tests and operations of the same production type. Also, since operations change the situation, the process can shift among tests temporally in an order that does not correspond in any simple way to the seemingly linear order in which the productions are written down. It is not straightforward to identify means and ends in productions. In one sense, however, the immediate end of any production is the operation itself. That is, if the situation passes the test, the aim is to do something described by the operation.

TOTE units may be those of a single person or they may be distributed among persons in a "social plan," a coordinated or joint action of several persons. An *intention,* at any given time, is given by the incomplete parts of a plan whose execution has already begun (Miller et al., 1960:61). Values are involved in the choice among alternative plans that might be executed.

2. *The DSE unit* (Kuhn, 1974): As a foundation for setting out a general systems logic for the analysis of social systems, Kuhn specifies three component processes in any cybernetic system. Two processes relate the system to its environment and one is a purely internal process. The system detects (*D*) events or states of its environment, yielding information input into a selector (*S*) component that involves values or preferences that assess the information to yield a goal that is the basis for the effector (*E*) output to the environment in an ongoing *DSE* cycle. Kuhn models interaction of two cybernetic systems as a coupling in which communication, transaction, and organization are analytical types of interaction corresponding to *D, S,* and *E* functions, respectively. Each main *D, S,* and *E* consists of micro-level *d–s–e* subsystems. When *E* is "rewritten" into its *d–s–e* subsystems, this is analogous to the spelling out of an operation via a series of linked TOTE subunits except that it has a more abstract quality to it.

3. *The quantitative control system model* (Powers, 1973): This author adopts directly the quantitative negative-feedback model of engineering control systems. There are three functional components, as in Kuhn but stated and related a little differently. There is an input function (in the mathematical sense now) that transduces an external signal into an internal signal, changing the quantities from external units to internal units. Powers is interested in cybernetic hierarchy, an ordered system of such feedback loops, as a theoretical model of how the brain generates behavior as the control of its inputs, its perceptions. At the lowest level of the hierarchy of control that Powers considers, this involves a transformation to and from physical signal units and neural current units.[3] There is a computation of a difference between the internal form of the input signal and a reference signal. Then the fundamental dynamic of the system is: The output function operates with the rule of attempting to *reduce* this difference. This or-

dinarily changes the input signal, hence its internal form, hence the difference, hence the continuing behavior. Since the input is subject to disturbances, due to events outside the control of the loop and the reference signal itself is dynamic, being the output of higher level control loops, the whole system is constantly generating behavior. In general, *behavior is the control of perception, where perception refers to the internal form of the input.*[4]

These three variants of cybernetic control conceptions have similarities and differences. Conceptually, the TOTE hierarchy conception is attractive. It is a qualitative and organizational way of thinking of control. Also, the production system mode of control seems to be a very promising way of thinking about the structure of social action. Kuhn's DSE model closely corresponds to Powers's formal model. Both are focused on negative-feedback mechanisms, corresponding to the first type of TOTE unit. Combining Kuhn, Powers, and the first type of TOTE unit, we obtain essentially a single general model of negative-feedback control. In this section, for definiteness, I employ this model, whereas the production system model will be emphasized under the category of structural–generative action theory later in this chapter. This separation is somewhat artificial and is only a tactical step in sorting out the problems of action theory with the eventual aim of a consistent and unified treatment of action and social order, drawing upon multiple traditions of general theoretical sociology. This chapter is only a start on this task.

What is the model object required for the representation of negative-feedback control? The diagram in Figure 3.1 shows the fundamental logic: a loop organization of subprocesses characterizing a system that acts or behaves in an environment.[5] (The symbols in this diagram are explained in detail in what follows.)

The three subprocesses are:

1. A read input function (detect)
2. A write output function (effect, operate)
3. A comparison function (select, test)

The term *function* here has a double meaning. On the one hand, in the mathematical model there are indeed three mathematical functions or mappings. The read input function maps the external input into an internal form. The write output function maps an internal form into an external effect or product. The comparison function has the internal form of the input and a reference standard as its inputs, and it has some difference as its output.

On the other hand, a function is a *recurrent subprocess of a recurrent process* (Miller, 1978). Since the three processes are all subprocesses of the basic feedback process and we envision them as recurrently executed as the system relates to its environment, they qualify as functions in this second sense.

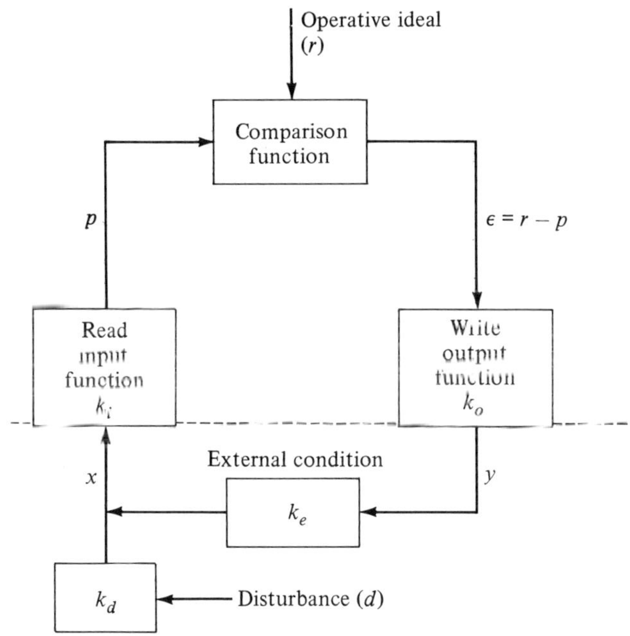


Figure 3.1. General negative-feedback control system

The logic of control is as follows. The organization of these subprocesses in a system so as to constitute one process is a *negative-feedback loop.* A situational object is in some actual or potential time-varying state described as an *external condition,* which is subject to actual or potential *disturbances.* We can describe the loop by beginning anywhere in it. Suppose we start with the external condition at a given time. It is "read" by the input subprocess, so that the external condition $x$ is the input to the system. The input function transforms this external input into an internal form ($p$, as in perceived state). The internal form of the input is compared with what I call an *operative ideal.* The essential point is that according to the model, all action involves operative ideals that control the flow of process. For variety it sometimes will be called a *reference standard* ($r$). (The terms *value* and *norm* are not used because they will be regarded as particular interpretations of the general idea.) The comparison results in a difference ($\epsilon$) that is transformed (to $y$) via the output subprocess into some (possibly negligible) effect on the external condition that is read by the input subprocess, which is where we began in describing the loop.

The fundamental law that the loop embodies is that of reducing the difference.

It is this law that makes the process one that involves a dynamic *normative* logic. In a generalized sense, this law is what justifies the term operative ideal contrasting with the real or perceived value of the input. The output increases with the difference between this operative ideal and the mapped value of the input.

The generic interpretation of what I call the operative ideal is imperative: For any internal form of the input the dynamic normative logic amounts to a command: Make it like *r!* By virtue of this dynamic normative control, the system helps shape the character of its own inputs, both in external and internal forms. So it modifies both its situation and its perception of the situation in the direction of *conformity* with its operative ideals.

But this is not all. Since the situational component of the feedback loop has its own dynamic elements, there is a *reality base* to the system's interaction with its situation. Also, any situational object is subject to what are, from the point of view of the operative ideal, disturbances.[6]

Analytical action theory requires a dynamic conception of how normative control works. Parsons (1951) speaks of ''normative orientations'' to the situation in a rather crippled way: The dynamic element stressed in the preceding logic of control is lost. The feedback model restores the necessary subsumption, under a process worldview, of this basic idea about human action.

To sum up:

> *The control principle of action (negative-feedback form).* The actor in a situation is a negative-feedback system, and a unit act is an episode of negative-feedback control.

The causal source of the operative ideal is a matter separate from the basic logic of the mechanism. It is a fundamental proposition of classic sociological theory (via Durkheim, Mead, Freud, and others) that social control is internalized. This classical framework presupposes a given social order and explains how an individual's own internal control system is constituted by learning the operative ideals already characterizing that actor's environment. It does not explain how novel common operative ideals arise, which requires not an actor–situation model but a dynamical social system model based on the coupling of such models. I shall return to this topic later.

The logic of dynamic normative control can be coordinated to two recent developments in theoretical sociology. First, Heise (1979, 1986) employs a control system model. The basic idea is that momentary affective states are under the control of more enduring sentiments. His ''fundamental sentiments'' are instantiations of operative ideals, whereas his momentary affective meaning states are the results of read inputs. These are compared with the fundamental sentiments from moment to moment in the affect control process. Behavior is the control of affect via the feedback loop. Undoubtedly this is the best developed empirically applicable cybernetic model in the history of theoretical sociology.

Jasso (1980, 1986) treats justice via a formula that can be interpreted in terms of the logic of normative control, although her model is not directly couched in its terms. Her fundamental formula states that the justice evaluation (made by an actor) is given by an expression involving logarithmic transformations:

$$\text{justice evaluation} = \ln(\text{actual}) - \ln(\text{just})$$

The "actual" term refers to the amount of some resource controlled by the actor. Different models can be employed to suggest the form of the corresponding just term. From the control system viewpoint, the important point is that the evaluation takes the form of a *difference* between actual and just. The logarithm, akin to utility functions over quantitative resources, represents an external-to-internal transformation with a decreasing marginal-value property. In this interpretation of Jasso's formula, a particular level of resource is then the operative ideal, dependent on a higher-level control through some moral value conception of social justice. According to the control system model, this difference between the subjective meaning of the actual state and the operative ideal is consequential in behavior through the reduce-difference law. Thus, an implied dynamical control system pervades this justice model and might be the basis for developing it further. Because Jasso is concerned with the macrosociological problem of the properties of resource distributions in social systems, her work is also quite relevant to formal macrostructural theory as discussed later in Chapter 4.

The control principle of action sets the framework for what follows in the remainder of this section: an application to the presuppositional level of discourse in action theory; a mathematical statement of the model, with translated derived results about the elements of action in situations; the application to cybernetic hierarchy; and a discussion of the implied problem of social order.

### *3.2.3. Application to presuppositions of analytical action theory*

A great deal of contemporary discussion among theorists is concerned with the presuppositional level of theory. The way in which I have framed the control principle of action helps illuminate one aspect of this level of discourse. Consider the subject–object dichotomy. The control principle of action provides an intrinsic bond, or loop, that connects the two sides of this dichotomy. It ties elements on one side of the boundary to elements on the other side. It thereby ensures the voluntarism that Parsons (1937) argues is necessary for general action theory: The normative (or ideal) elements and the conditional (or external elements) are dynamically interrelated. They are not related in some purely accidental ad hoc way. They are aspects of one entity, and so long as that entity is described in terms of the control principle of action, these two elements must both be included as two sides of one relation. Theorists who juggle subject and object terms without a relational model create metatheoretical confusion.

Nor is the subject–object dichotomy the only such instance of loss of relational wholeness with its attendant metatheoretical difficulties. Alexander (1982), in his discussion of the presuppositions of theoretical sociology, employs five such dichotomies. In each case, we have an instance of two terms connected by the loop postulated by the control principle of action:

| | *Actor cluster* | *Situation cluster* |
|---|---|---|
| 1. | Internal | External |
| 2. | Normative | Conditional |
| 3. | Ideal | Material |
| 4. | Subjective | Objective |
| 5. | Voluntary | Constraining |

The whole force of Alexander's argument is that classical and contemporary theorists have struggled to be ''multidimensional.'' This means avoidance of exaggerated explanatory force to terms in one cluster over those in the other. The solution to this metatheoretical problem, or at least a firm start toward the solution, is use of the control principle of action.

With the control principle of action, each of the respective terms in the preceding conceptual clusterings describes connected components or aspects of a *single relation, namely, the feedback loop and its components:*

1. What is *internal* is in a loop with what is *external,* given the actor–situation system is a control system.

2. The *normative* standard, or operative ideal, exerts a control that tends to shape the external situation. But what is external has its own structure and dynamics, situational *conditions* the actor cannot unilaterally alter.

3. The normative standard is an operative *ideal* relative to real external states; the latter are *material* in that they are actualities given for the control process.

4. Relative to the actor–situation boundary, one side of this boundary is *subjective,* comparing an ideal with an internal map of the external state; the other is *objective* in the sense of givenness for the actor.

5. The *voluntary* element consists in the fact that as a matter of implication of the control principle of action, to interpret the behavior of such a single actor is to regard it as effort to get the situation into a form that corresponds to the operative ideals – purposes, in a broad sense. But there is also *constraint* of two types: (1) The actor's action is part of the situation of other actors who, in apply-

ing normative standards acquired in social interaction, make efforts to bring this behavior – now as external condition – into a form corresponding to their norms; and (2) owing to learning processes in a particular social environment, the actor's normative standards are, in part, internalizations of norms that have emerged in that environment so that there is both external and internal constraint.

A final point about voluntarism is important. We must distinguish between substantive and formal voluntarism, to use a useful distinction introduced by Alexander (1978). Formal voluntarism corresponds to the normative *element* in any action: the logic of normative control as such. No particular values, norms, or the like are implicated in this generalized theoretical characterization of action. Substantive voluntarism concerns the sorts of operative ideals that govern action in particular cases, whether in some particular social situation of some particular actor or in some period of history with respect to some set of societies and their normative culture.

These statements, though made in reference to Alexander's metatheoretical discussion, have a bearing on the work of Parsons. Namely, they show that the control system model of the actor–situation system coordinates to the foundations of the voluntaristic action framework spelled out by Parsons. It does so in such a way as to make clear that apart from the fact that Parsons could not have used a terminology that had not yet been invented (in 1937), he nevertheless conceptualized human action in intuitive control system terms – as shown in his quoted statement given at the outset of this section. Provided "norm" is generalized to "operative ideal" and the distinction is made between general element and substantive value of the element, the statement should be seen as a sound basis for theory development in the analytical (Paretan) sense. The normative orientation is embodied in the description of the loop with a normative element entering into the comparison process *for any act,* given the representation principle defining the framework of the theoretical system.

### *3.2.4. A mathematical treatment*

The next two tasks are, first, to formulate the basic negative-feedback mechanism in mathematical terms and, second, to interpret it in terms of analytical action theory. For simplicity, two restrictions are introduced in the presentation of the mathematical model. First, a one-dimensional treatment is presented, although a vector description could also be formulated. Second, the properties of the implied steady states are the focus of attention.

Let $x(t)$ be the value of the input variable at time $t$ and let $y(t)$ be the value of the output variable at time $t$. The reference standard, or operative ideal, is a parameter $r$. The disturbance term is represented as $d(t)$. A *dynamical control system* is specified by:

$$dx/dt = f_1(x, y, d) \tag{3.2.1a}$$
$$dy/dt = f_2(y, \epsilon) \tag{3.2.1b}$$

where $\epsilon = r - k_i x$ and $k_i$ is a coefficient involved in the transformation of the external $x$ into an internal form.

These equations can be interpreted in terms of my earlier discussion of equilibration as adjustment (see Section 2.4). In equilibrium, both $dx/dt$ and $dy/dt$ are zero. Then the first equation implies an adjusted value of the input $x$ for every pair consisting of the output and the disturbance; the second equation implies an adjusted value of the output for every difference $\epsilon$, which depends on the parameters $r$ and on $k_i$. Thus in system equilibrium, where both $dx/dt$ and $dy/dt$ are zero, the values $(x, y)$ that satisfy *both* equilibrium equations depend on the parameters and on the disturbance term. For the elementary case, parameters $r$ and $k_i$ are assumed time invariant, but the disturbance term $d$ is assumed to be time varying. Hence the system equilibrium is moving in time: Depending on the precise values of constants that determine the speeds of the adjustments, the inputs and outputs have time-varying magnitudes generated by the negative-feedback mechanism incessantly adjusting to disturbances. Following the usual usage in control systems thinking, let us call these time-varying equilibrated values of $x$ and $y$ the *steady state* of the dynamical control system (3.2.1). For a linear system, the steady-state equations (without the equilibrium notation) are given by

$$x(t) = k_e y(t) + k_d d(t) \tag{3.2.2a}$$
$$y(t) = k_o \epsilon(t) = k_o[r - k_i x(t)] \tag{3.2.2b}$$

The constants $k_o$, $k_i$, $k_e$, and $k_d$ are positive.

The term $k_i x$ is the system's internal form of the external condition, $x$. Although $x$ is subject to control via difference-reducing outputs $y$, the comparator can only work with the internal form and the operative ideal. Thus, we can obtain an interesting consequence by using a generalization of the key idea presented by Powers (1973), who considers control of perception as implied by the loop. Namely, write $p = k_i x$. Then, in the steady state of the linear feedback mechanism,

$$p(t) = k_i[k_e y(t) + k_d d(t)] = k_i(k_e\{k_o[r - p(t)]\} + k_d d(t))$$

Solving for $p(t)$,

$$p(t) = [1/(1+G)][Gr + k_o d(t)] \tag{3.2.3}$$

where $G = k_i k_e k_o$, which is the product of the adjustment constants as we go around the loop. Engineers call it the loop gain coefficient. Suppose there were no disturbance. Then a high $G$ implies that $p$ will be nearly equal to $r$ according to formula (3.2.3). More generally, for any given level of disturbance, the greater the gain, the closer $p$ is to $r$. Thus, *perception* – the internal form of external conditions – tends to be brought into correspondence with the reference standard, the operative ideal, by the system's behavior, its output. Also, the higher is $G$, the less the disturbance contributes to the internal form. So $G$ is a basic quantitative property of the simple negative-feedback mechanism.

Similarly, the behavior of the system depends on $G$ as follows:

$$\begin{aligned} y(t) &= k_o[r - k_i x(t)] \\ &= k_o\{r - k_i[k_e y(t) + k_d d(t)]\} \\ &= k_o r - G y(t) - k_o k_i k_d d(t) \end{aligned}$$

Solving for $y(t)$,

$$y(t) = [k_o/(1+G)][r - k_i k_d d(t)] \tag{3.2.4}$$

Thus, if there were no disturbance, the steady-state output would be directly proportional to the reference pattern, the operative ideal. Also, the higher the gain (the better the system adjusts in all respects), the less output needed. Finally, the input itself – the external condition that is read – depends on the parameters of the loop, and using a similar calculation to the preceding, we obtain

$$x(t) = [1/1+G)][k_e k_o r + k_d d(t)] \tag{3.2.5}$$

If there were no disturbance, then in the steady state the external condition would be proportional to the reference pattern $r$. But, in general, it depends on both $r$ and the disturbances.

This completes the presentation of the abstract mathematical model. Now let us interpret some of these mathematical consequences in terms of the action domain, employing the control principle of action. The use of the mathematical model here parallels somewhat the way that Stinchcombe (1968) employed the logic of homeostasis to show that functionalism involves some definite types of propositions corresponding to relationships in the model. In his interpretation, the negative-feedback system represents a social activity that has the objective consequence of maintaining some homeostatic variable. His "activity variable" is the output term $y(t)$ and his "tension" variable is the disturbance term $d(t)$. His homeostatic variable has the internal dimensionality of $p(t)$, $r$, and $\epsilon(t)$, but his model obscures the crucial comparison operation and the relevant operative ideal. Formally, however, his $H$ is $\epsilon(t)$, that which is magnified by disturbances and reduced by the activity or behavioral output. In the present case, the interpretation is action theoretical in intent: We are explicating a normative logic intrinsic to the action frame of reference. The operative ideals functioning in the comparison process are fundamental.

By reference to the formal representation of the negative-feedback mechanism, we obtain these further implications of the control principle of action:

1. In the dynamic normative control relation between the operative ideals of the actor and the conditions of the situation, if there were no disturbances, then the operative ideals would completely control the form that the latter take for the actor (equation [3.2.3]).

2. In the dynamic normative control relation between the operative ideals of the actor and the conditions of the situation, the actor's observable behavior depends on the ideals but also on conditions beyond the actor's control: the disturbances, which might also be called constraints (equation [3.2.4]).

3. In the dynamic normative control relation between the operative ideals of the actor and the conditions of the situation, the form that the external conditions take depends to some extent on the actor's operative ideals but, also, to some degree on the constraining disturbances, with the degree a matter of properties of the actor and the situation (equation [3.2.5]).

Given the control principle of action, the logic of a dynamic normative control mechanism is incorporated into a model object. The fundamental task of this subsection is now complete. For the future of analytical action theory, what we require is theoretical work on the logic of coupling actor models that are dynamical normative control systems. There are two possibilities for coupling: *horizontal,* between autonomous actors, and *vertical,* in which control at one level is set through output from "above." The vertical case means a hierarchy internal to a single actor, with theoretical priority to the individual type of actor. Section 3.2.5 treats this vertical mode and Section 3.2.6 discusses the horizontal mode.

### *3.2.5. Cybernetic hierarchy models*

Consider the formal representation of cybernetic hierarchy. As a start on the formal treatment of this topic in analytical action theory, I first treat the fundamental new entity that arises: the coupling of two negative-feedback mechanisms, one above the other. Second, I discuss the four-level case of particular interest in the work of Parsons.

Formally, in the hierarchical relation, one mechanism's output becomes the operative ideal for the other, as shown in Figure 3.2.

Let us consider a simplified example of constructing a two-level model. In analytical action theory, by meaning postulate, values are essentially "at a higher level," so that for a given value parameter, a number of norms can develop that are specifications of it as functional exigencies and situations change. This sug-

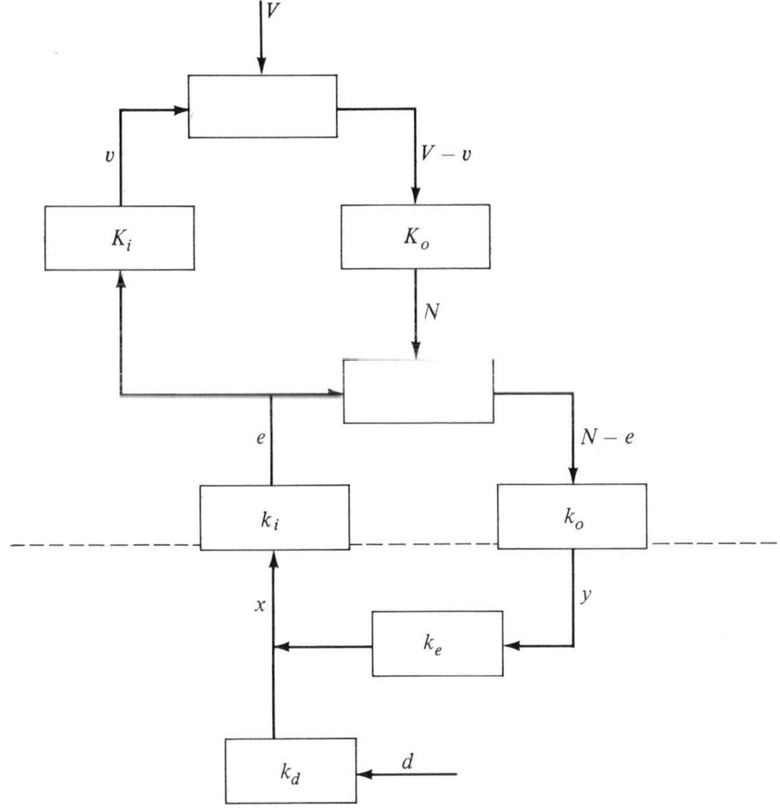


Figure 3.2. Forms of two-level cybernetic hierarchy

gests a pair of levels of negative feedback such that the upper level has a value ($V$) as its operative ideal and the lower level has a norm ($N$) for its operative ideal. By the coupling and the intended interpretation, $N(t)$ will vary dynamically as an output term from the reduce-difference process at the value level. So $V$ will be a constant parameter for this model, but its functioning in a higher-order control position makes the lower level operative ideal variable over time.

In fact, at this point it is useful to make explicit the implied *memory* function involving storage and retrieval of patterns such as $V$ and $N$. Such entities are not reemergent in each occasion, so some subprocess of retrieval is required. When the input is read, it enters not only the comparison function but also the memory function, activating some $V$. Then, at the next level down, the value-level output enters the memory function with the result that $N$ is activated. This means that our cybernetic model now has four functions in the sense of recurrent subprocesses of a recurrent process: read input, write output, compare or test, and retrieve/store.

The interpretation of $e$ is that it is an *expectation* derived from ''reading'' elements in the situation of action. Dimensionally, expectations and norms are in the same units, so a norm is an expectation ''setting'' or control parameter derived from the valuation control process. As input to the upper level, $e$ is interpreted in value terms, giving rise to a specific ''valuation'' $v$. Both $v$ and $V$ are in the dimension of valuation, with ''value'' as a setting or standard for valuation, a given parameter in this sketch. The comparison yields $V-v$ and its output translation, which is generated to reduce this evaluative difference, is an adjustment of the normative expectation parameter $N$. The reduce difference operation on $N-e$ then yields an output to the situation of action, denoted $y$. There is also a disturbance term $d$. Applying the method of the prior section to the upper loop, we obtain

$$e(t) = [1/(1+G)][GN(t) + k_d d(t)] \tag{3.2.6a}$$

$$N(t) = K_o[V - v(t)] = K_o[V - K_i e(t)] \tag{3.2.6b}$$

We can solve for $v$:

$$v(t) = [K_i/(1+G')][K_o GV + k_d d(t)] \tag{3.2.7}$$

where $G' = 1 + G + K_o K_i G$.

Let us see what the model says about action.

In a steady state, according to (3.2.6a), the expectation based on actual behavior is proportional to the norm and to disturbances. Without disturbances, the expectation would approach the norm more and more closely as the gain $G$ increased. Equation (3.2.6b) shows how the norm is adjusted in terms of feedback control at the upper level. To the extent that the expectation is under the control of the norm (which depends on $G$), it is governed by what ought to be the case rather than by a purely realistic cognitive process (Luhmann, 1976:509).

Also in the steady state, by equation (3.2.7), the valuation $v$ will be a function of the given value commitment $V$ and situational exigencies $d$. Thus, the dominant and given value commitment $V$ shapes the actual evaluations made.

The parameters of the loop as a whole will vary with the type of situation. Hence the steady-state equations formulate an infinite family of forms of action keyed to situational variation while yet realizing the value commitment $V$. This is so without the presumption that actual behavior and expectations based on it are exactly conformable to norms. By virtue of the $G$ term, more or less conformity is generated. But no matter what the empirical values of the parameters, a whole family of possibilities is described by the control principle of action and its consequences for cybernetic hierarchy.

Because of the various constants associated with the functions in the control systems, there is plenty of conceptual space for situational variation and actor variation in these processes. But this is an actor–situation model. The (correct) Parsonian argument in *The Structure of Social Action* (1937) and in *The Social System* (1951), however, is that arbitrary variability of these actor–situation components of the total system is incompatible with order. In other words, the social system is unstable unless the properties characterizing distinct actors satisfy some conditions. The necessary conditions stressed by Parsons are those that impose some commonness at the value level. Then the norms, which are more immediately responsive to situational and functional variability, should have derived conditions of their own corresponding, for instance, to the idea of shared but role-differentiated norms as components of stable social relations.

This statement reflects my interpretation of Parsons's work. In the negative form, this interpretation amounts to a rejection of a widespread opinion that Parsons's various statements about values are purely metatheoretical or epistemological (Bershady, 1973; Alexander, 1982). On the contrary, according to the interpretation proposed here, such statements are conjectured theorems related to the types described in the preceding chapter and to be further specified in what follows. They are insights into the possible forms of theorems linking social structure possibilities to cultural elements.

An even more complex cybernetic hierarchy can be constructed that corresponds to analytical action theory's required four levels. The main conceptual scheme and corresponding dynamical control system can be discussed by analogy with the formal case of two levels without introducing more mathematics. The four levels can be characterized in terms of a chain of operative ideals: from values to norms to goals to operations, the last directly controlling biophysical structures generating physical behavioral events.[7] The memory function implies that there are stored patterns corresponding to each of these types of operative ideals. For example, a learned mode of multiplication of numbers is a stored cognitive operation that can be activated by some output from the goal level of control. Similarly, a need disposition or goal is activated through the normative level output.

Recall that an operation can be quite complex, with its own embedded ends and means, subgoals, and suboperations. Also, an operation may be only a thought process (e.g., adding two numbers mentally) or an observable behavior as well (e.g., adding two numbers on a piece of paper).

The following general rule is formulated in regard to cybernetic hierarchy:

*The rate rule.* In a cybernetic hierarchy, if an operative ideal is set by the output of a higher level control mechanism, then its rate of change is faster than that of the higher level operative ideal.

An immediate consequence of the rate rule for the four-level chain of controlling operative ideals is that since lower level ideals change more rapidly than higher level ideals, behavioral and/or thought operations change faster than goals, which change faster than norms, which change faster than values. These comparisons must be within the appropriate hirerarchy. For instance, any subgoals set in the performance of a cognitive or behavioral operation (such as multiplying numbers or writing a letter) cannot be compared with the operation itself, since they are a phase of its constitutive process structure.

### 3.2.6. *Implications for basic theory*

Assume, without formal construction, a four-level cybernetic hierarchy model of the individual actor–situation system. Then a social network of individuals corresponds to a system defined by *coupling* such individual action systems in the horizontal mode. This means that they are connected externally through reading each other's behavior and not internally through normative control in the sense of vertically coupled control units. I call this a *social coupling of dynamical normative control systems* or, for brevity, simply *social coupling*. For a pair of individual level models, say $M_1$ and $M_2$, the social coupling is defined by $x_1 = y_2$ and $y_1 = x_2$: The input to $M_1$ is the output (behavior) of $M_2$ and the output of $M_1$ is the input to $M_2$. The effort to get another individual to do something, for instance, is an *input* to the other, not a direct setting of the other's operative ideals. In this way, Parsons's (1969) modes of social control have much relevance as ways in which one actor can exert control over another: through coercion, persuasion, inducement, or activation of commitments. All except coercion rely upon some element of order in the nexus of the actors.

Hence, the consequence of a social coupling is the highly problematic character of social order. *Social control* now means that the dynamic normative control exerted by one or more actors is with respect to the situation of one or more other such actors. There is nothing quite like this in the literature of control systems theory that Powers (1973) drew upon because engineers would avoid the implied "craziness" of autonomous control systems trying to control each other's behavior. Engineers design order. By contrast, in our application of formal control systems logic, there is no givenness of social design.

The complexity of such social coupling of cybernetically described actors is probably what accounts for the conceptual complexity of Parsons's writings.

Each actor model has four levels with four cybernetic functions, making for sixteen subprocesses. We want to "home in" on the coupling to focus on the problems of social structure. But how? What shall we assume about communicative order, which refers to common symbolic systems governing the reading of each other's behaviors? More generally, what shall we assume about what is commonly stored for retrieval through the memory function? While these "cultural" questions are important, I first want to concentrate on the central conceptual point about this social control problem to show how it is at the core of theoretical sociology. I shall place the social system in its wider action context when I discuss the AGIL scheme in the next section.

If the relevant operative ideals are free to vary at random at the very top (the value level), the coupled normative control processes are likely to result in mutual attempts to gain advantage over the other and, potentially, to the use of force to do so. This situation is not improved if we add some substantive ideals that might be given for social interaction, such as a value placed on communicative order or goal states involving food, shelter, and water. That is, if we assume some operative ideals arise simply because we are human organisms who interact symbolically and if we add scarcity, we obtain the Hobbesian initial situation or state of nature. In short, *starting from the control principle of action, what comes to be expected is not order but conflict and coercion in the social coupling of dynamical normative control systems.*

Hence, the theoretical problem is: Given a human world in which enduring forms of social action exist – implying enduring forms of coordinated action of individuals – how is this order really possible? To answer at some level of generality requires the setup and study of theoretical models and the formal investigation of them from the standpoint of demonstrating a certain type of theorem. In terms of the general types of theorems described in Chapter 2, the theorem type involved is a combination of Types 1 and 2: a *social order theorem.* Such a theorem responds to the problem of how enduring social structure is possible given the potential conflict and coercion in any network of social couplings.

To invoke any collective entity as a proposed solution to the order problem, such as the state, misconstrues the problem. For any such entity is an outcome of social interaction. The question is how a matrix of social couplings, a social network, can be described in generative terms such that it possesses attractor states. Any such attractor state corresponds to (1) a social structure because of the underlying social network and because of the equilibrated character of the dynamics and (2) a really possible such structure because it is an attractor and not a repellor of the dynamics. More specifically, the problem is to discover, by reasoning deductively about the defined model or by simulation studies of its properties, under what parametric conditions such an attractor state exists.

So the problem must be abstracted from its concrete locus in the world to a more generalized theoretical plain of inquiry. The classical attention to institutionalization and internalization processes finds its niche here, one in terms of the upper level of control and the other in terms of the lower level of control relative to the level of expectation states.

In Chapter 2, the critique of the idea of a general dynamical social system pointed in several directions, given the conceptual problems located. Among these were the action problem and the network problem. The derived needs were for (1) action principles from which generators of social dynamics could be derived and (2) retention of the network aspect in studying social dynamics. With the presupposition that we require models that are generative, the work of this section has involved the statement of a representation principle and the study of a corresponding model from the point of view of providing a conceptual resolution to these two problems by reference to the heritage of work by Parsons. Within this hierarchical structure of theory, part of which is formal and part of which is not, we can state the following derived basic result in terms of the conceptual problems.

> *Template for social generators.* The generator of general social dynamics has the form of a matrix of social (horizontal) couplings of dynamical normative control systems.

In more formal detail, we model each actor as a multilevel dynamical normative control system with corresponding vector input (**x**) and vector output (**y**) terms. (Vectors allow multiple inputs and multiple outputs, useful for a general statement.) An $N$-actor system is mapped, first, into a set of $N$ such model objects. Then the couplings form a matrix of 0's and 1's in which rows and columns correspond to these model objects, in which a 1 indicates that an output of the row model object is an input to the column model object. Such a matrix is time dependent in the general case. Note that for certain purposes, we might want to include 1's along the main diagonal to include self-reference (I read my outputs) to embody the dynamics in symbolic interaction. The way Heise (1979) treats the self–other dynamics might provide a clue as to this and related problems in implementing the template.

The point of this template is not one of constituting in itself a testable theoretical model or hypothesis. But this does not make it "merely metatheoretical," as some overly positivistic interpretations would have it. Like analogous templates in other theoretical sciences, it defines a general form, which it is the business of theoretical model building to translate into particular instances of models satisfying the form. Such model building will need to be conducted with a strong emphasis on the value of simplicity at the level of specific theoretical models, in some tension with realist-driven requirements to be sure (Heckathorn, 1984). Other relevant cognitive values are generality and conceptual relevance. Relevance arises here from the background of Chapter 2: The template preserves the network representation but grounds it in a principle of action. Generality is attained through the abstract and generalized definitions and notations.

## 3.3. Analytical action theory: dynamical system sketches

Analytical action theory as a branch of action theory within sociology has made a number of contributions to general theoretical sociology. Three are particularly worth noting: the conception of normative control, the AGIL scheme, and the conception of generalized symbolic media. Although the latter are important and equally worthy of attention, for reasons of space, only the former two are being treated. The first conception was treated in the prior section. In this section, the AGIL scheme is the focus of attention. My procedure will be first to discuss this scheme in conceptual isolation from the control principle and only afterward to relate it to that principle. Still later a conceptual problem about their connection will be discussed.

The AGIL scheme was initiated from studies of small group processes (Parsons, Bales, and Shils, 1953). Four problems were said to face any group: *adaptation* (*A*) to the environment, group *goal attainment* (*G*), social *integration* (*I*) of the participants, and *latent pattern maintenance* (*L*), a fusion of cultural and motivational problems of group process. Subsequently, the scheme was generalized by Parsons: Any model of action is defined in terms of an action space defined in terms of adaptation, goal attainment, integration, and latent pattern maintenance.

From the present perspective, this work is interpretable as focused on behavior manifolds characterized in terms of the AGIL dimensions. An underlying social coupling is presupposed, but its details are treated only later to focus now on the logic of the dynamical system. So there are four *dimensions of action space* (Parsons et al., 1953).

We let $\boldsymbol{\alpha} = (\mathbf{L}, \mathbf{I}, \mathbf{G}, \mathbf{A})$ be the abstract action state vector, and we let a set of nonaction conditions be described by what I call the biophysical parameter and denote by $\mathbf{b}$. The generic abstract dynamical action system is of the form

$$d\boldsymbol{\alpha}/dt = \mathbf{f}(\boldsymbol{\alpha}, \mathbf{b})$$

For each possible value of $\mathbf{b}$, there is a set of possible action structures (possibly empty in some cases) given abstractly in the form that instantiates expression (2.3.4):

$$\{\boldsymbol{\alpha}_{eq}\} = \mathbf{g}(\mathbf{b})$$

So a structure of action is a set of action elements adjusted to biophysical conditions, and a really possible action structure is one for which the biophysical conditions satisfy certain stability requirements. Note that nonlinearity can be expected to imply that there are plural really possible action structures under given biophysical conditions.

This abstract system is further specified through the AGIL scheme so that it is rewritten as the *abstract AGIL dynamical action system:*

$$d\mathbf{L}/dt = \mathbf{f}_1(\mathbf{L}, \mathbf{I}, \mathbf{G}, \mathbf{A}; \mathbf{b}) \quad (3.3.1a)$$
$$d\mathbf{I}/dt = \mathbf{f}_2(\mathbf{L}, \mathbf{I}, \mathbf{G}, \mathbf{A}; \mathbf{b}) \quad (3.3.1b)$$
$$d\mathbf{G}/dt = \mathbf{f}_3(\mathbf{L}, \mathbf{I}, \mathbf{G}, \mathbf{A}; \mathbf{b}) \quad (3.3.1c)$$
$$d\mathbf{A}/dt = \mathbf{f}_4(\mathbf{L}, \mathbf{I}, \mathbf{G}, \mathbf{A}; \mathbf{b}) \quad (3.3.1d)$$

Treating (3.3.1) as a formal system, we ask, What are its intended interpretations? Two problems of interpretation require treatment. One problem is to relate the system to the action frame of reference. In what sense are we treating a system of action? For instance, not concrete acts but *elements* in them, varying in magnitude, are assumed here. Which elements? The discussion of this problem will be postponed, as indicated earlier, but the prospective answer is through the control principle of action. The second problem of interpretation concerns the sociological meanings of the abstract dimensions. For instance, Parsons (1969) interprets the goal attainment state sometimes as a motivational state and sometimes as a political state. Neither of these is precisely the same as the original small group process meaning.

The idea of addressing the problem of social order, as suggested toward the end of the last section, suggests a focus on a particular interpretation of the dimensions among all those that are possible. The interpretation is supplied through a sequence of notational conventions as follows.

Any single one of the AGIL dimensions of state description can itself be analyzed into substates with the same abstract form. So, for instance, **L** = (**LL, LI, LG, LA**) is a breakdown of the **L**-state into four substates. Then any of these can be broken down into their substates. For instance, we can let **LI** = (**LIL, LII, LIG, LIA**).

Now if we assign a definite interpretation to the main states **L, I, G,** and **A,** the meanings of the substates are constrained and even suggested by the general nature of the abstract dimensions as referring to generalized pattern maintenance, generalized integration, generalized goal attainment, and generalized adaptation.

The primary interpretation of the dimensions of the general action state $\boldsymbol{\alpha}$ and of some of their substates may be indicated as follows, where indenting shows the way in which given meanings constrain lower level meanings:

**L:** action pattern maintenance = cultural dimension

**LI:** cultural integration = value dimension

**LII:** value integration = moral value dimension

**I:** action integration = social dimension

**IL:** social pattern maintenance = fiduciary dimension

**II:** social integration = communal dimension

**IG:** social goal attainment = political dimension

**IA:** social adaptation = economic dimension

**G:** action goal attainment = motivational dimension

**GI:** motivational integration = conscience dimension

**A:** action adaptation = cognitive dimension

**AI:** cognitive integration = mental model dimension[8]

This chart of functional nomenclature highlights an important element of systematic ambiguity in our natural language usage of the term *social.* A social relation can mean **I** or it can mean **II.** If the former, then an attractor state of a dynamical social (**I**) system includes economic and political role relations as well as communal (gemeinschaft-type) relations. If the latter, then structures of social (**II**) relations are attractor states of social (**II**) processes. These do bind people to one another (social integration function), whereas economic (**IA**) relations do not. Of course, concrete individuals enter into multiplex relations, containing strands of **IA**-type and **II**-type role relations (plus two other types). This point coordinates to Figure 2.4, which now should be relabeled so that **I** becomes **II** and **A** becomes **IA.**

As this partial tabulation shows, our primary interest is in the integration dimension itself and the integration subdimensions of the other states of action. For instance, institutionalization links **LII** and **I:** In terms of the control principle, moral values are potentially translateable (in the process of social interaction) into operative ideals that normatively control expectation states in social interaction (institutional norms). Internalization links **L** to **GI** and **AI** since both conscience and cognition are based on internalized cultural codes. The level **L** is the crucial locus for the embedding of interaction in a sea of given meanings that enable additional meanings to be generated. To take as one's topic the social generation of cultural meaning systems widens the scope of general theoretical sociology. But generation of those meanings that enter back into the social process that generates, regenerates, or destroys social structures is within the scope of the field as I have defined it. The next section sketches one dynamical system that incorporates some of this AGIL logic.

### 3.3.1. The general dynamical social action system

It will be useful to write out the abstract form of the general dynamical action system implied by the expansion of the integration component. The following is called here the *general dynamical social action system:*

$$d\mathbf{L}/dt = \mathbf{f}_1(\mathbf{L}, \mathbf{I}, \mathbf{G}, \mathbf{A}; \mathbf{b}) \tag{3.3.2a}$$

$$d\mathbf{IL}/dt = \mathbf{f}_{21}(\mathbf{IL}, \mathbf{II}, \mathbf{IG}, \mathbf{IA}; \mathbf{L}, \mathbf{G}, \mathbf{A}; \mathbf{b}) \tag{3.3.2b}$$

$$d\mathbf{II}/dt = \mathbf{f}_{22}(\mathbf{IL}, \mathbf{II}, \mathbf{IG}, \mathbf{IA}; \mathbf{L}, \mathbf{G}, \mathbf{A}; \mathbf{b}) \tag{3.3.2c}$$

$$d\mathbf{IG}/dt = \mathbf{f}_{23}(\mathbf{IL}, \mathbf{II}, \mathbf{IG}, \mathbf{IA}; \mathbf{L}, \mathbf{G}, \mathbf{A}; \mathbf{b}) \tag{3.3.2d}$$

$$d\mathbf{IA}/dt = \mathbf{f}_{24}(\mathbf{IL}, \mathbf{II}, \mathbf{IG}, \mathbf{IA}; \mathbf{L}, \mathbf{G}, \mathbf{A}; \mathbf{b}) \tag{3.3.2e}$$

$$d\mathbf{G}/dt = \mathbf{f}_3(\mathbf{L}, \mathbf{I}, \mathbf{G}, \mathbf{A}; \mathbf{b}) \tag{3.3.2f}$$

$$d\mathbf{A}/dt = \mathbf{f}_4(\mathbf{L}, \mathbf{I}, \mathbf{G}, \mathbf{A}; \mathbf{b}) \tag{3.3.2g}$$

In the intended interpretation, (3.3.2) defines four coupled dynamical systems for the analysis of action, and one of these is further analyzed into four subsystems. The *action environment* of the social system, which is represented by the dynamical subsystems for the **I** process as a whole, is processually described by the three other major dynamical systems (for **L, G,** and **A**). The *nonaction environment* is represented by the biophysical parameter **b.**

How does the general dynamical social action system (3.3.2) relate to the similarly named entity of Chapter 2? As mentioned earlier, in the reference to Figure 2.4, if we abstract from the way in which the dimensions are specified in terms of definite modes of state description, we can treat the adaptation–integration subsystems of (2.8.1) as corresponding to the **IA** and **II** dimensions. So Homans's external system is **IA,** and his internal system is **II.** This captures the special ''social'' (**II**) aspect he wanted to represent through this system and that I previously related to Durkheimian depth sociology. Parsons (1977) has referred to **II** as the *core* of the social system, and this also captures its special social integrative functional significance within the whole roster of AGIL components set out earlier.

When Blau (1964) treated these processes, he pictured social differentiation and social integration as two structural facets generated from the elementary exchange processes relating actors. Exchange is initiated through extrinsic interests in others as sources of rewards and, in the process of social integration, shifts to an intrinsic interest in the other as a diffuse source of rewarding association.

Thus, if we combine Parsons, Homans, and Blau, relying particularly on the latter's clarifying discussions of the pattern variables and Homans's clarifying characterizations of instrumental (external, substantive, adaptation, economic) and expressive (internal, ceremonial, social–integrative, communal) systems, we arrive at a reasonably convergent picture of this **IA–II** "axis" of the general dynamical social action system.

Similarly, the other two dynamical social subsystems may be interpreted as follows. The **IG** system arises because the social interaction process gives rise to attempts to define *collective* goals. These are ends that the entire referent social network is to employ in the production of an act, constituting itself as a single collective actor. The social network, under the social integration process, can become at once one collectivity and a network of subgroups. As a single collectivity, it can act in its environment – provided that somehow the control of action permits it. Two analytical elements then arise. First, the various goals of the various actors must mesh so as to constitute a basis for collective action. This may be called the *organizational* element. So the network has a self-organizing aspect. Second, the definition of such a collective goal is a matter of interactions among actors who may propose distinct goals. This gives rise to leadership, negotiation, compromise, conflict, and so forth. We may term this the *political* element. Thus **IG** includes the elements of organization and politics. In this regard, a good example of a contribution to modern analytical action theory is that by Etzioni (1968), who draws attention to the complex cybernetic subprocesses involved in the production of acts by collective actors.

Finally, we come to the **IL** dynamical subsystem. The generic reference is to *socialization* processes producing actors with values, norms, motivation, and operational skills to take roles in social structures. The emergent structures here, for instance, include educational institutions. From the point of view of cybernetic hierarchy, a critical aspect of this "reproductive process" is the possible regeneration of actors whose conscience (**GI**) is controlled by the parameters defining the moral values institutionalized in the social structure (**I** attractor state and perhaps **II** as most significant).

In all aspects of the dynamics no process simply does something unconditionally: There are necessary conditions framed in terms of the other processes. Hence, the generic concept of functional analysis as described in Section 2.8 holds: The problem is to show how the conditions necessary for a steady-state process are generated in the environment of that process.

The various states of processes adjust to each other. For instance, the political state **IG** equilibrates to the other social states and to the conditions of the action and nonaction environment. Given the network presupposition, an equilibrium state of **IG** is a *political structure*. There is a set of possible political structures (possibly empty) corresponding to every possible combination of its social, action, and nonaction environmental states and conditions. Similar remarks hold for *fiduciary structures* (**IL** equilibria, such as educational roles and collectivities), *communal structures* (**II** equilibria), and *economic structures* (**IA** equilibria). If we consider all these four substructures together, then only a subset of them are *mutually compatible* or *noncontradictory*, to use the Marxian terminology. As a visualization of this consideration, imagine that any two are selected and visually represented by $x$ and $y$ axes, as in Figure 2.1. When adjustment in one direction is considered, the possibilities for structures are functions of the other variable, and when both are considered simultaneously, the effect is to consider the intersections, thus reducing the possibilities. Thus, some political structures that are possible when we let the economic state be arbitrary are not possible when we set the economic state to *its* possible structures. Thus, as successive social dimensions are considered, we get fewer and fewer possible total social structures.

So we are led to the following: For each configuration of other action states and nonaction conditions, there exists a set (possibly empty) of possible social structures: They are possible in that under the conditions, they are equilibrated internally (i.e., polity to economy, economy to polity, polity to community, etc.) and also externally to the conditions. This is shown formally by an expression that instantiates the general expression (2.3.4):

$$\{(\mathbf{IL}, \mathbf{II}, \mathbf{IG}, \mathbf{IA})_{eq}\} = \mathbf{g}(\mathbf{L}, \mathbf{G}, \mathbf{A}; \mathbf{b}) \tag{3.3.3}$$

Some of these structures are *really* possible in specified action and nonaction environments in that required stability conditions are satisfied: They are attractors rather than repellors of process. But some of the action and nonaction conditions might have been generated in prior social dynamics, for example, the content of the conscience term **GI.** Really possible social structures, in all generality, are not constrained by particular motivational states produced by particular social dynamics even though as initial conditions they would so constrain social order. On the other hand, *general* properties of the action environment do constrain the social structural possibilities. For a sound interpretation, we require reference to the control principle of action.

### *3.3.2. Action and order implications*

The question to be addressed now is whether some intelligible connection exists between the two foundation elements of the theory, the control principle of action and the AGIL scheme. This is one aspect of the problem of the action interpretation of the system just set out. In another aspect, it is the problem of the implementation of the template derived earlier through the control principle of action.

Let me first say what would be ideal and then look at what we have. Ideally, we would apply the derived template rule for constructing social generators, from Section 3.2. This would give us a theoretical model for network dynamics based on a social coupling of dynamical normative control systems representing the actors. Then propositions answering to the general problem of social order would be logical consequences: arrived at, ideally, by formal study of the model object, given the assumptions about it, along the lines of the Simon–Homans models. Now the reality: Not in the literature, not here, will one find such a connection. This is for the future, if it is possible at all. I shall return to this point later.

Short of this strong type of connection, two sorts of links between the control principle and the AGIL scheme can be suggested.

First, there is a conceptual link that provides a partial interpretation of the state variables of the general dynamical social action system. Namely, the dimensional states of the AGIL scheme can each be interpreted as lists of *pairs* of states: (actual, ideal). Also, the ideal term can be in a latent state, saved in memory, or in the active state, retrieved from memory. This follows from the cybernetic hierarchy model. If actors *A* and *B* are socially coupled, for instance, then each has a description at four levels in the model. At each level, an "actual" term is the input to the comparator along with the ideal term, the difference being the basis for output terms. The general correspondence that is suggested, then, is that a state variable in the AGIL scheme describes the *state of a normative control mechanism with all its component cybernetic functions of input, output, comparison, and memory.*

Let us use the particular model in which the hierarchy runs from values to norms to goals to operations. We identify the value level for social interaction as *moral* values, and so the correspondence is with **LII** in the general action system model. At the next level down, involving control of social expectations through norms, the correspondence is with **I.** Functionally differentiated norms then correspond to the four substates of **I.** Then the goal level might be identified with **GI** (with unspecified internal differentiation for simplicity). Here the operative ideal constituting the social conscience monitors and controls certain momentary social feeling states derived from below. The lowest level might be taken as **AI,** where the synthesizing operations of cognition are involved, generating and interpreting self–other behaviors through feedback control.

So, what all this means is that the control principle of action provides an action interpretation of the dimensions of action space. These dimensions refer to the levels of normative control and the states of control mechanisms linked to each other in a hierarchy. The social coupling is through the input–output linkage between actors, each with this state description. The overall state of the system as a whole is a set of "locations" in action space, as Parsons et al. (1953) put it. Each actor at each moment occupies such a location. Attractor states or cycles provide a concept of stable locations or orbits for actors in relation to each other. The problem of order concerns the conditions necessary for such attractors to exist. This leads to the second type of link between the control principle and the AGIL scheme.

This second type of link corresponds to derivations that would follow from the setup of models satisfying the social coupling and the AGIL conceptual link. If we relax our standards and ask whether in analytical action theory there are propositions that, although not strictly derived properties of a theoretical model, play an analogous role and serve as conjectured order theorems, the answer is that there are such statements.

One major theorem conjecture consists of a group of statements found in one of Parsons's most difficult papers (1960). They incorporate much of the intuition of the traditional discourse about the dimensions of social systems. These statements treat the relations between the four action dimensions and the famous pattern variables in all generality. I shall discuss only the case of the social dimensions (**IL, II, IG, IA**). Correspondingly, pattern variables are not given their widest possible meanings.

The centrality of operative ideals at the moral value level in the hierarchical normative control systems is what suggests the need for generalized concepts to describe them. This problem is addressed through one specification of the generalized meanings of the pattern variables. Each pattern variable is interpreted here as a pair of covariables. For instance, universalism–particularism is a pair of variables such that, in a definite context, only one variable applies. Then it varies in magnitude to allow for our intuition of ''more universalistic than,'' for instance. The qualitative distinction between the pair of covariables can be thought of as a boundary in the appropriate cultural subspace so that it would be a catastrophe, in the technical sense of Chapter 2, if the meaning dynamics moved the state from the universalistic region to the particularistic region or conversely. Indeed, people do respond to movements of this sort as very serious problems of conduct.

Next, the problem is how these conceptualized value parameters relate to the problem of social order, that is, of really possible social structures (those that are attractors of social dynamics). The moral values are operative ideals, cultural substates (**LII**) in a parametric role for social dynamics.

The complete conjecture has four parts, corresponding to the four social subdimensions, but I treat only the economic dimension and the communal dimension. In addition, I focus on only two pattern variables in the formal conjecture, merely mentioning the others in the discussion that follows. The conjecture states moral value conditions necessary for stable social structures (hence, instances of social order) corresponding to the economic (**IA**) and communal (**II**) dynamical subsystems.

> *Moral normative control and social stability* [conjecture] (Parsons, 1960). (1) A necessary condition for the existence of a stable economic structure is that its controlling moral values are characterized by universalism and specificity. (2) A necessary condition for the existence of a stable communal structure is that its controlling moral values are characterized by particularism and diffuseness.

An economic structure, an **IA** substructure, is best interpreted as a structure of "instrumental" roles defined by relational institutional norms in some division of labor. The basic unit of this substructure is a generated role relation immanent in the complete interactive nexus of some concrete pairs of persons in interaction. But what do we mean by *role relation* in this context? We mean, by coordination to the social coupling, the specific states of the **I** level of the cybernetic hierarchy: the norms controlling the interactive expectation states *plus* those states. So in the case of **IA,** the normative control of expectation states in this generated role relation involves norms that are based on instituted values of competence or skill (universalism) and self and other obligations to do one's part in the division of labor (instituted specificity value). At the same time, affective neutrality (as contrasted with affectivity) and performance (as contrasted with quality) also become relevant operative ideals.[10]

A communal structure is a **II** substructure in (3.3.3). It can be interpreted as a structure of *expressive* or (in one sense of the word) *social* roles in a *gemeinschaft* aspect of the complete social system. Once again, the role relation refers to the social coupling at the **I** level, as differentiated. For **II,** the normative control of expectations is based on moral values of loyalty (instituted particularism) and on ceremonial exchanges or ritual interactions based on trust and so on unspecified obligations (instituted diffuseness). Both of these elements were key themes in the work of Durkheim. Also, Durkheim (1915) stresses the importance of the occasions of ritual celebrations as generating emotions focused on symbols that represent the group feeling even when the members are not gathered. These symbols of the group can call out the affectivity bound to the membership status: This is the affectivity–quality pattern relevant to the integration case.[11]

There is another and more familiar way of stating this theorem conjecture. *Order* is stable structure, framed now in the context of the general problem of order. Moral values that are universalistic–specific may be termed *rational* in at least one sense of this wide-ranging term.[12] Those that are particularistic–diffuse are often termed *nonrational* without the implication that they are "irrational."[13]

Hence, economic order requires rational values, whereas communal order requires nonrational values. The total order of the system, its enduring form, requires both rational and nonrational values. This statement is essentially the same as Durkheim's various arguments about the limits of rationality in social life.

These remarks perhaps can help to clarify a vexing issue in the tradition of general theoretical sociology that will be taken up again in Section 3.5. There is a tendency in the literature to portray the exchange-theoretical subtradition as containing two wings (Collins, 1985). Accepting this portrayal provisionally in order to frame and respond to the issue, let me characterize the two wings. Collins associates one wing with what in this book is called Durkheimian depth sociology. The keynote is ritual solidarity [illegible], [illegible] exchange relations. The other wing features the works of such theorists as Homans, Emerson, Blau, and Coleman. Here the characterizations are usually distorted. This wing is frequently mislabeled "utilitarian" in a sense that confuses a formal principle of action with a substantive value or norm. This terminology also neglects the differences between nineteenth-century ethical and economic utility theory and modern utility theory, in which utility is simply a numerical representation of any structure of preferences satisfying certain consistency conditions. (See Section 1.3.1.) In terms of Parsons's conjectured theorem, the Durkheimian wing of exchange theory stresses the necessity of the existence of nonrational values so as to govern the communal component of interaction. Polemically, as in Durkheim's critique of Spencer, it contrasts this side of the theorem with the other side. A nonrational foundation for social life is required. But in no way does the contemporary Homans-type wing presuppose anything contrary to this side of the conjectured theorem. Properly characterized, it stresses constructions and deductions based on a general principle of action. In short, its logic is that of Parsons, when both are seen as employing the procedure of coupling actor–situation models to derive social system models. In Section 3.6.2, as a demonstration of this procedure and as a means of further clarifying the point being made, it will be shown that a gemeinschaft-type social relation can be derived from a model constructed on a basis in which the general principle of action is that of adaptive rationality.

Two diagrams will help sum up some of the content of this section. First, using the form of network representation explained earlier for Figure 2.4, Figure 3.3 shows the simplest form of the adaptation–integration structure of roles generated by a dynamical social system (i.e., the **IA–II** connected substructures). In this diagram, the solid lines are the relational ties of social structure. The diagram may be interpreted in terms of social coupling and the cybernetic hierarchy model (focusing on the **I** level of control). Nodes represent expectation

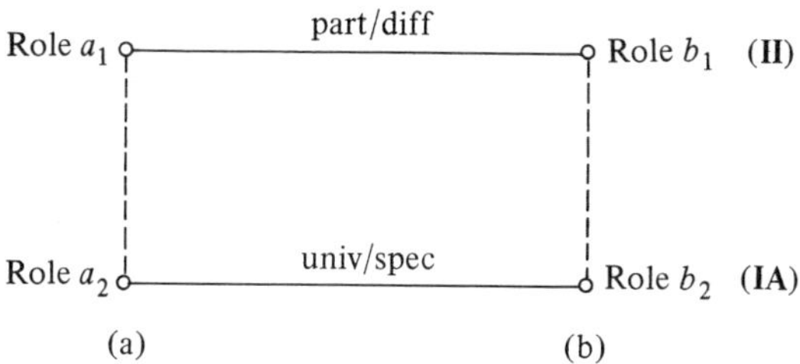


Figure 3.3. Values and types of social relations

control mechanisms, internal to the actors, constituted by the actual–ideal dual representation state description: (1) actual self–other expectations, which may vary dynamically from moment to moment in the same situation, and (2) norms controlling those expectation states of interaction. That is, when there is social order in the sense of an attractor state, actual expectations are kept near the norms through the control process. Because of the actual–ideal dual state, a role relation is not *only* normative, but its intrinsic character involves the social coupling of dynamical normative control systems. In turn, the norms are "set" through the control process involving the moral values at the cultural level of cybernetic control. The types of moral values stated in the Parsonian conjecture are used to label the relational lines between actors.

Then the model of the concrete relationship between actors *a* and *b* is a system with two ingredient social relations, as shown. Roles switch on and off as interaction proceeds so that the structures endure as properties of the interactive nexus, whereas their activation can be quite irregular. When the roles are "off," they are in memory as symbolically stored patterns, as stressed in what follows for structural–generative action theory. When they are activated, this means that the associated norms are activated and control expectation states. Note that a variety of different norms controlling interactive expectations can realize the same institutionalized moral values so the norm level is distinct from the value level of control. For instance, the **IA** norms may vary with specialized functions in the production process and with specific contexts of interaction, all realizing the general universalism–specificity value pattern.

Figure 3.3 can be embedded within a more complete structure representable in a second diagram corresponding to the social coupling of two cybernetic hierarchies (Figure 3.4). It is more complex but shows the cybernetic control hierarchy model of each actor. For simplicity, only the direction of normative control and not the reverse-feedback flow is shown. Also only differentiation at the **I**

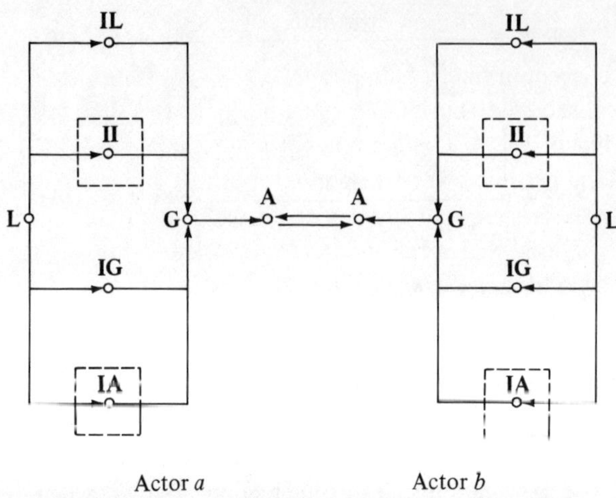


Figure 3.4. Social coupling with social relation aspect

level is pictured. The four role nodes of Figure 3.3 are shown in the four dashed boxes in Figure 3.4, each with a subsystem label to make the diagram easier to understand. With common values, the **L** nodes of actors *a* and *b* actually meet at the crown of the two hierarchies so that they interpenetrate (as discussed in the next section). The coupling is the input–output connection, where it must be recalled that the **A** nodes are complete normative control mechanisms. So each is linked to the situation through input and output functions, and it is through these that the social coupling occurs. Of course, the pair coupling is itself only one particular such connection from the complete social coupling matrix associated with the template for social generativity.

Before closing this section, let me remind the reader that the general cybernetic hierarchy is a model of the single actor. This has two interpretations, individual and collective. In the preceding discussion, primacy was given to the individual case because the problem of social order was the focus. We cannot assume *given* collective actors that are cybernetically organized to generate collective action, if our aim is the theoretical one of deriving or conjecturing theorems about the conditions required for social order, that is, stable social structures including collectivities as aspects of them. When collective actors *are* modeled by cybernetic hierarchy and then a social coupling matrix is considered, a problem of social order arises once again in reference to some potential structure emergent in their interaction. Sufficiently abstract theorem conjectures then reapply at this level.

### *3.3.3 Interpenetration and action theory*

The general concept of interpenetration recurs in various guises throughout general theoretical sociology but especially in the context of analytical action theory (see, e.g., Münch, 1982). It was a fundamental principle of Whitehead's (1929) metaphysics and became a key interpretive construct and presupposition of Parsons's theory. A brief formal explication of the general concept will be given here with an application to social structure as understood through the ideas stated earlier. (For a detailed mathematical treatment in the context of structuralist research, see Fararo and Doreian, 1984.)

A partial-identity relation betwen entities that share components is called *interpenetration*. Formally,

$$aIb \quad \text{if and only if} \quad \text{part-of-}a = \text{part-of-}b \tag{3.3.4}$$

Thus, interpenetration holds between a pair of entities *a* and *b* when some component (part) of *a* is identical with some component or part of *b*. Quantitatively, there is a *density* of shared components since a number of distinct components may be shared. A useful physical exemplar of interpenetration exists when a molecule is characterized by the so-called bivalent model. A molecule consists of atoms bonded by their shared electron density: Parts of one atom are also parts of the other. The atoms interpenetrate through the sharing of electrons. This interpenetration is the concrete character of the emergent entity, the molecule. *An emergent whole is given by the sharing of subparts by the entities that are the parts.* I refer to this statement as the *principle of structural integration.* It describes a generalized feature of the actual world (Fararo, 1987a).

An entity is *organic* to the extent that there is no stable state of the connectedness of its own parts that can exist when it is isolated from its whole. In other words, the whole is required for the part: Without the whole, it disintegrates into its constituent parts, the subparts of the relevant whole. These, in turn, if they are organic, will disintegrate. So we have *organic decay.* Atoms are not organic, because they can exist as stable structures of electronic–protonic entities when not bound to each other in a molecular arrangement.

There are two important types of applications of interpenetration in analytical action theory and in theoretical sociology in general. The discussion may be framed in terms of Parsons's (1966:18) discussion of the community, an interpretation of the **II** subsystem of the general dynamical social action system. It consists, says Parsons, of two complex components, what he calls a collectively organized population and a normative order. We can interpret whole, part, and subpart and the principle of structural integration for each of these components.

In each instance, Figure 2.2 can be used to supply a relevant network representation using three types of nodes.

First, consider the normative order. Here the operative ideal elements of the social coupling of dynamical normative control systems are relevant. At the most elementary level of analysis, we can let the emergent whole be the role relation. The theorem conjecture that *common* moral values are necessary for an attractor state suggests that at the value level the two cybernetic hierarchies meet. There will be a certain type of such a common value in accordance with the theorem conjecture on social stability and moral-normative order. So the emergent whole is the social relation, the parts are the actors (in the sense of two cybernetic hierarchical control systems), and the subparts are the moral values. Not all moral values need to be shared for the interpenetration to hold: There is a density of shared values just as there is a density of shared electrons.

But atoms are not organic. Are the actors in such social wholes organic? Translating: Could the necessary conditions for the real existence of a person (as more than a biophysical system) be fulfilled without the person's entering into social (**II**) relations? No, say Marx, Durkheim, Cooley, and other classical theorists. The individual is a social being. Indeed, the AGIL scheme and some of the concepts brought out in the prior section are intended to embed this idea in a theoretical system.

Second, consider the collectively organized population. This means that (1) the whole system may be a single collectivity (a nation, tribe, or whatever) and (2) various subcollectivities exist. It will be useful to postpone the discussion of the problem of structural integration of such a complex system until Chapter 4, where it is the topic for formal macrostructural theory and can be addressed in terms of the formal properties of social networks.

### 3.3.4. Critical discussion

A number of critical comments will conclude this development of ideas from analytical action theory. It is not my intention to undertake a critique of Parsons's entire theory. Indeed, there is no shortage of such critiques. The problem may be in the other direction. Parsons is the anti-Teflon theorist. All criticisms of his theoretical work seem to stick to it no matter how invalid or ill-informed. One function of formalization is explication of theoretical ideas that are at the core of a theory (Berger et al., 1962). Dynamic normative control has been treated here as the core concept of analytical action theory. One goal of the preceding work was to present this idea in a truly dynamic framework and to explore some of its implications. But such formalization also can bring into focus certain problems that give rise to legitimate concerns about the theory. Three such difficulties will be discussed.

First, from the perspective of Durkheimian depth sociology something is missing. The cultural-level values (and symbols, one should add) have not been exhibited as *generated* through social interaction. They have been treated as simply given, albeit with a feedback loop from social structure. This is not so much an intrinsic deficiency of the control principle of action and the AGIL scheme as a path that is easy to take if one follows Parsons's lead. Another aspect of this problem is that at the lower levels of normative control there are *constants* and *mechanisms* that are simply *givens* for the overall normative control process. For instance, Parsons (1951) speaks of the inherent tendency to optimize gratification. This suggests a constant feature that social-level control must accommodate. Hence, passing to the AGIL dimensions, this suggests that in each dimension there are givens that other levels must "learn to live with." The point is to avoid an "oversocialized" model of the actor in framing the specifics of the social–motivational nexus (Wrong, 1961). Conceptually, this caution can be observed if in the cybernetic model the constraints and feedback flow from below are retained.

Just as Parsons's work yields a kind of "downward" descriptive bias in the interpretation of the complete cybernetic loop, the ideas of Marx would yield an "upward" descriptive bias. The economic subsystem (**IA**) is the real foundation on which a political superstructure (**IG**) arises. The fundamental superior–inferior social relations that permeate the normative order of the societal community (**II**) arise on this basis and themselves are sustained through socialization (**IL**) of individuals to the ruling ideas (**L**) of the ruling class. In turn, this social system, arising from the economic production situation, controls the form taken by human nature in that social environment – especially the goals people have (**G**) and their rational adaptation (**A**), given such goals and the structure of the social system. The conceptual point is that the preferred mode of thought should be linked to the cybernetic model object, with its loops connecting and relating the downward flow of normative control and the upward flow contributing to the formation of the operative ideals at each level.

A second problem that arises is conceptual. An effort has been made to provide an action interpretation of the AGIL scheme by employing the control principle of action. All indications are that Parsons (1977:Ch. 10) intended the AGIL scheme to be coordinated to control system ideas: In his view, his four functions *are* the cybernetic functions.[14] Yet, if we look at the four cybernetic functions in the general control system model, they are memory, comparison, input, and output. The following seems to be the most natural identification: $L =$ memory function, $I$ = comparison function, $G$ = output function, and $A$ = input function. Does it "work?" In one sense, the answer is positive. It makes sense to think of culture as symbolic patterns that are saved and retrieved, a collective memory, for instance. But, in detail, it seems incoherent. Recall that in the four-level cybernetic hierarchy model, the output is behavior in the environment via the lowest level of control, the operational level. This corresponds to $A$ in the natural mode of interpreting the AGIL scheme as four levels of the cybernetic hierarchy. But when we turn to the mechanisms at any one level and so the four cybernetic functions, $A$ corresponds to input. These two identifications lead to the absurd result that the output (behavior) is generated via the input function. It is the attempt to have it both ways with regard to $G$ and $A$ as output and input and $G$ and $A$ as hierarchical control relations that leads to the absurdity if we try to identify the Parsonian and the cybernetic four functions. We may regard this as an unresolved conceptual problem of the framework consisting of the AGIL scheme together with the control principle of action if these are linked by identifying the AGIL functions and the control system functions. To avoid this conceptual problem, I did not employ the Parsonian identification rule. The two schemes were treated as distinct and then related, but not equated.

Finally, there is a third problem to consider. This more specifically concerns passing from comprehensive theory with its template of social coupling to more specific theoretical models. The problem is one of coupling actor models to derive an interaction generator. In this context, this means starting with the four-level cybernetic hierarchy of the actor–situation unit. Suppose, as we are apt to do in theoretical model building, that we approach the problem in its simplest form. Also, there is an empirical phase of model building to be considered in this context.

Consider the minimal entity of interest from the standpoint of the social coupling of dynamical normative control systems, a pair of actors in a common situation. One simplified sketch of the ingredients in such a model has been shown in Figure 3.4. Note now that only the lowest level of control is in direct contact with the nonaction environment of the actors through the production of bodily movements (including no movement as a meaningful act in terms of the higher level controls). For a definite coupling, we assume that the behaviors generated are "read" by each party, initially at the level of the immediate interface with the environment, that is, through the input channel of the lowest level. This is fine for the actors, but what about the scientific observer? Applying a strict behavioral criterion, it is only what happens in this environment that is a matter of empirical observation. All the rest is internal processing that, in the realist philosophical mode, we have treated as the legitimate subject matter of analytical action theory. Action theory tries to model the underlying structure of processes that generate such behaviors. But this is just the problem. No specific generator that really yields definite observable behaviors as outputs under given conditions has been constructed.

Accordingly, Figure 3.4 suggests several possibilities for next steps. First, one might directly represent the social coupling in a model that is embodied in a computer program and then "run" the model with various stipulated parameters and initial conditions to see what happens. Second, one might first try to work out a formal derivation using some simplifying assumptions (such as linearity in each cybernetic mechanism) followed by simulations of the derived interactive model assuming it would still be too complex to learn much about analytically. Finally, a third tactic suggests itself. We might begin to solve the problem of generating interaction from actor models by working on a model of coupled adaptation processes. That is, we might temporarily abstract from the whole hierarchy of control processes to study the nearest linkage to observations, how two actors adapt to each other. To be sure, the analysis will not tell us much about generativity through chains of normative control. It will, however, serve to initiate formal analysis of the coupling problem defined as the problem of showing how the generator of interaction and so the generator of social structures can be derived from the coupling of actor models. Moreover, it turns out that this idea of coupling adaptive processes of two actors is precisely the point of view that approximates that of another wing of action theory in sociology. This is the topic – adaptively rational action theory – of Sections 3.6–3.7. Given the experience with social coupling at its simplest level, we can return and add layers of normative control. At least, this would be the strategy if all the models in this chapter were constructed within the framework of a single mode of representation. They are not, so some of the learning may not carry over.

Before moving on to my treatment of interpretive sociology, there is one additional topic I shall consider: how various analytical perspectives on action and social order can be conceptually located in the framework of the general dynamical social action system.

### 3.3.5. Analytical perspectives on action and order

The general dynamical social action system given by (3.3.2) suggests that there is a set of partial *analytical perspectives*. These perspectives are derived by using two ideas. First, the four abstract types of theorems for dynamical systems are potential foci of attention in *any* dynamical system theory. The derived possibilities for order must be carefully interpreted, however, along the lines suggested in discussing the substructures of the social system. In other words, each perspective usually requires formulations involving the omitted dimensions of action to clarify the scope of its knowledge claims. For a useful discussion of scope problems see Cohen (1980). Second, the dynamical subsystem of special interest to theoretical sociology is the social system. Hence, the focus is on **I**, the social dimension. For this purpose, the internal substates of **I** need not always be considered. When **I** takes the analytical role of parameter, we use the terminology introduced in Section 2.10.2. By contrast, when **I** takes the role of state variable, we use the term *structuralism*. A partial listing is:

1. **I** as parameter: ''theoretical sociology of . . .''
   Theoretical sociology of culture (**L**)
   Theoretical sociology of motivation (**G**)
   Theoretical sociology of cognition (**A**)
   Theoretical sociology of the environment (**b**)
2. **I** as state variable: ''. . . structuralism''
   Cultural (**L**) structuralism
   Psychological (**G**) structuralism
   Cognitive (**A**) structuralism
   Biophysical (**b**) structuralism
      Biological structuralism
      Ecological structuralism

Concerning the ''theoretical sociology of'' perspectives, note that each defines a dynamical system with **I** as formal parameter. Hence, there are theoretical problems concerned with the emergence, stability, comparison and change of cultural structures, motivational structures, and cognitive structures as dependent on social conditions.[15]

Concerning the ''structuralist'' perspectives, cognitive structuralism might be one way to think of the approach of Lévi-Strauss (1963). Psychological structuralism is similar to but not quite the intention of Homans (1974), at least as interpreted later in this chapter. Cultural structuralism is close to the special interests of Parsons in all his work. I shall comment more extensively on the last category of biophysical structuralist perspectives.

According to (3.3.2), social action dynamics and so social structures depend on the biophysical state **b** as a parameter: hence, there are four types of theorems in this field as special cases of general social structure types of theorems. The biophysical structuralism category requires further discussion in terms of two interpretations. One is biological, the other ecological.

In the biological interpretation, parameter **b** concerns genetic components that define species. Then social structure varies with species. This is obviously important in terms of comparative statics, which corresponds to such empirical tasks as showing how wolf packs differ from chimpanzee groups or flocks of birds. The attempt to describe possible social structures as adjusted to such genetic variations is an extremely important task and should not be denigrated by those whose interests gravitate toward cultural structuralism or the sociology of culture. It is one legitimate path in the vast problem space associated with the dynamical action system.

The parameter **b** also may be interpreted to include certain elements favored by ecological sociologists. The *POET* model (Duncan and Schnore, 1959; Stinchcombe, 1983) suggests that social organization ($O$) depends on states of population ($P$), environment ($E$), and technology ($T$). Of course, by general mutual dependence, they depend on $O$ as well. We can interpret $O$ as corresponding to **I** in the general dynamical social action system. From this perspective, element $T$ consists of two sets of elements. One set (call it $T$–$L$) relates to knowledge, which is an element of cognitive culture. The dependence of $T$–$L$ on $O$ is treatable under the sociology of culture rubric. The dependence of $O$ on $T$–$L$ is treated by cultural structuralism. The other set of elements in $T$ can be placed in **b,** where the reference is to the state of material culture produced using technological knowledge. Of course, as Lenski and Lenski (1982) have shown, it is also an important way to understand variations in the social state, particularly the distribution of power and privilege. Continuing with the *POET* model, element $E$ includes parameters of the physical territory and its relevant ecological properties, making for one or another type of economy (as discussed in detail in Stinchcombe, 1983). An important component of the Durkheimian tradition, partly represented in the work of the ecologists, shows how important population size ($P$) is in terms of the social structure. Since we are counting human organisms, a case can be made for agreeing with Parsons (1937) in treating $P$ analytically as within **b.** This brief discussion shows there is some correspondence between aspects of $P$, $E$, and $T$ with **b** whereas $O$ corresponds to **I** and other elements of $T$ correspond to elements of **L.**[16]

## 3.4. Interpretive sociology and structural–generative action theory

Action theory has a number of branches, starting from classical authors who influenced contemporary theorists. One branch was initiated by Parsons on the basis of his interpretations of the works of Pareto, Durkheim, and Weber. This is what I have called analytical action theory. A second branch or wing has some common roots with analytical action theory, especially Weber's action foundations for sociology and Mead's contributions. But it has other roots, especially the phenomenology of the social world (Schutz, 1973). It is often called *interpretive sociology*. In this section, I begin by indicating some key ideas of interpretive sociology. Then I pass to a description of a formalism that can help us to represent the phenomena of action as understood from the interpretive perspective. Finally, I discuss the relationship of all this to analytical action theory from the point of view of formalization and unification as primary concerns of the comprehensive tradition of general theoretical sociology.

### 3.4.1. Elements of interpretive sociology

There is not space here to review all the many elements and aspects of interpretive sociology in its classical and contemporary phases. Hence, some brief capsule points are stated as drawn from works that have shaped my understanding of this subtradition. For convenience I list these points under the names of the authors.

1. Schutz (1973): Science builds models of the phenomena it treats. Such models are constructs. Social phenomena, in contrast to physical phenomena, are predefined by constructs of the actors. These are called *first-order* constructs. They consist of typifications of things, people, events, and the like. Social science models are *second-order* constructs. They attempt to understand the social world in the sense of a world that is predefined by the commonsense apparatus of thought with its typification schemes. So the data of social science are not sense data but meanings, especially those paramount meanings defining the texture of everyday life.

2. Mead (1934, 1936): Some of Mead's ideas have led to the approach of Blumer (1969), discussed in what follows, especially the idea of the self. Other aspects of his ideas have been synthesized with phenomenology, also discussed in the following, especially the concept of institution. According to Mead, institutions are types of habits that are handed down from one generation to another. The structure of social life lies in these habits and "only in so far as we take these social habits into ourselves can we become selves . . . If institutions are social habits, they represent certain definite attitudes that people assume under certain given social conditions" (Mead, 1936:375–376). So habitualized acts are crucial. A third aspect of Mead's viewpoint actually coheres well with the dynamical control system standpoint of the previous sections. As behaviors, acts are not just the observed behavior but also events going on in the central nervous system that inititate and organize the behavior. Acts are such that "the later stages of the act are present in the early stages – not simply in the sense that they are all ready to go off, but in the sense that they serve to control the process itself . . . the act as a whole can be there determining the process" (Mead, 1934:11). Thus, as would be expected from a process philosopher whose work is based on years of thought at various levels, Mead's corpus can function as a classical inspiration for unification of interpretive and analytical branches of action theory.

3. Berger and Luckmann (1966): Synthesizing Schutz and Mead, social reality is constituted through institutionalization, a process that yields reciprocal typification of habitualized actions by types of actors in types of situations. When passed on beyond their originators, such typifications acquire objectivity: They are *given* for new actors and internalized by them to constitute a mode of their cognitive orientation to the world. Any such typification scheme is an institution. Social reality is made up of institutions. They are the primary mode of social control, namely, control through the definition of social reality. Thus, in a certain sense, social reality is constituted by social knowledge structures.

4. Blumer (1969): Between the situational stimuli and the actor's behavioral response there is a process of interpretation of meanings. This process involves self-indications. The actor indicates to the self the things toward which he or she is acting. We can interpret Blumer as saying that particular things are tacitly assigned to types, drawn from the schemes of typification. Also, through the interpretation process, actions may be halted or aborted and new lines of action taken up. Social life consists of networks of action: "A network or an institution does not function automatically because of some inner dynamics or system requirements; it functions because people at different points do something, and what they do is a result of how they define the situation in which they are called on to act" (Blumer, 1969:19).

5. Garfinkel (1967) and Cicourel (1973): See, especially, Mehan and Wood (1975). The actor may be modeled as a reality constructor. Two types of components define such a model. The first type of component is tacit social knowledge. This is Schutz's idea of first-order constructs. They define the normal forms of entities. In the social case they are the Berger–Luckmann schemes of typification, which are both what these entities are and what they should be. Entities not fitting the model are strange or bizarre and, in the case of actors and acts, potentially immoral. For instance, a person who is not a man or a woman but somehow both is not only bizarre: He/she *should* be an embodiment of exactly one of these two institutional typifications, not both. The second type of component of the model of a reality constructor is an *interpretive procedure*. This is a *tacit* cognitive procedure. In combination, sets of such procedures are used like rules of grammar to generate or understand social action. For instance, the "et cetera" procedure includes "let it pass," in which another's talk is not interrupted for clarification despite its vagueness. The actor assumes some clarification will develop in the course of the talk. "Searching for normal form" is another such procedure. This suggests a succession of tacit attempts to match the situational features to some constructs that normalize them for the actor.

6. Giddens (1984): *Social practices* ordered across space and time are the subject matter of social science. These practices are recursive: They are continually re-created by the actors in such a way as to reproduce the conditions that

make these same activities possible. This involves knowledge, but not "discursive" consciousness so much as *practical* consciousness involving the stocks of knowledge the actors have as mutual knowledge and not directly accessible to consciousness. That is, it is simply the capability to go on with the routines of everyday life. *Structure* consists of *rules and resources* implicated in social practices, rules that both constitute meanings and regulate conduct. Instantiations of structures in action contribute to the reproduction of the structures. Rules are essentially procedural, referring to practice: procedures applied in the enactment of social practices. These rules are distinct from *formulated rules* found in laws or in bureaucratic organizations. The core of knowledge as the "constitution of society" is the awareness of these rules in practical consciousness terms. Thus the structural properties of social systems across time and space are the institutionalized features of these systems, providing *solidity* across such time and space. Social systems involve situated activities of concrete actors. Structures, on the other hand, are "out of time and space" except as instantiated in such situated activities.

Giddens uses these concepts to formulate what he calls the "theorem of the duality of structure." I prefer to call it a principle so as not to suggest any rigorous deduction:

> *Principle of duality of structure* (Giddens): "Structure is not 'external' to individuals: as memory traces, and as instantiated in social practices, it is in a certain sense more 'internal' than exterior to their activities in a Durkheimian sense. Structure is not to be equated with constraint but is always both constraining and enabling." (Giddens, 1984:25)

He goes on to add that this means that structure has no existence apart from the knowledge that agents have about what they do in their day-to-day activity.

One other statement by Giddens will be given here and addressed primarily in Chapter 4. The fundamental question of social theory is formulated by Giddens as a *reconstructed problem of social order,* "to explicate how the limitations of individual 'presence' are transcended by the 'stretching' of social relations across space and time" (Giddens, 1984:35). In my dynamical systems viewpoint, something like this problem arises in terms of Parsons's treatment of social order because in Parsons's (1951) treatment of relational institutions, the discussion identifies the generated social structure, the stable equilibrium of social interaction, with the idea of a relational institution. But as Parsons himself notes, an institution is not a collectivity: It has the property of embodiment in multiple collectivities through space and time, at least potentially. Analytically, the spread of such a form of interaction through successive possible embodiments is an analytical problem in its own right. This is my interpretation of Giddens's recon-structured problem of order. More generally, the Parsonian treatment of institutions glosses over some significant features highlighted within the interpretive sociological tradition.

### 3.4.2. Toward a formalization of interpretive sociology

Can interpretive sociology be formalized? And if so, can it be unified with analytical action theory? A program with these two features of formalization of elements of interpretive sociology and unification with analytical action theory I call *structural–generative action theory*. It is more a hope than an accomplishment, an operative ideal guiding certain conceptual and formal developments more than a real feature of the situation of theoretical sociology. But such as it is, this and the following sections attempt to provide a brief explication of it. The emphasis is on the helpfulness of certain notations and the conceptual possiblities of a certain representation principle. Details of the technical elements of formalism together with examples and connections with various other sociological ideas are provided in a series of papers starting from Axten and Fararo (1977) and continuing in Axten and Skvoretz (1980), Skvoretz and Fararo (1980), Skvoretz, Fararo, and Axten (1980), Fararo (1981a), and Fararo and Skvoretz (1984a). The entire research program is discussed in conceptual terms and in relation to theoretical issues in Fararo and Skvoretz (1986a). The abstract algebraic development of action theory, pursued especially by Skvoretz (1984), is closely related to the work of Nowakowska (1973) on the formal theory of action.

What is required for the program of structural–generative action theory is a mode of formalization that is able to represent knowledge structures, including procedural knowledge and interpretive procedures. The general type of formal entity to be used is a rule applied to generate strings of symbols representing components of action in situations. A model has the form of a set of such rules.

It is helpful to know a little about how linguistic theory defines such models. The most relevant form of linguistic theory is called the *generative–transformational* mode of representation or model building introduced by Chomsky (1957, 1965). A grammar is conceived to be a finite set of rules such that (1) every legitimate utterance is derivable through some chain of ''productions'' using the rules, (2) no illegitimate utterances are so derivable, and (3) every utterance has a structure given by the possibilities for its productive generation, each of which assigns a structural description to the utterance. Since a given utterance might be generated in multiple ways, it can have more than one structural description, in which case it is ambiguous. Via the concept of ambiguity, the theory anticipates that speaker–hearers of the language may interpret one utterance in several different ways. The generative part of such a grammar yields strings of the element of utterances by virtue of rules employing categories that are not part of the ultimate utterance, mainly grammatical categories such as noun and verb phrase. Thus, the generative part of the grammar features two categories of symbols: terminal (used by the speaker–hearers in the generated utterance) and nonterminal (appearing only in the rules that generate the ultimate utterance).

In linguistics, there are rewrite rules, of the form $A \rightarrow B$, where $A$ consists of nonterminal symbols and $B$ consists of either type of symbol. Some such rewrite rules are one-to-many mappings of a nonterminal symbol to its many legitimate substitution instances in the terminal vocabulary of the language. For instance, that ⟨noun phrase⟩ may be rewritten as ⟨article⟩+⟨noun⟩ is one type of rewrite rule, involving only nonterminal symbols. That ⟨article⟩ may be rewritten as *a*, *an*, or *the* is another type of rewrite rule, taking one nonterminal symbol into the specified terminal symbols. The speaker is conceived to select the legitimate substitution instances from the options, but it is not the task of the theory to try to predict which of these instances will be chosen. Rather, the task of the theory is framed as follows. There exists an infinite set of legitimate utterances constituting a specific language as a conceptual totality. The problem is to account for all the variant members of this totality in terms of the finite grammar. As described, the grammar has a generative component. It also has a transformational component in which the rules transform one structure (i.e., a pattern of nonterminal symbols) into another structure before the ultimate rewrite rules taking these symbols into terminal elements are applied. In this way, the generation of an interrogative form of a declarative utterance is a kind of special side-trip along one of the paths of possible generation. The path of generation shows how a family of overt utterances are related as variants having structural descriptions that are all possible transformations of an underlying structure, a kind of ''kernel'' form obtained through generative rules.

These syntactic structures and their generation illustrate a much more general approach to human action systems. As philosopher Margaret Boden (1980:Ch. 7) notes in her critique of Piaget, there are two forms of cybernetics. The first form uses the negative-feedback concept, and both historically and presently it is associated with quantitative representations and equilibration conceptions. This was the form employed in formulating the control principle of action as one of the key framework ideas of analytical action theory.

The second form of cybernetics involves generative rule structures of various sorts, including the rewrite forms of formal linguistics. I will call the type of control that is involved *computational* control, also called *instructional* control. The reader will recall that in the discussion of the TOTE unit concept in Section

3.2, two variants of that concept were mentioned. One variant corresponds to the negative-feedback model, now embedded within the second cybernetics. The other variant corresponded to production rules, the form of which was shown earlier as TEST → OPERATE, such that if the test passes, then the corresponding operation phase is initiated. These production rule systems will be the core of the formalism employed in this and the following sections.

Thus, the model of the actor here is essentially that framed in modern cognitive science. Miller, Galanter, and Pribram (1960) framed the conceptual scheme that both synthesized the emerging second cybernetics and provided an impetus for its continuation by many others in this field today. The actor is an information-processing system (Newell and Simon, 1972). The subprocesses of reading input and writing output still apply, and so does the comparison process and the memory function. Overt behavioral events are understood on the analogy of what is displayed on a monitor or written out by a printer connected to a central processing device. Most of the work is internal, involving instructions that accomplish the reading of symbols, the processing of them, and the translation of them into overt form (printing, displaying, behaving).

So we have a *computational model of mind* (described in Section 1.4) as the key idea from a realist philosophical standpoint. The social network of coupled individual action systems is based on the cultural level of communication among actors represented in terms of the computational model: Contingently, actors are able to *interpret* each other's displays or printouts by virtue of shared symbolic systems. But interpretations cannot flow from nowhere; they must be generated. The process viewpoint holds.

In the spirit of seeking integrative formulations, the action principle here will be framed as a variant of the control principle of action. In this way, it will be apparent that there is a commonality between interpretive and analytical action theory at one level with differential specification of it in the detailed formulations. Hence we have:

> *The control principle of action (computational model form).* The actor in a situation is an information-processing system, and a unit act is an episode of computational control.

In developing the consequences of this representation principle for the formalization of interpretive sociology, the focus will be on two types of production rules.

Some production rules are *constitutive* in the sense of introducing types of entities. Complexes of such rules yield rich structures of linked types of entities that actors employ to draw commonsense inferences about situations. Other rules imply actions as conditional on situational states defined in terms of such constitutive rules.[17] In what follows, I first treat constitutive rules and then treat situation–action rules.

In the constitutive type, the rule is similar to a rewrite rule. For instance, consider Garfinkel's (1967) study of the management of "gender passing" by "Agnes." Garfinkel's core points include the fact that there is a critical but little-noticed feature of everyday social interaction. Namely, a member of a collectivity is either a man or a woman but not both:

$$\langle\text{member}\rangle \rightarrow \langle\text{man}\rangle | \langle\text{woman}\rangle$$

Angle brackets are used to denote *typified entities*, those of the actors or those of the analyst. The vertical bar indicates mutually exclusive substitution instances for the type of entity on the left. This particular rule is an item of everyday social knowledge. At the same time is has normative significance, the second point emphasized by Garfinkel. This is typical of institutional typifications illustrated here with the gender institution.

A set of constitutive rules that define and relate various types of entities defines a "space" from the point of view of specifying a model object. For instance, the model object for the higher education institution might include ⟨university⟩, ⟨department⟩, and ⟨professor⟩ as component typified entities. The first two types of entities are normal forms of collectivities; the third is a normal form of individual in the higher education institution. To model a particular embodiment, an instance, additional definitions can be added to the space. For instance, the various departments of a particular university each instantiate ⟨department⟩ and constitute part of the social reality of that university. Similarly, each particular person assigned the identity ⟨professor⟩ embodies this typified entity. Any such typification can be regarded as an institution in its own right, since we can model it with its own proper subspace. For instance, ⟨professor⟩ is in one sense a role in higher education, but in another sense it is an institution with component typifications such as ⟨course load⟩, ⟨publications⟩, and ⟨committee memberships⟩. Since actors have these linked structures of typifications as differentially distributed ordinary social knowledge, actors embody *expert systems,* to use a fashionable word from knowledge engineering, by which they draw inferences about entities from given data about them. For instance, if told that something is a department of sociology, the academically knowledgeable actor will infer immediately that it is located in some faculty of arts and sciences in some college or university.

This first type of rule represents a static aspect of schemes of typification. The dynamic aspect, the generation of action, is represented by a second type of rule, which will be called a *situated action production rule* (and also simply production rule if the context is clear). Collections of such rules produce situated actions making up normal forms of interaction. This type was first introduced by Newell and Simon (1972) in a cognitive science context[18] and by Axten (in Axten and Fararo, 1977) in a sociological context. In the form we require for the latter, such a rule takes the form

$$\langle \text{situation-type} \rangle \rightarrow \text{ACTION}$$

This sort of rule is *not* ordinarily an object of orientation in the situation of action. As coordinated to the interpretive sociological tradition, it is a tacit form of procedural knowledge.

A situated action production rule may be interpreted as a latent state of some recurrent form of situated action. It must be "triggered" before it generates an instance of ACTION.[19] The latter is a primitive entity but is assumed to be stored in memory in the form of some *subproduction system* so as to constitute the particular form of action as latent and potentially recurrent. This element, that production systems are latent objects stored in memory, coordinates to Giddens's duality-of-structure principle. In one aspect, social structures are distributed production systems: Each actor has a part of a more comprehensive production system that generate normal forms of interaction comprising some institution.[20]

The triggering of a production rule is a consequence of an ordinarily tacit *matching* of the perceived situation of action to the template ⟨situation-type⟩. Practical consciousness is some stream of events in the nervous system (cf. Mead as in the preceding) that consists in the activation and processing of information through such "programs of the mind." In particular, therefore, one should *not* interpret a production as saying that the situation causes a certain form of action. There is the necessary intervening tacit interpretation made by the actor. Both situational knowledge and the generic types are expressed in terms of the typified entities in the space. We also allow the situation type to include goal states of the actor. Hence, a tacit (nonconscious) interpretive process intervenes between the external stimulus and any observable behavior instantiating ACTION.

This element of the intended interpretation of the model object is consistent with the symbolic interactionist understanding of social interaction. The self-indications that Blumer (1969) stresses occur in this interpretive process are specific cognitive events assigning typified entities to instances such as self as instance of ⟨professor⟩ and other as instance of ⟨student⟩. Blumer's self-indications occur so rapidly that the processing must be in terms of rapid-firing systems of production rules that process information. The actor is conscious and self-conscious but not of the rules so much as of their immediate cognitive products, which are the meanings of situational features.

However, a production rule representation does not rule out conscious choice as an element that may enter into the generation of action. This depends on the particular action. Institutional actions called for are frequently *decisions,* so the production calls not for a specific choice but for the act of choice itself. An example is REGISTER, called for in a certain situation for someone in the role ⟨student⟩. A student is called upon to register and has a large menu of alternative course combinations in the choice set. The choice of some courses is enabled by the existence of the complex structure that is the institution of higher education. This is an aspect of Giddens's simple point that structures should not be thought of only as constraining action. Another related point is that productions keep changing the situation of interaction, triggering other productions in a flux of circumstances depending on particular choices within the institutional menus such that there is no necessary obvious stereotyped sequence. The rituals, with their stereotyping (Collins, 1981), are an important class of special cases that are readily comprehended in terms of production rules. In all cases what is required is an ordered collection of such rules.

A *production system* is a model consisting of a collection of situated action production rules with some relationships among them. The assumption is that the complete model object includes a space and a production system. Roughly speaking, the production system generates interaction "in the space." Put another way, the space is analogous to the behavior manifold, the production system to the generator in dynamical system models.

Some production systems are associated with one role, whereas others are associated with plural roles of actors in interaction. Production systems are not limited to roles, however. Newell and Simon (1972) use them to model cognitive problem solving. From the present point of view, such heuristic problem solving means that actors have the generic capacity to develop novel procedures within the social situational boundaries created by institutions. For instance, a professor will develop his or her own personal procedures for realizing the institutional activities of teaching, writing, committee work, and so forth.

Valid examples of production systems are very difficult to state because action is contextual. The effort to state roles in production system terms shows that "et cetera" makes its appearance over and over. The actors know things that we cannot readily put into models because neither we nor the actor know them as discursive knowledge. Nevertheless, in principle, *some* base of production rules is the presupposition of this mode of modeling action. This includes production rules representing the interpretive procedures stressed by ethnomethodologists. So some such rules are general action rules, procedurally organizing evey social setting; others are institution specific, including specified roles.

Granted the difficulties, the reader may permit me to state a *very simple* example to illustrate the concepts without pretense of completeness. This example illustrates the way that production rules are distributed to distinct actors and yet mesh to generate a normal form of interaction. It also illustrates some notational features to be discussed. Suppose that two types of actors are introduced in the space:

$$\langle \text{actor} \rangle \rightarrow \langle \text{driver} \rangle | \langle \text{passenger} \rangle$$

Three types of action are also introduced:

$$\langle \text{action} \rangle \rightarrow \text{OPEN} | \text{GO-TO} | \text{EXIT}$$

For present purposes, it is unnecessary to list the various physical objects, their states and relations that are assumed in the following, so let me simply state two situated action productions of a miniature system:

DRIVER: ⟨passenger⟩ wants-exit & bus at stop→OPEN [door] (passenger)
PASSENGER: want-exit & bus near stop→GO-TO [door]; EXIT

This is an example of a production system with two productions in relationship. The particular relationship here is that the action of one production produces situational features to which the other is responsive as it recognizes these features as instances of normal forms.

Note that the roles are indicated in two different ways. DRIVER is the name of a body of procedural knowledge organized in terms of situated action productions, whereas ⟨driver⟩ is a type of social object. An entity such as ⟨driver⟩ does not *do* anything, whereas DRIVER is an action generator.

In a given occasion, normally only one actor is socially assigned the identity ⟨driver⟩ of a particular bus, whereas numerous actors will take on the identity ⟨passenger⟩ in a continuous stream of entering and leaving the situation of the person who is the driver. If the actors are denoted actor1, actor2, . . . , then the identities are such that, say,

$$\text{actor1} \leftarrow \langle \text{driver} \rangle$$

This means that some institutional process prior to the actual occasion has made actor1 an embodiment of ⟨driver⟩. He or she is a driver (of a bus). This does not mean that the person is at this instant simply driving the bus. It means a standing definition that incorporates the normative meaning of being entitled to do so and being expected to do so. The other role is taken by immediate situational action that could be modeled with other production rules: One enters the vehicle and pays. The payment makes one a passenger:

$$\text{actor2} \leftarrow \langle \text{passenger} \rangle$$

Any person not paying is on the bus but not really a passenger because the normal form of the latter is assigned only after a certain payment ritual occurs. (These remarks must be modified for bus institutions that have different payment procedures.)

This reverse-arrow notation refers, then, to outcomes of institutionalized processes in which actors are routinely assigned identities. Some of these identities are transient, as with ⟨passenger⟩, others are more permanent, as with ⟨driver⟩.[21] Blumer's self-indications are not necessarily congruent with the institutional definitions. They are aspects of immediate cognitive definitions of the situation, one definition per actor. For instance, assuming congruence, in a normal interaction on a bus we have the two types of cognitive definitions of the situation:

actor1: self←⟨driver⟩, other←⟨passenger⟩
actor2: self←⟨passenger⟩, other←⟨driver⟩

The entities that count as instances of relevant typified objects such as the door for exit are also parts of immediate cognitive definition of the situation normally congruent with the standing institutional definitions.

So a general statement holds, in the spirit of the reality construction point of view characterizing one element of interpretive sociology. To state it, some further notation is needed. An instance of ⟨driver⟩ is not the type but a typified instance. Such a typified instance is denoted *driver*. In general an instance of ⟨role⟩ is *role*.

> *Social reality rule*. An actor is a *role,* an instance of ⟨role⟩, if and only if there exists an institutional process in which the outcome is the assignment of that actor to that identity. We denote this by
>
> actor←⟨role⟩

This rule serves to distinguish between the *appearance* and the *reality* of typifications of actors (and other objects). An actor may "get away with" counting as an instance of ⟨role⟩ in some subsystem of the widest collectivity of reference while not really being such an instance at all. The force of *really* is that of the preceding principle or rule.

A second general statement may be made:

> *Matching conjecture*. A necessary condition for a steady state in interaction among a set of actors is that, for each actor in the set, when the actor is a *role,* the actor embodies ROLE.

A mismatch creates a failure of the production subsystems assigned to distinct actors to coordinate. For instance, when Garfinkel (1967) assigned his students to do breaching experiments, he sometimes asked them to activate some ROLE that did not correspond to their social ⟨role⟩. For instance, BOARDER might be activated at home, where the identities are ⟨son⟩, ⟨brother⟩, and other kin categories. Family members feel the vertigo of interacting with someone of the type ⟨boarder⟩.

The conjecture seems to hold also for collectivities. The notational convention by which ⟨role⟩ refers to a type of social object and ROLE refers to a production system may be extended to collectivities. Then ⟨department⟩ refers to a social object and DEPARTMENT refers to a production system distributed among the members. That is, ROLE1, ROLE2, . . . , ROLE*n* are embodied in members assigned, respectively, to ⟨role1⟩, ⟨role2⟩, . . . , ⟨role*n*⟩. The object role list is part of the social definition of ⟨department⟩, whereas the production subsystems are model components of the production system model DEPARTMENT. Put another way, the capitalized entities are sets of procedural knowledge rules embodied in members of the collectivity so that their meshing in actual occasions generates the behavior of the collectivity.

Normal forms of interaction are subject to disturbances through errors made by actors, through lack of the appropriate knowledge, and through deliberate disruption. Interpretive procedures are invoked in these occasions. We may think of an interpretive procedure as a production or a production system that is part of the constitution of each socialized member of the referent collectivity. The mode of response to a disruption depends upon the interpretation of a detected difference between the normal form and the observed form of action. But since normal forms of interaction are generated in the context of stable social structures, the responses tend to return the interaction to where it would have been in the normal form. The general process exemplifies *normalization,* in ethnomethodological terms. A simple example of such normalization processes in interaction will serve to illustrate how interpretive procedures may be represented by production rules.

Assume, in the driver–passenger interactive episode, that the driver has neglected to check the state of the situation in terms of indications of passenger intentions to exit the bus. This means that from the standpoint of a passenger ready to exit, a departure from normal form exists: The bus is not stopping as expected, or it has stopped but the door has not been opened by the driver. The knowledge state of the passenger now includes

*open door* by *driver* due

That is, the action of the driver production is due. This condition has the generic situation-type form

⟨action⟩ by ⟨role⟩ due

An appropriate production applying to such a situation type may be written as

⟨action⟩ by ⟨role⟩ due→FIND-REASON [role, action]

That is, the interpretive procedure generates an interpretation as to the state of the situation with respect to the particular action due by the particular other in the relevant role. It involves a search process, seeking a reason for the departure from normal form. The possible interpretive outcomes are shown by

⟨reason⟩→error|ignorance|deliberate

The relevant knowledge state of the passenger if the outcome is that the driver has simply made an error may now be

*open door* by *driver* due & error

The details of the situation and the subproduction process involved in processing the information to arrive at one or another of these possible reasons are probably topics for cognitive science rather than sociology. Of interest is the fact, however, that another production must make the response conditional on the outcome of this process; that is, the situation type now includes ⟨reason⟩. The form of a relevant production might be

⟨action⟩ by ⟨role⟩ due & ⟨reason⟩→SELECT-RESPONSE-MODE [reason, action, role]

Note that the particular knowledge state satisfies the template or pattern of situation type that occurs in the production. The mode of responding, then, depends on the reason assigned as to why the given action due was not performed by the other person in the given role. Probably the normal form of response to the attribution that the other's behavior represents no more than a momentary error is the activation of REMIND. If this production does not yield the action due, however, the interpretive process may recycle to produce the *deliberate* outcome, and the response mode may move toward some other mode.[22]

All these productions and interpretive procedures are not conscious knowledge states of the actor but rather modes of largely tacit processing of such knowledge states to generate action. If we are generally correct about this mode of representation, then these production rules are indeed part of the cognitive constitution of the actor as a member of a collectivity. If explicit knowledge states are identified with Giddens's "discursive consciousness," then production rules are identifiable with his "practical consciousness." They have something of the character of habits in Mead's social behavioral language. But they rest on the social knowledge base and are expressed in its terms, that is, in terms of the schemes of typification constituting institutions in the Schutz, Berger–Luckmann, and Garfinkel sense.

The examples given are only illustrative. Ethnomethodologists have specified a variety of interpretive procedures that might be represented in the formalism of production systems and related formal procedures. "Searching for normal form" is another such procedure, which implies that typified constructs are employed to "see" the social world. A failure of such a typification to work creates what information-processing theorists (Newell and Simon, 1972) call "generate and test." That is, some space of possible normal forms is generated and tested against the situation as the actor searches for a way to come to terms with the situational objects.

In general, then, interpretive procedures can be represented as productions that are *applicable in every situation*. Here we arrive at the interesting idea that ethnomethodology's model of the actor is intended to have universal validity. It is not the analogue of a grammar of English but of an underlying universal grammar. A production system model of the driver–passenger institution is analogous to the *particular* language. What ethnomethodology treats is not some particular procedural knowledge or institution but a universal competence. Following Garfinkel (1967:57, footnote 8) as he draws upon Parsons (1951), we could say that ethnomethodology models ⟨member⟩ of ⟨collectivity⟩ no matter what the instance of ⟨member⟩ or of ⟨collectivity⟩. Such a member not only invokes interpretive procedures but is normatively expected to do so. In Garfinkel's terms, the use of procedures is sanctioned. A member will arouse hostility when the interpretive procedures are not employed. Garfinkel's important indexicality principle (Collins, 1975) is involved here: Not everything can be made explicit, and demands for such explicitness arouse anger. This is illustrated by LET-IT-PASS as an incessant operation invoked during conversations. An actor who calls upon another to be clear at every point, who fails to "let it pass," will arouse anger if the failure is interpreted by the other as deliberate.

The fundamental representation principle implied in all this may now be formally stated. The empirical entities are institutions as the key structural ingredients of action networks, and the formalism involves the production system ideas and notations, as already discussed.

> *Production system principle.* An institution is both a social space defined by constitutive rules and a set of normal forms of interaction within it that are generated by a distributed set of situated action production subsystems linked to universal interpretive procedures.

An observable action domain ordinarily will realize multiple production systems. People may switch from one context to another in a single encounter. They put on different "role hats" involving distinct productions. This creative capability not only is consistent with the orderliness of production systems that constitute the latent and enduring organization of interaction, it also is enabled by it.

Consistent with the realist model of explanation, the "goodness" of science here is not in being able to predict the next action. It is in properly representing the generative powers, the mechanisms, that constitute the enabling basis for the observables. It is a corpus of normal forms of interaction analytically dissected from an empirical mixture of acts generated through plural generators that is the entity to be generated. This generativity is social. Formally, the various production subsystems represent actor–situation units, and the whole system is given by the coupling of these subsystems.

No one actor includes the entire generative basis of an institution. But together they embody it in multiple realizations or embodiments in time or space. When these actors look out on the situation of action, they find themselves to be units in a local collectivity that is often only one of many such collectivities included in a wider social system. The types of actors of which they are instances are replicated throughout the environment of this collectivity, which in fact is part of a wider social system. The multiple embodiments over time arising through member turnover constitute another such "environment," now found in the relevant history of the collectivity as interpreted both locally and in the wider social system. Giddens's reconstructed version of the problem of social order in process terms is the diffusion of a production system through a network such that various subnetworks become local embodiments of the spread of the institution. This topic will be taken up in Chapter 4.

Giddens's duality-of-structure idea can be clarified in terms of a philosophical implication of the approach taken here. The generators of normal forms of interaction are internal to the actors, distributed among them. In a latent state, they indeed have the ontological character of existing as "memory traces," as Giddens puts it. But the interpretable corpus of forms of interaction they generate is external to each of them, though internal to the network of interactions they constitute. Social structure is a state of a social network with two phases: latent and active (Bates and Harvey, 1975). A *recurrent* process passes between latency and activity and hence, in its latent phase, is a structure awaiting activation whereupon it *is* a process generator. It is precisely because a computer program is a latent state of a process involving operations on symbols that the computational model of mind has philosophical appeal. In this image, human society is a vast network of activity (process) self-generated through a structure of production systems distributed among people. Such structures are a problematic topic for general theoretical sociology, not ultimate givens. It should be clear that this image is not far from that derived within analytical action theory in connection with the social coupling template. (See Sections 3.2.6 and 3.4.3.)

Passing to a more empirical level of analysis, it may be possible to provide a very rigorous approach to some quite interesting phenomena from the standpoint of sociology's world-historical interest in the modern world. Many institutions are common to the entire global system, multiply embodied across the entire world. For instance, ⟨nation-state⟩ is such an institution. But of special interest is that preeminently Durkheimian institution we may denote by ⟨individual⟩. In keeping with the notational conventions of structural–generative action theory, ⟨individual⟩ is not a concrete entity but a scheme of typification. It corresponds to a production system INDIVIDUAL. The latter we may assume is internalized by persons socialized in modern social environments and who are expected to be and behave as instances of the institutional form ⟨individual⟩. Thus, this institution might be the subject of interesting production system model building. For one thing, it is an institution relevant to the world system (see Thomas et al., 1987) and also to the ritual interactions of daily life throughout the world, as was emphasized by Goffman (1967) in his generalization of Durkheim's idea of institutionalized individualism. By virtue of linking the microsociological and the macrosociological realms, this particular institution might serve as an exemplar for a new mode of sociological analysis. This mode of analysis would combine the comparative empirical approach of Meyer, the conceptual scheme of Giddens, and the formal orientation of structural–generative action theory. Such research would meet the felt demand for a more compelling example of the power of production system model building.

Let us admit, however, that constructing models under the production system principle is not so simple. The fundamental difficulty of constructing a production system and especially the universal interpretive procedural component is that the situation type part of the production rule seems inaccessible to us. But why not take the approach of theoretical model building: Suggest situation types and, through model rules, develop the consequences to see if we are on the right track? For instance, we do not really know the left-hand side of the following:

$$\langle \text{situation-type} \rangle \rightarrow \text{LET-IT-PASS}$$

In such cases, the problem is to specify some candidate situation pattern for ⟨situation-type⟩. Similarly the other interpretive procedures require hypothetical specification in productions so as to form a production system constituting our model of the reality constructor. Then two such models can be coupled and superimposed on production systems for "the surface of interaction" (e.g., DRIVER and PASSENGER) to generate interactive event episodes to be compared with observations of "organized social activities" (Garfinkel, 1967). The necessity for such universal productions, over and above procedural knowledge for specific institutions, is one of the key insights of ethnomethodology that is incorporated into the production principle.

What structural–generative theory rejects is the attitude sometimes found among ethnomethodologists that their claims about interpretive procedures are somehow not to be taken as part of "standard" sociology and its concern to represent social phenomena. The view taken here is that we can be wrong about the universal grammar of interaction, about interpretive procedures, just as we can be wrong about a lot of other things. Hence, ethnomethodological ideas are regarded as suggestions for theoretical model building, albeit adopting a mode of representation especially suitable to it and other elements of interpretive sociology.

One final point requires discussion. An important feature of the production system principle is that it implies *recursive generativity* of action. The simple examples given were not sufficiently rich in structure to allow this feature to be exhibited. An example exists in the literature (Axten and Fararo, 1977) but is too complex to be described again here. Instead the reader is asked to look back at Figure 2.3. There it will be seen that there is an action structure in which the unit acts are *S, W,* and *I* and we can interpret *E* as some environmentally located unit act providing inputs to the system and accepting its outputs. The action structure provides an example of recursion without the pain of trying to set out all the situated action information-processing details. For note that the structure represents possibilities of the flow of action, not any one realization. As noted in Chapter 2, the possible strings of action generated by the network include (without arrows): *EWSIE (standard form), EWSISIE, EWSIWSIE, EWSIWSISIE,* and so forth, corresponding to the choices made by the actor of the *I* unit act. This act, it will be recalled, amounts to rejecting or accepting the soldered product; if it is accepted, it goes to *E,* whereas if it is rejected, it goes back to soldering *(S)* or wiring *(W),* at the discretion of the inspector. Just as, in principle, formally legitimate sentences arise by self-embedding features, so too formally legitimate action sequences arise by self-embedding. In this case, the action strings *SI* and *WSI* can be self-embedded. And just as pragmatic interactive considerations effectively make unlikely any very long utterance from the infinite set generated by a generative–transformational grammar, so pragmatic interactive considerations make unlikely any considerable self-embedding of action strings. We have to distinguish between the infinite conceptual totalities that are generated by production rules with their enormous fund of *possible* strings from the *really possible* strings based on considerations of social order.

### *3.4.3. Analytical action theory revisited*

Next let us consider the relevance of the production principle to analytical action theory. Consider the following two questions that arise in reading Parsons on action systems. Action systems are sets of acts in various relations. But this conception raises the first question. Are the acts *actual* or *potential?* An ambiguity in reference to the one or the other runs through the work of Parsons (1937, 1951). Any conception of a structure of an action system requires recurrent acts. So in some occasions, a particular type of act is actualized, constituting an event with meaning. In other occasions that type of act is not realized. Yet the act as a type remains part of the structure of the action system even when not literally actualized. But then a second question arises: By what mechanism is a recurrent act activated so as to be appropriate to the situation of action? Somehow what is required is a linkage of situation pattern to act type.

This suggests that the fundamental units of the structure of an action system are at once latent rather than actual and also keyed to potentially recurrent elements of situations. A stable action structure is an action structure such that the ultimate nodes are *latent situationally conditional unit acts*. Such a node represents a stable connection between a type of situation and a meaningful type of behavior. The term *latent* coordinates not only to Parsonian analytical action theory (Parsons, et al., 1953) but also to a recent conceptual statement in a more structuralist vein by Bates and Harvey (1975). Thus, we are led to a model of an action structure in which the ultimate nodes, representing recurrent unit acts, are production rules. Starting from the analytical theory of action and asking certain questioins about the structural representation of action systems required for the theory, we are led to production systems as models of the structure of action systems.

How can we adapt production system models to this context of action theory? That is, the context is one in which we envision a network in which the nodes are production rules (or subsystems) connected processually. We require two additional elements in a production rule: inputs or resources needed to realize or implement the action called for and outputs or products normally generated by the successful accomplishment of the action. The expanded form of the action production is

$$\langle \text{situation-type} \rangle \rightarrow \text{ACTION[resources]} \qquad (\rightarrow \text{products})$$

When the production is triggered, an act realizing the type ACTION occurs if the actor has gained control over the required resources or ''inputs'' from some sources. The generic types of resources required to produce ACTION may be called *factors of production.* Thus, action transforms factors into products. But products reappear in other production rules in the guise of factors. This reappearance is not automatic but a feature of the structure. Namely, a recurrent process exists in which the actors who require a resource for the action called for in their roles convert products into factors. Exchange, in the sense of a recurrent subprocess of the structure of the action system, is the reverse movement of some quantity of symbolic medium that rewards the producer for the given supply of products.

Hence one type of tie among these action production units is output becoming input: The output or product of a production $P$ is one of the resources or inputs required for the action of production $Q$. This is where Parsons's (1969) symbolic media theory fits into structural–generative action theory. Actors spend money, power, influence, and value commitments to gain control over the factors of production of the actions they are called upon to enact institutionally. (For further discussion, see Fararo and Skvoretz, 1984a.) The node $P$ of the network and the node $Q$ of the network are in the functional relation of product $y$ of $P$ recurrently becoming factor $x$ in $Q$ via the recurrent (structural) exchange process. This exchange process itself, since it is recurrent, is represented by a production system. The concrete terms of exchange arrived at in a particular interaction are analogous to items chosen from a menu or to a particular way of realizing an action called for. These terms presuppose the structure of social action. A primary topic for future structural–generative theory is to convert the intuitive and often obscure ideas about "interchange" of products and factors in analytical action theory into definite model objects. Here, as elsewhere in action theory, it will be essential to move toward the network branch of structuralism with its conception of an extended interlocking set of relations. In the current context of a functional network, manifest functions correspond primarily to direct ties, but paths of indirect ties are likely to generate latent functions. Thus latent-function analysis becomes an aspect of the study of action networks.

Three conceptual entities have appeared in this section and in Sections 3.4.1 and 3.4.2: interpretive sociology, production system models, and analytical action theory. The intent of what I call structural–generative action theory is to forge some links between two strands of action theory in a unification process through the use of production system models. That is, interpretive sociology and analytical action theory are both bodies of ideas about the same class of model objects. In the analytical action theory case, the production rules represent nodes of functional action structures. This representation is fully compatible with interpretive sociology. What the latter adds are other elements of action that are readily coordinated to and represented in the production system form.

This is not to say that there are no conceptual problems arising in the program of structural–generative action theory. The negative-feedback model object associated with the control principle of action in Section 3.2 has not been coordinated to the production system representation of control discussed in this section. At this point, negative-feedback cybernetic hierarchy and production systems are two independent control system formalisms. This is not a satisfactory state of affairs. One plausible bridge between the two is simply the assertion that the abstract logic of read input, compare, and write output holds in both cases. Sometimes the comparison involves acting to reduce a difference and sometimes it involves acting on the basis of a match.

But the deeper problem is twofold. Formally, one model was presented in the classical quantitative variable form whereas the other is in terms of discrete symbols. Conceptually, one model stresses operative ideals and normative control, whereas the other stresses knowledge of constitutive rules and interpretive procedures.

Keeping the models separate, every purely structural model in analytical action theory could presumably be given two interpretations of its ultimate nodes: through the negative-feedback control model and through a computational or instructional control model, each implementing the control principle of action. For instance, Figure 3.3 can be interpreted with each node as named by ⟨role⟩ and as constituted by ROLE for the four specific roles involved in the two role relations. Figure 3.4 can be interpreted as a linked series of ROLEs, where the links are representations of a control relation between production systems. Cybernetic hierarchy holds, but now in the context of the second cybernetics in which a key feature is the *explicit* representation of the symbols implied by symbolic interaction and symbolic media. Mind is to brain as culture is to network of human organisms: A computational model of mind passes over into a computational model of culture. This sketch does not resolve the problem of multiple representation principles so much as indicate how one may explore various formal interpretations within action theory.[23]

In a looser sense, the intuitions associated with dynamical systems and with negative-feedback control can be applied to the situations of action modeled by production systems, making use of several formal and sociological sets of terminology simultaneously. The result is to draw the two branches of action theory, interpretive and analytical, into some closer nexus than is often perceived in metatheoretical discussions of sociological theory. In particular, one then blends the normative and the interpretive conceptual foci of the two theories.

Consider a simple example. In the preceding section, the ethnomethodological conception of normalization was illustrated in the instance of interpretive procedures invoked when an action due is not actualized. Recall that the response is conditional on the interpretation and has the functional effect of tending to restore the flow of interaction to the normal state, that is, to the state in which meshing productions are generating normal forms of interaction. No conscious sense of using rules is involved: Production rules are tacitly employed to restore order. In the tradition of Durkheimian depth sociology, an instance of this process occurs in "ritual disequilibrium" (Goffman, 1967). As when a high dignitary has a momentary unintended loss of proper demeanor, the audience generally interprets the action as an unintended event. They disregard the lapse, allowing time for recovery to normal form. In other cases, some specific actions are taken. In either case, there is a return to the normal flow of interaction, constituting it as a ritual equilibrium. From a dynamical systems point of view, this is a stable equilibrium or attractor of social interaction process. In other words, *attractor state* and *normal form of interaction* and *ritual equilibrium* are strongly overlapping ideas. In this context we invoke the control principle of action in its negative-feedback control system form to clarify the relationship between the generation of action and interaction and the normative element of such action. [illegible] we have in an instance of a problem of stability, where the equilibrium involved is the normal social interaction flow. [illegible] In Durkheim, the reaction to departure from a normal form so as to restore the normal form suggests a normative element. In the context of the negative-feedback model such an element is the operative ideal that enters into the comparison process.

Hence, we obtain our main tentative response to the conceptual problem of linking the normative and the interpretive foci of the two action theories:

> The steady state of interaction has a dual character: It is a production process backed up by the comparison process that keeps it on track. This leads participants and observers to say that certain actions are ''called for''; they are not only cognitively expected but should occur.[24] And the sanctioned character of interpretive procedures is an aspect of the steady state of any interaction system.

This conceptual sketch cannot pretend to have solved the problem it addressed. It is offered in the spirit of integration of ideas that are not yet fully clear and where the respective formalisms are very different.[25] I shall return to the problem of formalization and unification in action theory in concluding this chapter.

## 3.5. Adaptively rational action

In Section 3.4 the theory took its problem to be that of generating interaction from given social structure represented in the form of interconnected modules of productions. The latter are items of tacit everyday social knowledge in the form of conditional situated action rules.

In this section, we turn to the reverse problem: generating emergent social structure from interaction, where interaction is formally represented by coupling models of actors. Depending on the model of the actor–situation unit, we get different mechanisms that drive the change of state of the dynamical social system, and hence potentially different answers to the questions of the possible social structures and of their stability properties. The main subtradition of general theoretical sociology that will be drawn upon is that represented by the later work of Homans (1974) and also developed by Emerson (1981). The theoretical project is to show how interaction of individual actors, each satisfying a general actor model, generates social structures. From the standpoint of analytical action theory, as pointed out at the end of Section 3.3, this is an abstraction from the broader control hierarchy representing each actor. So, with only partial success, there are a number of ingredients mixed and partially blended in this section and Section 3.6: (1) the most general elements of the perspective represented by Homans and Emerson, the foundation of which is the idea that the action of an actor dynamically adapts to the situation of action; (2) a process model of such adaptive behavior; (3) the procedure of coupling actor models to derive a dynamic model of the interaction of actors, which is investigated from the standpoint of dynamical systems properties; and (4) the control principle of action.

A mathematical model is explored because it permits an elucidation of the general logic of the study of coupled adaptive behavior models in *process* terms. It stems from the same behavioral tradition that provided the empirical basis for the Homans–Emerson perspective. This meshing of the mathematical model with the behavioral ideas associated with Homans and Emerson, with suitable interpretations, is a theory of adaptively rational action.

There are some immediate issues that must be addressed, given the current state of metatheoretical discussion in sociology. A number of recent commentators have dismissed the work of Homans. These writers share my aim in fostering the ideal of a general theoretical sociology (Alexander, 1982; Collins, 1985). But these authors and many more like them may not have the informed intuitions associated with the dynamical system ideas I have used to interpret the earlier work of not only Homans but also Parsons. These intuitions also enter into the interpretation of the later work of Homans, although the interpretation involves other issues about which informed analysts disagree. Let me present my own viewpoint.

The main problem relates to the methodological and content presuppositions of the Homans framework in its *apparent* or seeming double departure from the vital Durkheimian subtradition of general theoretical sociology.

First, this framework seemingly denies that individuals are social beings since under one misleading interpretation, it attempts to generate ''society'' from ''individuals.'' In fact, this would violate not only Durkheim's presuppositions but also those of Marx, Mead, and many other classical and contemporary theorists. Second, it seemingly denies the Durkheimian argument that rational action alone cannot be a ''foundation'' of social life.

In short, its *methodological individualism* and its seeming adoption of a *rationality postulate* seem to place this so-called exchange perspective in conceptual opposition to important elements of the comprehensive tradition of general theoretical sociology. Each of these issues is a large one, but for my present purposes what is important is to clear up an obfuscation connected with each of them.

### *3.5.1. Methodological individualism*

The first issue concerns methodological individualism. There are two very different meanings intended when sociologists refer to this notion. One meaning is intended by structuralist-oriented sociologists when they criticize research programs based on traditional survey analysis at the empirical level. Namely, the relations that link individuals are not sampled. Social structure slips through the empirical procedure as so much background information used to interpret individual responses, typically mapped into some regression equations. This meaning of the term is not relevant to the present discussion, since at no point does the perspective of this chapter imply such a "focus on the individual," as it is sometimes put.

But there is a second meaning of methodological individualism. In this second sense, it is a principle that coheres with the view expressed in this volume that we should develop action principles that permit us to construct models of interaction by coupling actor models. (See Section 2.11.) The principles of action are those that lead to the actor models. Methodological individualism is the commitment to explanations based on the discovery and formulation of such principles. But neither is this really a focus on the individual, since the main reason for the action principles is instrumental: One wants to have definite theoretical models of action in order to derive definite theoretical models of interaction. To merely propose and study an action model is not sociological, not focused on social structure. To carry out the coupling procedure and shift the focus to the generativity of social interaction, that is sociological and that is what requires some principles of action. Strictly speaking, this logic of coupling applies both to individual and collective actors in interaction. But as a general metatheoretical principle, methodological individualism adds that since collective actors are special states of social structures requiring generation from dynamical social systems, it follows that the ultimate principles of action are those applying to individual actors. For an extended defense of this position in the context of analytical Marxism, see Elster (1985).

And there is more. For the sake of a *comprehensive* dynamical social systems framework, such individual action principles must have the intended scope of applying to *any* human being at all in any time or place. Just because so much of the *content* of a human being as a social being is socially generated, for that reason the *general principles of individual action* must be highly abstract and relatively content free.[26]

### 3.5.2. Adaptive rationality I: dynamic utility

The second issue concerns the notion of rationality. In Section 3.3.2, reference was made to exchange theory and to the fact that it is often portrayed as having two branches, one associated with Durkheim and the other with Homans. I shall return to the Durkheim–Homans issue in Section 3.5.4. At present what I want to emphasize is that the "Homans side" of this division within exchange theory itself has two wings in terms of the nature of the theory of action employed. One, associated with Homans since 1961 and later also with theorists such as Emerson, stems from the study of behavior of organisms by experimental psychologists. The other wing, associated with theorists such as Blau (1964) and Coleman (1986), stems from economics.[27] In the context of an interest in dynamics, these two wings define two meanings for adaptively rational action.

The economic or rational choice model is based on the concept of a utility function. The latter is a numerical representation of preferences. Preferences satisfy axiomatic conditions such as those outlined in Section 1.3.1. This type of model can definitely be developed to implement the theoretical procedures recommended in this book. To illustrate, let us consider a simple exchange example developed in mathematical detail by Rapoport (1960) and also described in another context by Fararo (1978). The method is similar to that used by Coleman (1973). The basic idea is to *fuse utility theory and dynamical systems thinking.*

Suppose that $A$ and $B$ are two actors, each of whom controls the quantity of production of some good. Let $A$ produce amount $x(t)$ and $B$ amount $y(t)$ at a given time. There is a parameterized rule that says that each keeps a fraction, say, $p$, of the product and gives the remainder to the other in exchange. So at a given time, actor $A$ has $(px, qy)$ and $B$ has $(py, qx)$, where $q = 1 - p$. The underlying axioms of preference and indifference described in Chapter 1 are now assumed to hold over these composite bundles obtained in the exchange process. Using the numerical model, we have two utility functions defined over all the possible bundles, one for $A$ and one for $B$, respectively:

$$u_1(px, qy), \; u_2(qx, py)$$

We now posit that in the small, each actor changes the variable under control in the direction of increasing utility for that actor.

Thus, the coupled system has the generic form

$$A\text{'s behavior:} \quad dx/dt = \partial u_1 / \partial x$$
$$B\text{'s behavior:} \quad dy/dt = \partial u_2 / \partial y$$

We can think of this system as a template for a class of dynamical interaction models. Rapoport (1960) inserts definite utility functions by supposing that each has the form of a positive aspect of the bundle minus a negative aspect (which he takes to be the work involved in production).

The important conceptual point is that in a small time interval the actors shift production by certain amounts in certain directions so as to change the state of the system. All the ideas of Chapter 2 now apply, and four types of theorems about the production and exchange process are derivable for each family of models. A portrait of all the possible outcomes exists in terms of what these outcomes are as the parameters (such as $p$) vary. In Rapoport's theoretical model the generated production and exchange structures are: no-production "structure," exploitation structure, and egalitarian structure.

To repeat, the basic presupposition is that of rational action in the sense of utility theory, which in turn means that preference and indifference relations satisfy various consistency properties such as transitivity. This is a presupposition because in this context the point is not to test such an assumption but to deploy it to construct theoretical models. Should the models fail on empirical grounds, the more specific functional forms are likely to be challenged, rather than the underlying general assumptions about preferences. The general representation principle of this version of adaptively rational action theory is that *change of action is in the direction of increasing utility*. This is a powerful idea that can be employed throughout social science. The Rapoport model is one particular theoretical model within the broad framework defined by this principle. In turn, this theoretical system is only part of the whole modern rational choice framework that even includes most of normative social theory (including Rawls's [1971] theory of social justice).

### *3.5.3. Adaptive rationality II: the behavioral model*

The behavioral model proceeds from a different standpoint. The experimental background studies that initiated the research tradition focused on the dynamics of behavior as contrasted with the usually more static settings of classical utility theory. The psychologists were skeptical of the assumptions embodied in the preference–indifference axioms, such as transitivity of indifference. (I am indifferent between any given amount of sugar in my coffee and that amount increased or decreased by one grain, but this implies, if transitivity holds, that I do not care how much sugar is in my coffee!) In fact, some of the consequences of the experimental research show that people do not act as an optimizer would act (see the articles and discussion in Hogarth and Reder, 1986).

Staying closer to the data of choice, psychologists were led to describe the state space in terms of probabilistic dispositions toward various possible activities in the given environment. Adaptation means the shifting of this distribution over time until some adjusted state arises, if such a state is possible in the given environment.

Sociologically, this model can be abstracted from the organism–environment frame of reference and given the content of the action situation frame of reference. The problem is how the actor's action adjusts to the givens of the situation of action. Empirical situations may not be very stable, but the theoretical model can accommodate this by a Type 4 theorem: the continuous adjustment of the adjustment process as the parameters of the situation change.

The version of adaptive rational action theory developed in the remainder of this chapter is in the tradition of the behavioral approach, which is the background for the theoretical perspective of Homans and Emerson.[28] It is not based on any rationality postulate if this means any of the following: (1) conscious deliberation with a view to selecting the best means, an act oriented to a rational norm; (2) conscious calculation involving maximization of utility; or (3) unconscious processes that amount to behavior as if optimizing and therefore representable as utility maximization. A type 3 model *might* be obtained as a special case of a behavioral model, as Homans (1974) thinks, but even this assumption is not necessary. Thus, without attacking the attractiveness of the economics or rational choice approach to adaptively rational action, I want to explore this alternative. It represents an important subtradition within general theoretical sociology that grew out of Homans's earlier focus on "the internal system," which in turn (I claim) is in direct continuity with the important Durkheimian depth sociological subtradition.

### *3.5.4. Adaptive rationality III: the Durkheimian issue*

This brings us to the substantive aspect of the issue of rationality in sociological theory and its relation to Homans's theory. Durkheim's polemic against Spencer and the utilitarians is against the theory that there could be a stable social structure in which all interactions are of the instrumental type in the sense of universalistic–specific or rational norms. Parsons, as we saw in Section 3.3.2, conjectures that social systems have both integration (internal) and adaptation (external) stability conditions. The Spencerian error is to neglect the integration stability conditions, those associated with particularistic ties and diffuse expectations. But this Durkheimian argument remains intact under an adaptively rational action theory. Indeed, we have already seen in Chapter 2 that Homans (1950) built the internal system construct to map the particularistic–diffuse elements of social systems. His subsequent theory is largely a matter of showing how such integration structures *can arise* under given conditions. It most definitely is not anti-Durkheimian in substance.

In fact, allowing for idealization, either version of adaptively rational action theory would seem to be compatible with the Durkheimian subtradition. If either of these two bases for a model of action is adopted, their concepts are not inevitably restricted to application to the social adaptation dimension of social systems. There is no reason to think that two actors who change their action in the direction of increasing utility (as a formal representation of whatever their substantive preferences may be, provided only they satisfy consistency axioms) or who change their probabilistic dispositions as a function of the sanction significance of their actions cannot generate gemeinschaft-type norms and corresponding interactions.

Returning to the behavioral theory of adaptively rational action to be treated formally in what follows, we note that it is not a theory that all action follows rational norms. It is most certainly not a theory postulating an actor busily calculating things. It is simply a theory of how the *probability of an action changes with its consequences in terms of the sanction significance of those consequences, whether positive or negative*. This statement will be called the *behavioral principle of adaptive rationality*. The theoretical models are inherently dynamic. And since the adjustment process is based on actual consequences for the actor, there is, in a broad sense, an element of rationality. But it may not be intendedly rational action.[29] So this is both a dynamic and a limited rationality. From the standpoint of a more knowledgeable observer, even if given enough time and experience, the adaptive actor may not make the best connections. The actor is not ideally rational.

Does intention figure at all? Can it do so in this sort of model derived from the behavioral tradition? In an integrative spirit, we can propose that each of the possible actions is represented by a TOTE unit. The adaptive process is shifting the probability distribution of activation between a set of situationally relevant but mutually exclusive plans. Whenever a TOTE unit is active but incomplete, the intention is given by the incomplete character of the plan it represents. For instance, if "mail a letter" is one action and "make a telephone call" is the disjoint alternative, each is a TOTE unit. If the probabilistic generator activates the first TOTE, then until the test criterion for having mailed the letter is satisfied, the intention is to mail the letter.

The term *adaptively rational actor* is used here even though the justification is not as clear as in the case of the rational choice model of Section 3.5.2. As used here, the term always envisions a spreading out of action over a series of occasions, not a one-shot isolated choice. The models are constructed to recursively generate the behavior in these occasions. This conception agrees with the framework proposed by Emerson (1981) for what he terms "exchange theory." The coupling of actor models on the basis of an adaptive process on the part of each actor will constitute a model of social interaction. As Emerson points out, such a model will be part of the truth but not the whole truth about social interaction. That is, each wing within adaptively rational action theory is one stream of developments within action theory that needs eventual unification with the other streams.

## 3.6. Adaptively rational action: behavioral models and theoretical procedures

This section begins with a formal statement of a model object representing an actor–situation unit and states the generic mechanism of adaptive rationality in mathematical form in terms of certain operators. The model is then used to provide mathematical interpretations of the most fundamental concepts occurring in the postulates of Homans's (1974) theory. Then the discussion moves to the procedure of coupling actor–situation models to derive a dynamical interaction system. Discussion of the derived system is in terms of generating novel social structure under given initial conditions of interaction. For a pair of interactants, this is an emergent social tie. Finally, after noting the analytical complexity of the interaction model, a series of "thought experiments" are conducted by computer simulation, referring to the iterated Prisoner's Dilemma as the social situation of interest.

### *3.6.1. An adaptive behavior model*

The basic model of the actor–situation system to be presented was initially developed by Bush and Mosteller (1955) as one of a family of models of behavioral change that emerged in the 1950s and 1960s. Later, it was explicated in rigorous terms by Sternberg (1963) and in very intuitively appealing terms by Lave and March (1975). Also, Atkinson and Estes (1963) consider it within a broader family of "stimulus sampling" models developed within mathematical psychology. I have made use of all of these sources in the following presentation, with a language shift to embed the ideas within the action systems terminology of the tradition of general theoretical sociology.

The following is a description of the conceptual components of the basic type of model object in the action framework interpretation:

1. There exists a set of alternative actions of an actor in a situation.
2. The state of the actor is described in terms of a time-varying probability distribution over the alternative actions.
3. There exists a fixed set of possible contingent reactions by one or more actors in the situation. These will sometimes be called outcomes for the actor. They have *sanction significance* for the actor, positively or negatively.
4. The state of the situation is described in terms of a possibly time-varying probability distribution over the possible reactions.
5. A set of possible events is defined in terms of all the logically possible combinations of action and reaction. For each event, there is a probability of that event given by the product of the probability of the action and the probability of the contingent reaction.

To fix ideas, it is useful to have in mind a conception of a pool of actors in the same institutional conditions but in distinct group settings. A collection of elementary school teachers each in a different classroom situation would be an example. Despite the close institutional control over the conduct of elementary school teachers, the institutional menu leaves considerable "space" for choices by the actor in the situation. The adaptive behavior model can be thought of as applicable to the choices from the menu. This is not the only possible interpretation, but it is useful for explicating the basic ideas. Because each social situation and social background of each concrete teacher is somewhat different in detail from every other and because teachers are not identical in cultural, personality, and cognitive states, variability is an intrinsic feature of the realization of the institution. This variability is represented in the model and also generated by it. First, as a matter of representation, each teacher is described in probabilistic terms. Actions in a latent state are dispositions with probability weightings. Second, as a matter of recursive generativity, each teacher's own experience in the situation transforms the initial probabilistic state in a particular way. Thus, even if all teachers are identical in probability state to start with – which only says that in some sense, despite their variability, they come from some common population with its own uniformities – they will not be identical any longer as the situation of each unfolds.

To continue with the example, suppose that in teaching a given subject, the teachers are permitted to select a particular strategy or some alternative. For each of the teachers, then, the five components of the model object are identified, for this example, as (1) a strategy of teaching a certain subject versus some alternative method; (2) a probability of using the strategy, its compliment referring to the alternative, as a function of time (experience); (3) two possible outcomes, such as "learning occurs" and "learning does not occur," having the significance of positive sanction in the first case and negative in the second, given a situation in which the given goal is effective teaching; (4) the conditional probabilities of the possible learning outcomes for each of the two strategies; and (5) the four possible events, each defined by the conjunction of a possible strategy and one of its possible outcomes.

Let us call the two possible actions $A_1$ and $A_2$ and the two possible outcomes or reactions $R_1$ and $R_2$. The four events are then defined by the four combinations as follows:

$E_{11}$: strategy 1 ($A_1$) and learning occurs ($R_1$)
$E_{12}$: strategy 1 ($A_1$) and learning does not occur ($R_2$)
$E_{21}$: strategy 2 ($A_2$) and learning occurs ($R_1$)
$E_{22}$: strategy 2 ($A_2$) and learning does not occur ($R_2$)

The probability of each of the events is given by the probability of the action multiplied by the conditional probability of the reaction. Depending on which event occurs, the actor's relative dispositions toward doing $A_1$ rather than doing $A_2$ will change. In the theoretical model, stated in what follows, this will be done by calculating a new probability of each act using an "operator." Each event corresponds to a distinct operator since it has distinct meaning in terms of sanction significance. Thus the theoretical model will be a dynamical model of the stochastic type in which the state variables are probabilities.

The simplest theoretical model is the only one I discuss here. As in the preceding example, the model object has two alternative actions and two possible reactions defining four events. Let us further assume that the reactions are such that the first reaction has positive sanction, or reward significance: It increases the probability of the action it follows. The second reaction decreases the probability of the action it follows. We can call it a nonrewarding outcome, or a punishment, or a negative sanction.

We let $P_1(t)$ be the probability of action $A_1$ at time $t$ and $P_2(t)=1-P_1(t)$ be the probability of the other action at that time. The mechanism that defines the theoretical model deals with how these action probabilities change over time as a consequence of the events that occur. Again, for a simple model, I take the contingent reaction probabilities as properties of the situation that do not vary over time as the actor adapts to the situation. We let $\pi_1$ be the probability of reaction $R_1$, the reward, when action $A_1$ is taken and $\pi_2$ is the reward probability for the second action $A_2$. The equations take the form of postulated *linear operators*, one for each possible event:

1. If $E_{11}$ occurs at $t$, then $P_1(t+1)=P_1(t)+a[1-P_1(t)]$.
2. If $E_{12}$ occurs at $t$, then $P_1(t+1)=P_1(t)-bP_1(t)$.

3. If $E_{21}$ occurs at $t$, then $P_2(t+1) = P_2(t) + a[1 - P_2(t)]$.
4. If $E_{22}$ occurs at $t$, then $P_2(t+1) = P_2(t) - bP_2(t)$.

The first equation says, if the event occurs in which the actor's first action is followed by the situational reaction $R_1$, then the probability of that action increases. The increase is determined by the application of a linear operator: The new probability is a linear function of the given probability. The amount of increase depends on the parameter $a$. This parameter varies between zero and 1, and the higher it is, the greater is the increase in the probability of the rewarded action. The second equation says that if the event that occurs involves action $A_1$ followed by the $R_2$ reaction, then the probability of that action will decrease linearly by an amount that depends on parameter $b$. Parameter $b$ also varies between zero and 1, and the greater it is, the greater is the decrease in the probability of the negatively sanctioned action. In a similar way, the third and fourth equations are interpretable for events involving the second action.

It is useful to rewrite the expressions in 3 and 4 in terms of $P_1$. Since the sum of $P_1$ and $P_2$ is unity for any $t$, we obtain:

3′. If $E_{21}$ occurs at $t$, then $P_1(t+1) = P_1(t) - aP_1(t)$.
4′. If $E_{22}$ occurs at $t$, then $P_1(t+1) = P_1(t) + b[1 - P_1(t)]$.

Considering equations 1, 2, 3′, and 4′, we see that depending on which event occurs, one of four linear operators applies to transform the state of the system.

The following parameters describe the contingent reaction probabilities or outcome probabilities:

$$\pi_1 = P(R_1|A_1)$$
$$\pi_2 = P(R_1|A_2)$$

In terms of these parameters and the actor's state at time $t$, the probabilities of the four events at $t$ are

$$P(E_{11} \text{ at } t) = P_1(t)\pi_1$$
$$P(E_{12} \text{ at } t) = P_1(t)\ (1 - \pi_1)$$
$$P(\mathrm{E}_{21} \text{ at } t) = P_2(t)\pi_2$$
$$P(E_{22} \text{ at } t) = P_2(t)\ (1 - \pi_2)$$

In particular, note that the event probabilities change over time as the actor adapts to the situation and changes state. Actors who undergo different event histories will have different probabilities of actions generated during the process. The result is a *recursive bifurcation process.*

As in the example of the teachers, it is useful to imagine a pool of actors and to posit also that they start with some initial uniform probability of actions $A_1$

and $A_2$. Then after one time unit passes, in which an action is taken and a reaction is generated, the uniform pool bifurcates into four distinct subpopulations, each internally uniform in probability state, corresponding to the four possible events. The first pool, for instance, consists of all those actors who selected the $A_1$ action and received the rewarding reaction. Their new probability of action $A_1$ is generated by equation 1. Similarly, after a second time unit, each of these four pools bifurcates into four subpools so that there are then sixteen distinctive subpopulations of actors. In this way, if we consider any common institutional situation (say, teaching arithmetic to elementary school pupils) and consider a population of settings embodying that situation, the event histories within the institutional situation lead to bifurcation upon bifurcation of the pool of actors into experientially distinct subpopulations. Although mathematically complicated, this recursive bifurcation picture of the "microworld" is quite compatible with our empirical knowledge of it.

There is also an "average process," obtained by averaging at each time before generating the next event. If there are sixteen pools at a given time, each with its own probability state, the total probability of the $A_1$ action is the summation: Sum over all pools the probability of being in the pool multiplied by the probability of the act, given one is in the specified pool. The resulting total probability of the act at that time characterizes the initial pool of actors without regard to the internal differentiation by experience. This average process also can be represented by an operator. As Bush and Mosteller (1955) show, the *average process is generated by a nonlinear operator*. To see this intuitively, consider the average probability of $P_1(t+1)$. We have to sum a weighted combination of linear operators, namely, those specified by statements 1, 2, 3′, and 4′. Call the operator that applies when $E_{ij}$ occurs $L_{ij}$. Then the average of $P_1(t+1)$ is given by:

$$P(E_{11} \text{ at } t)L_{11} + P(E_{12} \text{ at } t)L_{12} + P(E_{21} \text{ at } t)L_{21} + P(E_{22} \text{ at } t)L_{22}$$

The first term alone is given by

$$P_1(t)\pi_1\{P_1(t) + a[1 - P_1(t)]\}$$

Hence the square of a probability term arises, and so the complete expression for $P_1(t+1)$ as a function of $P_1(t)$ is nonlinear.[30] The average process characterizes the original pool of actors without regard to their internal differentiation according to experience in the situation. It tells a story about adaptive behavior, a typical story rather than the complex differentiated story told by the bifurcation process.

The general form for the adaptive behavior model is

$$\mathbf{P}(t+1) = f[\mathbf{P}(t); \mathbf{X}(t)] \qquad (3.6.1)$$

Here **X** represents the stochastically generated events $E_{ij}$ in numerical form: (1, 1), (1, 2), (2, 1), and (2, 2) are the possible values of **X** in the example. The map $f$ of (3.6.1) is defined by the family of linear operators, one per possible event. When **X** takes the value (1, 1), for instance, $f$ is the first of the four linear operators listed earlier. Which linear operator applies at a given time depends on the outcome of an internally generated stochastic event.

Let us now interpret some of the concepts involved in these dynamic equations in terms of the language of Homans (1974).

1. *Rewards:* These are reactions or outcomes in the situation of action that have positive emotional significance to the actor. For example, a reaction might be an act of approval or an outcome might be a monetary gain. The tagging of a reaction as a reward implies that the action probabilities satisfy equations of types 1 and 2.
2. *Success probability:* This is the probability that a reward will follow a given action. This is the contingent reaction probability for the case of a rewarding reaction, the parameters $\pi_1$ and $\pi_2$.
3. *Value of the reward:* This can be measured by the parameter that appears in the equation that produces an increase in the probability of the corresponding action that obtained that reward. This parameter governs the magnitude of a shift in probability following an event that involves a reward. For action $A_1$, for instance, parameter $a$ measures the value of $R_1$ as reward, as shown by the linear operator corresponding to event $E_{11}$. When a sanction is negative, it produces a decline in the probability of the action. Let us identify the negative of parameter $b$ with negative value. With uncertain outcomes, in doing either action, there is a risk of the negatively valued outcome. Taking the mathematical expectation of $a$ and the negative $b$, we obtain an *expected net value*. For action $A_1$, the expected net value is

$$\pi_1 a - (1 - \pi_1) b$$

The expected net value for action $A_2$, similarly, is

$$\pi_2 a - (1 - \pi_2) b$$

4. *Cost of an action:* This can be defined as the expected net value forgone. Thus the cost of $A_1$ is the expected net value of $A_2$.
5. *Profit:* The profit of an action is the expected net value less the cost. For $A_1$ this is given by $(\pi_1 - \pi_2)(a + b)$. In the present model, which is not the most general model, of course, the profit of $A_2$ is the negative of the profit of $A_1$. Thus, if the contingent reward is more likely for $A_1$ than for $A_2$, there is some profit in doing $A_1$; otherwise, there is a loss.

Several points about values in this theory are worth noting. First, note that Homans's idea of "value of reward" is interpreted here in terms of a parameter that helps account for behavior. It is not interpreted in phenomenological terms. That is, the theory does not claim that the actor consciously regards a certain reward as having a certain worth. The theory is not about conscious evaluative thought, except as that thought may become the action under analysis, one that is sanctioned by certain situational outcomes. Second, the idea of a preference structure, which looms large in rational choice theory, is not directly represented in this type of model. One might regard "value of reward" as approximately the same as "utility of outcome." Such preferences are revealed in the patterning of choices over time, especially after a stable probabilistic state is reached. When the value parameters are estimated, these estimates are analogous to measures of utility. Third, all this implies that people's evaluative orientations are measured by what they *do* (in repeated occasions over time) rather than what they might say in some artificial situation constructed to measure them. And finally, "value of reward" is not conceptually equivalent to values as cultural-level standards in the cybernetic hierarchy model. Any connection between them is a problem for theory and research.

It is easy to see how some of Homans's general propositions (see Section 1.3.1 for the basic listing) are implied by the model. The success proposition is reflected directly in the operators that increase the probability of action in a situation given the reward event occurs. For any operator representing the effect of the action–reward event, successive applications of the operator produce smaller and smaller increments in the likelihood of the action. This would be one way to interpret the satiation proposition. The value proposition is direcly reflected in the increment term for the reward-type operator. This covers three of the five propositions. The other two, treating stimuli and emotions, are more complex but are comprehended within the general theory from which the operator model can be derived (see notes 31 and 33).

It is relevant to remind the reader that the present model is a model of an actor–situation system, not a social system. No coupling is involved. When the theoretical model is applied to a class of actors in an institutional type of situation, there are deductions about the average process and about the bifurcating classes of actors having probability states varying over time as a function of their event histories in that situation. These deductions are expressed in terms of the parameters $a$ and $b$, the initial state $P_1(0)$, and the reward probabilities $\pi_1$ and $\pi_2$. Given appropriate data, then, $a$ and $b$ are estimated, given known $P_1(0)$, say. That is, we learn the best-fitting values of the constants that account for the data on action changes over time in the type of situation. In other words, we do not really know the value of the reward for these actors until we estimate it from model that describes their behavior correctly.

A philosophical model of theory structure is useful at this point to see the logi of this situation. Recall that, as explained in Chapter 1, the model guiding th work of this book has three meaning levels below the level of general presup-positions. At the topmost of these levels is the fundamental representation prin-ciple that defines the entire approach through a nonhomogeneous statement whose subject is an empirical domain and whose predicate refers to a formal mode o representation. The next level down consists of theoretical models constructed within this framework. And the last level consists of invariants discovered in the study of the models, including their empirical tests.

Applying this philosophical conception of theory structure to the present con-text, the basic principle of the theoretical system is that the actor is adaptively rational. We can think of the formal side of this principle as represented by expression (3.6.1) for definiteness. Each type of model constructed within the framework defined by this principle leads to a particular version of (3.6.1). This is the theoretical model level. Various derived formulas and parameters of the model exist. Parameters estimated from appropriate data descriptively character-ize empirical phenomena within the scope of the model. Potentially, some such derived formula or some such parameter can function as an important invariant, the last of the levels in the structure. (A simple example is formula [3.6.2].)

The theoretical model is empirically testable and may be wrong even though we are in no position to know the values of parameters $a$ and $b$ beforehand. The degrees of freedom exist even after the best-fitting parameters are estimated. One can also think of functions of the form $a=f(x, y)$, where $x$ and $y$ are external variables that are postulated to effect the value of the reward. For instance, $x$ may be a binary 0–1 variable that indicates whether the actor is a woman or a man or, more generally, belongs to a certain social category or not.

One type of deduction from this sort of theoretical model involves the equilib-rium state as a function of the parameters of the process. Bush and Mosteller (1955:288) indicate that it can be shown that if $a=b$, then the equilibrium aver-age probability $P_1$ of action $A_1$ in the preceding model is given by

$$P_1=(1-\pi_2)/(2-\pi_1-\pi_2) \tag{3.6.2}$$

Since $P_2=1-P_1$, we see that in this case the following holds:

$$P_1>P_2 \quad \text{if and only if} \quad \pi_1>\pi_2$$

But, then, according to the derived formula for the profit in doing $A_1$, previously shown as point 5, we obtain

$$P_1>P_2 \quad \text{if and only if} \quad \text{profit}(A_1)>\text{profit}(A_2)$$

At least for this special case, our intuitions are satisfied: In equilibrium of the adaptive process, on average, our actors have discovered a rational relation of means (actions) and ends (values of outcomes, given some goal). Namely, if the profit of $A_1$ exceeds that of $A_2$, then the probabilistic disposition to do $A_1$ exceeds that of doing $A_2$. This is not to say that actors are *consciously* trying to increase profit. Granted this, however, we find that through the adaptive process they adopt a mode of behavior (a probability distribution over possible actions) that is adjusted to the parameters of reward in just such a way as summed up in formula (3.6.2).

The main way that this theoretical model connects with Homans's theory, apart from the way it permits us to interpret his concepts, is that Homans's five axiomatic propositions have a logical status as actual or prospective *derived* propositions within a comprehensive adaptive behavior theory. I shall not try to demonstrate this claim but only sketch the reasoning that underlies it.

The adaptive behavior equations are a special case of consequences proved from a general set of axioms that characterize behavior change over time.[31] We can interpret Homans's success proposition[32] as indicating that the probability of an action adjusts to its reward probability in such a way that an increase in the reward probability produces, after adjustment to the new circumstance, an increase in the likelihood of the action. Formally, it is a matter of the partial derivative with respect to a reward probability term in an expression such as (3.6.2). This is a comparative statics proposition. Practically any dynamic model of adaptation would imply this result when its asymptotic probability of a behavior is derived and then differentiated with respect to the relevant reinforcement rate parameter of the model.

This is my main point: Homans is taking as assumptions about the dynamics of individual action some propositions about how action states adjust to parameters of situations.[33] And these propositions, in a mathematical framework, report derived properties of theoretical models constructed within a general adaptive action comprehensive framework.

### *3.6.2. The coupling procedure*

I turn now to the logic of the analysis of interaction as the coupling of actor models. There are (at least) two actors in each other's situations so that each reacts to the other and each actor is described in terms of the adaptive action model. This is exactly Homans's domain once we interpret his main conceptual strategy as one of coupling two or more actor–situation systems. Hence, Homans's substantive claim will be interpreted as follows: Social structures, equilibrium states of dynamical social systems, are *generated* by *coupled adaptively rational action systems*. These systems are models satisfying (3.6.1) through the procedure of writing down one linear operator per possible stochastic event generated by the actors' actions.

From the standpoint of Homans's theory of interaction, in any interactive occasion of two persons *A* and *B*, the action of each is a contingent reaction to the action of the other. The element of sanction enters directly into this ''exchange.'' The same general idea, of course, is part of the foundation of analytical action theory (Parsons and Shils, 1951). It constitutes *double contingency* and requires a conceptual move to the system of interaction from the starting point of the actor–situation unit.[34] It is essential to try to conceptualize this interactive nexus dynamically. For the purposes of general theoretical sociology, the theoretical interest is not in a one-shot act and react but a sequence of occasions involving the same two actors. Thus each will adapt to the pattern of contingent reaction provided by the action of the other. The promise of a conceptually mobile point of reference, the actor–situation unit, must be carried through in detail: We require a model of each acting unit and a coupling of the actor models to generate interaction over time, yielding equilibria interpretable as emergent social structures, enduring (if stable) social relations comprising patterns of interaction.

Most real interactive encounters, regarded as a stream of occasions involving the same actors, do not present the identical situation in each encounter. Theoretical model building, however, proceeds on the basis of initial simplicity with gradual extension to more complex cases. The simplest case is that in which each encounter involves ''the same situation'' in the relevant aspects.

Hence, the idea of action and reaction dynamics of a pair of actors in repeated encounters in a given type of situation will be embodied in a theoretical model.[35] The basic model object of the interactive nexus is characterized as follows:

1. For each actor, there exists a finite set of alternative actions in a situation of a given type.
2. The state of each actor is described in terms of a time-varying probability distribution over the alternative actions.
3. Each actor is in the situation of the other, providing the contingent reactions for the other.
4. A set of possible *interactive events* is defined in terms of the logically possible combinations of action and reaction, and there is a probability distribution over these interactive events that depends on the action probabilities of each actor.
5. Each actor adapts to the situation in accordance with the linear operators of the Bush–Mosteller adaptive behavior model.

Using the simplest type of adaptive behavior model, I shall illustrate how such an interactive model is constructed. Consider two people who engage in a sequence of intermittent conversational episodes. In Collins's (1981) terms, we have an interaction ritual chain of conversational encounters. For instance, they meet daily and converse for a while that day and then meet again the next day. For definiteness I shall make this the interpretation of the time variable: day 0, day 1, and so forth, with a definite state of the system for each day. For the purpose of this illustration, we focus on socioemotional elements in their conversational behavior. In particular, for simplicity, we assume that each actor can choose to be agreeable and supportive of the other or not. In the latter case, the emotional tone conveyed is disagreeable or discouraging. These are the two alternative actions. An interactive event is defined as a choice of one of the two action alternatives by each actor. Thus there are four possible events on any day. Three brief points about this example should be kept in mind. First, the same model could be applied to a more microtemporal analysis of conversational encounters by identifying the time variable with smaller durations. Second, in general, it would not be necessary for the action alternatives of the two parties to be the same, as they are in this example. Third, the choice to be supportive is not the same as the reading of the generated behavior *as* supportive by the other actor. For simplicity, this model assumes a matching of the two meanings, or alternatively, one might regard the missing interpretive elements as part of the basis of the stochastic character of the process.

The action alternatives of actor $A$ may be denoted

$A_1$: supportive
$A_2$: nonsupportive

Similarly, the action alternatives of actor $B$ are

$B_1$: supportive
$B_2$: nonsupportive

Thus the possible interactive events each day are

$E_{11}$: $A_1$ and $B_1$
$E_{12}$: $A_1$ and $B_2$
$E_{21}$: $A_2$ and $B_1$
$E_{22}$: $A_2$ and $B_2$

For each actor supportiveness from the other is rewarding (a positive sanction) and nonsupportiveness is nonrewarding (a negative sanction). Now note the following in terms of the consequences of the various possible events for each actor:

1. If $E_{11}$ occurs, then $A$'s supportiveness is rewarded by $B$'s supportiveness and $B$'s supportiveness is rewarded by $A$'s supportiveness.
2. If $E_{12}$ occurs, then $A$'s supportiveness is negatively sanctioned and $B$'s nonsupportiveness is rewarded.

3. If $E_{21}$ occurs, then $A$'s nonsupportiveness is rewarded and $B$'s supportiveness is negatively sanctioned.
4. If $E_{22}$ occurs, then both $A$'s and $B$'s nonsupportiveness are negatively sanctioned.

We model each actor by the four adaptation equations of the prior section. Let $a$ and $b$ be the parameters for $A$ and let $c$ and $d$ be the parameters for $B$. Let $P_1(t)$ be the probability that actor $A$ does $A_1$ at $t$. As before, $P_2(t) = 1 - P_1(t)$. Let $Q_1(t)$ be the probability that actor $B$ does $B_1$ at time $t$. We write $Q_2(t) = 1 - Q_1(t)$ for the probability of $B_2$. The probability of event $E_{ij}$ at $t$ is the product $P_i(t)Q_j(t)$.

The initial state of the system is given by $[P_1(0), Q_1(0)]$. The subsequent states of the system are recursively generated from the eight equations that follow. The consequences of the four types of events on day $t$ for the states of the actors at the start of day $t+1$ are given by

1. If $E_{11}$ occurs at $t$, then

$$P_1(t+1) = P_1(t) + a[1 - P_1(t)]$$
$$Q_1(t+1) = Q_1(t) + c[1 - Q_1(t)]$$

2. If $E_{12}$ occurs at $t$, then

$$P_1(t+1) = P_1(t) - bP_1(t)$$
$$Q_2(t+1) = Q_2(t) + c[1 - Q_2(t)]$$

3. If $E_{21}$ ocurs at $t$, then

$$P_2(t+1) = P_2(t) + a[1 - P_2(t)]$$
$$Q_1(t+1) = Q_1(t) - dQ_1(t)$$

4. If $E_{22}$ occurs at $t$, then

$$P_2(t+1) = P_2(t) - bP_2(t)$$
$$Q_2(t+1) = Q_2(t) - dQ_2(t)$$

In the tradition of Homans (1974) and Emerson (1981), such an interactive system is described as an exchange involving sanctions. At any time, we can define an *exchange ratio* between the pair of actors. To see this, let us show the relation of the preceding model to the notation used by Emerson (1981) to describe exchange relations. Emerson emphasizes, as does the presentation here, the time-extended character of the interactive nexus constituting a relation. His notation takes the form $[A_x; B_y]$, signifying that $A$ has or produces $x$ that is a benefit for $B$, that is, is a reward. Similarly, $B$ produces $y$, which is a reward for $A$. Emerson's "mutual contingency" is the double contingency of action and reaction of the interaction model. For the preceding model, $x$ and $y$ can be relaced by 1, so that $[A_1; B_1]$ is the exchange relation in which $A_1$ is a reward for 3 and $B_1$ is a reward for $A$. In the concrete example, each finds the other's upportiveness to be a reward. Thinking of $x$ and $y$ as quantities and probably envisioning an equilibrium state, Emerson (1981:42) defines the exchange ratio as $x/y$. In the present context, the acts as such are rewarding and their relative frequencies are the quantities. Hence, we take $P_1(t)/Q_1(t)$ as the exchange ratio. Thus, in generating the over-time behavior of the state of the system, the preceding equations also generate a time-varying exchange ratio. Note that the expected net value and the corresponding expected cost associated with an action will vary over time, since these terms involve mathematical expectations computed with respect to the state of the system, that is, the pair of prevailing probabilities.

Consider a population of such pairs of interactants each modeled by the above process with the same initial state on a given day 0 and each independent of the others. (I discuss networks of exchange relations in what follows.) According to the recursive bifurcation property of the model, the initially homogeneous population of pairs repeatedly splits into subsets. Each subset arises from a particular interactive event that generates a particular new probability state of the pair. On any day, therefore, the various interactive events are generated with varying probabilities depending upon the event histories of the particular pair. We can imagine that the pairs are chosen to be independent realizations of interaction in certain roles, say, roles $A$ and $B$. The parameters can be thought of as associated with the roles since they remain invariant as the process generates distinctive event histories.

As an example, consider the process for particular initial conditions. Let $a=c=.5$ and $b=d=.7$ and let the initial state of the system be (.8, .8), so that each actor is initially inclined to be supportive but with some chance of nonsupportiveness also. It can be shown that one obtains convergence toward the state (1, 1), that is, the state of mutual supportiveness, under these givens.[36] Thus, if the parameters and initial state were as indicated, then the dynamical interactive system would converge on mutually supportive behavior. As an equilibrium condition of the dynamical social system under analysis, it qualifies as a social structure. In Collins's (1981) terms, the *interaction ritual chain* has generated a solidary group. Since it involves only a dyad, what has been generated under these conditions is better regarded as a type of social relation, where *social relation* implies some invariant patterning over time in the interactive nexus between two actors. Since our empirical interpretation imagined the pair to be in an institutional role relation to start with, the generated social relation is an emergent of the interaction "in the internal system." It is an expressive bond, a little gemeinschaft.

From the standpoint of Homans's theory, this example may serve to illustrate the idea of showing how enduring social relations are produced in interaction between actors. Interaction generates structure. However, repeated applications of a simulation procedure, with varying initial conditions, are needed to obtain any analytical results of generality. (A further discussion and illustration of simulations of dynamic exchange relations will be given shortly.) Let me put this discussion in the context of the systems ideas of Chapter 2. We are dealing with a dynamical social system, albeit in terms of states that are probabilities of actions and, for convenience, in terms of discrete time. Hence, the theoretical problems are those noted in Chapter 2. This implies that any simulation analyses would be aimed at discovery of any general results of the four types: parametric conditions for the existence of probabilistic equilibria, parametric conditions for the stability of any such equilibrium; how any stable equilibrium varies with variation in a parameter on which it depends; and finally, how the dynamical system behavior varies with over-time variation in the parameters of the system. Thus, as theoreticians we are interested in the four types of theorems, and analysis has its tasks set out for it once a family of theoretical models is specified in such a way that we recognize an instance of a dynamical system. In the present case, the dynamical system is a stochastic coupled adaptive behavior process, a coupling of (at least) two component dynamical systems.

The general form of the model that arises by such a coupling procedure may be written in a form that generalizes expression (3.6.1), namely,

$$\mathbf{S}(t+1)=\mathbf{F}[\mathbf{S}(t);\mathbf{X}(t)] \tag{3.6.3}$$

Here **S** is a matrix in which each column contains the probability states of a particular actor. For instance, in the two-actor model, column 1 contains $P_1$ and $P_2$ and column 2 contains $Q_1$ and $Q_2$. Selecting a row entry from each column and multiplying these, we obtain the probability of an interaction event at a given time, the indices of which constitute one value of vector $\mathbf{X}(t)$. The mapping **F** corresponding to this event is the set of linear operators updating the matrix **S** by transforming each probability distribution. In this general case, one way to define the linear operators is by averaging.

For instance, consider any arbitrary actor with probability $P_1$ of a certain action and $P_2$ of its alternative. Suppose there are $n$ other actors in the network with whom that actor "exchanges." Then the sanction significance for our actor of the action of any one such alter, say, $j$, is associated with linear operator $L_j$, and we define the transformation of $P_1(t)$ into $P_1(t+1)$ as the average $\Sigma z_j L_j$, where the $z_j$ form a probability distribution over the $n$ alters. If $k$ of the $n$ opera-ors are of the rewarding type and $n-k$ of the punishing type, then this average can be shown to yield

$$P_1(t+1)=(1-\beta)P_1(t)+\alpha[1-P_1(t)]$$

Here $\beta$ is the average of the negative-value terms over all $n-k$ "punishing" operators and $\alpha$ is the average of all positive-value terms over the $k$ rewarding operators. The special cases $\alpha=0$ and $\beta=0$ recover the two main forms of the linear operator, now interpreted as an aggregated effect on our actor as a consequence of the combination of sanction significant reactions of the others. For some systems, parameters $\alpha$ and $\beta$ will be time-variable. As an example, consider studying the emergence of norms. If $A_1$ is a symbolic expression of a normative sentiment and $A_2$ is some alternative, then the network process is generating a time varying system state $S(t)$ of probabilistic dispositions concerning a potential group norm. With the reactions of alters varying with time (agreement counting as reward), the numbers $k$ and $n-k$ will be outcomes that are functions of time, producing time-varying $\alpha$ and $\beta$. Granted the complications, by such procedural extensions of the coupling procedure to the general case, we can derive generative models of emergent social structure.

Obviously, there are problematic aspects of this otherwise attractive approach to the theoretical analysis of dynamical interaction systems that may serve to deter the potential analyst from employing it.

First, even the relatively simple basic adaptive behavior theoretical model is sufficiently complex as to make it difficult to derive any definite theorems about it. With eight equations, the tasks are mathematically even more formidable with just two actors. Thus, the first problem is that the sheer mathematical complexity that arises in even the simplest models makes it difficult to derive general propositions.

Second, I showed earlier that there is a way to interpret Homans's general propositions in relation to the adaptive behavior model. But this was in the form of tentative suggestion rather than the construction of a theoretical model simultaneously incorporating all the elements (e.g., situational similarity, expectations, and the effects of emotional elements). Thus, in the interactive model just presented, these additional mechanisms were not included; only the basic adaptive mechanism was postulated for each actor. The first problem is thus compounded. Without the additional mechanisms, we do not have a comprehensive theory, the sort of formal apparatus that would accomplish what Homans is trying to do. In a sense this is a critique of Homans, for if we find it so difficult to deduce the behavior of the system using mathematics or computer experimentation, what can words accomplish that mathematics or computation fails to do?

The answer is not far away: It can persuade us without rigorous demonstration that some consequence is likely. Thus, Homans's ''deductive systems'' of explanations (Homans, 1974:8–13) are, as he indicates, ''explanation sketches.'' What Homans failed to reckon, however, was that without a formal representation of these basic mechanisms, the whole theory would be received as an exercise in tautology. In defense, in his 1974 revision that responds to some criticisms of the 1961 effort, Homans notes that some of the same charges could be made about forces in classical mechanics, with the same invalidity. And I think he is right: If you frame the foundational ideas of adaptive behavior in mathematical terms, you do get testable consequences, there is no doubt about it. You generate the trajectory of the state over time and, in some cases, you discover analytically what may be expected by way of equilibrium. Also, you measure the values of the rewards: Certain parameters are estimated in the process of applying particular models. Thus, *in principle*, Homans's basic idea of generating the properties of dynamical social interactive systems from coupled dynamical adaptive systems makes sense. It is the complexity of it all that makes continued efforts so daunting and makes the other wing of adaptively rational action theory appear all the more attractive. On the other hand, the situation of analytical complexity will arise in any theoretical tradition, and one should not retreat from it on such grounds.

What we are faced with is a set of assumptions, expressed formally, without a clear idea of what they imply about the dynamics of interaction under given conditions. For such cases, the modern development of high-speed computation implemented on microcomputers as well as larger mainframe computers can be a tool for thought experiments. A theoretician can conduct thought experiments with a model in the sense that by setting the parameters to certain values and specifying the initial conditions, what-if questions become answerable. At present, we cannot ask for programs that answer general questions such as: Under what parametric conditions is a specified equilibrium state stable? Thought experiments, instead, take the form: Suppose the initial conditions were such and such. Then what would the dynamics of interaction be? Would a particular equilibrium state be approached? Would there be oscillations? At present most theorists in sociology think of computers as handmaidens of data analysis and as having little or nothing to do with theoretical work. The point of what follows is that for the future development of general theoretical sociology, the use of computers by theorists is essential. Even so, a full-scale simulation study will not be undertaken here. Instead, I shall highlight some important elements of such a computer-assisted analysis of a theoretical model.

What is the logic of the analysis? The model object, as a formal entity, is embodied in a computer program. Parameters are specified; and initial states,

| | $B_1$ Cooperate | $B_2$ Defect |
|---|---|---|
| $A_1$ Cooperate | $E_{11}$ $(R, R)$ | $E_{12}$ $(S, T)$ |
| $A_2$ Defect | $E_{21}$ $(T, S)$ | $E_{22}$ $(P, P)$ |

Figure 3.5 Prisoner's Dilemma

set. ''Runs'' of the program tell us what event histories emerge under those conditions. With probabilistic models we must repeat the process and look at the event histories and the averages. We conclude with some statements that in some sense summarize the ''data'' generated by the theoretical process.

On the one hand, we are learning something about the implications of the theoretical system as it was implemented in the particular theoretical model. On the other hand, we are learning something about the world in a hypothetical form: If the world were to operate as posited, then such and such would be the results. This latter step provides some *insights* into the nature of the world via the study of the model.[37]

### *3.6.3. Computer-assisted analysis of theoretical models: an example for the iterated Prisoner's Dilemma*

To illustrate the idea of the computer experiment as a tool of theoretical investigation that complements mathematical analysis of a model, I select a particular abstract type of situation that has been of special interest to social scientists, the iterated two-person Prisoner's Dilemma.

Although general *n*-person versions can be constructed, the typical focus in Prisoner's Dilemma analyses is on the two-person case in which each person has a choice between two actions. One way to describe the actions (see Boudon, 1981) is that the choice is between being cooperative or being aggressive. Another and similar interpretation, employed by Axelrod (1984), is that each actor has a choice between cooperating and defecting. Figure 3.5 shows the way in which the game matrix is structured using Axelrod's terminology and notation.

Axelrod notes that the payoffs must satisfy the condition:

$$T > R > P > S$$

The dilemma can be seen from $A$'s viewpoint, which is symmetric with $B$'s viewpoint. Suppose that $A$ knows that $B$ will be cooperative. Then by selecting action $A_2$, defecting, $A$ can gain because payoff $T$ (temptation) exceeds the reward $(R)$ for mutual cooperation. Now suppose that $A$ knows that $B$ will defect. Again, it pays $A$ to do action $A_2$ because the sucker's payoff $(S)$ is worse than the punishment $(P)$. Thus, it would seem, it is ''rational'' for $A$ to defect. Symmetrically, it is rational for $B$ to defect. But then mutual punishment occurs. This outcome is ''irrational,'' since by cooperating they could have guaranteed better payoffs for each. This, in a nutshell, is the dilemma, with its fascinating abstract resemblance to the collective irrationalities of arms races, for instance.

In a brilliant study of the logic of this situation, Axelrod uses a thought-experimental or simulation approach somewhat different than the one I use. He solicited recommended optimal strategies for repeated plays of this game under the same conditions. Computer programs embodying strategy recommendations were sent to him, and he used them to simulate repeated plays, calculating the benefits to the simulated players. The fundamental result is that the simplest possible strategy, ''tit for tat,'' wins over all competing strategies. It is the best of the many strategies submitted for doing as best as one can as a player in this type of game. At each time, the tit-for-tat rule is simply this: Cooperate on the first play of the game, and then, if the other player cooperated last time, cooperate with the other now; if the other defected last time, then defect now. Axelrod's study represents a rational action approach to the problem of theoretical analysis of the iterated Prisoner's Dilemma game.

The approach taken here is to model this situation by supposing that each actor is adaptively rational in the sense of the behavioral model. No optimization is involved.

We need to identify the forms of the linear operators for each of the four possible joint events. The action process for $A$ is described in terms of the adaptive model with $P_1$ and $P_2$ as the probabilities of $A_1$ and $A_2$, respectively. The action process for $B$ is described in terms of the adaptive model with $Q_1$ and $Q_2$ as the probabilities of $B_1$ and $B_2$, respectively. Payoffs will not be employed directly. Instead the parameters of the equations, with their value interpretations, correspond to the various sanction significances of the payoffs. Corresponding to the positively evaluated outcomes $R$ and $T$ are positive-value parameters denoted $a$ and $c$, respectively. Corresponding to the negatively evaluated outcomes $S$ and $P$ are negative-value parameters denoted $-b$ and $-d$, respectively. To reflect the ordering of the payoffs, we must have the ordering $c > a > -d > -b$.

Parameters are subscripted to indicate that they need not be the same for the pair. The probability of the event $E_{ij}(t)$ is given by the product $P_i(t)Q_j(t)$ for any $t$.

The four sets of adaptive action equations, one set per possible joint event, are

$E_{11}$: Both cooperate ($A_1$, $B_1$).

Since both are rewarded, the adaptive behavior equations are

$$P_1(t+1)=P_1(t)+a_1[1-P_1(t)]$$
$$Q_1(t+1)=Q_1(t)+a_2[1-Q_1(t)]$$

$E_{12}$: $A$ cooperates, $B$ defects ($A_1$, $B_2$).

Player $A$ gets the sucker's payoff, which corresponds to the negative-value term $-b_1$. Since $B$ gets the temptation ($T$) payoff, $B$ is rewarded, and this reward has greater value than in the $R$ case as reflected by the value parameter $c_2$ being greater than $a_2$. Thus action $B_2$ is reinforced, and by using the relation $Q_1=1-Q_2$, we write the equation in terms of $Q_1$ (with similar procedure in the other cases to follow) so that the system state ($P_1$, $Q_1$) can be traced out over time:

$$P_1(t+1)=P_1(t)-b_1P_1(t)$$
$$Q_1(t+1)=Q_1(t)-c_2Q_1(t)$$

$E_{21}$: $A$ defects, $B$ cooperates ($A_2$, $B_1$).

The argument is symmetric to that given for $E_{12}$, with parameter $c_1>a_1$.

$$P_1(t+1)=P_1(t)-c_1P_1(t)$$
$$Q_1(t+1)=Q_1(t)-b_2Q_1(t)$$

$E_{22}$: Both $A$ and $B$ defect ($A_2$, $B_2$).

Each is punished. The punishment is not, however, as severe as in the case of sucker's payoff; so the negative-value parameter for the sucker's payoff is greater in absolute value than that for mutual defection (i.e., $b_i>d_i$, $i=1, 2$):

$$P_1(t+1)=P_1(t)+d_1[1-P_1(t)]$$
$$Q_1(t+1)=Q_1(t)+d_2[1-Q_1(t)]$$

Note that the probability state $P_1=1$, $Q_1=1$ is an equilibrium state of the system. For if this is the state, then $E_{11}$ is sure to occur. But then each of the two operators implies that the probability remains unity. However, it it unlikely that this is a unique equilibrium.[38]

Let us explore questions related to this implied equilibrium state of certain mutual cooperation. Is it stable? This question is not well put, however. We know that in investigating dynamical systems, a general problem is to investigate the parametric conditions under which a given equilibrium is stable. Unfortunately, the current model is too complex to permit a mathematically general answer, a theorem. Instead, we resort to simulations to investigate the behavior of the system near equilibrium. But this we can do only under *particular* parametric conditions. With a full-scale simulation study, we can carefully explore all the regions of parameter space suggested by theory as potentially distinct. Short of that and by way of illustration of the logic of this kind of computer-assisted theoretical analysis of the model, we can answer the particular question, Is the specified equilibrium state stable under these conditions? Even here particularity intrudes: We have to select a variety of initial states and see if, no matter what the initial state, the process gravitates toward the equilibrium state. But, again, this is a serious problem of careful analysis of regions that might be chosen, that is, by specified distances from the equilibrium state. Short of that, we can look at simulated interactions that begin to suggest the existence of stability or negate it.

*Experiment A*. Suppose each person in a dyad has the identical value parameters given by

$$a = .6, \quad b = .8, \quad c = .7, \quad d = .5$$

Suppose further that such persons interact over a series of occasions, say, 30, starting more or less near the equilibrium state of certain mutual cooperation. Then what would happen? We consider 25 pairs in the identical initial state and let each interact over 30 occasions. We select as initial states the following three sets of values:

$$\begin{aligned} &\text{Experiment } A_1: \quad P_1(0) = .9, \quad Q_1(0) = .9 \\ &\text{Experiment } A_2: \quad P_1(0) = .5, \quad Q_1(0) = .5 \\ &\text{Experiment } A_3: \quad P_1(0) = .1, \quad Q_1(0) = .1 \end{aligned}$$

A program was written to embody the model. We insert the parameter values required for experiment $A$ and do three experiments. Each experiment has 25 pairs of simulated actors interacting 30 times from the specified initial conditions.

The results are interesting. In experiment $A_1$, where initially the pair is near equilibrium, after a short transient period of only a few times, *each* of the 25 pairs moves quickly toward the probability state (1, 1), that is, toward mutual cooperation. Only one pair showed any oscillations of probability states over an extended time period, but even here by time 20 the probabilities had returned to the original values and then moved rapidly toward unity. The average probability of cooperative action by player $A$ and also by player $B$ drops initially but then climbs rapidly to over .9 by $t=6$ and then increases, although not monotonically, toward unity. The exchange ratio (earlier defined as $P_1/Q_1$) is unity in equilibrium. For each pair, it is also usually close to unity before equilibrium is reached. For the average probabilities, it is very close to unity at all time points.

In experiment $A_2$, the initial state is one of equally likely orientation to cooperation and defection. In 23 of the 25 pairs, the behavior is that of more or less rapid approach to certain mutual cooperation, probability state (1, 1). In two of the pairs, oscillations characterize the interactions for an extensive time period. In one case, after an initial transient period, the oscillation is an alternation between approximately .55 and .15 for each actor, accompanied by $E_{21}$, $E_{22}$, and $E_{12}$ events, until an $E_{11}$ event is generated and the probabilities jump to above .9 at $t=28$ and then generate further $E_{11}$ events that further increase the cooperative orientation, that is, $P_1$ and $Q_1$. In the other case, the process again showed alternation between .5 and .1, with accompanying events involving defections; then at $t=23$, an $E_{11}$ event occurred and carried the cooperative orientation to above .9 in likelihood for each actor. Then, even though this was followed by the highly probable $E_{11}$ once again and even though this further increased the cooperation probabilities, at $t=29$ the unlikely happened: $E_{21}$. This increased the probability of defection by each party followed by an $E_{12}$ event that further reduced the cooperative orientations. At $t=30$, when the process was halted, this pair had gotten into the drastic condition of nearly .9 probabilities for *defection* on each side. Of course, since both are punished by mutual defection, the model implies they will increase their probabilities of cooperation. But at least as far as the exchange was taken in time, the pair did not move into, or even near, the equilibrium state of mutual cooperation. The average probability state over time drops initially from (.5, .5) and then climbs above it by $t=4$, after which it climbs toward unity but not monotonically. For instance, the average probability of the cooperative action at $t=10$ is about .85 for both $A$ and $B$, but at $t=11$ it is about .73 for each, climbing back up to about .82 at the following time. As in experiment $A_1$, the exchange ratio is usually close to unity throughout the process.

Experiment $A_3$ begins far from *this* equilibrium state (1, 1). I emphasize the particular equilibrium because, in general, we suspect multiple equilibria, and so we may have selected an initial condition close to some alternative equilibrium state of the system. But in 21 of 25 pairs, there is more or less rapid absorption into the state of certain mutual cooperation. Of course, in these pairs, the exchange ratio stays close to unity throughout the process. One pair alternates from high to low probabilities of cooperation by each actor throughout the duration studied. At $t=10$, for instance, $P_1$ sinks to .02, although it had been .96 at $t=6$. The problem is that even though it was unlikely, a defection occurred at $t=7$, ''bouncing'' the ''sucker's'' orientation away from cooperation (from .96 to .29). Of course, the magnitudes of such bounces, or jumps, in state depend on the values of the actors, the particular parameters. The bounces also throw off the exchange ratio, so that it oscillates from about 1.5, favorable to *B*, to about 0.7, favorable to *A*, since each is favored by the generation of more probable cooperative action by the other. Another pair exhibited this sort of oscillation or bounce until about $t=20$, when a long string of events involving some defection was broken by a cooperative event $E_{11}$ that increased the cooperative orientations of each actor. Thereafter, the process approached the equilibrium state, with corresponding equal exchange, that is, an exchange ratio of unity. Two other pairs showed similar behavior. The curve of average probabilities quickly moves to the (.5, .5) region in a couple of occasions, then .6–.7-type orientations prevail for a few time periods. By $t=10$, the average probabilities are in the region around (.8, .8) and by $t=22$, they are near to (.95, .95). Again, there is a ''secular trend'' of increase but not a strictly increasing function of time. The exchange ratio for this average process is close to unity at all time points.

Our first thought experiment seems to point toward the stability of mutual cooperation under the particular parametric conditions. Although some variation by initial state exists and within any given initial state the stochastic process generates some exchange relations that may take a very long time to reach equilibrium, the hypothesis suggested by the experiment is that for the particular parameter values, no matter what the initial state, the process eventually takes the state of the system into mutual cooperation.

But this immediately raises a question leading to our second thought experiment: What if the values of the actors were quite different from those underlying the parameters of experiment *A*?

*Experiment B*. This experiment uses the parameter values

$$a=.2, \quad b=.4, \quad c=.3, \quad d=.1$$

Also, two initial conditions are considered:

$$\text{Experiment } B_1\text{:} \quad P_1(0)=.5, \quad Q_1(0)=.5$$
$$\text{Experiment } B_2\text{:} \quad P_1(0)=.9, \quad Q_1(0)=.9$$

A third experiment was not done because these two were sufficient to answer the question. That is, if we can find *any* reasonably nearby initial conditions such that the process does not move toward the equilibrium, we know that it is unstable.

Absorption into state (1, 1) occurred in only one of the 25 pairs in experiment $B_1$. The problem appears to be that even when $E_{11}$ occurs, it does not have the sort of jump effect as a mutual reward as in experiment $A$, given the low value of $a$. Similarly, $E_{22}$ is just not that punishing, comparing $d$ here to $d$ of experiment $A$. The result is that the pairs do not show initial oscillation followed by "homing in" on the mutually rewarding behavior. The average probability curves (for $P_1$ and for $Q_1$) reflect this: Each is fairly stationary, varying between about .3 and .4. Although a lot of detection is occurring, it does not mean as much, in sanction terms, as under the earlier parametric conditions. The exchange ratios behave quite differently than in experiment $A$: The usual pair shows an undulating curve in which there is a phase favorable to actor $A$ followed by a phase favorable to $B$ and back again. Thus, the exchange ratio exhibits a cyclic behavior. For the average probability states, this cyclic behavior is concealed: The relatively small variations in the averages create a nearly unity exchange ratio throughout the process.

Experiment $B_2$ begins close to equilibrium. It confirms the instability of this equilibrium under these parametric conditions in terms of leaving an even smaller neighborhood of certain mutual cooperation. The problem is that with such relatively small values placed on cooperation, even a long string of $E_{11}$ events produces not so much a bounce as a slow growth in cooperative orientation. Similarly, the low negative value of mutual defection does not generate a bounce toward cooperation, only a positive marginal increase. For instance, in one pair, the state at time $t=11$ was (.12, .15), and this was followed by a string of five $E_{22}$ events, taking the state to (.48, .50), that is, only equal likelihood of cooperation or defection on each side. This was followed by a string of six $E_{11}$ events yielding a state of (.86, .87). However, an assortment of successful temptations ($E_{12}$ or $E_{21}$ events) dropped the state back down to (.13, .18) only a few time periods later. Eleven of the 25 pairs, however, approached equilibrium. They typically began with a string of the highly probable $E_{11}$ events that made such future events all the more likely. Yet, a few cases illustrate the stochastic element dramatically in terms of "anything can happen" as long as cooperative actions are not certain. In one pair, the initial string of $E_{11}$ events carried the state to (.95, .95) by the close of occasion $t=3$. Yet a successful defection occurred ($E_{12}$) at $t=4$, dropping the state to (.57, .66). Although it later climbed back up into the .8 region on each side, when the process was halted, the pair was in the .2 region on each side. In another such case, the highly improbable did in fact occur: After a string of $E_{11}$ events from the start to $t=20$, bringing each state variable into the .99 region, a successful defection ($E_{21}$) threw off the process, and at the close the state was (.24, .33). The remaining 14 of the 25 pairs exhibited no convergence and showed the pattern of cyclic undulation of exchange ratio. The average probabilities show a slow secular trend downward from the initial .9 on each side to the .6 region on each side, with near unity of the exchange ratio.

The first experiment showed that for some parametric conditions, the state of certain mutual cooperation is stable; the second experiment showed that for some parametric conditions, that equilibrium state is unstable. What the limited computational character of the thought experiments cannot show is the general rule for how the configuration of parametric conditions determines stability or instability. Only a vastly more complex simulation study could possibly suggest such a rule. A third thought experiment, called *C*, was natural to explore a question that arises: So far we have assumed equal parameters for each actor, but what if we assume they are different? In particular, suppose one of them has values like experiment *A* and the other like the *B* case? On one side, the parameter configuration would favor a mutual cooperation stable equilibrium; on the other side, an unstable situation would be likely. What will happen if two such actors interact?

*Experiment C.* This experiment is defined by the parameter configuration:

$$\begin{array}{ll} \text{Actor } A\text{:} & a_1 = .6, \quad b_1 = .8, \quad c_1 = .7, \quad d_1 = .5 \\ \text{Actor } B\text{:} & a_2 = .2, \quad b_2 = .4, \quad c_2 = .3, \quad d_2 = .1 \end{array}$$

Two initial states were explored:

$$\begin{array}{ll} \text{Experiment } C_1\text{:} & P_1(0) = Q_1(0) = .5 \\ \text{Experiment } C_2\text{:} & P_1(0) = Q_1(0) = .9 \end{array}$$

Experiment $C_1$ yielded no convergence in any of the 25 pairs. The process bounces considerably for actor *A*, whose greater value parameters produce greater change of state than in the case of B given the same event. Thus, although there is in-phase oscillation, in the sense that they rise and fall together, the magnitudes of the highs and lows are more extreme for actor *A*. The exchange ratio in most pairs exhibits a very rapid fluctuation from favoring A to favoring B and back again. Yet the magnitudes of favorability are not equal. This shows up in the average states: The exchange ratio for the averages is greater than unity at every time point $t \geq 2$. (It stays in the neighborhood of about 1.4.) Thus, actors in the *A* role are generating, on average, more cooperative behavior than they get in return. The process is biased in favor of actor *B*, who is more indifferent. This closely resembles the *principle of least interest* advanced by Waller and Hill (1951:191): "That person is able to dictate the conditions of association whose interest in the continuation of the affair is least.'' [The principle is a famous one, quoted by Thibaut and Kelley (1959:103) and then by Homans (1974:73).] Thus, the simulation suggests that the theoretical model has a set of parametric conditions under which the exchange relation is biased in favor of one party over the other.[39]

Experiment $C_2$ begins close to the equilibrium state of certain mutual cooperation. It appears that the probability of absorption into the equilibrium state is about one-half, since 13 of the 25 pairs did exhibit convergence to (1, 1). The others exhibited the pattern of oscillation found in Experiment $C_1$. The bias in favor of actors in the $B$ role continues to show up, in terms of the average probabilities, but takes a little longer to display itself and is not as strong: The exchange ratio is about 1.1 for all $t \geq 8$. The reduction in the amount of bias obviously is a consequence of the fact that half of the pairs rather rapidly developed the pattern of equal exchange, which is the certain mutual cooperation state of the system.

This concludes my illustrative examples of thought experiments by computers, the simulation method of studying theoretical models. Further such study of the iterated Prisoner's Dilemma situation using coupled adaptively rational action models seems a quite interesting task to put on the agenda for future work. Also, with better reflection of Homans's comprehensive theory of adaptive behavior in the interactive context, the element of emotional reactions might be included, treating them along lines suggested in note 33. The results of such a full-scale simulation study could be compared with the theory and results of Axelrod (1984), as well as with efforts to model game situations in the framework of a dynamic utility principle. (See, e.g., Rapoport, 1966:Ch. 10.)

## 3.7. Concluding discussion

This chapter has consisted of three contributions to action theory. Within the comprehensive tradition of general theoretical sociology, we cannot say that we possess some uniquely accepted theory of action. Instead, there are some ''branches'' that possess some common roots in classical theory but diverge at various points.

What I have called analytical action theory is rooted in the classics and the convergence argument made by Parsons. He tried to wed the action frame of reference to the idea that a theoretical science must deal with a class of systems. My interpretation treats these systems in terms of the logic of dynamical systems analysis. Within this framework, the most important single idea of analytical action theory is expressed by the control principle of action in its negative-feedback form. Action is subject to dynamic normative control. This implies that there is no such thing as action apart from some normative element. But as was made clear in the formal model, there is no such thing as action apart from some situational condition element. The balance of ideal and real, subjective and objective, voluntarism and constraint can be maintained if the proper model object is adopted and all reasoning about single actors and about social interactive systems is about complexes of such coupled models.

The use of the control principle to model cybernetic hierarchy leads to a picture of successive layers of normative control running from values to norms to goals to operations yielding outputs to the situation of action that have the meaning implied in this generative process. This led to the idea that the control principle of action implies a network of active hierarchically organized actors. The nodes are actor–situation units engaged in dynamic normative control of each other's conduct. The important implications of this representation principle, in reference to the problems described at the end of Chapter 2, include the derivation of a template, a generic form for the social generator.

The representation of the AGIL scheme as an abstract form of a class of dynamical systems led to a discussion focused on what was called the general dynamical social action system. In particular, it was shown how the adaptation–integration dimensions of the dynamical social system of Chapter 2 can be embedded within a set of four social subdimensions. An attempt was made to provide an interpretation for such AGIL models in terms of the control principle of action. This included the statement of an interpretable social order theorem conjecture based on Parsons's work. Finally, the topics of interpenetration and analytical perspectives based on the AGIL scheme were discussed. Various criticisms of the framework were suggested: Most important, a certain incoherence arises in trying to relate the four cybernetic functions to the four Parsonian dimensions.

Structural–generative action theory, as I call it, has its roots in modern developments in cognitive science and in the realist philosophy of science that has been congenial to the understanding of this approach. But it is readily adapted to an interpretive sociological mode of thought. The underlying model object is not a behavior manifold but a space of constitutively defined types of entities with situated action productions organized into systems. The focus on operative ideals normatively controlling action, typical of analytical action theory, shifts to interpretive procedures as productions operating with features of tacit knowledge structures. A variety of connecting links were tentatively proffered between elements in the heritage of interpretive sociology and the idea of generation of action via production rules.

The same formalism of production systems applies to analytical action theory to represent the structure of action systems. In fact, if we consider analytical action theory as presented by Parsons and by current neofunctionalist authors (Alexander, 1985), the striking absence of any sort of representation of concrete structures of social action is remarkable. The word *concrete* here refers back to Parsons (1937:Ch. 1), where he discusses modes of conceptualization. One mode involves types of concrete units and their structural relations. A second mode involves analytical elements (state variables and parameters) and their analytical relationships. Structures rooted in the production rule as the elementary concrete unit of situated action have the sort of concreteness that characterizes network representations, now widely recognized as vital to our field.[40] In Section 3.4.3, the representation of the structure of a social action system in terms of production rules as nodes was shown to lead to the idea of a functional network in which nodes are in an important processual relation: The products of one production reappear as factors of action in another production via some structural exchange process. Such a concrete representation of action structures is necessary from the point of view of structural–generative action theory.

Neither the discussion of analytical nor of structural–generative action models provided an opportunity to explore in detail the idea of coupling actor models to derive a dynamical social system generator. The adaptively rational action theory, covered in its behavioral form in Sections 3.5 and 3.6, provides a basis for this mode of generativity.

In my interpretation, there are two types of theories that treat action change as adaptively rational action. One is in the rational choice or utility theory tradition and is best represented within sociology by Coleman (1973). The other is the behavioral type developed especially by Homans (and also Emerson) on the basis of ideas drawn from the general analysis of behavior. In the versions presented here, I only sketched one example of a utility-based exchange theory. I tried to explicate the basic idea of fusing utility theory and dynamical systems with the principle of action change in-the-small in the direction of increasing utility.

The major effort was with the second type of theory. The representation principle is that the probability of action changes as a function of the sanction significance of its consequences for the actor. This amounts to a single-actor model of adaptive action described by stochastic linear operators. In the coupling procedure, each actor in the interactive nexus is described by a set of such operators. The coupling arises through the common situation and the fact that the action of each counts as a sanction-significant reaction to the other. This whole process was illustrated through the study of the implied dynamics and equilibria of a coupled adaptive interaction model for the iterated Prisoner's Dilemma. In this context, the methodological point was stressed that computer-assisted analysis of theoretical models is vital to the further development of general theoretical sociology.

At present, no claim is made that these three wings of action theory neatly fit under one comprehensive action theory. But neither are they mutually exclusive alternatives for such a role. I have already discussed (in Section 3.4.3) some elements of the connection between the analytical and interpretive branches of action theory when viewed in the context of structural–generative theory. Adaptively rational action theory – in its behavioral manifestation – might be regarded in two ways relative to the other two.

First, its equilibria could be interpreted to correspond to novel productions. After all, for a given situation each actor is adapting and eventually (under some parametric conditions) stabilizing behavior. The resulting pairs of situation–action links are stochastic, that is, in the situation an action occurs with a certain probability. This is not quite the same as our institutional interpretation of productions, but it is close enough to make one think that the two can be connected with further formal and conceptual work. Stochastic production systems would be analogous to the probabilistic grammars suggested within formal linguistics (Suppes, 1969:Ch. 23).

Second, if the action is goal oriented and the goal is given, then the adaptive process is concerned with the discovery of actions that are adaptively rational with respect to the goal. Such goals serve to define which outcomes count as rewards or successes and which do not. Thus, they are a kind of higher order entity. Then we can interpret the adaptive process as corresponding to the *A*-dimensional level relative to an immediately superordinate *G*-dimensional level in a Parsonian AGIL cybernetic hierarchy single-actor model. Such a connection seems reasonable. Obviously, this is no substitute for the conceptual and formal effort to genuinely integrate the two modes of approaching social action. If the action is expressive, then an explicit goal is probably irrelevant; in Parsons's (1937) terms, the means–end connection is symbolic, not intrinsic. This was the case, for instance, in the example of the exchange of supportiveness (or not) considered earlier. Here the model seems to provide the action basis for the development of the internal or integration system of a more complete dynamical social system. Indeed, the exchange of supportiveness or warmth, if it occurs, is a Collins-type interaction ritual chain spread over time that yields an integrative bond. It is a particular case of ritual solidarity, the key feature of Durkheimian depth sociology. The actors are in a ''social'' relation in the sense of a pattern of interaction found in their repeated encounters, a pattern characterized by diffuseness and affectivity, a reciprocity of supportiveness. We might add particularism in that they come to feel a membership relation to the collective entity they constitute. Then they are a little community in the precise sense of the integration or communal subdimension of the social dimension in the AGIL scheme. A related point is that the line of development of Homans's own thought from the 1950 systems concept of the group to the 1961 first edition of the exchange theory of interaction is nothing but a twofold step: (1) simply take the external system state as given and (2) show, via interactive coupling, how the internal system generates emergent social structure. The passage to verbal axiomatics and the polemical philosophical remarks are relatively unimportant compared with these substantive elements.

For a three-way synthesis we would require conceptual consistency and formal unification of (1) the AGIL scheme and the negative-feedback interpretation of the control principle of action, (2) the production principle of institutions with accompanying universal interpretive procedures, and (3) the adaptively rational theory of action with its stochastic operators. Each of these ingredients is not yet well developed. Also, the corresponding subtraditions include extensive ramified applications of the general ideas to all sorts of topics, corresponding to the theoretical model level in the image of theory presented in this book. Most of these topics have not been treated here, for good reason: The formalisms are at the baby stage, whereas from an empirical viewpoint, none of the three theories has really "proven its mettle" (Popper, 1959). Thus, real work on unification would be premature. (For a related discussion, see Section 4.9.3.)

Finally, the dynamic utility type of theory sketched in Section 3.5.2 must be considered in any overall assessment of the possibilities for a unification episode. Its analytical power is attractive to formal theorists, but there are other reasons for taking it seriously, as I explain in closing this chapter.

Sociologists such as Coleman (1973, 1986) and Lindenberg (1985, 1986) are making a strong case for some version of the rational choice approach as a workable action-theoretical basis for sociology. In his writings, Boudon (1981) tried to show that a generalized rational theory is implicit in the classics. Rational choice theorists have shown ways to incorporate self-interested motivation and collectivity-oriented motivation into the quantitative utility framework (Margolis, 1982). The work of Schelling (1971, 1978) has been a powerful exemplar in demonstrating the conceptual beauty and payoff of the approach. Contemporary sociologists who use a generalized rational choice theory stress that they wish to "bridge" (Wippler and Lindenberg, 1987) macrosocial conditions and the analytical components of a choice situation. Essentially, this means using the model by supplying a specific social menu of possible actions and, for instance, rooting the preferences in social position, including group memberships. Surprising aggregate results are obtained from such uses of the rational choice model. For instance, Schelling (1971) shows how a slight preference to live near one's own social kind can generate, over time, a completely segregated residential area. Another example of a model with surprising aggregate or emergent outcomes is Granovetter's (1978) collective behavior model, which was inspired in part by

Schelling's work. And in the work of Coleman (1973) contemporary rational choice theory builds a relational element into the framework. So we have action, we have dynamics, and we have a social structural focus. And the key principle stated earlier, that action change in-the-small is in the direction of increasing utility, is analytically powerful. Thus, at its best the approach exhibits the logic advocated in this book: Start with a dynamic action model and then couple models of actors to derive social systemic outcomes.[41]

This brief discussion of rational choice as an action theory for sociology will serve to remind the reader that despite the variety of concepts and methods treated in this chapter, only a portion of the vast proliferating developments of relevant theory have been the focus of formalizing efforts here.[42] Also, although linkages among the frameworks have been made and others suggested, none of this is an example of effective theoretical unification. This raises a question: What are the requirements for such an effective unification episode? In the next chapter, this question will be addressed in another theoretical context. The formalization occurs within a framework defined by structuralist presuppositions and a representation principle that will be found to have wide scope. Two theories are formalized as families of theoretical models within this framework, and then a unified theoretical model is displayed. It will be a particular episode of realization of the twin objectives toward which all the work of this book points: formal modes of representation and theoretical unification.

# 4. Structuralism and unification

## 4.1. Introduction

In Chapter 1, a philosophy of theoretical sociology was set out. A process worldview was described, and the claim was made that it, or some very similar process philosophy, is a high-order component of the research tradition of general theoretical sociology. In Chapter 2, this process worldview led to a conception of dynamical social systems. Four types of theorems were described, each an aspect of the analysis of any dynamical social system model. These theorems concern the emergence and forms of social structure, the attractor or repellor classification of such structures, the systematic comparison of attractor structures, and the change of such structures, including both smooth and catastrophic transformations over time. Employing the emerging "do's" and "don'ts" of the general theoretical sociology tradition, two conceptual problems were noted in this development of dynamical social systems theory. These two problems provide the foci for the investigations, respectively, in the preceding chapter and in this chapter.

The two problems pertain to action theory and structuralism, respectively. The first problem leads to a call for an intelligible explanatory basis for theoretical sociology. Formally, we require generativity. Substantively, we require a model of the single actor entering into interaction. This focus on generativity and action was the basis for the studies in action theory in Chapter 3. It must not be thought that the concern with action theory is in some way a *lack* of concern with social structure. The dichotomy is a false one. Action theories employ action principles instrumentally to make intelligible conceptual moves to the level of interaction. The focus is on how social interaction generates social structure or how social structure shapes or guides the process of social interaction. Thus, as a matter of orientation, theoretical models of this sort have been framed as intrinsically concerned with social structure. *Nevertheless,* as pointed out at the close of Chapter 2 and shown in detail in Section 3.6, when definite model objects are set up and the procedure of coupling is employed, the logical starting point is the *pair* of actors in interaction. There is no permanent commitment to this level, but it is a natural starting point because it is the simplest social system within the scope of the general problem. Then the complexities of the approach even at this starting point, as shown in the case of coupled adaptively rational action models, tend to inhibit rapid movement toward larger systems.

This takes us to *structuralism* and the present chapter. To locate the work to be undertaken in this chapter, a preliminary background discussion of various structuralist approaches and their relation to the approach taken in this book is required.

In Section 1.4.2, in the context of discussing the realist philosophical model of explanation, three modes of generativity were described: combinations of [illegible] defining generators of dynamical systems, combinations of rules defining grammars that generate formal or natural languages, and hybrid systems of production rules that generate normal forms of interaction.

The third type of generativity was the basis for what was called structural–generative action theory in Chapter 3. It uses the computational model of mind and provides a realist model of society as a vast hierarchically organized system of distributed systems of production rules generating normal forms of interaction and keeping them on track through universal interpretive procedures. It was argued in Chapter 3 that this type of realist model provides a potentially significant basis for formalization of the key ideas of both interpretive sociology and their unification with analytical action theory.

The second type of generativity has not been utilized in this book. It is part of the wider zeitgeist that emerged after World War II in which explicit studies of symbol systems through formal models became prominent. The fundamental idea is, to use Harré's (1970) distinction, that the *source* of models is language, whereas the *subject* is any conceptual totality of cultural items represented as what is generated by something like a generative–transformational grammar. So structuralism in one of its meanings has exactly this model-building strategy as its core theme with efforts to model such cultural entities as literature, art, music, myth, and kinship (Levi-Strauss, 1963; Lane, 1970). As such, in this book, this form of structuralism is part of the background for some of the ideas of interpretive sociology as well as for the structural–generative approach itself.

The first type of generativity has been the conceptual basis for Chapter 2 and parts of Chapter 3. This mode of generativity in theoretical model building is not ordinarily regarded as structuralist. Indeed, if variables are defined and related dynamically, nothing about this procedure is especially structural in focus. But in Chapter 2, the whole point was to define such a generative approach relative to an underlying social network over which a behavior manifold is defined. The system state is a complex of substates that ultimately refer to the activity and sentiment elements characterizing interactions between persons or other social units. Social structures are attractor states of such dynamical social systems that may be themselves dynamically varying by virtue of changing parameters, either through internal feedback loops or exogenous sources. This viewpoint incorporates the intuitions of structuralism in the sense employed in this chapter but embeds them in a broader process worldview and corresponding generative process implementations. For this reason, the term *structuralism* was used in Section 3.3 in describing those analytical perspectives that focus on the dynamical social system, understood always in terms compatible with the underlying network image of Chapter 2. In one sense, then, this book has been structuralist in a variety of senses. For this reason the approach, taken as a whole, has been designated *generative structuralism*. What, then, is the special character of the present chapter?

The term is used in this chapter to denote modes of thought whose presupposition levels dictate, through chains of more specific principles and procedures, two fundamental do's and don'ts for sociological analysis:

1. *The theoretical model rule:* Construct theoretical models about social relations, about ties or connections and corresponding processes. Derivations should be about such entities and not about individuals.
2. *The empirical operations rule:* Design empirical studies such that relational data are obtained rather than only data on unconnected units.

The structuralism characterized by these two methodological presuppositions is now coming to be called *structural analysis* by some sociologists.[1] But my interpretation is somewhat wider, leading me to retain the term *structuralism*.

Structuralism, as a research tradition, is often understood primarily in terms of one of its don'ts – implied especially in the empirical operations rule but also in its theoretical model rule – its opposition to an *individualistic* approach in empirical research. This is an individualism totally different from either *institutionalized individualism* (a property of modern social systems) or *methodological individualism* (a property of a theoretical procedure that in this book is represented by coupling single-actor models to derive social interactive models). Unfortunately, there seems to be no distinctive name for it. We might think of it as *research individualism*. Since the 1950s, *empirical social research* had come to mean, in many circles, one thing: the technology of survey research. You take a random sample of a population, ask some questions, get some *background* data, and use statistical inference to draw some conclusions about the population. Actual existing social relations drop through the empirical net back into the ocean of society, whereas the researcher grapples with all the technical issues of drawing inferences about masses of aggregated data about individuals.[2] In this process, the accompanying theories treat social structure as a set of independent variables to explain the dependent variable, which is individual behavior: The theoretical model rule is violated.

Even theorists who feel alienated from the resulting statistical empiricism may internalize this research-individualistic logic and define our problem as one of trying to predict individual behavior. (See, e.g., the early work of Collins, 1975.) Nor are the conceptual limitations of research individualism in any way eliminated if the research produces data on nodes that are organizations, communities, or nations. The resulting formal entity, the model of the data, is still a set of isolated nodes with various measured properties. It is a result of violating the empirical operations rule. It is the data realization of a substance–quality metaphysics as contrasted with the network data realizations of a process worldview (as discussed in Chapter 1) in which the most fundamental features of the actual world are simultaneously processual and relational. To believe this and not act on it, that is the problem of research individualism as a component of the tradition of sociology with its widely accepted process worldview.

The lapse on the part of some theorists toward the conceptual limitations of research individualism is also directly related to their failure to understand the idea of a dynamical social system. And this failure may be a consequence of the near death of the subtradition of Pareto–Homans–Simon. Both Homans and Simon, after the 1950s, developed into action theorists. In fact, Simon became fully committed to the study of the ultimate acting unit with his research shifting to a focus on the cognitive subsystem of the individual actor. Homans retained the focus on social structure, but the logic of the action-theoretical coupling procedure and its difficulties kept the work at an "elementary" level. General theoretical sociology went into its epoch of "paradigms," and a commitment to it as a comprehensive framework with a built-in unification dynamic was all but abandoned.

Thus, neither fundamental theory nor basic research held to the vision of a science of the dynamical social system and its analysis in terms of the four key problems of the emergence, maintenance, comparison, and change of structures of such systems. Structuralism is a reaction to this apparent dual failure. Fortunately, today the problem is no longer one of bringing structure back in. Instead the flowering of structuralist-oriented research presents a problem of sorting it all out. But the present chapter does not aim to provide contributions that relate to all the diverse lines of research in this tradition. For my purposes, two branches of structuralism can be delineated that are not only quite distinct but even to a certain extent in some tension with respect to each other. One basic contribution of the chapter is to forge a link between the two via an episode of unification that follows upon two formalization efforts. These will be described in detail later. At this point I want to provide a brief metatheoretical overview of this suggested image of structuralism and how it relates to the wider image of general theoretical sociology as a single comprehensive research tradition.

The two branches are *network analysis* and *macrostructuralism*. The latter is much simpler to characterize than the first, which involves a number of interrelated research programs that have time-extended histories. By macrostructuralism I mean the commitment, added to the two rules of structuralism, to build theory at a macrosociological level of analysis. Although relations are still a focus, another element looms large: the distribution of units into groups and into strata. Analytical elements are required to describe the properties of such macrostructure, and relations among groups must be defined in terms that appropriately aggregate the relations among their units to arrive at rates. The analytical elements are such that the values they take are invariant when individual units shift position or relation without altering the numerical distribution or rate. The basic theory here is due to Blau (1977) and will be discussed in detail in Section 4.6.

Network analysis adds to the two rules of structuralism a commitment to the study of both direct and indirect ties. The image of a social relation is extensional. That is, the image is one of the pattern of all ties of the given type as simultaneoulsy realized in a population of units. We have not only unit $a$ in relation $R$ to unit $b$ but $b$ in relation $R$ to $c$ and hence an indirect link between $a$ and $c$ that might coexist with a direct link if the relation is "transitive." Not only one but multiple types of relations can be studied from this point of view. So network analysis focuses on the logic of interrelated social ties as such. In short, it starts with *interlock* – the dynamics of any pair depends on the states of other pairs – and builds outward to more complex social structures from the fundamental *triadic* unit in which this phenomenon first makes its appearance. Thus, network analysis addresses quite directly the second conceptual problem, relating to structure, discussed at the end of Chapter 2. Perhaps most typical of network analysis is its insistence that relations have properties: They can be transitive to some degree, symmetrical to some extent, and as realized in a population, characterized in terms of other such formal properties. In turn, a patterning of such properties indicates whether the network takes a certain form, such as a hierarchy.

Network analysis has a long and complex history with many research programs that overlap various disciplines and with many unsettled issues. Leinhardt (1977) includes a sampling of classical papers in this tradition by sociologists, anthropologists, and psychologists. Berkowitz (1981) provides a conceptual survey of some of these developments. Wellman (1983) argues for network analysis as a form of theorizing. Some sense of this history may be given by noting both the empirical content and the formal techniques that have been employed.

A variety of empirical content has characterized the networks studied: kinship analysis (White, 1963); studies in community power structure (Freeman et al., 1963); studies of structures of interpersonal sentiments that ultimately go back to sociometry and structural balance theory (Newcomb, 1953; Cartwright and Harary, 1956) as well as cluster theory (Davis, 1967); studies of diffusion in networks (Rapoport, 1956; Coleman, Katz, and Menzel, 1957) including related mathematical studies from the point of view of stochastic processes (Coleman, 1964; Bartholomew, 1982); studies of structures of relations in markets and other economic contexts (White, 1981; Mintz and Schwartz, 1985); studies of social roles, going beyond role sets (Merton, 1968) to study local networks of families (Bott, 1955); and, to conclude this partial list, studies of the implications of strength of ties among members of a social system (Granovetter, 1973, 1982). In the past decade, Ronald Burt has been especially active in a mode that combines theoretical interests and fine-grained network data analysis [for a sampling, see Burt (1982, 1987)].

The element of formal technique is especially relevant in the present context. The use of graph-theoretical concepts and methods (Harary, Norman, and Cartwright, 1965) has been important. It underlies a large number of distinct contributions, too numerous to begin to cite (see Freeman, 1984). Abstract algebra has been an important tool. In fact, what we might call the *algebraic sociology* of systems of social relations has advanced remarkably. It began when White (1963) went into exhaustive detail on possible kinship structures based on a set of axioms. On this basis and with the inspiration of the work of Boyd (1969), a generalized algebraic approach was described by Lorrain and White (1971). This evolved into block models and related algebras (White, Boorman, and Breiger, 1976). In the following decade, block models were built into empirical research, and algebraic sociology continued to elaborate on the earlier work. (See, e.g., Breiger and Pattison, 1986.)

A formalism combining some aspects of graph theory with a probabilistic approach characterizes much of this chapter. It is *biased network analysis.* The statistical properties of large-scale networks of social relations come under analysis. The approach negates the idea that network analysis is mainly useful for small social systems. Although this idea is valid with regard to many of the computational techniques developed in the network analysis tradition, it misses the conceptual thrust of network analysis and overlooks the notion of structure statistics inherent to the biased network mode of analysis. In a sense, within the broader structuralism tradition with its two rules stated earlier, this biased network framework has the potential to combine the added emphases of macrostructuralism and network analysis, respectively: The intended scope is the very large-scale social system, and the treatment is in terms of the formal properties of patterns of relations within it.

How do we regard structuralism from the comprehensive standpoint of the process worldview? Generally speaking, the most influential contemporary modes of structural analysis focus on structures in abstraction from the generative dynamics that produces such structures. This is both an expedient of scientific division of labor and a reflection of the complexity of dynamical social systems. Ideally, we want a unified theoretical framework in which we can show how under specified conditions the generator yields (1) various possible social structures described by structural analysis (Type 1 theorems); (2) both attractors and repellors in a configuration associated with parametric conditions (Type 2 theorems); (3) varying stable structures according to parametric conditions, which typically would be cultural or biophysical (Type 3 theorems); and (4) dynamical transformations of social structures under continuous change of parameters that control these possible forms of social systems of interaction (Type 4 theorems).

Although contemporary structuralism is relatively weak when viewed in terms of this dynamical system standard, in another sense it does analyze social processes. Namely, the conception of a stable background of parts-in-relations, a social structure, is used to examine social processes conceived as having a fast dynamic against this stable background.[3] For instance, a piece of information, such as a rumor or an ideology, may be conceptualized as moving through a given structure, its movement shaped by that structure. The point is that the processes seen against a stable background can be used to illuminate that background: By watching processes, we can map structures, at least to some extent. In fact, in the study of large-scale structures, it turns out that in the biased network tradition there is a way to analyze these structures that mimics the analysis of a process shaped by a structure. We study an as-it-were process of flow or spread of something through a network. Such an as-it-were process will be termed a *tracing process*. It is not a replacement for the setup and analysis of true dynamic models, but it has a kind of recursive generativity that is suggestive of what might occur in a real process as it informs us about the structure in this particular way.

To sum up this overview of structuralism: Its frameworks are governed by two major presuppositions: the theoretical model rule and the empirical operation rule. Macrostructuralism is one branch of structuralism, and network analysis is another. In turn, network analysis exhibits internal variety both in terms of the empirical content studied and the formal analytical tools employed. From the standpoint of this book, the theoretical aspects of structuralism define a subtradition of the comprehensive tradition of general theoretical sociology, albeit one that interpenetrates other disciplines. As such, the theory in structuralism comes under the superordinate presuppositions of the process worldview. As implemented in our philosophical model of explanation (Section 1.4.3), this puts a premium on trying to develop models featuring generative mechanisms. We seek to implement *generative* structuralism. From this standpoint, structuralism has been relatively weak. The notion of a tracing process analysis is an attempt, probably only partially successful, to implement generativity in a structural analysis context.

In terms of this overview, the topics to be treated in the remainder of this chapter may be outlined.

In Section 4.2, the biased network research program of the social networks branch of structuralism is introduced. The objective is to show how the study of *diffusion* of anything at all against a presumed background of a stable social structure leads to a mode of characterization of that structure. The theoretical method is given by the construction of biased net models. In turn, this leads to the tracing process viewpoint.

In Section 4.3, the conception of spread in a network is related to the concept of *institutionalization,* conceived as a diffusion process in which the object of diffusion is a cultural entity of the social type, that is, a mode of typification with production rules that moves through the social system from some points of origination.

In Section 4.4, the biased network approach is taken a step farther to treat *weak-ties theory* and what is termed the *dilemma of integration* of social systems: Local integration and global integration are in a trade-off relation. The context for exploring this idea involves the demonstration of the theorem on the strength of weak ties, namely, that the strength of such ties lies in global integration even though the weakness implies less integrative local ties.

In Section 4.5, I discuss some other contributions to formal social network analysis. This section is only an attempt to summarize a few basic results that closely relate to the ideas in the preceding section.

Section 4.6 takes up the second branch of structuralism, namely, macrostructuralism. The focus partially shifts to dimensions of social structures, but there is an important continuity with the preceding sections in the use of bias parameters leading to the deduction of the main principles of the theory. In other words, formal macrostructural theory is presented in such a way as to be embedded within the analytical framework of biased networks. The focus is on heterogeneity, inequality, and consolidation as properties of distributions of actors in a multidimensional space of social positions. Such properties help account for the patterns of social relations among institutional groups and strata in complex social systems.

In Section 4.7, an example is given of *unification* of previously separate lines of theory in structuralism. It will be shown that we can generate a formal theoretical system that unifies weak-ties theory from the social networks branch of structuralism and formal macrostructural theory from the macrostructuralism branch. The unifying substantive theme is the way in which both properties of social relations and parameters of distributions of actors over dimensions of social structure relate to the problem of social integration of a complex social system.

Section 4.8 presents an application of the unified theory to the problem of *small worlds*. The global connectivity of large scale acquaintanceship networks is approached through a derived nonlinear model that theoretically traces linkages in and between subgroups of a heterogeneous population of nodes linked by strong and weak ties. The tracing process interpretation holds here: We are describing a form that process might take in which the formal variable $t$ is interpreted not as time but as network distance from the nodes that originate the process. The nonlinear form of coupled equations defining this "dynamical system" provides a further illustration of the use of computer thought experiments to study the implications of the model, as explained in Chapter 3.

Finally, in Section 4.9 a second type of unification is discussed and illustrated, namely, an integration of theoretical methods of two research programs. The aim is to combine more closely the element of generativity with the commitments of structuralism. There is a sense in which the unification episode presented here shows how one can combine concepts and procedures from action theory and from structuralism. From action theory comes the theoretical procedure of coupling actor–situation units. From structuralism, especially social network analysis, comes the focus on a network of such couplings. Finally, from the overarching dynamical social system viewpoint comes the effort to show how social structures are generated in a dynamic process. The method is illustrated with the construction of a modest theory to explain the emergence of hierarchy among interacting animals, incorporating a triadic bystander mechanism. Thus, with this final contribution, the book closes on the note of commitment to unification of separate streams of contributions to general theoretical sociology.

A key theoretical procedure used in this chapter involves the postulation of sociologically significant bias parameters that account for departures of social structural phenomena from a random net baseline. The next section uses the context of diffusion to introduce the random net concept and the principle that social structures are biased networks.

Table 4.1. *Observed tracing data and random net predictions for Project Revere*

| $t$ | 0 | 1 | 2 | 3 | 4 | 5 | Total |
|---|---|---|---|---|---|---|---|
| $H(t)$ | 42 | 69 | 53 | 14 | 2 | 4 | 184 |
| $210P(t)$ | 42 | 66.6 | 55.8 | 22.3 | 5.5 | 1.1 | 193.3 |

## 4.2. Biased networks: diffusion in a social structure

Let us begin with an example of an empirical study of diffusion, an experimental field study in the early 1950s called Project Revere (Dodd, Rainboth, and Nehnevajsa, 1955). The discussion of this study will lead us into biased net methods for the parsimonious characterization of complex social structures. As discussed in a further analysis of the data by Rapoport (1956), the aim was to trace the "tellings" of information in a network via spread from some initial starters. In a village of 210 housewives, the investigators told 42 of them about a brand of coffee and asked them to tell other housewives, providing some monetary incentive for doing so. Thus there were 42 "starters" of the diffusion process in a network with 210 nodes. In a follow-up survey, the investigators canvassed the village to discover which of these women knew the information and, if so, from whom the information was obtained. Thus, the relational tellings were part of the data.

One type of summary of such relational data is done as follows. Let $t$ stand for the *step removed* from the starters, who are said to be at step $t = 0$. Those who hear directly from the starters are at step removed $t = 1$. Some may have been starters themselves, but a subset are newly reached at this step. Similarly, those who hear directly from those who are newly reached at step 1 are at step 2. Again, a subset of these persons is newly reached. In general, we count the number of persons hearing the information at step $t + 1$ from those who first heard it at step $t$ removed from the origin and who did not hear it at any earlier step. The form of such data is shown in the $H(t)$ row of Table 4.1. (The other row is generated by a model to be described in what follows.)

In the empirical study, the term $H(t)$ is the number of housewives in the village hearing the information about the coffee *for the first time* at $t$th-hand, that is, at the step removed $t$ from the starters. We see that the numbers $H(t)$ at first rise from the start and then decline. Also note that the total number hearing the information is less than the total that might have heard it in the population of 210 housewives.

There is an abstract type of problem here for theoretical sociology. That problem is to conceptualize and to represent formally the generic process of the spread of anything in a socially structured population of social units, that is, the diffusion of anything in a social network. Anatol Rapoport (1951, 1956, 1957) approached this problem by asking an interesting *baseline model* question: What would the data look like if the spread occurred by random contacts? This introduces the important concept of a *random net,* by which we mean that each node contacts a certain number of others as if independently selecting a sample of them at random; that is, each possible sample has the same probability. One says that the population is *completely intermixed* (Coleman, 1964:Ch. 17). The number to be contacted is treated as a parameter of the network, denoted $a$ and termed the *contact density*. It is estimated from the data in terms of the average number of contacts per node.[4]

The general approximate recursion formula for a tracing process in a random net with contact density $a$ is a given by (see Rapoport, 1951, for a derivation)

$$P(t+1)=[1-X(t)]\{1-\exp[-aP(t)]\} \tag{4.2.1}$$

for $t=0, 1, 2, \ldots$ The function $\exp(x)$ is the exponential $e^x$. The term $P(t)$ is the probability that a node is reached for the first time at step $t$, and the term $X(t)$ is the corresponding cumulative probability of being reached on or before step $t$. The givens for the formula are the parameter $a$, which is the contact density, and the given fraction of the population that has the object of diffusion initially, the starter fraction $P(0)$. Given these two terms, $P(1)$ follows from (4.2.1). Given $a$ and $P(1)$, the formula generates $P(2)$, and so forth.

As applied to the Project Revere data, the initial condition is $P(0)=\frac{42}{210}$, and the parameter $a$ is estimated in terms of the average number of tellings per node, in this instance about 2. From (4.2.1), the derived expected values of $H(t)$ for step removed $t$ are given by $210P(t)$, for $t=1, 2, \ldots$. These are displayed in the third row of Table 4.1, below the corresponding values for the data. We see that the random net model predicts somewhat less of an initial rise of $H(t)$ and a somewhat less sharp subsequent decline beyond step 2 than occurs in the data. It also predicts somewhat more people will ever hear the information than actually do. But the initial impression is that in a first approximation one can model the diffusion process in the social network as if it were occurring by random contacts among the housewives, each of them contacting an average of two others.

Solomonoff and Rapoport (1951) show that formula (4.2.1) implies that a limit exists that in general depends on $a$ and $P(0)$. If $P(0)$ is small, then an approximate relation between the limit and the density logically follows. I call the limit in question the *connectivity* and denote it by $\gamma$. Thus, in a random net we have approximately the tabulated values shown in Table 4.2. The connectiv-

Table 4.2. *The connectivity of a random net as a function of the contact density*

| $a$ | 1 | 2 | 3 | 4 | 5 |
|---|---|---|---|---|---|
| $\gamma$ | .13 | .59 | .80 | .94 | .98 |

ity is a monotone increasing function of the contact density and approaches unit in the limit as the number of contacts per node increases. For surprisingly smal values of the density, the connectivity is nearly unity.

After the initial development of these ideas, attention turned to applying the to sociograms, thought of as imperfect maps of social structures (Rapoport an Horvath, 1961). One can regard the real social structure, of which such a socio gram is an observational depiction, as being a social network within which var ious diffusion processes may occur. Each such diffusion process will be initiate from some set of starters and then either all subsequent spread is purely by inter nal contacts or there is a mixture of contact and ''broadcast'' from outside th network (Lave and March, 1975:Ch. 7). Disregarding the latter in this context to characterize the structure in terms of how internal diffusion processes *migh* occur is the basic idea.

The objective is to map out the properties of the social structure, using the analytical tool of the random net baseline. Only sociograms of large size are o interest here, although the general idea of a baseline random structure has wide scope. The tracing of a network via ''steps removed'' whether the stepwise de- velopment is in real time (as in the Project Revere case) or not (as in studying a sociogram) is what I call *tracing process analysis*. The $t$ in the formulas in no instance represents any clock time. The ordinal sequence of values of $t$ corre- sponds to ''removes from the origin,'' not to minutes or hours or any unit of time at all. Yet the formulas have the formal property of recursive generativity: Starting from some initial conditions, we recursively calculate the successive values of the *structure statistics,* that is, the successive terms $P(0)$, $P(1)$, . . . . The full set of structure statistics is a description of a social structure in such a form as to be suggestive of the possibilities for process, that is, for the spread of anything along the links in the network, given the assigned contact density. The latter may be imposed by the analyst or it may correspond to an average number of ties activated per node where free variation was possible.

The analysis of the Project Revere data illustrated tracing process analysis in the context of a real diffusion process, where our analysis is in terms of a tracing of relational tellings through steps removed from the origin. Let us consider an example of a tracing process analysis of a structure where there is no real diffusion process, at least none that constitutes the data.

In Fararo and Sunshine (1964) the entire population ($N=417$) of a junior high school was investigated in terms of nominations of friendships. Each student was asked to name exactly four others, an imposed contact density parameter. The actual average number of nominated friends was 3.94, which is the value of $a$ for that sociogram. Tracing data were obtained by the following tracing procedure done on a computer. Linkages are traced from an initial starting set determined by randomly sampling a small number of nodes (four in the study), recording all nodes nominated by them. Deleting any already reached at $t=0$, we have the set of nodes reached for the first time at step $t=1$. In general, we trace to step $t+1$ from the new contacts at step $t$ and delete those already contacted at any earlier step; the remainder constitute the new contacts as step $t+1$. The tracing halts when no new contacts are reached at a given step. This tracing procedure is then repeated with another sampled small set of starters. The tracing data are averaged at each step, and samples are taken until the average stabilizes. Thus the tracing statistics associated with the network take the same form as the Project Revere data except that the entries are averages over repeated tracings. These descriptive averages, which are based on counts over concrete social relational ties, are the structure statistics of the network. Corresponding to the empirical values of the structure statistics are the random net model's calculated expected structure statistics, the expected fraction of new contacts at step $t$, for every $t$, as a function of the starter fraction and the contact density.

In the particular study, three levels of friendship nominations were used to define three corresponding sets of structure statistics: the first two friends only, the first three friends, and all four friends. The cumulative fraction of nodes reached as a function of step $t$ is shown in Figure 4.1 for the first two friends (with $a=1.98$). Also shown is the random net predicted values and those of a "biased" net model, which I shall discuss shortly.

It is apparent that the observed structure statistics are far below the random net values. Also note the connectivity results: Although a typical tracing in a random net with density 1.98 will reach nearly 80 percent of the nodes in the course of the tracing, the real situation is that less than one-third are reached. This is a general regularity in the study of sociograms via structure statistics, illustrating how the baseline model functions in our empirical recognition of a phenomenon, that is, a regularity, that needs to be explained.

So we ask *why* we generally reach a smaller proportion of the network in empirical tracings of real networks as compared with tracings of random nets. The specification of an explanation leads to a generalized model that turns out to have far-reaching connections with sociological theory.

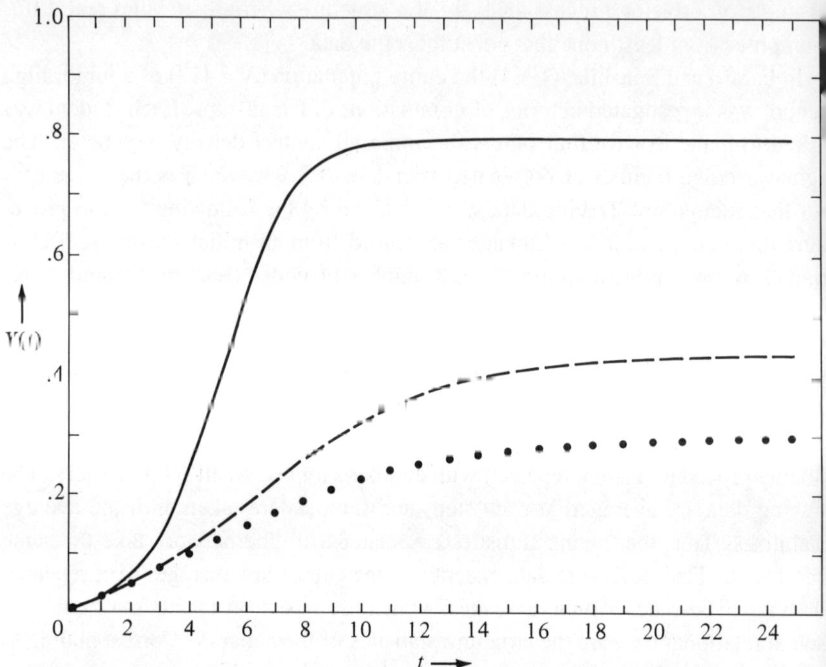


Figure 4.1. Cumulative structure statistics: data (points), random net (solid curve), biased net (dashed curve)

The general explanation takes the form of employing the general principle that *social networks are biased nets*. This representation principle introduces a formal idea that functions as a general model of a class of phenomena and allows us to analyze particular cases of such phenomena (as discussed in philosophical terms in Section 1.3). I mean by a *biased net* a network characterized by a model that *generalizes* or *extends* the random net model. What this means is that the postulates that define a random net with contact density *a* are modified by introducing *bias parameters* in such a way that (1) the bias parameters reflect real social structural tendencies in social networks; (2) we derive formulas that are probabilistic but not purely random, in that the bias parameters appear; and (3) when the bias parameters in any such formula are all set to zero, we recover a corresponding random net formula.

In particular, Foster, Rapoport, and Orwant (1963) suggested that the general form of the bias explanation not only of the connectivity but of the entire structure statistics of empirical sociograms might be captured by parameters relating to two properties of any social relation: its symmetry and its transitivity. Recall

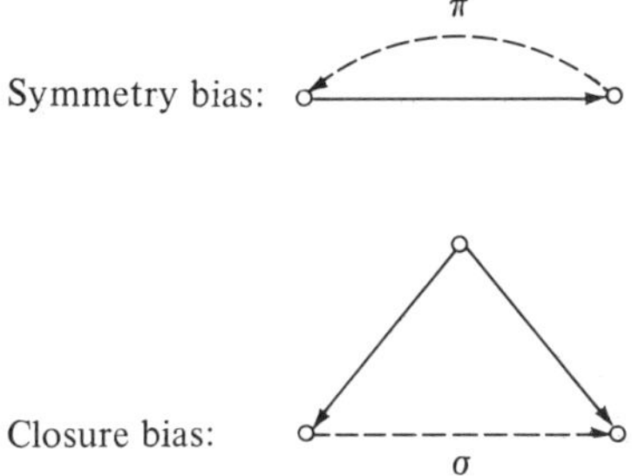


Figure 4.2. Bias parameters

that a relation $R$ is symmetric if $aRb$ implies $bRa$ for all nodes $a$ and $b$, and $R$ is transitive if $aRb$ and $bRc$ implies $aRc$ for all $a$, $b$, and $c$. (Reflexivity – defined by the property that $aRa$ for all nodes $a$ – is not trivial, but for the type of model being considered it is usually taken as irrelevant, as when we do not ask if a person is acquainted with himself or herself.) If a sociometric relation is both symmetric and transitive, then the net falls apart into a set of disjoint, unconnected subsets. In the case where each node is $R$ related to exactly $a$ others, the subsets are each of size $a+1$ (Fararo and Sunshine, 1964). But then if we traced such a net, the tracing would quickly terminate as no new nodes would be reached at step $t=2$. Thus, for large networks the fraction ultimately reached would be very small indeed if we assume that the density $a$ is very small compared with $N$, the number of nodes in the network.

This provides the basic intuition, then, for introducing bias parameters related to symmetry and transitivity for networks where these properties are not completely realized in the relations, that is, where in some sense degrees of symmetry and transitivity are present. Such parameters provide a quantitative basis for generating the structure statistics from a generalized tracing formula. This implements the idea of a tracing process analysis in which we use a derived tracing formula to recursively generate the successive values of the $P(t)$ terms from the given initial state $P(0)$ and the parameters (the density and the bias parameters).

The exact definition of these bias parameters had been a minor problem, but it is not of any concern here. (For details, see the sequence from Foster et al., 1963, to Fararo and Sunshine, 1964, to Fararo, 1981b, to Skvoretz, 1985, where the most up-to-date versions are presented.) Except for the exact conditions required to define the bias components of the events in question, one can see the meanings of the biases in terms of the diagrams in Figure 4.2.

Denoting the *symmetry bias* by $\pi$ and the transitivity-related *closure bias* by $\sigma$, one simple approximation formula that shows the logic of generalizing the random net to the biased net is given by the tracing formula (derived in Fararo and Sunshine, 1964):

$$P(t+1)=[1-X(t)]\{1-\exp[-\alpha P(t)]\} \quad (4.2.2)$$

for $t=1, 2, \ldots$, where the *reduced density* $\alpha$ is derived in terms of the bias parameters:

$$\alpha=a-\sigma(a-1)-\pi \quad (4.2.3)$$

The general principle is as follows:

> *The correspondence theorem*: For a given value of $P(0)$, the derived structure statistics for a biased net with parameters $a$, $\pi$, and $\sigma$ are the same as those for a random net with contact density $\alpha$.

In fact, for any particular formula for $\alpha$ that is accompanied by the recursion formula (4.2.2), this principle holds. I mention this because (4.2.3) is only a first approximation. What is important is the conceptual idea that the correspondence theorem asserts: The tracing process in which we imagine an as-it-were flow of something (an emotion, an idea, an institutional type) through a social structure behaves in a calculable way as does the analogous process in a random net. The measurement of the biases and the density supplies the relevant data to find the structure statistics corresponding to an initial seeding of a fraction $P(0)$ of the population with the entity to be spread.

The contact density might be quite small, as in the examples given, as arising from the nature of a particular spread process itself (the coffee information diffusion process) or from a decision of an investigator studying a given structure from this point of view (the friendship net). Real existing social structures, however, might have quite high densities. People in modern societies are usually acquainted with a much larger number of people than they realize, often in the hundreds (Pool and Kochen, 1978). Thus, in theory, we want to include the case of very high densities and very small starting fractions for tracing processes.

As a numerical example, consider a society's acquaintanceship structure such that $a=279$, $\pi=1$, and $\sigma=.10$. If the initial fraction starting off the process is set at $P(0)=.00000001$, then we generate the structure statistics as follows: First, we find that $\alpha=250$ by using (4.2.3). Second, we insert this value of the reduced density, together with the starting fraction, into formula (4.2.2) to generate recursively $P(1)=.00000250$, $P(2)=.00062480$, $P(3)=.14452170$, and $P(4)=.85485100$. Summation shows that the connectivity is unity given the large density that was presupposed. Note that $\pi$ was set to unity on grounds of meaning postulate: When we say that $a$ is an acquaintance of $b$'s we want to mean that $b$ is an acquaintance of $a$'s. A real diffusion process would not ordinarily activate all the acquaintances of any person, so what this tracing process provides for us is a structural description of the whole network as an existing entity. That is, it is characterized by its structure statistics, which remain invariant with small changes in the initial starting fraction so that it is derivable essentially from its two fundamental parameters: the contact density and the closure bias. One can think of the structure statistics as successive reachability proportions from an arbitrary person in a network with such parameters. With such a high contact density, eventually everyone is reachable from any person despite the enormous size of the population and the element of bias parameter. Even though such large density networks may often or almost always possess a connectivity of unity, they will differ in their profiles of structure statistics because of differences in density and in the bias parameter.

In empirical studies in which people tell us who their acquaintances are, we do not have symmetry, since $a$ can say that $b$ is an acquaintance whereas $b$ does not "reciprocate." For example, suppose that the empirical net in a sociometric study has the parameter values given by $a=4$, $\pi=.5$, and $\sigma=.5$. Then (4.2.3) yields $\alpha=2$. Thus the empirical net's connectivity is predicted to be the same as that of a random net with contact density 2, which is 80 percent. In practice, we have to estimate the bias parameters from the data, after which formula (4.2.2) provides a derived set of structure statistics to compare with the observed values. For the data underlying Figure 4.1, the estimated bias parameter values were $\pi=.41$ and $\sigma=.29$. The derived values of the cumulative structure statistics (the $X(t)$ terms) are shown along with the corresponding data and baseline random model. The gap between the biased net calculated values and the observed values shows that the model is still not perfect but, as compared with the random net model with the observed rather than reduced density, is much closer to the data.

## 4.3. Theoretical significance of biased networks and diffusion processes

In the preceding section I outlined an approach to structural analysis that began as a model for diffusion in social networks and now is a mode of characterizing structure in terms that relate to its propensity to inhibit or foster the spread of anything through a network. From the standpoint of general theoretical sociology there are two questions that arise in reflections on this approach:

1. How do we fit the idea of a biased network into the general tradition? For instance, how do we relate it to the conception of the nature of the equilibria of general dynamical social systems?
2. What is the theoretical significance of diffusion processes?

Taking up the first question, the reader is reminded of the analysis in Section 3.3 that drew attention to the convergence of Homans, Parsons, and Blau on a portrait of the emergent structures of general dynamical social systems. The three-way correspondence consists in a set of matched contrasts, one side of the contrast pertaining to social adaptation to the action and nonaction environment and the other to the social integration of the system. These were Homans's external and internal systems, respectively, Parsons's economic and communal systems, respectively, and Blau's economic versus social exchange, respectively. The internal side is characterized by social values of the particularistic–diffuse type. The patterning of ties of this kind constitutes the basis for whatever level of integration is attained in the particular environment. In the small group, particularistic diffuse ties are those of positive and negative interpersonal sentiments. They are indicated in patterns of friendship that occur within the broader context of the division of labor and other aspects of the adaptation of the small social system to its environment. For instance, friendships arise in the context of work that provides the initial conditions of interaction that are the starting mechanism for the buildup of interpersonal sentiments.

In general, passing beyond the small group, within the givens of the particular environment, individuals are brought into contacts that lead to the formation of friendships or, at least, acquaintanceship. Thus, an acquaintanceship network is a dynamical outcome of interactive events occurring under certain social conditions. It is one of the possibilities for voluntary pair associations adjusted to those conditions. In Blau's (1964, 1977) terms it is a structure of social associations. What the random net model says is that such an equilibrium structure of social associations will reflect merely random mixing of such ties.[5] The whole structure is then a pattern of possibilities for the spread of something through it, and a particular such pattern in the form of the structure statistics of a random net is derivable from the contact density and initial starting fraction of any such process. The biased network model adds to this analysis the known properties of such associations, above all the tendency to transitivity as reflected in the closure bias. In either case the parameter of contact density strongly coordinates to the Durkheimian depth sociological focus on this analytical element. In the random model, the relevant density is simply that which is empirically the case; in the bias model, it is the "corrected" or reduced density, taking account of the structural properties of the social association relation.

The interpretation this suggests, then, is the following:

> A biased network model describes aspects of the equilibrium of the integration process of a dynamical social system, especially a large-scale system. The social associations generated are characterized by particularistic–dif-

> fuse operative ideals defining the type of tie usually called acquaintanceship or friendship (depending on the strength). Its fundamental parameters are the density of such ties and the closure bias.

This interpretation can be amplified somewhat by noting that the closure bias is a function of the strength of the ties. This point will be taken up in Section 4.4.

We know that a variety of phenomena such as those of the economy are "embedded" in such integratively significant networks (Granovetter, 1985). For instance, when two organizations engage in sales negotiations involving million-dollar contracts, interstitial structures of social association emerge, as was stressed in the analytical study of contractual relations by Parsons and Smelser (1956). As we would expect from the general dynamical social system sketch as involving an interplay of adaptation and integration processes, the former adjusts to the structures generated by the latter. Ideally, we should have a much closer link between the ideas on dynamical social systems in Chapters 2 and 3 and the biased network idea. Failing that, we at least have a way of "placing" the biased network models within the comprehensive tradition of general theoretical sociology.

I turn now to the second question. What is the theoretical significance of diffusion processes? Two sorts of entities are especially important to consider with regard to diffusion in networks. First, emotional states can spread. In the Durkheimian depth sociology subtradition, such spread of states is remindful of the "effervescence" by which solidarity is reconstituted in a collectivity. In a large system, the periodic renewal of feelings of membership in the collectivity cannot be accomplished by a single ceremonial meeting of the entire membership. Instead, there is a mixture of emotional broadcast process and interpersonal diffusion. For example, in modern systems, somber ceremonial occasions in which there is public recognition of the meaning of the death of soldiers or leaders are shown in the television media. The associated feelings are induced directly from such viewing and spread and are reinforced through contacts with others in the same population. The spread process has the character of a tracing except that at every moment there is a constant new seeding through broadcast as well as stepwise passage of the emotional feeling through the population. But in the same way that a feeling that renews solidarity can be spread, a feeling of loss of collective meaning can be spread. In short, the diffusion of sentiment elements of membership can be construed as an integration mechanism with a variety of possible outcomes under varying conditions.

A second type of entity that can spread through a social network is a cultural object. One type is a familiar though significant topic of research, the spread of new technology. But as we are theoretical sociologists, our interest in such diffusion is in its implications for social structure. Thus we are led to the topic of spread of cultural objects that are typified forms and can become constitutive of social structures. But this means institutions as typified entities. Thus we can think of the process of institutionalization as the spread of a social-type cultural entity – thought of as a scheme of typifications of social and other objects and corresponding production systems, as discussed in Section 3.4 – through a population of local social systems that become the multiple embodiments of the institution. For instance, successive local schools acquire instances of ⟨guidance counselor⟩ in a time-extended process culminating in the general constitutive rule that ⟨high school⟩ includes ⟨guidance counselor⟩ in the same sense that ⟨football⟩ includes ⟨quarterback⟩: Without it, you are not an embodiment of the game or institution.

For further discussion we require two levels of network: local and global. The *local network* is the set of units of the local social system and some types of relations among them through which interactions are mediated. The *global network* level has these local social systems as subnetworks with some social relations that function as the linkages along which the cultural object can flow and be inhibited or not in its spread through a population of potential embodiments of the object. For instance, for an educational institution such as ⟨guidance counselor⟩, each community is a local network and the global network is a system of communities tied through connections between the groups making up the communities (Bates and Harvey, 1975).

It is natural to define the degree of institutionalization in this global network as the ultimate fraction, the connectivity, of a tracing process from the starters. The starters are the originators of the institution, and there can be more than one. Assuming that each local network has some direct contacts with a number of other such local networks yields an interpretation for the contact density $a$. Then a random net model predicts the degree of institutionalization as a function of this density and the initial starting fraction. It is the expected fraction of local networks that could adopt the institution that do in fact adopt it when the spread has reached equilibrium. A theoretical model of the local process by which the institution is adopted or not would be possible, but the main structural interest would lie in the global process by which it is spread throughout the network of local embodiments so as to ultimately constitute an institutionalized procedure in the social system of which each local network is a part. The biased net model would ask for estimates of the density of contacts between the local networks and of $\pi$ and $\sigma$. This would translate by the correspondence theorem into a reduced density of the global network that, together with the starting fraction, would produce a presumably more accurate account of the tracing and the ultimate institutionalization of the procedure. In reality, the reduced density $\alpha$ would also be reduced by nonadoption of the spreading pattern within some local networks, requiring an additional term in transforming the contact density of the random net into the actual density in the spread process.

In this way, the diffusion process as seen in terms of the tracing process associated with the biased net framework is one answer to Giddens's (1984) "reconstructed problem of social order" (discussed in Section 3.4): The time–space separation of concrete actors (with memory traces of distributed procedural knowledge constitutive of the generators of institutions) is bridged in terms of the spread of typifications and of associated production rules.

The biased net models and the study of tracing statistics for social networks do not exhaust the topic of how diffusion relates to social structure. Diffusion processes relate to the family of continuous time stochastic processes involving "contagion" terms and the like that were developed by Coleman (1964). The logic of the whole family of processes was outlined by Jaeckel (1971). Theoretical sociologists ought to make much more use of these ideas in formulating theoretical models for the spread of anything through a network that has differentiated subpopulations. These models should be linked to ideas in the theory of biased networks. It is hard to believe how *little* we have done with all these processes except in terms of the fundamental stumbling block, that is, the training of sociologists in statistical algorithms but not in theoretical procedures, including formal methods, by which ideas about social structures and processes can be cast in the form of postulates about definite model objects with derived properties. One component of theorizing ought to be the study of such objects with a view to deriving interesting theorems. There is an opportunity for a whole new sociological synthesis of ideas and data dealing with social structures in terms of institutionalization viewed as produced through various types of diffusion mechanisms.

## 4.4. The strength of weak ties and the dilemma of integration

From the approximation formula (4.2.3) we see that the lower the value of the closure bias $\sigma$, the less is subtracted from the contact density $a$ to produce the reduced density $\alpha$. Now $\gamma$, the connectivity, depends on $\alpha$ in the biased net in the same way that it does in a random net: The greater is $\alpha$, the greater is $\gamma$. So the lower is the closure bias $\sigma$, the greater is the density term $\alpha$ and hence the greater the connectivity. This means that in a social network characterized by contacts that are less likely to close up to form transitive triads (lower $\sigma$), the more units will be reached by the objects of diffusion, other things equal. This idea is the basis of Granovetter's (1973) "strength of weak ties." Empirically associating "weakness of a type of tie" with "less likely to be transitively closed," we see that what is strong about weak ties is that the object of diffusion is less likely to get trapped in a tight pocket of local social structure and thus is more likely to branch out to reach other parts of the global network.

In this way, Giddens's reconstructed social order problem (see Section 3.6) of how separated entities get connected is solved in principle. Namely, the objects of diffusion, among them potential candidates for institutional embodiments throughout the global system, are spread beyond localized networks through weak ties that bridge them. The implication is that if all the ties were of the strong type, there indeed would be mutual separation and isolation of subsystems and thus a lack of integration of the global system. Thus, weak ties have positive integrative consequences for the global system. This is just one special case of the general idea that in studying biased networks we are focused on Homans's "internal system" writ large. Weak and strong ties are both particularistic and diffuse in type. They differ in magnitude. Both are ways of describing social relations in terms of their integration significance for one or another level of social system, local or global.

Among types of relations, perhaps "acquaintanceship" is the clearest referent for "weak type of tie." Kinship or close friendship is a reasonable referent for "strong type of tie." Other identifications of the weak–strong polarity can be made, of course, but I employ acquaintanceship–friendship as the empirical interpretation. In these terms, the axiom of weak-ties theory is as follows:

> *Weak-ties axiom* (Granovetter, 1973): When two people are both friends of a third person, they are likely to become either acquaintances or friends themselves.

Granovetter employed the idealization in which "they are likely to become" was replaced by "they become." In this form he showed that the fundamental consequence of this axiom is, as we have seen, that weak ties provide the connections among otherwise locally separated subnetworks and hence the social "bridges" for diffusion between them.

This consequence can be obtained as a theorem within the biased net framework. The model begins with an assumption of symmetric relations (acquaintances or friends), so that the symmetry parameter is set to unity in (4.2.3). Thus,

$$\alpha = (1-\sigma)(a-1) \qquad (4.4.1)$$

Formally, the nodes reached at step 1 in a tracing all "reciprocate" their contacts from the starters, using up at least one contact each to leave at most $a-1$ per node to trace forward to step 2. If the relation is so strong as to have $\sigma = 1$, then no such contacts are traced forward because "cofriends" – other friends of the starters – will be contacted. This minimizes the connectivity. On the other hand, if the relation is so weak as to have $\sigma = 0$, then from step 1 forward we have a random net with contact density $a-1$. So, for instance, if $a=4$, then about 94 percent of the nodes are reachable in a tracing from an arbitrary small set of starters. (As shown in Table 4.2, for a density of 3, the connectivity is approximately .94.)

Now assume that the network is a mixture of acquaintanceship and friendship ties. Think of the former as weak. One can visualize them as dotted links connecting various pairs of nodes symmetrically. Think of the latter as strong and, visually, as solid links connecting other pairs of nodes symmetrically. No pair may be connected in both ways, and some pairs are not connected by either type of link. We represent the total bias parameter as an average of the two closure biases, one for the weak type of tie and one for the strong type of tie.[6]

$$\sigma = w\sigma_w + (1-w)\sigma_s \tag{4.4.2}$$

where $w$ is a parameter between zero and 1. The weak-ties axiom is represented in the form:

$$\sigma_w < \sigma_s \tag{4.4.3}$$

The two $\sigma$ terms are defined as follows: $\sigma_w$ is the bias component of the probability that two people who are acquaintances of a third person are themselves either friends or acquaintances; $\sigma_s$ is the bias component of the probability that two people who are friends of a third person are themselves either friends or acquaintances (with suitably adjusted meanings for other interpretations of the weak–strong polarity idea).

One definition of a formal parameter with the name "strength of weak ties" is $1-\sigma_w$. [Alternative forms of this idea are possible; see Fararo and Skvoretz (1987) for another version; the same paper uses a generalized version of equation (4.4.1).] Call this SWT. Fararo (1983) showed that

$$\alpha = [\text{SWT} - (1-w)S](a-1) \tag{4.4.4}$$

where $S$ is the absolute difference between $\sigma_s$ and $\sigma_w$. With this formal interpretation, it is clear that since the connectivity increases with the reduced density $\alpha$ and the latter, by this formula, increases with SWT, we have the result that the greater the SWT, the greater the connectivity. Stating this formally:

> *Strength-of-weak-ties theorem:* Given a social network with two types of ties, one weak and the other strong, and with contact density $a$, the greater the strength of weak ties, the greater the global integration as measured by the connectivity.

A second aspect of the weak-ties theory applies to the local–global contrast. Around any node, there is a set of other nodes directly tied to that node through acquaintance or friendship. Consider such a node in the role of a starter of a tracing process. The more that contacts remain in this local subset, the more integrated it is; but as SWT increases, contacts move out of this subset. Thus, increases in SWT have necessarily opposite, or trade-off, effects as between local and global integration.

Hence, we have the *dilemma of integration:* The greater the SWT, the greater the global connectivity but the weaker the local integration. This proposition holds ceteris paribus, since other parameters effect the reduced density $\alpha$ in (4.4.4), notably the actual contact density $a$ that could increase with increases in variables external to the set of parameters of the network.

This section has made quite definite the sense in which biased networks and diffusion processes have integrative functional significance for a social system. If we attempt to map the structure of modern social systems, we find economic, political, legal, familial, and other institutional components. According to the argument of the prior section, we should not forget that these components are always found embedded in concrete interactive situations in which emergent as well as given structures exist. These emergent patterns of social associations are the subject matter of biased network analysis. The sometimes illusive idea of a social integration system (Parsons, 1977) is made more concrete through this conception of a network of particularistic–diffuse ties. Whereas in Section 3.3 such types of relations were treated as conceptually isolated components of social structure, here they are studied as a network. These ties, we have seen in this section, vary in strength. In turn, this has provided us with intelligible theorems about the integration of complex social systems. The double element of treating the entire social network of such ties and of employing quantitative parameters to characterize them distinguishes the present structuralist treatment from the typical treatment found in analytical action theory. The analysis of the integration aspect of complex social systems continues in Section 4.6.

## 4.5. Related formal theory in the social networks tradition

Since the early 1970s, the social networks research tradition has exploded in a proliferation of research programs and accompanying modes of data analysis and theorizing. What I have discussed in the preceding sections is only an aspect of the literature that intersects some of my own efforts. Theoretical sociologists interested in recent readable overviews of the literature should consult Freeman (1984) and Marsden and Laumann (1984). A technical survey may be found in Burt (1980). The present section is a highly selective sketch of some contributions that relate to the topics just discussed.

In Chapter 1 I discussed balance as a property of $p$-centric relational systems involving unit-forming and sentiment relations as introduced by Heider (1946).

Then I interpreted Newcomb's (1953) *ABX* model. The formalization of Heider's concept of balance by Cartwright and Harary (1956) initiated a whole set of other developments of great theoretical interest to structural analysts. First, let me review the basic formal ideas in brief form. The formal context is graph theory as dealing with nodes and lines between nodes. For formal balance theory we have two types of lines, usually interpreted as positive and negative, so that the lines are signed and the graphs are called signed graphs. When the lines are directed, these graphs are called signed digraphs. I shall not try to be very rigorous in maintaining these distinctions, however. The key idea is that balance means that all the cycles of the graph have a positive product obtained by the sign rule of multiplication. This definition, and its generalization for signed digraphs, holds no matter how many entities are in the structure. A cycle is a path along the lines of the graph that starts at a certain point and returns to that point, never using the same line twice. The basic formal theorem that Harary and Cartwright proved is the following:

> *The structure theorem* (Cartwright and Harary, 1956): A signed graph is balanced if and only if its nodes can be separated into two mutually exclusive subsets such that each positive line is within a subset and each negative line is between subsets.

A special case exists in which one of the two subsets is actually empty because all links are positive. Note that unless all nodes are joined by lines (in which case we say that the graph is complete), nodes in the same subset need not be directly connected.

The structure theorem has great generality and intuitive appeal. In Chapter 1 it was shown how it relates to the processual conceptions of the *ABX* model: The derived equilibria of such a dynamical model may be expected to be balanced. Hence, they will satisfy the structure theorem. Taken together, these results constitute a step toward a Type 1 theorem concerning the existence and form of social structures.

It seems likely that more concrete constraints found in various institutional domains can be explained in terms of this sort of theorem. For example, Lévi-Strauss (1963:42) suggests a general rule for the interlock of elementary kinship units: "The relation between maternal uncle and nephew is to the relation between brother and sister as the relation between father and son is to that between husband and wife. Thus if we know one pair of relations, it is always possible to infer the other." His kinship diagrams of various possibilities (p. 45) are readily represented as graphs to which the structure theorem applies. There are four nodes, with plus and minus signs representing the institutionalized forms of sentiment connecting the types of actors in kinship terms. Some of these same kinship relations, with the same sorts of interlocks, were noted by Homans (1950:255), who suggested the general rule that "if the relationship between *A* and *B* is of a particular kind, and the relationship between *B* and *C* is close and warm, the relationship between *A* and *C* will tend to resemble the relationship between *A* and *B*." So, if *ARB* is restrained (negative), *ARC* is too.

Both the Lévi-Strauss rule for kinship structures and Homans's general interpersonal relations rule can be interpreted as special cases of balanced structures. The general idea is to envision some initial condition of signed sentiment relations among various actors and then to infer the signs of other relations in the same system. A vital premise in this type of argument is the existence of balance. But this premise is highly plausible because we are dealing with patterns of *institutionalized* interpersonal relations. Such a pattern has had to persist amid countless episodes involving concrete persons with concrete feelings about each other. Thus, the underlying premise is that an institutionalized structure of interpersonal sentiments is a component of the attractor state of a dynamical social system. Presumably, the underlying dynamics would be much like those proposed by Newcomb in his *ABX* model, with *X* as a social object; the setup and analysis of an actual dynamical system that would allow us to generate the social equilibrium with a number of interlocking pairs changing state over time is another matter. The point here is that social theorists have been discovering instances of institutional and subinstitutional structures that are satisfyingly comprehended under the (sociologically interpreted) structure theorem.[7]

Sociologists, however, have been apt to wonder if what this theorem asserts might be too strong. If balance is a state of equilibrium and the latter refers to possible social structures of dynamical social systems, then to say that the only possible structures of sentiments are characterized by either uniform positive sentiments or two disjoint subsets in a negative relation is to rule out quite a bit. It is true that the theorem does not necessarily imply polarization, because two nodes in the same subset may not even be directly connected; yet they are potential allies nonetheless whose positive linkage would not disturb the equilibrium. But what about the history of sociometry with its repeated finding of a number of cliquelike groups, not just two? We could interpret this to mean that all these studies were looking at nonequilibrium situations. More likely, however, at least some of these studies were mapping settled states, under given parametric conditions.

With this consideration in mind, Davis (1967) came up with the fertile idea of generalizing the Cartwright–Harary principle of balance. Davis works backward from the theorem. Suppose we have in a given graph representing some social structure a series of *plus subsets,* not necessarily two, such that positive lines are within such subsets, negative lines between. Call this configuration of plus subsets connected negatively a *clustering*. Now what does this imply about the structure?

> *Cluster theorem* (Davis, 1967): Given a signed graph, a clustering exists if and only if there is no cycle with exactly one negative line.
> *Corollary:* If a signed graph is balanced, then a clustering exists.

Because every case of balance is a clustering but not conversely, the clustering conception of equilibrium is a generalization of the balance conception. Davis points out that our intuitions on these matters are likely to be strongly related to the special case of completeness where every node is tied to every other negatively or positively. In such a case, the balanced situation is one of two cliques in opposition. Also, in this case, clustering holds if no *triangle* has exactly one negative link.

To see the difference in such a complete system between multiple clusters and balance, Davis asks us to consider the interpersonal sentiment aphorisms:

1. A friend of a friend will be a friend.
2. An enemy of a friend will be an enemy.
3. A friend of an enemy will be an enemy.
4. An enemy of an enemy will be a friend.

In each case, the aphorism can be interpreted as saying that *if* completion occurs (so that a relation directly links every pair), *then* in each case it makes the triangle a positive cycle. Thus, all the statements concur with the structure theorem. The first three also agree with cluster theory in that no triangle has exactly one negative line. But consider the fourth case. Clustering amounts to saying that an enemy of an enemy may be a friend *or* an enemy in equilibrium. Davis (1967:32) points out that Heider originally treated the all-negative triangle as a possible balanced case, albeit admitting that people exhibit some preference toward the case described by case 4. Another way that Davis puts it is that in the completion case, balance amounts to a tendency toward clustering *and* (case 4) a tendency toward coalition formation between people with a common enemy.

Davis's generalization of balance theory also relates to what I have called the dilemma of integration in Section 4.4. Let the nodes of the signed graph represent families. Interpret one type of link to represent the fact that two families know each other. To make the graph formally complete, let the second type of link represent that they do not know each other. Call the first type positive, the second negative. Consider clusters of families that know each other but do not know families outside the cluster. The condition for such a clustering (since the graph is complete) is that no triangle of families has a single negative line: If a pair of families are known by a third family, then they know each other. This is the extremely "close-knit" property that Bott (1955) used to characterize some of the networks of families she studied. Thus the community breaks up into a system of disconnected local networks of families but not just two such local networks. The situation corresponds to the closure bias $\sigma = 1$ in the biased net model. With a symmetric relation this in turn implies a partition of the network. If each family knows $a$ other families, then each local subnetwork or cluster has $a+1$ families. But then the connectivity will be quite small as we trace out from any one family. This is another instance of the trade-off between local and global integration. With arbitrary values of the bias parameter $\sigma$ we capture a range of cases intermediate between the special cases of $\sigma = 0$ and $\sigma = 1$.

The fact that Davis's cluster model fits in nicely with other elements of the structuralist tradition and yet captures balance theory as a special case heightens its theoretical significance.

It is clear that the concept of transitivity of a positive interpersonal sentiment relation is playing a strong role in all this work. A mathematical idealization that captures Davis's clustering idea as a special case was produced by Holland and Leinhardt (1977a). It turns out that this too can be connected with the biased network model and itself treated as a special case in which algebraic idealized relationships arise by setting bias parameters to their extreme values.

Holland and Leinhardt start from a single abstract relation denoted $C$ on an unspecified set denoted $X$. Relation $C$ should be thought of in Newcomb's terms as a positive interpersonal orientation relation. Let us idealize $C$ as transitive: If $aCb$ and $bCc$, then $aCc$. The idea is to explore the structure of positive sentiment on the basis of this idealization.

Relations $M$, $A$, and $N$ are defined as follows:

1. Mutuality: $aMb$ if and only if $aCb$ and $bCa$.
2. Asymmetry: $aAb$ if and only if $aCb$ and not $bCa$.
3. Null: $aNb$ if and only if neither $aCb$ nor $bCa$.

The mathematical result is:

> *Structure of positive-sentiment theorem* (Holland and Leinhardt, 1977a): If $C$ is a transitive positive-sentiment relation, then (1) relation $M$ divides $X$ into a set of mutually exclusive and exhaustive subsets called $M$-cliques, and (2) relations $A$ and $N$ generate a partial ordering of the $M$-cliques.

Holland and Leinhardt show that this general result includes the cluster and structure theorems as two of a number of special cases, including ranked clusters (or $M$-cliques). Mayer (1975) criticizes this model. He notes that the transitivity of $C$ implies that a certain type of triad (technically 210) that is empirically frequent (especially in large systems) is ruled out. Indeed, this is the case for which (with $\pi = 1$) the $\sigma$ bias relates to the tendency toward closure.

This last point suggests that it might be fruitful to connect the biased net framework to the *MAN* relations. This integrative connection was undertaken by Skvoretz (1985). In a conceptual move identical to that made in Section 4.4 in embedding Granovetter's weak-ties ideas in the biased network framework, Skvoretz passes from the strict transitivity of $C$ to a probabilistic interpretation. Then $C$ is characterized by the bias parameters $\pi$ and $\sigma$. It follows that there is a derived probability for each of the *MAN* relations expressed as a function of the bias parameters. The Holland–Leinhardt elegant algebraic characterization of the general form of structure produced by *MAN* becomes a special case. In the same paper, Skvoretz relates the bias parameter conception to the loglinear representations for relational data formulated by Holland and Leinhardt (1981) and Fienberg, Meyer, and Wasserman (1985).

## 4.6. Macrostructuralism

Beginning in this section, I apply the conceptual scheme and formal theoretical apparatus of the biased net framework to macrostructuralism. Recall from Section 4.1 that macrostructuralism shares certain presuppositions with network analysis: favoring theoretical models focused on relations and not individuals and requiring relational data. Where network analysis goes on to focus on patterns of indirect as well as direct ties and thereby to "relate relations," macrostructuralism goes on to focus on analytical elements characterizing the distribution of persons into various groups and strata. The corresponding attention to relations is in terms of how they relate the groups and strata. So the focus is on the problem of the integration of complex social systems.

In this and the next section, two tasks are undertaken that are significant in their own right and also as illustrations of two aspirations motivating the work in this book: formalization and unification. The formalization of a macrostructural theory, associated primarily with the work of Blau (1977), is the topic of the current section. The next section gives an account of a unification of the resulting formal macrostructural theory with the formalized theory of weak ties. In short, the biased net framework will have functioned as the basis for (1) formalization of weak-ties theory, (2) formalization of macrostructural theory, and (3) unification of the two formalized theories. In so doing, a link will have been forged between the two branches of structuralism. Following the presentation of the unified theory, an example will be given of an application of the theory to the small-worlds problem.

This section begins with some introductory remarks on the macrostructural theory, including the way in which it carries forward work on a general substantive problem that was a common focus of both Simmel and Durkheim. Then it moves into the formalization of macrostructural theory within a biased network frame of reference. Finally, the section concludes with some remarks on how the theory relates to recent contributions of other formally oriented theoreticians.

### *4.6.1. Introduction to macrostructural theory*

Macrostructural theory deals with the problem of integration of the general complex social system characterized by interrelated modes of differentiation of members (Blau, 1977). We are fortunate that so much of the research tradition of general theoretical sociology has treated this problem. Before presenting the formal theory, I want to review some of the classical theory and contemporary work that leads to it.

In the background for the work of this section are the seminal ideas of Simmel and Durkheim. The key common concern of both of these classical theorists was the characterization of social differentiation and the study of its relationship to social integration. Dynamic interest in the differentiation–integration relationship is particularly shown in Durkheim's (1964) discussion of the historical evolution of the division of labor, that is, from a relatively undifferentiated state to the highly differentiated state of the system. Structural interest in the differentiation–integration relationship is best seen in Simmel's essays dealing with cross-cutting ties and levels of interpenetration (see Levine, 1971). I dealt with this Simmelian theme in one way in discussing interpenetration in Chapter 3. Formal macrostructural theory combines this theme with two other key ideas in Simmel's work.

First, Simmel emphasizes that social structures have an intrinsic numerical aspect that is explanatory of aspects of social interaction: the number of members of a group, the amount of overlap among groups, and the like. From the present point of view, these numerical aspects are as central to general theoretical sociology as quantities of commodities are for theoretical economics. This is because the perhaps distinctive social structural focus of sociology is on the integrative processes of social systems that build and interrelate groups. In Simmel's own term referring to the process generating the novel unity (or system) constituted by interaction, this focus is called *sociation*.

Second, Simmel defined three branches of sociology: formal, general, and philosophical. The idea of formal abstraction, the key to formal sociology, involves Simmel's well-known distinction between form and content. This is strongly reflected throughout this book but especially in the work to follow. Although differentiation, as treated here, presupposes an institutional basis, the analytical concepts to be defined abstract from the content of such institutions, seeking formal elements and relations among them.

With regard to Durkheim's work on differentiation and integration, in the following there is formal abstraction from "division of labor" in the narrower sense of occupational differentiation. Durkheim intended that this phrase be given a broad meaning as social differentiation, although its economic institutional instantiation remains very significant for the evolutionary theory not treated in this chapter. No attempt will be made to directly formalize Durkheim's arguments about the causes and consequences of increases in social differentiation. To the extent that Durkheim meant to emphasize the role of density of interaction, the parameter $\alpha$ of biased network analysis directly incorporates this primary parameter. But Durkheim's phrasing reflects a narrowness of scope that has plagued the effort to achieve generality in social theory: The interest in *increases* in differentiation is related to the historical comparison of earlier and later types of societies as actually have evolved in "modernization." Analytically, we seek relations among formal variables that can be interpreted in terms *either* of increases *or* of decreases, depending on concrete cases of interest.

Similarly, Durkheim's two modes of integration, mechanical and organic, correspond to his typological map of the evolutionary process, from mechanical society to organic society. For general theoretical sociology – with its scope *not* restricted to the world-historical level of analysis – we want to alter this conception: Any social system has a mechanical aspect and an organic aspect with regard to its integration of parts. The mechanical aspect is based on similarity in social structural terms. This aspect is directly reflected in the theory to follow in a number of ways, as the reader will see, such as homophily bias to be introduced in this section and the unification principle stated in Section 4.7. The organic aspect of integration relates to the entire problem of this section: How is a complex social system with a variety of dissimilar parts held together? A central component of the theoretical answer provided in this chapter is summed up by a short answer: For a given density parameter, the answer is weak ties; for a given weak-ties parameter, it is density. These are the two key terms that, if they increase, produce direct increases in parameter $\alpha$ in formula (4.4.4). And increases in $\alpha$ yield increases in network connectivity.

This connectivity of complex social systems in terms of paths through networks of social bonds depends crucially on the existence of bridges between otherwise disconnected subgroups with their internal strong ties. These paths allow new culture to diffuse throughout the social system. In particular, novel schemes of typification can lead to systemwide institutionalization through making transitions along various paths connecting physically and socially remote parts of the system. In turn, the incidence of weak ties depends on the extent of heterogeneity, as we shall see. So organic solidarity depends on contact density and on the strength of weak ties.

In short, the theory of this and the next section addresses Durkheim's question using Simmelian methodology: There is formal analytical abstraction from institutional content but preservation of the key abstract questions that helped shape the origins of general theoretical sociology.

The contemporary development of macrostructural theory to be formalized here is due to Blau (1977). An important idea of the theory is that there exist what we might call either institutional groups or, simply as a variation of terminology compatible with disciplinary usage, *systemwide collectivities*. Also there are systemwide strata. For instance, all the blacks in the United States form a systemwide collectivity, as do all the women, all the Catholics, and all the professionals.

In Section 3.4 concepts and notations were introduced to help us represent institutions as typification schemes. Macrostructural theory abstracts from the structure of institutions but presupposes their existence. For instance, its institutional groups arise in the context of schemes of typification such as ⟨man⟩–⟨woman⟩. All the actors whose standing definition is ⟨woman⟩ form one systemwide collectivity, and all those with standing definition ⟨man⟩ constitute a second such collectivity. Together, by social definition, they exhaust the legitimate range of possibilities for the dimension of gender in our society. The systemwide strata are observer partitions based on the distribution of resources in the social system, and these are typically forms of wealth, power, and prestige. The point is that the constitutive social definitions and production rules that are the stuff of interpretive sociology are not denied by macrostructural theory. And nothing in macrostructural theory is denied by pointing out that the distributions studied in the theory rest upon categorization schemes that have arisen in prior social interaction and that are taken for granted in the given population. It is essential to realize that a science can be *one* and *many* at once, both a single comprehensive research tradition and a plurality of theoretical systems drawn upon to work at varying levels on varying specifications of the fundamental general problems of social structure.

Similarly, macrostructural theory is not really in competition with analytical action theory. If indeed actors are best described in terms of cybernetic hierarchies of normative control, then the pattern variables or other elements close to them in function loom large. But they can loom large and still not negate the abstract approach of macrostructural theory. In fact, the two modes of differentiation of the members of the social system emphasized by Blau, the groups and the strata, correspond to particularism and universalism in Parsons's (1951) pattern variable scheme. This is true not only as a claim made here but in the evolution of ideas in Blau's own work, where an important intermediate product was a study of Parsonian-type description of values in relation to macrostructural integration (Blau, 1964). A particularistic orientation implies a boundary, a separation: men and women, blacks and whites, Americans and Canadians, and so forth. A universalistic orientation implies ranking, having more or less of some valued resource. Some of these orientations involve treatment of the typifications as ascribed so as to be invariant objects over the dynamics of situations. Others involve an achievement element, implying situational variability in the typification of social objects. That we are dealing with socially constituted objects of orientation and not natural objects is a crucial feature of the approach of general theoretical sociology. But for macrostructural theory the prevalence of *institutional standing definitions*, as emphasized in Chapter 3, means that it is not necessary to continually refer to the institutions as such nor to the corresponding value orientations of actors. The social objects have been so constituted and are so maintained in the whole dynamical social system of reference that a mode of abstraction treating sheer distributions has relevance and merit. In short, macrostructural theory starts from the conception that individual and collective units are differentiated social objects of orientation for actors in an arbitrary social system.

In macrostructural theory, the two modes of social differentiation are referred to as *nominal* and *graduated*. Thus, a nominal dimension is an abstract way of talking about a set of collectivities with mutual exclusion of members. A graduated dimension is an abstract way of talking about a collection of strata with mutually exclusive ordered placement of social units. Given a specified set of such dimensions, each actor is located in the social space of such collectivities and strata. The nominal and graduated dimensions are "coordinates" of the space. These dimensions are ordinarily correlated to some extent, and their correlation, technically called consolidation, is a substantively crucial feature of the social system. Put another way, in macrostructural theory, "correlation" (consolidation) is not merely a vehicle of description of data; it is a theoretically significant parameter of the social system.

How do these dimensional conceptions relate to the problem of the integration of complex social systems? First consider the microanalysis of the system. The structure of the social system is a network of social relations adjusted to each other and to the environment. Social relations are subequilibria, that is, equilibrium states of pairs of members in a given social environment and with given parameters. Interactional events more or less closely approximate to the social relation as such (the attractor state in the stabilized case). The dimensional locations – standing definitions of the individual actors in terms of institutional groups and less stable but apparent stocks of resources – of the individuals are among the parameters or determinants of the parameters. For instance, these locations define a similarity between any pair of persons. Actor $A$ is an ⟨American woman⟩ with ⟨doctorate in economics⟩ and actor $B$ is a ⟨Canadian man⟩ with ⟨bachelor degree in electrical engineering⟩. The interaction between such actors, initiated from some given conditions such as work, yields a concrete tie, a social relation with its own distinctive direction and intensity of interpersonal sentiment. In terms of analytical action theory (Section 3.3) the pair realizes a dynamical subsystem with its own emergent equilibrium level of integration characterized by magnitudes of particularism–diffuseness (as well as affectivity–quality). Such relations are bonds between people. If we look at the whole set of such social relations, the social structure, at any time, we can ask nonlocal questions. In one perspective, that treated earlier in this chapter, the question leads out from the pair to the network of all individuals with the full pattern of bonds connecting various pairs.

But another nonlocal question arises. It characterizes the macrostructural perspective. Given the set of systemwide collectivities or institutional groups described by a given nominal dimension, to what extent do social bonds connect members of distinct groups? For instance, to what extent do Americans and Canadians marry? To what extent do friendships connect women and men, blacks and whites, Catholics and Protestants? Passing beyond only binary distinctions, what is the probability that a friendship tie connects two persons of different religious affiliation? Similarly, there are nonlocal questions arising with respect to resource distributions: Given the set of strata corresponding to a graduated dimension, to what extent do social bonds connect individuals more or less distant on the resource distribution? For instance, to what extent are the wealthy intermarrying with the poor? To what extent are the political elite socially associating with the powerless? What is the mean distance with respect to a resource between two nodes in the social relation? These nonlocal questions relate to the problem of the integration of the whole social system of reference and not to the problem of the formation of a social relation for a particular pair.

### 4.6.2. Formalization of macrostructural theory: I

Formal macrostructural theory – the theory to be presented here – has a conceptual scheme derivative from the preceding sketch of the basic ideas. The formal theory joins two basic types of model objects: the network and the space of positions with respect to the dimensions of social differentiation. The network contains the concrete social relations among the members of the social system of reference. The space is overlayed on the network, as it were, so that there are types of nodes. The node is labelled by its positional identification: ⟨man with income⟩, say. The fundamental formal analytical variables of the theory (Blau and Schwartz, 1984) are:

1. *Heterogeneity,* a quantitative property of the distribution of nodes with respect to any nominal dimension of social differentiation
2. *Inequality,* a quantitative property of the distribution of nodes with respect to any graduated dimension of social differentiation
3. *Consolidation,* a quantitative property of the joint distribution of nodes over multiple dimensions of differentiation

In the presentation here we add:

4. *Relation heterogeneity,* a property of the network in terms of the heterogeneity of the pairs of nodes in the social relation
5. *Relation inequality,* a property of the network in terms of the average distance between nodes in the social relation

Each of these key five terms will be given a specific quantitative definition in what follows. Essentially, the theorems are proven relations among these concepts, holding for particular classes of model objects defined by the number and types of dimensions of differentiation.

The formal ideas and results to be discussed at this point began as an attempt to formalize Blau's theory. That process was initiated with the publication in 1981 of a paper that showed how the heterogeneity part of the theory could be treated within the framework of biased net models (Fararo, 1981b). Shortly thereafter, Skvoretz (1983) elaborated on this idea and extended the heterogeneity models. Following these publications, we collaborated in Fararo and Skvoretz (1984b) and Skvoretz and Fararo (1986) to show how the whole approach was extendable to the inequality side of the theory. In Fararo and Skvoretz (in press) we employ the biased net parameter method to treat a variety of other problems in macrosociology not necessarily tied to Blau's theory. This latter effort shows how the framework permits a unification research program (see Fararo and Skvoretz, 1987, for an elaboration and also Section 4.7). The model objects and theoretical models within the biased net framework that Skvoretz and I have been working with are called *formal macrostructural theory.* Thus in this section I shall show that important and basic concepts and principles of Blau's macrostructural theory are represented mathematically within formal macrostructural theory.

Before discussing the principles of the theory, I shall indicate how the basic variables are represented in the model. As in Blau's empirical research, we represent heterogeneity, denoted $H$, by the probability that a pair of persons from the population are in distinct systemwide collectivities on a given dimension.

Equivalently, $H$ is the probability that a *random interaction* involves nodes in distinct systemwide collectivities. Each dimension gives rise to a particular $H$.

Also as in Blau's work, we represent the inequality of a graduated dimension over a population as the Gini measure of the distribution, denoted $G$. Each graduated dimension gives rise to its own $G$.

We represent consolidation in terms of derived correlation coefficients between dimensions of various types. This is in marked contrast with the work of Blau and Schwartz (1984) and others who have empirically applied the theory. Operating within the confines of a conventional (but deficient) dogma of "methodology," these authors have assumed that the choice of the correlation coefficient is not something we could ever expect to be dictated by theory. That this is false for this theory was first shown by Skvoretz (1983), and since that time a number of *required* correlation coefficients have been identified, with the requirement shifting with the particular form of the model object. More will be said on this point later.

The relation heterogeneity, denoted $H_{\mathrm{R}}$, is the probability that a pair of persons *in the relation* are in distinct institutional groups of a given dimension. Similarly, the relation inequality, denoted $G_{\mathrm{R}}$, is a Gini measure to be explained in what follows.

The five ideas are further clarified in the context of showing how we derive the three fundamental principles of the theory. These basic principles of macrostructural theory have been compactly summarized by Blau and Schwartz (1984:13–15). In what follows, I shall state each principle in words and then show how formal macrostructural theory permits the deduction of one or more formulas from which the principle can be "read off." The logic here closely approximates the theory structure suggested by the integrated philosophical model described in Section 1.3.3. The really general principle, in the nonhomogeneous sense of the representation principle, is that social systems are biased networks. The substantive theories are embedded within the analytical framework defined by this principle. Thus, the "principles" of macrostructural theory appear as corresponding to derived properties of theoretical models constructed within the framework. However, these deductions do not *explain* the propositions to which they correspond because there is no generativity (Section 1.4.3). They simply show that what is important in the theory is captured within the formal framework without any need for special assumptions.

The *first principle* is that heterogeneity promotes intergroup relations.

In formal macrostructural theory, *intergroup relations* refers to the analytical element $H_{\mathrm{R}}$, the relation heterogeneity. Just as $H$ is defined with reference to the population, $H_{\mathrm{R}}$ is defined with reference to the ties. When a tie is considered, either both parties are in the same institutional group with respect to the nominal dimension of interest or not. The probability that they are in distinct such groups is $H_R$. We represent the basic *homophily* propensity in social relations by a bias parameter, denoted $\tau$.

This parameter is defined as follows. Let $R$ be the social relation and let $E$ mean the event that two nodes are "equivalent" in the specific sense of being in the same institutional group. The probability of event $E$ if the two nodes are sampled at random is $P(E) = 1 - H$. The corresponding probability for the heterogeneity of ties is denoted by $P(E|R)$. Operationally, select a tie in $R$ at random and then see if the members of the pair are in the same group or not. With data, find the proportion of ties in which the two persons in the relation are in the same institutional group. So $H_R = 1 - P(E|R)$ is the chance that they are *not* in the same institutional group, which is the relation (as contrasted with the population or node) heterogeneity. It would be simply $H$ if the relation and the dimension were independent. The bias parameter is introduced under the assumption that, generally, people will have a propensity to form social relations with those in the same rather than different institutional groups. This provides the implicit definition of the bias parameter as this propensity, called the *homophily bias:*

$$P(E|R) = \tau + (1 - \tau)P(E) \tag{4.6.1}$$

Then, in terms of $H$ and $H_R$, this is equivalent to

$$H_R = (1 - \tau)H \tag{4.6.2}$$

Formally, this defines a transformation: The population heterogeneity is transformed into a network or relation heterogeneity.

From the formula, we see that no matter how strong the homophily propensity, the greater the value of $H$, the greater the value of $H_R$. In short, heterogeneity promotes intergroup relations as measured by heterogeneity of ties. Hence, the first principle of macrostructural theory is read off from a derived formula of formal macrostructural theory.

This formula can be used to measure $\tau$ for a particular network where the nodes are differentiated in one dimension. It is then given a near-tautologous interpretation since it can only be wrong if the heterogeneity of ties is greater than the population heterogeneity.

The formula also can be used in another way. Namely, suppose we have $K$ networks of the same content, that is, the same mode of differentiation and social relation type. For instance, in Blau and Schwartz (1984) the $K$ networks are the more than 100 SMSAs in the United States and the social relation is marriage. Then we have a set of more than 100 pairs of points $(H, H_R)$ that can be plotted in the plane. According to (4.6.2), with the homophily bias treated as constant, the points should lie on a straight line. This could well be wrong in a stronger sense: The slope might be positive without the relation's being linear. If the qualitative form of the data satisfies the formula, one estimates the slope, which yields an estimate of $\tau$.

In terms of the preceding concepts, by the *salience* of a nominal dimension one means the difference between the relation heterogeneity and the population heterogeneity:

$$S = H_R - H = \tau H \quad (4.6.3)$$

Hence, the greater is the homophily bias, the greater is the salience, and the greater is the heterogeneity, the greater is the salience.

The *second principle* of macrostructural theory is that inequality increases the status distance of associates (Blau and Schwartz, 1984:15).

As in Blau's work, in formal macrostructural theory, the inequality property is measured by the Gini index $G$. Let $X$ be some socially defined resource such as wealth or prestige. There are alternative formulas for various purposes (Allison, 1978). One such formula used by Blau (1977) is given here in terms of expected value notation used with probability concepts. Namely, if $X$ is a variable with a probability distribution, then $E(X)$ is the average computed with respect to that distribution, and using the same probability distribution, $E(D)$ is the average difference between every pair of members of the population with respect to the amount of the resource they have. Then the Gini index of inequality is given by

$$G = E(D)/2E(X) \quad (4.6.4)$$

The aim now is to sketch the parallel to the heterogeneity formulas, here in the domain of graduated dimensions of differentiation of social actors. For this purpose, note that $E(D)$ can be thought of as the expected distance in terms of the $X$ resource between a *random pair* from the population.

Now let $R$ be the social relation. Then by $G_R$ I mean the Gini inequality measure with $E(D)$ replaced by $E(D|R)$, that is, the expected difference in the amount of resource $X$ between members in relation $R$. Thus, to interpret $E(D)$, we think of a random pair from the population; to interpret $E(D|R)$, we think of a random tie from the relation (thought of as a network of concrete ties between pairs of members of the population). Hence,

$$G_R = E(D|R)/2E(X) \quad (4.6.5)$$

If the distribution of resource $X$ is independent of relation $R$, then $G_R = G$. This is a definition, and the quantity defined, $G_R$, is termed the *relation inequality*.

It is shown elsewhere (Fararo and Skvoretz 1984b) that a variety of models differing in complexity of assumptions generate formulas for which (4.6.6) is the "kernel" in the sense that a term $(1-\tau)G$ occurs in all such formulas and tends to be approached in certain limits. This formula arises from the simplest model, which assumes that with a bias event, associates of a person are restricted to those in the same stratum (treated as at distance $D=0$ in the model); otherwise, with no bias event occurring, each is selected at random from the distribution and so with expected distance $E(D)$. This yields the kernel formula

$$G_{\mathrm{R}}=(1-\tau)G \tag{4.6.6}$$

This is termed the *social relation inequality formula*. It can be thought of as a mapping of population inequality with respect to resource $X$ into social network inequality with respect to that resource (Fararo and Skvoretz, 1984b).

The salience is defined as the difference:

$$S=G-G_{\mathrm{R}}=\tau G \tag{4.6.7}$$

Now at last I raise a point that might have troubled the reader. It is awkward for theory to work with an arbitrary set of strata on what amounts to a resource distribution continuum. The more general situation seems to be as follows. Social relations are emergent or built up under given conditions, one of which is differential resource distribution. This yields a difference $D$, or dissimilarity, which we know makes it less likely that integrative social bonds will form. This is the similarity–sentiment–interaction nexus described by a proposition in Table 2.2. Hence, in equilibrium, we expect a social relation will be characterized by a situation in which the probability that a pair of actors in the relation will differ by $D$ in resource $X$ is a decreasing function of $D$. Assuming a continuum of values for $X$, we can represent this in a more complex inequality model by an exponential bias density of the form

$$b(D)=\beta e^{-\beta D} \tag{4.6.8}$$

where $D>0$ and $\beta>0$. Then in terms of expected values, we have the result

$$E(D|R)=\tau(1/\beta)+(1-\tau)E(D)$$

since the expected value of the exponentially distributed $D$ is given by the reciprocal of the exponential parameter. In turn, this implies that

$$G_{\mathrm{R}}=(1-\tau)G \;+\; \tau(1/\mu) \tag{4.6.9}$$

where $\mu=\beta[2E(X)]$. We can call $1/\mu$ the *bias radius*. As the bias radius decreases, the right-hand side of (4.6.9) approaches the right-hand side of (4.6.6), which illustrates the general point that $(1-\tau)G$ is the kernel of the transformation of $G$ into $G_{\mathrm{R}}$. (For further discussion of these compact statements, see Fararo and Skvoretz, 1984b.)

We see that no matter how large is the homophily tendency to associate with others near the self in resources, the greater the $G$, the greater the $G_R$. In short, population inequality increases the status distance of associates. Hence, the second principle of macrostructural theory is read off from a derived formula of formal macrostructural theory.

There is a mathematical complication that I address here, but without loss of continuity readers may wish to skip the mathematical note and pick up the thread of theory in Section 4.6.3.

*A note on a mathematical treatment of a complication.* There is a complication that arises in connection with heterogeneity and inequality. This pertains to the possibility that $\tau$ may vary with $H$ or with $G$. For instance, consider a social system with a rather homogeneous ethnic composition and a particular value $\tau_0$ of the ethnic homophily bias parameter. Now let the population become more heterogeneous. On empirical grounds one might expect the bias parameter to increase. But as the heterogeneity increases still further, it seems plausible to argue ethnic homophily might be reduced through the mixing that occurs as induced by the increasing heterogeneity. This suggests that $\tau$ is a function of $H$, which is at first increasing and then decreasing with some critical value of $H$ separating these two sides of the function. This suggests that (4.6.2) may be replaced by

$$H_R = [1 - \tau(H)]H$$

such that

$$d\tau/dH > 0 \quad \text{if } H < H^*$$
$$d\tau/dH < 0 \quad \text{if } H > H^*$$

An increase in $H$ produces an increase in $H_R$ if and only if

$$1 - \tau(H) > H(d\tau/dH)$$

From this we conclude:

1. If H is large, meaning above the critical level $H^*$, then any further increase in $H$ produces an increase in $H_R$: In highly heterogeneous systems, (further) heterogeneity promotes intergroup relations.
2. If H is not large, meaning it is below the critical level $H^*$, then it is possible for an increase in $H$ to produce a decrease in $H_R$: For highly homogeneous systems, an increase in heterogeneity may reduce intergroup relations by increasing the homophily bias.

A similar qualification holds for inequality. Formula (4.6.6) is replaced by

$$G_R = [1 - \tau(G)]G$$

such that

$$d\tau/dG > 0 \quad \text{if } G < G^*$$
$$d\tau/dG < 0 \quad \text{if } G > G^*$$

An increase in $G$ produces an increase in $G_R$ if and only if

$$1 - \tau(G) > G(d\tau/dG)$$

We see that the argument is formally identical to the $H$ case, although the intuition behind the critical value is not as clear. If one thinks of $G$ as reaching very high levels, then we expect the elite to socially associate only with the elite, implying a correspondingly high value of the homophily. This suggests that $G^*$ may be, in effect, infinite. In any case, if $G$ is less than the critical value, then an increase in $G$ may produce a decrease in relation inequality by virtue of its effect on increasing $\tau$. It seems that precisely these propositions may help explain some anomalies recently discovered in testing the macrostructural theory (Blau and Schwartz, 1984:49).

### *4.6.3. Formalization of macrostructural theory: II*

The formalization process in Section 4.6.2 concerned the most elementary propositions of the theory. These are encapsulated in the first two principles of the theory, which deal with a general single dimension of nominal differentiation and a general single dimension of graduated differentiation, respectively. Consolidation enters the theory when two or more dimensions, of whatever types, are considered simultaneously. This section treats this more complex analytical context corresponding to the third principle of the theory.

The *third principle* of macrostructural theory is that the extent to which dimensions of social structure are correlated modifies the effects of heterogeneity and inequality on intergroup relations. To the extent that such dimensions are *not* correlated, even homophily-generated associations (with respect to one dimension) will generate intergroup relations (with respect to the second dimension).

Using the term *intersecting* to mean lack of consolidation, Blau and Schwartz (1984:15) state this principle in the form: "Many intersecting social differences promote intergroup relations." They go on to mention that it incorporates Simmel's idea of cross-cutting circles, also stressed by Coser (1956) in his contribution to general theoretical sociology as an elaboration of Simmel's ideas. The integrative significance of such intersection was also treated by Galtung (1966) under the category "criss-cross."

For example, in university settings, there is a homophily bias: Staff socially associate with staff, professors with professors. But if professors vary substantially in ethnic background, their very proclivity to form social bonds with each other means people of heterogeneous ethnic background are forming such bonds. Thus the ethnic groups as such are being integrated as a by-product of choices of associates on a relatively uncorrelated dimension.

Formal macrostructural theory treats consolidation as a term that arises in derived formulas of multidimensional models of several sorts: (1) uniformly nominal dimensions, (2) uniformly graduated dimensions, and (3) mixed cases involving at least one nominal and at least one graduated dimension. In each case, various combinations of bias parameters can be introduced. The derivations of such formulas are quite complex. What they generate is not only a formula but a term in the formula that amounts to a formula specific required measure of correlation to represent the analytical element of consolidation. I want to indicate the logical structure and empirical interpretation of some examples of such derived formulas without reproducing the derivations here. For the earliest detailed derivation for one class of cases, see Skvoretz (1983). For another class of cases, see Skvoretz and Fararo (1986).

*Consolidation principle for two nominal dimensions.* With two nominal dimensions, we have three heterogeneity terms, one each for dimensions $A$ and $B$ and a heterogeneity of the positional or joint dimension $A \times B$. This is given by the probability that two nodes are in distinct positions in the multidimensional space generated by $A$ and $B$. Corresponding to these three population heterogeneities, there are three relation or network heterogeneity terms:

$H_{\mathrm{R}}^{A}$ = the probability that a tie in the network connects two nodes in distinct $A$ groups
$H_{\mathrm{R}}^{B}$ = the probability that a tie in the network connects two nodes in distinct $B$ groups
$H_{\mathrm{R}}^{J}$ = the probability that a tie in the network connects two nodes in distinct multidimensional positions (defined by $A$ and $B$)

The theoretical model for this case yields the three equations

$$H_{\mathrm{R}}^{A} = (1-\tau^{A})H^{A}(1-\tau^{B}\mathrm{Tau}_{A|0}) \tag{4.6.10a}$$
$$H_{\mathrm{R}}^{B} = (1-\tau^{B})H^{B}(1-\tau^{A}\mathrm{Tau}_{B|0}) \tag{4.6.10b}$$
$$H_{\mathrm{R}}^{J} = H_{\mathrm{R}}^{A} + H_{\mathrm{R}}^{B} - (1-\tau^{A})(1-\tau^{B})(H^{A}+H^{B}-H^{J}) \tag{4.6.10c}$$

Here the Tau terms are Goodman and Kruskal's statistic, obtained in the details of the formal derivation. (See Skvoretz, 1983, Appendix, although a somewhat different notation is used.) In the context of these and related equations, the Goodman and Kruskal statistic is always denoted by Tau, whereas the homophily parameter is always denoted by $\tau$.

The Tau statistic varies between zero (no correlation) and 1 (perfect correlation). The Tau term in the first of the two equations is based on predicting the $A$ group based on information about the $B$ group. The second has the reverse interpretation. Thus the two Tau terms together represent the consolidation of the two nominal dimensions. The effect of consolidation, however, depends on the homophily associated with the two dimensions as seen by the multipliers of the Tau terms. I emphasize that the Tau terms were not arbitrarily inserted into the formulas but emerge in the deductive process. They are the *required* mode of representation of consolidation if one works within the framework of the biased net representation of macrostructural theory. In this respect, as I promised earlier, these formulas introduce a rational or theory-driven choice of a statistic, which is rather unusual in sociology.

Let us now look at a few special cases to get a feel for what these formulas mean.

1. If the two dimensions are perfectly uncorrelated, both Tau terms are zero. Then the first two equations are independent or uncoupled examples of the basic heterogeneity equation (4.6.2). The third equation reduces the sum of the two heterogeneities in computing the positional heterogeneity by an amount that depends on the bias parameters.
2. If the two dimensions are perfectly correlated, then the Tau terms are both unity. Also, suppose that $\tau^B = 0$. Then

$$H_R^A = (1 - \tau^A)H^A$$
$$H_R^B = (1 - \tau^A)H^B$$
$$H_R^J = (1 - \tau^A)H^J$$

   Consider the positional dimension $A$ with values ⟨faculty⟩ and ⟨staff⟩ and the gender dimension $B$. The Tau assumption corresponds to an all-female staff, all-male faculty, for instance. Speaking purely hypothetically, in taking gender as dimension $B$, the homophily assumption is that it is not an "orientational" basis for social relations. That is, the actors do not seek out same-gender associates. Nevertheless, to the extent that the faculty–staff distinction is such a basis for social relations – faculty seek out faculty, staff seek out staff – rates of social association between men and women will be reduced, as shown in the second equation. In the limit, if the homophily bias along this dimension is unity, there is no social association between men and women even though in one sense ($\tau^B = 0$) it is unintended.
3. Suppose the dimensions are only moderately correlated at the level of each Tau = .5 and that as in case 2 the bias parameter $\tau^B = 0$. Then

$$H_R^A = (1 - \tau^A)H^A$$
$$H_R^B = (1 - .5\tau^A)H^B$$
$$H_R^J = (1 - \tau^A)H^J + .5\tau^A H^B$$

Using the same substantive example as in case 2, we see that the relational heterogeneity with respect to faculty–staff mixing remains the same, the mixing with respect to gender increases (since the effect of positional homophily is cut down by the .5 coefficient) and the relation heterogeneity by "joint location" with respect to $A$ and $B$ is increased by the factor shown in the third equation. This demonstrates the general point that a reduction in consolidation of dimensions is conducive to the building of intergroup relations. This is true in this case even though the basic propensities of professors to informally associate with each other and staff persons to associate with other staff persons have not been changed.

More abstractly, one can see by differentiation of the first and second equations in (4.6.10) with respect to their Tau terms that a decrease in consolidation produces an increase in relation heterogeneity. In turn, this result in conjunction with the third equation shows that a decrease in consolidation produces an increase in relation heterogeneity with respect to groups in distinct positions in the multidimensional space. This is the basic consolidation principle for the case of two nominal dimensions, each of which has a homophily bias.

*Consolidation principle for two graduated dimensions.* Consider two graduated dimensions, denoted $X$ and $Y$. The use of the simple model of strata in this case yields an analogous set of three equations with very similar interpretations and implications. I shall not present these, but I refer the reader to the relevant literature. (See Skvoretz and Fararo, 1986.) One new element is worth discussion, however. This arises in that the derived correlation coefficient between $X$ and $Y$, though of the PRE (proportional reduction in error) type, has no precedent in the literature of which I am aware. Namely, suppose we define a notation parallel to that for Tau in the preceding section:

$$\mathrm{Beta}_{X|0} = (G^X - G^{X|0})/G^X \tag{4.6.11}$$

This formula defines a correlation coefficient for expected status differences that have been converted into standardized forms so as to be Gini indices. The term $G^{X|0}$ means the conditional Gini inequality on $X$ given equality or zero difference on graduated dimension $Y$. A similar formula holds for $Y$: There is a conditional Gini term of the form $G^{Y|0}$ that is the Gini inequality with respect to $Y$ given equality or zero difference with respect to $X$. Thus, as with Tau, there are two Beta correlations that together formally represent the consolidation of $X$ and $Y$. Analysis of the derived triple of equations shows that the lower the consolidation of $X$ and $Y$, the greater the relation inequality between nodes. (Corresponding to the pair of statuses of a node, on $X$ and $Y$, we define a composite status as a weighted combination; then the consolidation principle also holds for the weighted status: The lower the consolidation of two graduated dimensions, the greater the average status distance between people who are in social association.)

*Consolidation principle for a mixed case.* Let us look at one case in which there are two dimensions, one of which is nominal with "antihomophily" with regard to the social bond and the other of which is graduated with homophily bias. Antihomophily means a bias in the direction of outgroup relation. The prototypical case is gender with regard to marriage. From the point of view of formal macrosociological theory, the statement that "gender is antihomophily with respect to marriage" is the representation of the fact that the relation is intergender. Rather than treating this as a nuisance factor for a theory based on a general homophily axiom (Blau, 1977), it is preferable to simply treat it as one empirical case that instantiates a formal possibility comprehended within the general framework. It is an institutional fact about marriage that it is intergender. There is no need to restrict ourselves to dimensions that are characterized by the $\tau$ bias only. We can introduce a second type of bias parameter as follows.

Let $\phi$ be the antihomophily bias parameter. It is implicitly defined by the expression

$$H_{\mathrm{R}} = \phi + (1 - \phi)H \qquad (4.6.12)$$

When $\phi = 0$, the relation and the dimension are independent. When $\phi = 1$, the probability is 1 that any tie of the given kind connects nodes in distinct classes on the given dimension. So, for instance, with $R$ as marriage and the dimension as gender, we set $\phi = 1$ to obtain complete marital heterogeneity with respect to gender.

For the general case under consideration in this section, we have nominal dimension $A$ with bias parameter $\phi$, which is the propensity to select associates in the *out*group for the given type of social association. We also have a graduated dimension $B$ with its assumed homophily bias $\tau$.

The heterogeneity of the nominal dimension $A$ is simply denoted $H$. The Gini inequality of the graduated dimension $X$ is denoted $G$. (Although there are two dimensions, we need no special subscripts or superscripts since the $H$–$G$ distinction will distinguish them in formulas.) Corresponding to dimension $A$, there is the problem of accounting for $H_{\mathrm{R}}$, and corresponding to $X$, there is the problem of accounting for $G_{\mathrm{R}}$. So a pair of coupled equations are derived in which $A$ properties have an effect on the term $G_{\mathrm{R}}$ and $X$ properties have an effect on $H_{\mathrm{R}}$ via the consolidation of the two dimensions. Once again the derivation yields a new correlation, now denoted Phi (for a discussion and derivation, see Skvoretz and Fararo, 1986). The two equations are

$$H_{\mathrm{R}} = \phi + (1-\phi)H[1-\tau\mathrm{Tau}] \tag{4.6.13a}$$
$$G_{\mathrm{R}} = (1-\tau)G[1+\phi\kappa\mathrm{Phi}] \tag{4.6.13b}$$

The Tau term involves prediction of the institutional group given the stratum on $X$. The Phi term involves prediction of the stratum on $X$ given the group. The constant $\kappa$ arises in the derivation and need not concern us. Note the coupling of the two equations via the consolidation terms. When Tau = Phi = 0, for minimum consolidation, the two equations simply become the generic forms for their respective types of dimensions and biases independent of each other. In general, the smaller is Tau, the greater is $H_{\mathrm{R}}$.

However, we see that the effect of Phi is different: The greater the Phi, the greater the $G_{\mathrm{R}}$. The critical point is that the correlated nominal dimension is *anti*homophily in character. Thus if $X$ is correlated with it, the effect will be in the same direction. Pairs of persons who select each other via outgroup membership on $A$ will, via the correlation, be selecting others different on $X$. This inflates the value of $G_{\mathrm{R}}$. But the effect of Phi, in turn, depends on the magnitude of the antihomophily bias term $\phi$, as the second equation shows. If $\phi = 0$, then we return to the kernel transformation $(1-\tau)G$.

For the case of marriage, we can take $\phi = 1$ as noted earlier, in which case the first equation reads $H_{\mathrm{R}} = 1$ and $\phi$ simply drops out of the second equation so that the multiplier of the kernel transformation is $1 + \kappa\mathrm{Phi}$.

A variety of other developments of the formal theory show the way in which the mathematical formulation of the theory is faithful to the original ideas of Blau but also goes well beyond them in various directions. Before concluding, one example will be treated. This concerns the derivation of a hypothesis put forward by Feld (1982), who argues that a great deal of what investigators have interpreted as in-group preference in the formation of social associations is due to *foci of activity*. In the context of Chapter 2 of this book, these foci are the givens of the external or adaptation subsystems of dynamical social systems. They are work and neighborhood settings, for instance. In fact, formal macrostructural theory implies a formalized statement of Feld's hypothesis that such settings involve disproportionately homogeneous sets of people.

The key to the derivation is to notice that a set of work departments, for instance, can be treated as a nominal dimension of differentiation. The intradepartmental homogeneity is with respect to some second dimension, such as age in Feld's data. Call this second dimension $A$ and let $B$ be the "departmental" or focus-of-activity dimension. So in terms of the present framework, *Feld's hypothesis,* to be demonstrated, states:

1. The population homogeneity of $A$ within $B$ groups tends to be larger than the overall population homogeneity of $A$.

2. This tendency gets reflected in the association rate so that some part of the homogeneity $(1-H^A_R)$ of the relation is *not* due to any homophily bias $(\tau^A)$ but to fact 1.

To derive part 1 of the hypothesis, we define the concept of conditional heterogeneity $H^{A|0}$ as the probability that two nodes are in different $A$ groups given that they are in the same $B$ group. It can be shown that:

$$H^{A|0}=H^A(1-\mathrm{Tau}_{A|0}) \tag{4.6.14}$$

Since the correlation varies between zero and 1, this implies the following about the conditional homogeneity:

$$1-H^{A|0}\geq 1-H^A$$

But this is part 1 of Feld's hypothesis. Part 2 follows from this first result (Fararo and Skvoretz, in press). It is the first part, as Feld surmised from various data, that is critical. The embedding of the problem within the framework of formal macrostructural theory amounted to no more than the typical stratagem of using a formalized framework: We *represent* the phenomenon of interest in terms of the framework and proceed to *show* that some otherwise isolated empirical hypothesis logically follows. This takes nothing from Feld, since the hypothesis not only still stands but is made even more secure by its derivation from basic theory.

Moreover, it turns out that if we elaborate on this idea of conditional heterogeneity a little further, we meet with and formalize another major idea in Blau's theory. In their listing of major theorems, Blau and Schwartz (1984:218) state what they designate as T-15: "The more society's heterogeneity results from the heterogeneity within rather than that among its substructures, the more it promotes intergroup relations." For variety of illustration, consider racial groups ($A$) and residential neighborhoods ($B$). If each neighborhood is racially homogeneous, then no relational heterogeneity – interracial contacts – will arise out of residence. Formally, notice the following: It is apparent that the conditional heterogeneity of $A$ is the average of a set of conditional heterogeneities, one per $B$-group. For each $A$-group (race), if all its members are concentrated in a particular $B$-group (neighborhood), then each such conditional heterogeneity of race within the neighborhood is zero and so is the average. Here the overall heterogeneity is due entirely to heterogeneity among, rather than within, substructures (neighborhoods). With a zero term on the left side of (4.6.14), the consolidation term must be unity. Hence, by (4.6.10a), the relational heterogeneity is zero. This corresponds to the intuitive case at the extreme. More generally, as the conditional heterogeneity of $A$ in each $B$-group increases, so does the overall conditional heterogeneity of $A$. This is simply a matter of averaging. Then, with the overall heterogeneity $H^A$ constant, the consolidation must decrease, according to (4.6.14), and hence, the extent of intergroup relations will increase, by (4.6.10a), also holding constant the other parameters in the latter formula. This is precisely what T-15 asserts. If we call the conditional heterogeneity on the left side of (4.6.14) the *penetration* of differentiation by $A$ into $B$ substructures, then the derived general statement corresponding to T-15 is that increases in penetration produce increases in the extent of intergroup relations. In the spirit of unification, we note that Feld's hypothesis and T-15 draw attention to the same idea. In analytical terms, the idea is represented through (4.6.14) and its consequences.

### [illegible]

The main burden of the preceding formalization was the task of showing that the three major principles of macrostructural theory, as well as subsidiary results, are logical consequences of quantitative definitions and the representation of homophily and antihomophily. In general, every abstract class of cases presents a new version of the problems just treated, such as the derivation of the proper consolidation formula. The developments described here have far from exhausted all the possibilities. Empirical tests of models have been initiated (Skvoretz, in press), but in the present context the more relevant question is potential theoretical developments and further unification efforts.

In particular, for the purposes of general theoretical sociology, we need to extend the theory to cover at least the three-dimensional cases such as the Weberian triple of graduated dimensions (wealth, status, and power) as well as more complex cases of intersecting/consolidating nominal dimensions. Some work has been initiated on the fully multidimensional formal macrostructural theory. (See, e.g., Fararo and Skvoretz, 1984b: Proposition 4.)

As an example of how advances in formal macrostructural theory can relate to other efforts in theoretical sociology, consider the recent work on societal stratification by Turner (1984). Many of Turner's admittedly awkward quasi-formal expressions could be upgraded in significance with the use of the quantitative concepts and procedures of formal macrostructural theory. For instance, what Turner calls "differentiation of homogeneous subpopulations" is simply the consolidation of a nominal social dimension with a nominal *cultural* dimension. The former defines mutually exclusive types of actors; the latter defines mutually exclusive types of beliefs, norms, values, and the like. The Tau consolidation terms replace Turner's symbol $DF_{HO}$, converting an abbreviation for a verbal term into an empirically meaningful quantitative concept.

In turn, this social–cultural nexus would relate to Collins's (1987:196) Durkheimian "principle of social density": "The more individuals are exposed to networks of social encounters that are diverse and cosmopolitan, the more their ideas will be abstract, relativistic, and concerned with long-term consequences. Conversely, individuals in localistic and enclosed networks think and speak concretely and particularistically." In its turn, this statement is suggestive of our upcoming topics of unifying weak-ties theory and macrostructural theory and applying the unified theory to the small-world problem.

Turner relates his propositions to comparative analysis of societal types of the kind described by Lenski and Lenski (1982). For formal macrostructural theory, the corresponding requirement is a theoretical comparative statics derived from the study of a dynamical social system, as discussed in Chapter 2. From this broader dynamic perspective, the formulas derived in the preceding represent statics without derivation from dynamics, decidedly an inferior mode of theory but not unusual in macrosociology. There is much to be done.

Thus, formal macrosociology is a frontier of theoretical sociology with much promise. Formal developments provide challenges to theorists of the type familiar in physics, that is, to reach out to each other in efforts of formal unification to arrive at more comprehensive theoretical systems.

Another example of such a possibility relates to the work of Jasso (1978, 1980, 1986). Her central construct, discussed earlier in connection with the control principle of action (Section 3.2.2), is a quantitative subjective justice evaluation, here denoted by $J$. There is a comparison process taking the form

$$J = \text{justice evaluation} = \ln(\text{actual}) - \ln(\text{just})$$

As Jasso uses this idea, the actual and the just elements are expressed in terms of observables, so that $J$ values can be computed once we are given certain data. Jasso's papers apply this construct in a variety of ways to generate deduced propositions.

There are two ways that Jasso's theory fits into the present context. What we have here is a theoretical construct with considerable potential for deployment in dynamic theoretical models. A gradient dynamic (minimize felt injustice as the mechanism) might be posited, and as suggested in Chapter 3, the model might be embedded within control systems theory. Then such theoretical models can be studied from the standpoint of their implications for social order. In this way, the fairness of distributions as it is subjectively represented by members can become a central aspect of the discovery of fundamental theorems of theoretical sociology. Therefore, I see Jasso's $J$ theory as an important contribution to general theoretical sociology.

There is a second and more specific way that Jasso's $J$ construct fits into the present context. Her evaluated entities, which she calls "quality-goods" and "quantity-goods" correspond to particular states of nominal and graduated dimensions, respectively. Then, any $J$ term itself, since it varies among the members of the social system of reference, can be regarded as an induced quantitative dimension. But this means that the Gini inequality measure $G^J$ makes sense. In fact, Jasso (1980) shows that for a number of theoretical distributions of quantity goods or graduated dimensions, the corresponding $G^J$ is a function of one or more parameters of the distribution. From the standpoint of the formulas of this chapter, this expression for the Gini in terms of the parameters of the distribution can be inserted into such formulas to predict the relational inequality of a network. The use of explicit distribution forms for theorizing, rather than unspecified forms, as in current formal macrostructural theory, is another advance. It makes the theory more powerful. For if we know that a certain resource can be assumed to satisfy a certain theoretical distribution form, the formulas of macrostructural theory become more exact and predictive.

To illustrate, suppose we know that income is distributed according to the Pareto distribution. This yields a $G^J$ value of $1/c$, where $c$ is Pareto's constant term occurring as a parameter of the distribution (Jasso, 1980: Table 1). Suppose we assume that similarity with respect to justice sentiments is related to the formation of social relations in the sense of a homophily bias. That is, people tend to form social bonds with others who feel similarly treated in the resource distribution. The exploited form ties to one another, for instance, and perhaps the overrewarded join in mutual efforts to allay any possible guilt feelings. Then $G^J = 1/c$ can be inserted into formula (4.6.9) to yield a calculation of the relational inequality in the social network, that is, the average justice sentiment distance for pairs of persons in the relation. If these ideas are linked to the potentialities for a dynamic approach based on the $J$ construct, then the unification of Jasso's $J$ theory with the ideas of macrostructural theory may be a step toward a dynamic macrosociology.

A still more general way of thinking of the place of macrostructural theory in general theoretical sociology is in relation to analytical action theory. Two points deserve brief discussion.

First, the reader may recall that in the discussion of interpenetration in Section 3.3.3, it was mentioned that Parsons delineates two complex aspects of the societal community with respect to which interpenetration exists. The type discussed in Chapter 3 was with respect to the normative order. The other type pertains to what Parsons calls the "collectively organized population." But this is exactly the subject matter of macrostructural theory. The relevant whole is the society as a collectivity in its own right. The relevant parts are the subcollectivities, which are the groups and strata of macrostructural theory. The subparts are the members of the society who are distributed among the parts and create a complex set of criss-crossing ties. This means that interpenetration becomes statistical in that a pattern of overlaps among groups defined in various dimensions constitutes an overall measure of it. Consolidation measures are the obverse of such interpenetration; in other words, what Simmel and Blau call ''intersection'' is interpenetration. Thus, in one aspect, we have been examining some quantitative features of interpenetration in the societal community.

The second point pertains to the AGIL scheme. For each of the AGIL dimensions of a society there exists a resource, expressed as a stock of a symbolic medium, which is distributed among members: wealth (*A*), power (*G*), prestige (*I*), and commitments to relevant values (*L*). Hence, there are six consolidation terms, each computed according to an appropriate formula, but for the present purpose the conceptual connection between theoretical frameworks is what is being stressed. Within this set of six consolidation terms, one stands out as of the utmost importance in the total structure. This is the consolidation of power and value commitments, as emphasized by Stinchcombe (1968:153), who gives the example of rules of civil liberty in the United States. Judges, who have the legitimate power to decide on such matters, are usually strongly committed to the maintenance of civil liberties, whereas many other actors in the society are not so committed but lack such relevant legitimate power. This is another way of stating that civil liberties are strongly institutionalized in the United States. Stinchcombe suggests that this is an illustration of the great importance of correlation concepts as *substantive* quantitative parameters describing social structures.

In a more strongly unified state of general theoretical sociology, we would want to show how such an institutionalization parameter could be defined and precisely interpreted in terms of the normative control hierarchy principle and articulated formally to macrostructural theory. We would have to be precise and rigorous about the underlying concepts and about the definition of the distributions along the graduated dimensions of value commitment and power. Of course, the conceptual and formal character of the normative control hierarchy itself would require more clarity and precision than are given in Chapter 3. To suggest the great significance of a particular form of consolidation, however, is not to denigrate the importance of the whole *system of consolidation,* as we may call it. This is the entire set of six types of correlation terms, one per pair of substructures of the complete structure. Here ''structure'' is interpretable as some attractor state of a network of units described in terms of the AGIL dimensions.

Among the other possibilities for such unification efforts, one stands out as immediately possible, the articulation of formal macrostructural theory with the network analysis branch of structuralism, which treats structures in terms of properties of paths of indirect ties. But the biased network framework includes this element, for instance, the focus on structure statistics and connectivity. In these terms, integration is studied in a more extended sense than is given by the rates of intergroup relations considered previously. In the earlier sections of this chapter, the key bias parameter (the transitivity-type closure bias $\sigma$) was formally related to the connectivity of a network. This culminated in the strength-of-weak-ties theorem. In this section, the bias parameters, mainly $\tau$, related to the classification of the nodes in terms of institutional dimensions. Since both efforts involve theoretical models within the identical analytical framework defined by the representation principle that social systems are biased networks, a natural idea is to articulate the models, providing a unifying formal theory. This is the task of the next section.

## 4.7. Unification of macrostructural theory and the weak-ties model

In Section 4.4, employing the method of bias parameters within the framework of random and biased nets, the strength-of-weak-ties theorem was demonstrated. For a social network with two types of ties, one weak and the other strong, the greater the strength of weak ties, the greater the global integration of the network. The strength of weak ties was represented in terms of a quantity $SWT = 1 - \sigma_w$, where $\sigma$ is the closure bias parameter in triads and the subscript w refers to the weak type of tie. In the prior section, in interpreting the concept of social association in macrostructural theory, I emphasized that the integrative significance of such social bonds depends on the system of reference. For the dyad thought of as a small social system, the buildup of expressive or social bonds has direct integrative significance: A bond is constructed between people who otherwise might be in purely instrumental relation. Thus, the greater the strength of this tie, the more integrated the system comprised of the pair. Classifying ties as strong or weak, for simplicity, weak ties do not create any deep sense of mutual identification, nor do they call out much by way of loyalty to the dyad. They have weak integrative significance for the dyad. Strong ties create solidarity, including a sense of some responsibility to the relation itself. Thus strong ties are conducive to the formation of local groups. But they do not create bridges (Granovetter, 1973) to other such groups. This function is performed by weak ties. So the integrative significance of these two types of ties reverses when we consider the broader or global social system in which they are embedded: Strong ties are weak for global integration; weak ties are strong for global integration. And, in this context, *global integration* means connectivity, the extent to which paths of ties permit information, attitudes, and other entities – including emerging typification schemes constituting aspects of institutions – to diffuse widely through the system.

In this section, we turn to the problem of relating this weak-ties theory to macrostructural theory, as dealt with in this chapter so far. This relation will take a special form, namely, that of *unification* of the two bodies of ideas. This idea of unification is of sufficient general interest to warrant some discussion prior to undertaking the task. (See also Fararo and Skvoretz, 1987.)

One effect of the current era of extensive and productive research on social structural analysis is that the sheer proliferation of the work appears to be too enormous and too diffuse to grasp as a whole. Thus, coupled with enthusiasm about particular lines of development of ideas, there is concern about the lack of clarity in the overall picture, if not downright dismay. Yet such a situation also presents opportunities, since it also generates the motivation to bring the disparate items together. Differentiated lines of research set up pressures for intellectual integration of the resulting theories and findings. Indeed, such integration is a basic aspiration of any theoretical science. It is one element in the overall philosophy of theoretical sociology emphasized in the approach taken in this book. Unification is especially desirable if the entities – principles or sets of ideas – to be unified meet all of the following conditions:

1. Each body of ideas is internally coherent, possessing some vision or picture in which the relatedness of various objects under discussion is clear.
2. Each is abstract and general and offers a range of explanations of various phenomena.
3. Each has successfully passed various empirical tests.
4. Each can be couched in mathematical terms.

These conditions are drawn from impressions of the situation in theoretical physics, a field with a unification dynamic built into it and motivating its fundamental theoretical work today.

In the case at hand, the two bodies of ideas satisfy the four conditions reasonably well, indeed much better than most theoretical formulations in social science. Certainly, nothing comparable was attainable in the treatment of action theory in Chapter 3. I shall discuss the two formalized theories, one focused on the weak-ties principle and the other on macrostructural analysis, in terms of the preceding four criteria.

Weak-ties theory measures up quite well in terms of the four criteria.

First, it represents a very coherent body of ideas. Its image of a complex of social relations in network terms is quite clear: There is a set of nodes and two types of ties indicated by two types of lines connecting the nodes. The unification process operates from where we are and moves us a step farther in an ongoing process; it does not claim to be an absolute attainment of some transcendent goal. In the case at hand, the unification starts from a version of weak-ties theory in terms of the formal treatment, in which "weak" and "strong" are two types of lines. An alternative and ultimately preferable starting point would assign a quantitative strength to each line, such that weak and strong are segments of values on a continuum.[8] The local-versus-global distinction is also reasonably sharp: On the one hand, we have a node and the set of nodes to which it is directly related by ties; on the other hand, we have the entire social network with its numerous paths of indirect ties and overall connectivity property. The principle highlights the importance of the weak type of ties for the overall connectivity.

Second, the ideas are abstract and general: They are not limited either historically or culturally since they are purely structural. Granovetter (1973) showed that the key idea may be employed to account for a variety of phenomena.

Third, further applications of the ideas have proved fruitful, and tests of derived hypotheses have been successful. (See Granovetter, 1982, for a summary and, in particular, Friedkin, 1980, for an example of an empirical test.)

Finally, as shown in this chapter, it has proved possible to embed this body of ideas within the framework of the theory of random and biased nets. This mathematical apparatus, we saw, permitted a mathematical representation of the strength of weak ties and of global integration with a corresponding derivation of the main theorem.

Macrostructural theory also satisfies the four conditions. First, it is quite coherent. Its analytical standpoint toward social structure is especially constructed for the structural analysis of complex social systems involving potentially millions and even billions of people. Its image is that such people are mapped into positions in a multidimensional space of dimensions of social differentiation. Sets of people in the same or similar positions constitute institutional groups and strata. Patterns of social relations are treated in terms of their integrative significance for the complex system that, in this aspect, is a system of partially overlapping institutional groups and strata. Second, the theory is abstract and general, by design, since it too is purely structural, albeit in a different sense than weak-ties theory. Based on this abstract generality, it can be exemplified or instantiated with respect to a wide variety of times and places, of dimensions, and even of concrete forms of associations among people. When so applied, it offers an account of comparative intergroup integration in terms of comparative rates of intergroup association by invoking differences in heterogeneity, inequality, and consolidation as explanatory ideas.[9]

Table 4.3. *Theory construction logic for unification of weak-ties theory and macrostructural theory*

| Theory | Nodes | Ties | Integration | Bias |
|---|---|---|---|---|
| SWT | Undifferentiated | Differentiated | $\gamma$ | $1-\sigma_w$ |
| Macro | Differentiated | Undifferentiated | $H_R$ | $\tau$ |
| Unified | Differentiated | Differentiated | Both | Both |

Third, the theory has survived various empirical tests or, where it has been shown to be deficient on empirical grounds, it has been revised so as to bring it into conformity with the data. (This is especially apparent in Blau and Schwartz, 1984, but also in Blau, Blum, and Schwartz, 1982.)

Finally, as this chapter has made clear, it has proved possible to embed the idea in the mathematical framework of biased nets so as to deduce its key principles.

Table 4.3 shows the theory construction logic that generates the unification effort. Once we see both theories in terms of the same generic model object – a network with potentially distinct types of nodes and distinct types of ties – we see a contrast like that shown in the table, which now will be discussed.

Weak-ties theory treats nodes as undifferentiated. Any differences between nodes arise from their location in the pattern of ties. Thus, a node connects two otherwise isolated subnetworks if it is tied to nodes in both subnetworks. This differentiates the node from others through the pattern of relational ties. This conception is the fundamental one for theoretical sociology, as outlined in the earlier discussions of social structure in relation to dynamical social systems (see especially Chapter 2). The point is that the concept of "position" is relative to a space of possible relational ties, including those that are actualized at any time. In all generality such ties and hence such positions are emergent outcomes of dynamical social systems, that is, aspects of the really possible adjusted states of interaction, activities, and sentiments. But for any real group, there is always a givenness with respect to institutions. These provide standing definitions of all types of entities, including the persons themselves independently of the particular group setting. When network analysis is applied to a field of such interconnected persons belonging to various groups in an institutional setting, we notice that in terms of such *given* differences among nodes, independent of the particular ties that are treated, weak-ties theory does not recognize any. Thus, people may be friends (strong tie) or acquaintances (weak tie), but there is no formal representation of any given institutional group locations within some scheme of typification that corresponds to a nominal dimension. On the other hand, macrostructural theory represents nodes as differentiated by such locations. Indeed this is its fundamental starting point. In this sense, it incorporates a key point of structural–generative theory (as discussed in Chapter 3) that cognitive definitions and local events are embedded within standing institutional definitions of situations, including types of actors and types of resources they hold.

Concerning the ties, formalized weak-ties theory employs a model object that has its two types of ties.[10] On the other hand, macrostructural theory treats just one type of tie, the relation of social association. There is an analogy to the differentiation of nodes contrast. The single type of tie in macrostructural theory does give rise to differentiated types of ties among institutional groups and strata in terms of the magnitudes of rates of social association between them. But so far as the formal theory is concerned, there is only one type of tie underlying these rates. In distinct applications the single type of tie may be given different empirical interpretations, such as intermarriage in one application and friendship in another. But this does not bear upon the matter at issue: Any statement or formula of the theory relates to a single type of tie and not to multiple types of ties simultaneously.

The unification effort is motivated in part by the complementarity of the two models: By integrating them, we can deal with (at least) two types of ties and (at least) two types of nodes. In other words, the theory treats model objects that are differentiated with respect to both nodes and ties.

Now let us look at the local and global properties represented in biased net terms. Weak-ties theory involves the transitivity type of bias, the closure bias $\sigma$, in the form of its complement as computed over weak ties. Thus, in the formal theory, $\text{SWT} = 1 - \sigma_w$ is the bias element in the probability that two nodes that are both weakly tied to a third will *not* become tied (weakly or strongly) themselves. This means their connections spread out and away from the third node's local network of nodes. In this way, social knowledge can spread away into other regions of the social network. Then global integration is characterized by the connectivity $\gamma$ of the network.

By contrast to the relational type of bias parameter needed to mathematically represent the weak-ties ideas, in macrostructural theory no relational bias parameters are employed at all. For direct correspondence to the Blau formulation, the key bias parameter is simply the homophily bias $\tau$. This is based on the institutional differentiation of the nodes and not on any relational property such as symmetry or transitivity. Nevertheless, in a sense it is "local," since it refers to an event connecting a pair of nodes: If the bias event occurs, then the two nodes are destined to form a bond, otherwise only chance dictates the formation of such a bond. At the macrostructural level, the theory requires a concept that deals with relations between aggregates of nodes. For this purpose, the concept of *relation heterogeneity* – which is the term used here for Blau's "intergroup relations" – was introduced and denoted $H_{\mathrm{R}}$. If one randomly samples a *tie* in the network of (undifferentiated) ties, then $H_{\mathrm{R}}$ is the chance that the two nodes so tied will be in distinct positions (or subgroups, depending on the dimensionality of the differentiation of nodes).

In developing the theory in formal terms, we see that this analytical element of relational heterogeneity does not really refer to global integration of the system. For one thing, it ignores indirect ties and their effects. For another, it is not immediately obvious in what sense the system is integrated by such relational heterogeneity except definitionally.

Hence, a required task of the unification theory is to synthesize the bias parameter representations ($\pi$ in one theory, $\tau$ in the other) to derive a relationship between macrostructural rates of intergroup relations ($H_{\mathrm{R}}$) and the implications of indirect paths generating connectivity ($\gamma$).

To see the link postulated between the theories, let the model object, the network, have two nominal dimensions of differentiation of the nodes and two types of ties, strong (ST) and weak (WT). Let the total relation $R$ be the union of the weak and strong ties. "Similarity" is a parameter of any dyadic dynamical social system that generates some equilibrium weak or strong tie. Let $\theta$ be the probability that a tie is weak rather than strong, given that the pair are in the same joint position or location, that is, the same in both dimensions of the model object. Let $\theta'$ be the probability that the generated tie is weak rather than strong given that they are the same in only one dimension, either $A$ or $B$. Let $\theta''$ be the probability that the generated tie is weak rather than strong given that the nodes are not the same on either dimension. The three given parametric conditions are decreasing in a parameter of similarity of the members of the pair, and so we should have

$$\theta < \theta' < \theta'' \tag{4.7.1}$$

The general principle is evident and represents the basic conceptual way in which the two theories are linked:

> *Unification principle:* The greater the number of dimensions along which two nodes in relation differ, the greater is the chance that the tie is weak.

The next step postulates a definite mathematical form that realizes the key relationship (4.7.1). Let us assume that each successive loss of dimensional similarity increases the weak-tie chance in a uniform manner. Start with $\theta$ for the case of identity of position in the multidimensional space of the model object. Then add a fraction $c$ of $1-\theta$ to $\theta$ to generate the chance $\theta'$ when there is a drop by one dimension in similarity. For the next drop in similarity by one dimension, add a fraction $c$ of $1-\theta'$ to $\theta'$ to produce $\theta''$. This is all we need for the two-dimensional model, but the idea is perfectly general.

Using the technique of tree-diagramming the possibilities (see Fararo and Skvoretz, 1987), we obtain the total probability that a tie is weak rather than strong. Namely, with $q=\mathrm{P}(\mathrm{WT}|R)$, we have

$$q=\theta+(1-\theta)c(1-c)(H_{\mathrm{R}}^{A}+H_{\mathrm{R}}^{B})+(1-\theta)\,c^2H_{\mathrm{R}}^{J} \qquad (4.7.2)$$

We know [from formulas (4.6.11)] that all three relational heterogeneity terms that appear in this formula increase when the corresponding population heterogeneity increases, decline when the homophily biases increase, and decline when the consolidation of dimensions increases. Therefore, formulas (4.6.11) and (4.7.2) together imply (1) the greater the population heterogeneity along a dimension, the greater is $q$; (2) the greater the homophily bias along a dimension, the smaller is $q$; and (3) the greater the consolidation of the two dimensions, the smaller is $q$. Each of these three propositions is obtained by partial differentiation of the function given by (10.7.2) and so is valid in the *ceteris paribus* sense. We now have to relate $q$ to the connectivity of the network via its relationship to the closure bias $\sigma$.

To take this step, we express the parameter $w$ of expression (4.4.2) in terms of $q$. Recall that $w$ arises in considering the total probability $\sigma$ as a weighted average of the closure bias terms for different types of ties. Actually, there are three types of situations to which the bias is relevant, depending on the strength of the ties of a node to two other nodes: two weak, two strong, and mixed. We now interpret formula (4.4.2) as an approximation in which the bias parameter in the mixed situation is treated as the same as $\sigma_{\mathrm{s}}$. (The general case, yielding the same qualitative conclusions, is treated in Fararo and Skvoretz, 1987.) So $w$ is actually the probability that two ties are weak. A first approximation to this probability is just the square of the probability that any one tie is weak. Therefore, substituting $q^2$ for $w$ in (4.4.2),

$$\sigma=\sigma_{\mathrm{w}}+(1-q^2)S \qquad (4.7.3)$$

From this formula, we see that the greater is $q$, the smaller is $\sigma$. But formula (4.2.3) implies that the smaller is $\sigma$, the greater is the connectivity $\gamma$, the global integration of the system. Putting this together with the three results from the analysis of expression (4.7.2):

1. The more heterogeneous a population is, the greater is the global integration of the network.
2. The greater the degree of homophily along a dimension, the smaller is the global integration of the network.

3. The greater the consolidation between the two homophilous dimensions, the smaller is the global integration of the network.

From the dilemma of integration (Section 4.4), in each instance the inference about local integration is the reverse, by the trade-off between local and global, for any given density.

Let us review the basic unification procedure. Call the two relatively well-confirmed structural theories with which we began $T$ and $T'$. Each was formalized as a biased net model, say, $B$ and $B'$, within the common mathematical framework of the theory of random and biased nets. Then the unification uses some basic sociological ideas (especially the well-confirmed connection between similarity and strength of ties) to formulate a generalized model, say, $B''$. Within theoretical model $B''$, both $B$ and $B'$ are special cases. Moreover in terms of the theoretical ideas, these are brought into coherent relationship in one broader theory that is inherently mathematical, although far from complete. The guiding image throughout is that of a social system as a vast social network in which there are both differentiated types of ties and differentiated types of nodes. In the interpretation favored here, the node differentiation corresponds to relevant standing definitions of actors as social objects in institution space abstractly characterized in terms of dimensions. The observer "colors" the nodes, as it were, to code their locations. Actors, as nodes, tacitly or even consciously attend to the coloring. The interaction among actors of *given* coloring then yields, by the generic logic of the dynamical social system as applied to any pair, an adjusted state or social relation. This is differentiated as to strength, essentially the magnitude of the diffuseness–affectivity dimension of their orientations to each other, as a function of the parameter of similarity of coloring in institution space. Of course, this microinterpretive element is then relationally aggregated so as to draw conclusions about the interpretation of the system comprised of many interlocking pairs, that is, the overall social network. In this way, the unification theory provides a thread of connection between *microstatics* (the state of the relational tie as a function of similarity parameter) and *macrostatics* (the connectivity of the network as a function of various parameters).

## 4.8. Small worlds: an application of the unified theory

Does the preceding section's unification of two sets of theoretical ideas from the two branches of structuralism have any implications for further theoretical model building? Does it permit us to analyze some problem that apart from the unification might not be connected with macrostructural theory? In this section, a positive answer is supplied in the form of an application of the theory to the small-world problem. (For a review of research on this problem, see Bernard and Killworth, 1979.) Small-world research was initiated by Stanley Milgram (see, e.g., Travers and Milgram, 1969) and by Pool and Kochen (1978) whose early manuscript in the area was not immediately published. The general phenomenon is on the surface of daily life: Two persons $A$ and $B$, initially unacquainted, meet and discover that they have a common acquaintance or friend. "Small world!" they exclaim. More generally, for any two people, they may be acquainted directly (a chain of length 1), or not directly but through some intermediary (a chain of length 2), or neither directly nor through some common acquaintance but through $A$'s knowing someone who knows someone who knows $B$ (a chain of length 3), and so forth.

We see from these remarks that the "smallness of a world" is the distance between two arbitrary members of that world, where distance is measured in terms of chain length. This amounts to saying that the smallness is the mean value of the length of the shortest chain of ties between two nodes in a given network.

Now note that if smallness is conceived in this way, it is read off from what I have defined earlier as the structure statistics of a network. This suggests that (1) a "world" is represented as a network of ties, some weak and some strong; (2) the study of that world proceeds by a tracing process to discover the nodes in the network first reachable at step removed or distance $t$ from an arbitrary starter or small set of starters; and (3) the corresponding fractions, averaged over various starters, are used to compute an average distance. Since the connectivity of the network may not be unity, the structure statistics – the successive values of $P(t)$, $t = 0, 1, \ldots$, where $P(t)$ is the probability of being newly reached at step $t$ from the starting set – do not necessarily form a probability distribution for the variable $t$. But if we consider the conditional probability of being newly reached at $t$ given the node is reached at all, then we have a probability distribution. Hence, we form the measure of smallness of a world, that is, of a network of nodes with weak and strong ties, via the expected value formula

$$E(t) = (1/\gamma)\Sigma tP(t) \tag{4.8.1}$$

Using this formula, the next result follows immediately from the implications of the random net tracing formula: A random net with contact density 3 has a smallness of approximately 6.1; with a contact density of 5, a smallness of approximately 4.4; and with a contact density of 7, a smallness of approximately 3.7. In fact, if we follow Pool and Kochen (1978) and imagine that people typically know hundreds of others, most on a weak-ties basis, then for densities in the range of 250–500 contacts per person, the approximate smallness of a random net can be shown to be between 3 and 4. In the cases of much smaller densities, the connectivity is not yet unity, so some pairs are infinitely distant even if among those who are connected to each other the chain length is fairly short. But for the larger densities (and even at a density of 7, the connectivity is .999), virtually everybody is connected to everybody else in the random network.

In his program of experimental research on the small-world problem, Milgram essentially employed a world corresponding to adults residing in the United States. Here is the procedure he used: An arbitrary set of starters was selected and also a specific ''target person.'' An attempt was made to generate an acquaintance chain from each starter to the target. Each starter was provided with a document describing the study and the target and was asked to move it along by mail toward the target, selecting one person known to the respondent on a first-name basis. (''Knowing on a first-name basis'' could be regarded as a correspondence rule for the meaning of *acquaintance* in American society.) The document emphasized trying to reach the target as the main goal. Information about the target was provided in the document: a man who was a stockbroker in Boston, having a certain place of employment, and so forth. With 296 starters selected, 217 actually participated by sending the document on to an acquaintance. Of these, 64 reached the target. The mean number of steps in these completed chains was 5.2. Among the other findings, an important one was the homogeneity within chains, that is, there was a strong tendency for people to select recipients similar to themselves with respect to two dimensions: occupation and gender. Also, once the document entered the finance field, it tended to stay there.

How does the unified theory apply to this type of problem? Basically, it provides a way to link the structural parameters of the population and the network to the smallness of the world involved. One type of structural parameter is the heterogeneity of the population with respect to nominal dimensions of relevant differentiation. A second basic type of parameter is the homophily bias associated with dimensions of differentiation, which is of critical importance in terms of the probability of ''cross-over,'' the movement of the document into a salient group from another institutional group (e.g., a woman's passing the document along to a man).

Next, the whole point of the strength of weak ties is relevant to small-world problems. A network with proportionately fewer weak as contrasted with strong ties, for a given density, will not have as many bridges between local groups, making passage of a document to a socially remote location in the social structure less probable. (The social remoteness of the location is the dissimilarity in the positions of the nodes in the multidimensional space of macrostructural theory.) In short, heterogeneity, homophily bias, and the weak-ties axiom are extremely relevant to the small-world phenomenon.

A simple unified theoretical model will be constructed to illustrate how the theory applies. The aim will be to derive propositions about how the smallness (4.8.1) depends on the structural parameters of the network. First, we assume that when a document is passed on from node $a$ to node $b$, node $b$ will not send it back to $a$. Thus we set $\pi = 0$ in formula (4.2.3) for the approximate biased net reduced density. This gives

$$\alpha = a - \sigma(a-1) \tag{4.8.2}$$

Next, we use formula (4.7.3) for $\sigma$:

$$\sigma = \sigma_{\mathrm{w}} + (1-q^2)S \tag{4.8.3}$$

Recall that $S = \sigma_{\mathrm{s}} - \sigma_{\mathrm{w}}$. Now we recall the expression for $q$. For a first exploration, I assume just one relevant nominal dimension of differentiation. Then formula (4.7.2) reduces to

$$q = \theta + (1-\theta)cH_{\mathrm{R}} \tag{4.8.4}$$

Finally, we recall that

$$H_{\mathrm{R}} = (1-\tau)H \tag{4.8.5}$$

Substituting in (4.8.2), we obtain:

$$\alpha = a - \{\sigma_{\mathrm{w}} + [1 - (\theta + (1-\theta)c(1-\tau)H)^2]S\}(a-1) \tag{4.8.6}$$

From the latter formula, we see that $\alpha$ is expressed as a function of several parameters of the network: (1) the contact density $a$; (2) the weak-ties closure bias $\sigma_{\mathrm{w}}$; (3) the difference in closure bias between strong and weak ties, namely, $S$; (4) the homophily bias $\tau$ of the dimension of differentiation; and (5) the heterogeneity of the population with respect to this dimension. To these, one could append the other constants in these equations, but this list is sufficient to indicate the logic of the model so far.

To derive the smallness for the network, we need to consider the biased net tracing formula. This means that the random net contact density is replaced by the biased net density in which the closure bias $\sigma$ is the only bias parameter for this model. Then the analysis of closure into its weak and strong components, the two types of ties, leads us to additional parameters, and the analysis of the relative frequency of weak ties leads us to the homophily bias parameter and the population heterogeneity.

Suppose that the dimension of differentiation defines two institutional groups, such as men and women. Denote these by $A$ and $B$. A tracing starts from within one of these two groups, say, $A$. Then the starter in $A$ passes along the document to a number of others, say, $a$. We can imagine instructing the person to contact this number of acquaintances. In the Travers–Milgram experiment $a = 1$, which would make our bias parameter and its consequences irrelevant, so I assume that the density term is at least 2. Also note that consideration of the goal-oriented action of trying to reach a specified target person is omitted: This was a feature of an experimental design to examine the small-world phenomenon, whereas the theoretical model deals with the nature of this phenomenon as defined at the outset of this section.

Let $p_A$ and $p_B$ be the proportions of the persons in the two groups. At any given step removed from the starters, some of the newly reached persons are in $A$ while others are in $B$. Let $P_A(t)$ be the probability that an arbitrary person in subgroup $A$ is newly reached at $t$, and let $P_B(t)$ have a similar meaning for $B$. Then $P(t)$, the probability that an arbitrary person is reached for the first time at step $t$, is

$$P(t) = p_A P_A(t) + p_B P_B(t) \tag{4.8.7}$$

A detailed analysis of the tracing possibilities of contacts in and between subgroups leads to the following pair of simultaneous recursive equations (see Skvoretz and Fararo, 1989, for a proof):

$$P_A(t+1) = [1 - X_A(t)][1 - \exp(-\alpha\{P(t) + \tau[P_A(t) - P(t)]\})] \tag{4.8.8a}$$
$$P_B(t+1) = [1 - X_B(t)][1 - \exp(-\alpha\{P(t) + \tau[P_B(t) - P(t)]\})] \tag{4.8.8b}$$

Recall that the initial condition is that $P_A(0)$ is some small positive fraction, whereas $P_B(0)$ is zero.

The recursion is as follows. At step $t$, we have a certain fraction of all the nodes that are new contacts at $t$, some in $A$ and some in $B$, according to (4.8.8). Tracing their contacts, a certain fraction of the A group is newly contacted at step $t + 1$, according to (4.8.8a) and a certain fraction of the $B$ group is also newly contacted at this step, according to (4.8.8b). By (4.8.7), with $t$ replaced by $t+1$, we find the expected fraction of all nodes that are newly contacted at $t+1$, and this is the start of the next recursion.

Let us examine the nature of these equations. First, note that they are *coupled*. This is clear from the terms in the exponential function in each expression. Next, note that they are nonlinear since each contains an exponential function. So what we have is a *discrete nonlinear dynamical system*. No routine solutions are possible. To explore the implications for the smallness of the world, a series of computer studies are needed. Such a study, with some modifications of the equations presented here, is provided in Skvoretz and Fararo (1989). Some numerical examples and results of this study will be drawn upon here to illustrate the type of behavior generated by the nonlinear dynamics.

In all of the computations, we set $a = 3$ and $p_A = .8$, which implies that $H = .32$.

For convenience, the state of the system is expressed in cumulative terms ($X_A$, $X_B$). The initial condition is (.00125, 0). We start with a random net and then superimpose various biases as indicated:

1. Random net. Let $\sigma_s = \sigma_w = \tau = c = 0$, $\theta = 1$.
   The dynamical system generates a rapid approach to equilibrium at (.94, .94), corresponding to the random net connectivity with a contact density of 3. In the $x$–$y$ positive quadrant that contains the state space, after about four recursions, the approach is along the 45° line in which $X_A = X_B$ at all $t$. The smallness given by the mean chain length of formula (4.8.1) is about 6.07 and is the same for reaching nodes in $A$ or in $B$.
2. Biased net. Let $\sigma_s = \sigma_w = 0$, $\tau = 1$, $c = 0$, $\theta = 1$.
   There is rapid approach to the cumulative equilibrium state (.94, 0). Because of the maximum homophily bias, nobody in group $B$ is ever reached, starting in group $A$. The mean chain length for $A$ is about 5.9.
3. Biased net. Let $\sigma_s = .5$, $\sigma_w = 0$, $\tau = .95$, $c = .5$, $\theta = .5$.
   After about twelve steps, there is an approach along the 45° line to equilibrium at (.89, .89). The mean chain length for reaching nodes in $A$ is 6.87, whereas for reaching nodes in $B$ it is 8.47. The average is 7.19.
4. Biased net. Let $\sigma_s = .75$, $\sigma_w = 0$, $\tau = .8$, $c = .25$, $\theta = .25$.
   After about thirteen steps, there is an approach along the 45° line to equilibrium at (.765, .765). The mean chain lengths are now longer: 9.34 for $A$ and 9.79 for $B$ with an average of 9.43.
5. Biased net. Let $\sigma_s = .75$, $\sigma_w = .25$, $\tau = .2$, $c = .1$, $\theta = .1$.
   After about six steps, there is an approach along the 45° line to equilibrium at (.65, .65). The mean chain lengths are almost identical, about 11.6.
6. Biased net. Let $\sigma_s = .90$, $\sigma_w = .25$, $\tau = .2$, $c = .1$, $\theta = .1$.
   After about eight steps, there is an approach to equilibrium along the 45° line at (.476, .476). Mean chain lengths are almost identical, about 15.8.
7. Biased net. Let $\sigma_s = .95$, $\sigma_w = .8$, $\tau = .2$, $c = .1$, $\theta = .1$.
   The equilibrium is a bare (.16, .16), reached as usual along the 45° line after an initial transient period. The mean chain lengths are very similar, 19.5 and 19.7, respectively, for $A$ and $B$.
8. Biased net. Let $\sigma_s = .95$, $\sigma_w = .90$, $\tau = .9$, $c = .1$, $\theta = .1$.
   After a run of thirty steps, the process was still not in equilibrium but appeared to be approaching (.11, .11). The average chain lengths differed: 18.7 for $A$ and 21.0 for B.

These calculations strongly suggest that under perhaps all parameter conditions, the ultimate fraction reached in each group tends to equality over a long enough series of recursions of the process. But by altering parameters such as those that determine the frequency of weak ties and the strength of such ties, the value of these connectivity-type statistics can be made more or less high. Also, the structure statistics reflect the way in which the parameters make for larger or smaller values of $\alpha$, which in turn influences the mean chain lengths. More elaborate studies accompanied by some analytical work with the pair of nonlinear equations should help us to put some of these results into general form. In other words, here as in other thought experiments with computers, the outputs are suggestive of, not demonstrations of, general theorems about the theoretical model.

The main aim here has not been to provide an exhaustive study of this particular model. Rather the focus is really on the general point of the procedure of unification. Earlier, I reviewed the unification procedural logic. The impression might have been given that the application of this logic is a sheer end in itself, providing an esthetic pleasure in integrating two theories. But the current section shows that in a *unification dynamic* approach to theories, the unified structure functions as a means to still further theoretical analysis. This process is unending. It recursively generates new theory. It *is* a process, a passage to a next state rather than a celebration of static arrival. In addition, this short section has provided another example of a pervasive fact about theoretical model building: Even if one initiates such work from operative ideals that include simplicity of formulation, the initial simple premises lead into nonsimple results. Simple rules or mechanisms generate complex dynamics. This is the fundamental maxim of dynamical systems. It is illustrated here in the postulation of relatively simple ideas for setting up the small-world model and then deriving a discrete nonlinear dynamical system. Finally, this *implied* complexity becomes the object of thought experiments using computers, as illustrated here very briefly and discussed as a point of theoretical procedure in Section 3.6.

The reference back to nonlinear systems and simulation studies is suggestive for the future of studies of large-scale nonlinear networks of *social couplings,* as the linkages among purposive nodes was called in Chapter 3. The suggestion relates to intellectual history and to currently active research frontiers of science. The mathematical theory of random and biased networks began after World War II with models of neural networks that its developers (especially Rapoport, 1951) thought of as potentially applicable to any dynamic network with many nodes. Today, cognitive scientists are moving in the direction of building complex dynamical system models of neural networks characterized by parallel distributed processing. (See, e.g., the studies by Rumelhart et al., 1986.) This is one component of a scientific research program, now known as the interdisciplinary field of *neural networks,* that may be a source for further advance in the study of the dynamics of social networks. As Durkheim (1974:Ch. 1) indicated in his essay "Individual and Collective Representations," there is an analogy between neural networks and social networks. In the likely next developments that exploit this analogy, a key role will be played by nonlinear simulation models of the type that constitute the core of this neural network science. For this reason and for the reasons discussed in Chapter 3, a good guess as to the near future of productive theoretical model building in our field is easy to make: An important if not dominant element of it will involve the construction and study of complex network simulation models based on coupling models of action. This work is likely to give us a better perspective on the significance of biased network models and to help to bring it, or its successor formalism, in closer connection with the action-theoretical foundations of general theoretical sociology.

## 4.9. Generativity via *E*-state structuralism

In Chapter 2, interlock was defined in a dynamical-systems setting: The state of the relational process of any pair depends on the states of other pairs in the same system. The division between the action approach and the structuralist approach to social phenomena has been the difficulty of really generating social structure on an action foundation. For example, the dyadic action–reaction adaptive equations of Chapter 3 already become sufficiently complex even in the ''average'' process, which takes a nonlinear form, so as to make extension to genuine networks of least three actors analytically difficult. The point of this section is to simplify sufficiently at the action or behavioral mechanism level to engage the interlock problem and to show how a dynamic process can generate a stable social structure. A key feature of modern structural analysis that finds expression here is the treatment of the formation and transformation of relational systems. Finally, since the problem treated is to generate a phenomenon reliably reported as an empirical generalization about dominance relations, the *explanatory* payoff of *generativity* is demonstrated. So, here in this final section, we study a mode of integration of ideas from the action subtradition and the structuralist subtradition of general theoretical sociology. From the former, as interpreted in this book, is the idea that recursive generativity is implemented through *acts* as the fundamental units of process. From the latter, as interpreted in this chapter, we take the presuppositional theoretical model rule and the corresponding empirical operations rule that models and data should focus us on social relations and not on disconnected units.

It will be recalled that the approach taken in this book has been called generative structuralism. Not all of its characteristic ideas can be drawn together in any one context, but a variety of ideas permeating the book culminate in this section, where they are synthesized to construct a theoretical method. Three such ideas relate to the dynamical system concept. First, the state of a dynamical social system should be thought of in matrix or network terms. Second, the mechanisms of the system specify how a change of state occurs in a small time interval. Third, the behavior of the system is generated through the recursive application of the mechanism to each new condition it produces. A compact statement of these ideas, in a context intended in part as preparation for this section (so that the *E*-state idea was employed), was given in Section 1.4.3.

Still further elements focused on in various ways in earlier sections of this book are involved in the work of this section. By the first and third points, the dynamical social system implies a generative process by which the network state is recursively changed over time. Although this is implied in the concept of the general dynamical social system defined in Chapter 2, in that chapter the theoretical models were limited to cases in which the mode of aggregation made such recursive generation of network states impossible. In the action theory developments undertaken in Chapter 3, none of the three types of theoretical models could be developed sufficiently to incorporate this feature. Finally, up to this point in this chapter, structuralism has been actualized in a form in which the structure is *given.* A focus on tracing process has meant some sort of actual or potential spread or flow within a given and analytically fixed social structure state. So the paramount importance of deriving recursive change of state of a network from first principles is a key accomplishment of the method worked out in this section.

The confluence of ideas leading to the developments to be discussed includes still other important strands of argument developed in earlier chapters. For instance, the realist philosophy of science, which is an element of the philosophy of theoretical sociology of this book, is implemented in that the meaning of "to explain a phenomenon" becomes "to generate that phenomenon." This implies that since a social structure is interpreted as an equilibrium state of a dynamical social system, to explain a social structural phenomenon means to generate that phenomenon as an aspect of the implied equilibrium states of the system.

But how shall the mechanism of the dynamical social system be obtained? By mere postulation of some equations, which is hardly satisfactory on theoretical grounds, or through some deductions from . . . what? This is where the ideas of Chapter 3 apply concerning the logic of coupling actor models to define interactive network models.

So to derive the mechanism of the dynamical social system from first principles, one should use the *coupling procedure* by which one first posits some simple mechanism or principle at the actor–situation level and then shows how the dynamical social system is constructed on the basis of the coupling of actor–situation models.

Finally, we arrive at a complex issue that is nevertheless at the core of the theoretical method to be described. The operative ideal of simplicity in scientific work, as a doctrine of successive approximations starting from simpler formulations and proceeding to more complex cases, is without doubt a major significant ideal that has *not* been institutionalized in the tradition of general theoretical sociology. How is it relevant to a process worldview and to the accompanying effort to represent social phenomena in dynamical terms with a focus on social structure?

In a dynamic context, one way that the ideal functions is as follows. Suppose that a set of observables, collectively denoted $X$, are observed to vary over time and that a dynamical system is to be formulated with respect to these phenomena. As a first approximation, one might derive a process mechanism directly in terms of $X$. But consider the following property discussed in Chapter 2 as the principle of state determination. Given the relevant parametric (including input) conditions over a time interval, the state at the end of the time interval follows from the state at the start of the interval. No information on states occupied before that initial time is required. We also say that a state space concept has been formulated: It incorporates into itself whatever effects history has had that still matter to the behavior of the system. Thus, simplicity considerations often lead to the initial formulation of dynamical systems in terms of observables, and this implies that these observables are construed to satisfy the principle of state determination. However, experience with Markov chains – probabilistic dynamical systems used frequently in social and behavioral science since the 1950s – shows that this initial step leads to incorrect predictions about the observables at the end of relevant time intervals. That is, wide empirical experience indicates that *observables do not generally satisfy the principle of state determination.*[11]

The theoretical method to be discussed in this section adopts the procedure of postulating *unobservable latent states* as *theoretical constructs*. As part of the meaning of such a construct, it satisfies the principle of state determination. That is, the derived models will be Markovian (in a probabilistic context). If the models fail on empirical grounds, what is revised are particular assumptions formulated in using the procedure, not the fundamental state determination property of the states. State determination is a meaning postulate for the state space concept to be introduced. So to arrive at such a state space concept requires that we do what sociologists often find difficult to do, that is, eliminate phenomenology and consciousness as ''natural'' ways to characterize states of actors in interaction. Instead, the state description is chosen to enable us to conceptually represent the dynamical system in conformity with the principle of state determination while yet satisfactorily reproducing the observable interactions. Whether theoretical sociologists who are not formal in orientation will appreciate the logic of this approach is an open question. In any case, this section adopts it.

Even these numerous considerations do not exhaust the intuition, the theoretical procedures, the conceptual points, and the explanatory aims that enter into the present effort. But they suffice to indicate that in a certain sense, this section provides a natural culmination of the entire thrust of this book. It is not that it is a *canonical form* for doing general theoretical sociology to which all are asked to conform. Nor is it that no other section of this book attained anything of comparable scientific worth. Rather, the particular confluence of theoretical logic involved in the analysis to be reported provides a good *illustration* of the way in which formal means can be adopted to work on problems of general theoretical sociology.

The procedure to be described and illustrated is termed *E-state structuralism* (Fararo and Skvoretz, 1986b). In recent years, sociologists who are interested in the development of formal theory have shifted their attention from the sheer format of statements to such theoretical procedures (Willer, 1984) that enhance the effectiveness of theoretical analysis. Other such sociologists have stressed the importance of building relations among theories of a noncompetitive kind, relations that can lead to a more cumulative science (see, especially, Wagner and Berger, 1985). One such relation is integration or consolidation of theories. In this book I have used the term *unification* to cover a wider sense of modes of synthesis. (See especially the related discussion in Section 2.11.)

Two modes of unification should be distinguished. One type involves the integration of theories as such. This is what was exhibited in Section 4.7, where a common biased net theoretical framework and method was the vehicle for the formal unification of weak-ties theory and macrostructural theory. The second type involves integration at the level of theoretical method. This is the mode of integration illustrated in this section. Instead of unifying theories as such, the aim is integration of theoretical procedures.

On the one hand, I propose a particular theoretical procedure and illustrate its application to the construction of a theoretical model intended to explain a certain modest range of phenomena. The generic method, in contrast with the illustrative application, should be applicable to other episodes of theoretical analysis. On the other hand, the method involves a synthesis of two prevailing theoretical procedures used in distinct theoretical contexts. Hence, this section exhibits an integration of certain methodological components of two research subtraditions of general theoretical sociology. One of these is the network analysis branch of structuralism. The other is expectation states theory. (For a recent review of the theory see Berger, Wagner, and Zelditch, 1985, and for an earlier interpretation of its logic see Fararo, 1972b.)

### *4.9.1. Formulation and application of the theoretical procedure*[12]

Four steps will accomplish the objective of this section. The first step is a brief review of the general presuppositions of network analysis. The second step involves a more elaborate statement with regard to the expectation states research program. This will be a general statement of the ideal logic of this type of theory combined with a stress on generativity. Then the third step is the procedural integration, which will be termed *E*-state structuralism. Finally, the theoretical method will be discussed in terms of its use to formulate a theoretical model explanatory of a particular range of phenomena, as shown in detail elsewhere (Fararo and Skvoretz, 1986b).

*Step 1: presuppositions of network analysis.* Network analysis is grounded in the two presuppositions of structuralism: the theoretical model rule and the empirical operations rule. It adds to them, distinguishing itself from the macrostructuralist branch of structuralism, the focus on both direct and indirect ties and so on interlocking patterns of relational ties. It will be convenient to employ the philosophical models of theory and explanation described in Chapter 1 (especially Sections 1.3.3 and 1.4.3) to characterize and contrast the two research programs: network analysis and expectation states theory. Accordingly, the key aspect of discovery in theoretical science involves the element of formal techniques implemented in the construction of theoretical models. Representation principles state how empirical phenomena in a certain class are mapped into modes of formal representation that involve such techniques. Network analysis utilizes the mathematics of graph theory and related formalisms such as biased networks to represent structures; the model says that social structures are bundles of interconnected social relations, each represented by a type of tie in a graph or other such object; and explanations of particular phenomena use such modes of representation.

*Step 2: presuppositions of expectation states research.* The second research program takes the social *situation* as its basic unit of analysis. In situations, characterized abstractly, given social relations shape interaction outcomes, and conversely, it is in concrete social situations that social structures emerge. Essentially, EST (expectation states theory) formulates discrete theories of recurrent interpersonal processes with the objective of accounting for the fundamental sociological features of social systems as these can be seen to emerge in social interaction. What the various theories have in common is a presuppositional commitment to an abstract and generalizing approach to social situational analysis, featuring the deployment of the theoretical construct "expectation states." The commitment to generalized formulations means that the focus is on the development of theoretical statements, stated in abstract terms, that apply whenever certain abstractly stated scope conditions are satisfied in a social situation.

The commitment to expectation states formulations means several things, and this aspect of EST will be drawn upon in the next step. On the one hand, expectation states contrast with observable behaviors. The relationship is this: At any moment, behavior by $A$ toward $B$ is a function of (properties of) expectation states of $A$ vis-à-vis $B$ and possibly toward other parties; such expectation states arise in a feedback loop from the consequences, for the actor, of observed actions taken toward $B$ (and possibly others) at earlier times. In short, behavior is a function of expectation states and such states arise in prior social interaction. On the other hand, ''expectation state'' as a theoretical construct contrasts with phenomenologically available states of expectation. That is, if $E$ is an expectation state, it is not an epistemic requirement on $E$ that the actor to whom the researcher attributes $E$ be able to say, in so many words, that $E$ is his or her conscious state of expectation. In the language of present day causal model building, expectation states are latent variables connected to observables by postulation. The confirmation of such postulation occurs through the theoretical linkages that allow predictions about the observables that may be shown to be in good agreement with the facts. The use of the expectation state construct, then, is a theoretical procedure by which one attempts to construct abstract and generalized theories of interpersonal processes that are either induced within a given social structure or are productive of an emergent social structure. Clearly, EST is definitely concerned with structure, such as prestige and power hierarchy and the conditions under which it emerges. How, then, does it differ from the social networks research program?

Let us deploy the philosophical model of theoretical science once again. The fundamental principle of EST may be said to be: Observable behavior in social situations is generated through information processing involving internal relational states connecting cognitive units representing elements in the situation. An expectation state is such an internal relational state connecting cognitive units. This principle is connected to the formalism of graphs, as is structuralism in the social networks research tradition. In other words, it can be interpreted as a representation principle that governs the form that theoretical models take.

But although both traditions employ graphs, the models are ordinarily quite different. For social network analysis, the focus is on chains and webs of interrelated relations among actors. There may be chains of acquaintanceship, for instance, as in the treatment of the small-world problem. The minimal relational structure of interest for purposes of network analysis is a triad, not a dyad, because only in triads do we find the relevance and ramifications of such phenomena as closure, as explored earlier in this chapter.

For EST, the graph is $p$-centric (as discussed in another theoretical context in Section 1.3) and the analysis is in the actor–situation frame of reference.[13] The graph represents a bundle of mental relations among cognitive units, such as those of perceived ability (''alter is better at the task than self''). Thus, in terms of the formalism, although the inference tools in both cases use counting processes on graphs (see, e.g., Berger, Fisek, and Norman, 1977), since the interpretations of the formal techniques are so different, the research programs rarely cross paths.[14] The EST theorists aim to explain how certain recurrent features of social life, such as status orders, *arise* from social interaction.

In sum, EST focuses on underlying or latent relational states that can be interpreted as *relational orientations* of actors in the sense of Parsons (1951). Its theoretical procedure of postulating such states as connected in mutual causation with observable social behavior is an important component of the program that can be drawn upon by theorists unwilling to follow it into the confines of the laboratory or into the elaboration of information processing models of the actor. The key element is the unobservable, postulated character of these states and their dynamic character as they both arise in and subsequently shape concrete social interaction. So this element refers to the state space concept and the principle of state determination discussed previously. It is this core element that will be unified with a structural analysis perspective by concentrating on a procedure by which the interlocking states of relatedness of the social units is directly addressed.

In this context, recall, interlock is associated with dynamics, with the coupling of otherwise analytically independent processes involving pairs of units. The more customary notion of interlock in network analysis assumes such processual coupling of pairs but is generally invoked in the context of static algebraic analyses associated with block models.

*Step 3: the unification procedure.* The next step is to outline the generic character of the unified theoretical method that involves combining elements of these two research programs. The present discussion does this in an abstract and general way, but an example will be provided later in this section.

The principles of the E-state structuralism are as follows:

1. An *E*-state is a relational construct, not an observable, but it is formally connected to observable social behaviors in the form: Behaviors depend on *E*-states, and among the consequences of social behaviors are changes in *E*-states.
2. A social structure is an equivalence class of patterns of complementary or contradictory *E*-states of multiple actors.
3. Structural change is derived, in the logical sense, from a dynamic model formulated in terms of *E*-states, and stable equilibrium is a special such derivation.

Behind these principles, which will be illustrated shortly, lies a *hierarchy of abstraction* as follows:

Social behaviors
*E*-states
Social relations
Patterns
Structures

The observable data are social behaviors in social situations, from which we infer the existence of *E*-states as cocausal with such behaviors, from which we explicate relations among units as conjunctions of such *E*-states (and that then account for the regularity of the observable *inter*action connecting any such pair); a configuration of such relations we simply call a pattern, and from patterns we construct structures as classes of such patterns according to some specified criterion of grouping patterns into classes. Thus the relational data presupposition of network analysis is reinterpreted: Relations reappear as in the middle of an abstractive hierarchy in which the more primitive data would be *E*-states (were they observable) and still more primitive data (which *are* observable) are the social behaviors.

For conformity with the dynamical system concept of social structures defined in Chapter 2, not every class of patterns will constitute a possible social structure. As we shall see, certain pattern classes are simply transient states, whereas others are adjusted to the parametric conditions and define possible structures. Evidence of structure is based on evidence of patterns, which involve relations; the *constitution of* relations – not evidence for – is a matter of *E*-states, but evidence for *E*-states ultimately comes from confirmation of theories using *E*-states to make predictions of observable social behavior. Hence, the behaviors have an epistemic priority in terms of the nature of evidence, but this does not at all threaten the premise of structural analysis that behaviors depend on structure: The interpretation of the *E*-states as causal generators of behaviors toward others and the interpretation of structure as (a class of) patterns of relations constituted by such *E*-states merely affirms this premise.

From the perspective of *E*-state structuralism, social network analysis has been a bit too skewed toward a data analysis focus. The tie to basic problems of general theoretical sociology is not always evident in such research. The fascination with indicators of social relations and their patterning leads to a preoccupation with devising numerical measures and discovering correlations among network properties. As others have pointed out (Anderson, 1979; Granovetter, 1979), network analysis that is too skewed toward data analysis has no theoretical cumulation, only a growing and impressive armory of technical tools of analysis. As connected with a structural focus on networks and their properties and especially in their dynamic character, *E*-state structuralism constitutes one attempt to shift the focus to explanatory analysis.

On the other hand, the potential of the theoretical construct method as used in expectation states theory has been slow in actualization beyond the research group that routinely applies this construct to experimental data. Thus $E$-state structuralism is a theoretical method – a set of formal procedures associated with the formulation of theories and with methodological principles guiding their use – which is *one* way of integrating these two sets of commitments and ideas.

*Step 4: discussion of an application of the procedure*. The example arises in the study of dominance hierarchy formation in animal groups, a topic of interest both to biologists and sociologists, dating back to Allee (1938) and currently best represented in the work of Ivan Chase (1980, 1982a,b). Our reason for writing *E-state* instead of *expectation state* is that there is reason to believe – or at least that is the premise of this illustrative theoretical model – that some of the same general ideas worked out in sociology for human groups will apply to other animal groups. (For a persuasive and fascinating account of social relational dynamics among chimpanzees, see De Waal, 1982.) The use of the concept in the EST tradition ties it to the concept of the self. In a Meadian tradition, this in turn ties the concept to the symbolizing capacity level of human language. Hence, to allow application of this theoretical method to any structural problem, not just human social structural phenomena, the *intrinsic* tie between the theoretical construct and the concept of the self must be broken. *All expectation states are E-states, but not conversely*. That is, in some species, $E$-states are relational constructs that do not necessarily presuppose self–other conceptions and evaluations. At the same time, the possibility that models involving postulated self–other evaluations might provide better explanations for social phenomena among primates, say, than models without such self–other processes it not ruled out. Our $E$-state formulations are validated, as scientifically significant, if they function in theories that make predictions about social behavior and social structures that are verified.

With this said, the illustrative theoretical model will now be outlined. Although mathematical techniques play a central role in carrying out the procedure, the focus here is on the conceptual character of the method. (For details, the reader is referred to Fararo and Skvoretz, 1986b, 1988.)

A basic regularity in the comparative study of social structures among various social species is the emergence of hierarchy in animal groups. In particular, a dominance hierarchy is often found in which each animal has its place in the group. Chase (1980) showed that attempts to derive this regularity by a procedure based solely on dyadic encounters are not successful. Instead, he proposed a focus on triads. This is what makes his work and the current illustration so much a part of the structural analysis tradition. The basic relation property of *transitivity* comes into its own only with the triad. Recall that a relation, say $R$, is said to be transitive over a domain of entities if whenever $xRy$ and $yRz$, then $xRz$ for any $x$, $y$, and $z$ in the domain. Chase proposes that when an encounter between two animals occurs, there might be a third animal present that is not directly involved in any aggression that takes place but is affected by it. He suggests that structure is built up in terms of sequences of interactions involving triads as the basic building blocks. To see this, think of three animals $A$, $B$, and $C$. Suppose that $A$ comes to dominate $B$. Then suppose the next dominance relation to form involves $C$. The possible states of the triad after this second relation is formed are:

1. $A \rightarrow B$, $A \rightarrow C$
2. $A \rightarrow B$, $C \rightarrow B$
3. $A \rightarrow B$, $C \rightarrow A$
4. $A \rightarrow B$, $B \rightarrow C$

To complete the system, there will eventually be an encounter between the pair not yet related. However, whichever way this last relation is directed in terms of who dominates whom, the hierarchy is already made extremely probable. How can we see this?

Note that in state 1, if $B$ comes to dominate $C$, then transitivity holds because we have $A \rightarrow B$ and $B \rightarrow C$ and also $A \rightarrow C$; but also in state 1, if $C$ comes to dominate $B$ in the last relation to form, we have $A \rightarrow C$ and $C \rightarrow B$ and also $A \rightarrow B$, so transitivity once again obtains. Hence, in case 1, the transitivity of the eventual pattern of relations is already determined. (This assumes that no changes occur in the relations formed earlier.)

Similarly, in state 2, where two animals dominate the other animal, whatever the direction of the $A$ and $C$ dominance relation, transitivity holds. The other two states could give rise to either transitivity or to a cycle such as, from state 3, $C \rightarrow A \rightarrow B \rightarrow C$. Data cited by Chase (1980), however, show that states 1 and 2 are the most likely states to arise at the stage of the sequence involving the formation of the second relation in the pattern. Thus, a theory that can generate 1 and 2 much more frequently than 3 and 4 will be successful in explaining the tendency toward dominance hierarchy, featuring transitive dominance relations. In fact, we want to employ the same basic mechanism to explain nonlinear hierarchies as well as the strictly linear cases.

This means that the theory should propose some mechanism involving the *bystander,* any animal not involved directly in a particular episode of dominance struggle but in a position to observe it. This is the subject matter of the theory proposed here. It is the particular way in which the concern with interlock – the dynamic interdependence of relational processes – is manifested here.

The basic procedure involves assigning relational $E$-states to the animals such that these are not observable but dispose the animal to certain observable behaviors. The dominance *relation* is sharply distinguished from the observable behavior in a conceptual step involving the two levels, relation and behavior. The theory will assert that the animals participating in a dominance struggle and the animals observing it, the bystanders, may form $E$-states that mirror the directionality of the successful aggression. Thus, if $A$ attacks $B$, all three animals in a triadic system, $A$, $B$, and $C$, may form $E$-states: $A$ and $B$ may form $E$-states that are complementary and define their dominance relation, but also such states may form with respect to $C$. There is only a probability relation between the observable aggressive behaviors and the formation of such "permanent" dispositional states comprising social relations, but with repeated encounters, eventually a dominance relation — as a latent relational state — will form for all pairs. Because of the postulated mirroring of directionality, when $C$ observes $A$ as attacking $B$ in a particular encounter, if an $E$-state is formed by $C$ in reference to $B$, it will be that of dominating $B$, and if an $E$-state is formed by $C$ in reference to $A$, it will take the form of deference. For simplicity of a first theoretical analysis of this process using $E$-state structuralism, I shall idealize this process and assume that $E$-states form in complementary pairs.

The $E$-state definition of the dominance relation of animals $A$ and $B$ is as follows. Let $xE_{\mathrm{H}}y$ mean that animal $x$ is in the "high" state toward $y$, thought of as "ready-to-observably-dominate $y$." Let $xE_{\mathrm{L}}y$ mean that animal $x$ is in the "low" state toward $y$, thought of as "ready-to-observably-defer to $y$." Then if at any time we have both $xE_{\mathrm{H}}y$ and $yE_{\mathrm{L}}x$, we say that $x$ and $y$ are in the *dominance relation,* denoted $xDy$. It can be seen that this is an asymmetrical relation. If the $D$ relation does not hold at a particular time for a particular pair $x$ and $y$, I shall write $\overline{\mathrm{D}}$. As will be seen in the axiomatic presentation of the theory presented next, the behavior that depends on the $E$-state will be termed *attack.* This coordinates the theory to the data of Chase (1980), who arranged an experiment involving a number of chickens previously not encountering each other and now brought into a common area. For more general purposes, the *attack axiom* will be the *behavior axiom,* which describes how the observable social behavior depends on the $E$-state relationships. (For instance, the behavior could be a threat rather than an attack.)

The following are the axioms of the theoretical model.

*Axiom 1* (initial condition). At $t=0$, every pair is in the state $\overline{\mathrm{D}}$.

*Axiom 2* ($E$-state formation). At any $t$, if a pair is in state $\overline{\mathrm{D}}$ and if one member ($x$) of the pair attacks the other ($y$), then $xDy$ forms with probability $\pi$.

*Axiom 3* ($E$-state stability). Once $D$ is formed, it is retained: For any $x$ and $y$ and $t$, if $xDy$ at $t$, then $xDy$ at any subsequent $t' > t$.

*Axiom 4* (deference). At any $t$, if $xDy$, then $y$ does not attack $x$ at $t$.

*Axiom 5* (bystander). At any $t$, suppose an attack occurs, say, $x$ attacks $y$. Let $z$ be a bystander. Then:

i. if $x\overline{D}z$ before the attack, then $xDz$ after the attack with probability $\theta$,

ii. if $z\overline{D}y$ before the attack, then $zDy$ after the attack with probability $\theta$,

and events i and ii are independent and also independent of the event in Axiom 2.

*Axiom 6* (attack). At any $t$, given the constraint of Axiom 4, all potential attacks have the same probability of occurrence.

Note that in general in $E$-state analysis the *state of the system* is the set of all $E$-state relations. By virtue of the definition of $D$, this means the state of the system consists of the $D$ or $\overline{\text{D}}$ relations between every pair at a particular time. The axioms describe a process by which, starting from the state in which $\overline{\text{D}}$ holds for every pair, the system state is transformed over time.

Such a state of the system as in the preceding discussion is a dominance *pattern,* a set of (in this case complementary) relations each defined by a conjunction of $E$-states. Any such pattern may be represented by a 0–1 matrix where the entries indicate if a given relation exists at a given time. Hence, the axioms imply a transformation of the matrix state of the system and hence a transformation of the potentialities for interactive events over time.

To illustrate how the process works, suppose we start with three animals satisfying Axiom 1, so that no dominance structure exists initially. Thus, the initial pattern is represented by a matrix of zeros. For simplicity, think of marking off time $t$ by the sequence of observable attacks. Thus, when the first attack occurs, call that $t=1$, by Axiom 6 each of the possible six directed pairwise attacks (any one of three as the attacker, any one of the remaining two as attacked) has the same probability of being the one that occurs. Given the particular pairwise attack, the $D$ relation forms for that pair with probability $\pi$ according to Axiom 2. With the third animal observing this attack, Axiom 5 applies and says that after the attack, we may have the attacker dominating the bystander or the bystander dominating the attacked animal. We can also have both relations involving the bystander formed after this first encounter with probability $\theta^2$ by the independence assumption. These various possibilities give rise to a set of possible next states of the system described in terms of the $D$ or $\overline{D}$ state connecting each pair of animals. Each next state arises with a certain probability determined by the axiomatic description. For instance, suppose that animal $A$ attacks animal $B$, with $C$ observing. And suppose that as a result, $A$ now dominates $B$, but $C$ is still in relation $\overline{D}$ to $A$ and $B$. Since by Axiom 3 the $E$-state dominance relation is stable and by Axiom 4 the dominated animal never attacks the animal dominating it, $B$ will never attack $A$. This means that only five of the possible attacks can now occur, by Axiom 6. Note that $A$ can still attack $B$. Suppose such an attack occurs; then the $D$ relation remains in place between $A$ and $B$ but another opportunity for the $D$ relation between $C$ and $A$ or between $C$ and $B$ to form has been generated. Alternatively, $C$ may attack $A$ with probability .2. Then $B$ becomes the bystander, and the various possibilities for next states of the system are assigned probabilities by Axioms 2 and 5.[15]

In this way, a system of transition probabilities is defined between every pair of possible dominance patterns, the states of the system. Equivalence classes of such states are definable in dynamical terms. That is, the patterns in a given class have a uniform transition probability with respect to another such class; the states can be "lumped" or blocked. Hence, it can be shown (see Fararo and Skvoretz, 1986b) that the system of transition probabilities between the patterns reduces to a $6 \times 6$ absorbing Markov chain between various pattern classes. To say the chain of probabilistic events is Markov is to say that the probabilities of future pattern classes depend only on the current pattern class and not on the particular path by which is was arrived at. This is a direct consequence of the treatment of $E$-states as satisfying the principle of state determination discussed at the beginning of this section. That the process is absorbing means there exist some pattern classes that are equilibrium states: Once entered, they are not left. Hence, in terms of the way in which *social structure* was defined in dynamical system terms in Chapter 2, these absorbing states are the possible social structures under the given conditions. The six pattern classes are:

$S_0$: no dominance relations
$S_1$: just one dominance relation
$S_2$: one dominating two or two dominating one
$S_3$: $xDyDz$ but $x\overline{D}z$
$C$: cycle: $xDyDzDx$
$H$: hierarchy: transitive triple $xDyDz$ and $xDz$

The absorbing states of the Markov chain are $C$ and $H$. Hence, according to the theoretical model, $C$ and $H$ are the only possible social structures under the given conditions. Eventually a particular group will be in one of these two states. In fact, suppose we set the bystander probability $\theta$ to zero. The resulting process is one in which the two possible equilibrium states have probabilities of $P(C) = .25$ and $P(H) = .75$. Call this the baseline model prediction, since these are the probabilities for a purely random process (with parameter $\pi$ determining how long it takes to arrive at equilibrium). The fundamental property of the model is that as the bystander dominance relation formation probability $\theta$ increases from zero, the probability $P(H)$ tends to increase. (This result is not monotonic, however, since depending on $\pi$, there is a value of $\theta$ at which the increase ceases and a relatively small decline occurs.) Since in the data Chase (1980) reports, the hierarchy occurred in substantially more than 75 percent of the triads, the bystander effect is needed to explain this finding. The theoretical model provides a particular formulation of the way in which the *bystander mechanism* works and deductively demonstrates how it generates a hierarchy with greater than chance frequency. The empirical generalization that in animal groups a hierarchy tends to form (more frequently than expected by chance) is explained via *generativity*. That is, the equilibrium state descriptions, as derived theoretically from the dynamical model, correspond to the fact reported in the empirical generalization.

When the process description is applied to groups of more than three animals, the baseline probability of the hierarchy becomes much smaller than .75, making it even more essential to postulate the bystander mechanism. For the case of four animals see Fararo and Skvoretz (1988).

These properties of the theoretical model are reasonably impressive. But they are confined to the context of equilibrium analysis as derived from the dynamical system. The properties of the over-time development toward the social structure state, toward equilibrium, are not nearly as impressive in terms of empirical adequacy. A study of the predictions about the over-time data (Fararo and Skvoretz, 1988) indicates that Axiom 6 is no doubt wrong about the attack event constraints, given the pattern of $E$-states. Hence, as is typical in detailed mathematical model building, the evaluation is partly positive, partly negative, and suggestive of revisions of the underlying theory. The novel element here is that (1) the theory is formulated in axiomatic terms so that it is easier to see its logical structure and to derive consequences and (2) the theory itself and the derivation of consequences from it is produced using a generic theoretical method, $E$-state structuralism. It should be mentioned that Axiom 1 is not necessary to the theory, which is readily generalized to any initial state.

### 4.9.2. *Summary*

Theoretical sociology needs theoretical procedures or methods, just as empirical researchers need generic methods of design and data analysis. Although this need has been recognized by modern theorists, contributions explicitly intended to remedy the gap between what we need and what we have are too seldom found. The theoretical method described in this section is based on a unification of methodological components drawn from the "core sets" (Wagner, 1984) of two theoretical paradigms or research programs. From structuralism, in the social networks sense, is drawn the focus on interlock and on social structure as a network that emerges dynamically and exhibits over-time transformation in its state such that some states may exhibit equilibrium properties. From expectation states theory, the principle is taken that social behavior is a function of unobservable or latent states that are formed in social interaction and shape subsequent interaction. Then, *E*-state structuralism unifies these ideas and corresponding techniques, although it does not claim to unify theories invented in the two programs.

It is time to summarize the main principles of *E*-state structuralism and to indicate how they were employed in the illustrative theoretical model.

The first principle of *E*-state structuralism implicitly defines the idea that an *E*-state is a theoretical construct and that it is cocausal with social behavior. An *E*-state is a relational construct, not an observable, such that, on the one hand, it is emergent in interaction and, on the other hand, observable behavior is a function of the *E*-state. This principle is readily seen in terms of the illustrative theory. Bearing in mind that relation *D* was defined in terms of complementary *E*-states, note that Axiom 2 pertains to their formation consequent upon a behavioral episode; Axioms 4, 5, and 6 indicate how observable behavior depends on the *E*-states; and Axiom 3 postulates a stability element associated with them in order to generate the sort of phenomena we typically find: Social relations (such as *D*) usually settle into some stable state, and so the structures they exhibit also tend toward some stability. This assumption could conceivably be built into the principles of *E*-state structuralism, but we can let experience with the method decide such a matter.

The second principle of *E*-state structuralism is that a social structure is an equivalence class of patterns of *E*-states between various acting units that exhibits equilibrium behavior. In different theoretical models, this equivalence procedure may be defined in different ways. The pattern realizes or embodies a structure such as a cycle or a hierarchy.

The third and final principle of *E*-state structuralism is that we use assumptions about *E*-state formation and change to derive network transformations. In fact, this is exactly the purpose of the formal theory. Chase had already provided the basic explanatory idea of a bystander effect. Moreover, the effect was corroborated in independent studies of other animal groups. (See the papers in Barchas, 1984.) Thus, this mechanism may be considered a part of the stock of knowledge of structural mechanisms of groups. What the formal theory does is show how one can represent the process in formal detail (embodying in the representation the known basic mechanism) in such a way as to logically derive the main empirical finding requiring explanation, that is, that the group tends toward an interactive equilibrium that is a hierarchy.

To accomplish this derivation through $E$-state structuralism requires a dynamic model, one that shows how the state of some system of interest changes from time $t$ to time $t+1$ (or to time $t+dt$ in continuous-time formulations). In short, we are led to a dynamical system, albeit in probabilistic form. From such a theoretical model, typically, derivations about equilibrium fall out as special, albeit important cases. As I stressed earlier in this book (in Chapters 2 and 3), comparative statics – the study of how stable states depend on parameters – is a special case of dynamics. As the axioms of the illustrative theoretical model make clear, the *process is formulated in the small*, a method of great significance for theoretical sciences and not fully appreciated by nonmathematical theoreticians. What this means is that the basic assumptions are about events carrying the state of the system to some new state in a small time interval. ("Small" depends on the level of analysis. On the scale of small groups, an interval that is small for sociocultural evolutionary theory is incredibly large. For a further discussion of this idea, see Fararo, 1973, 1987b; and for a physical context, one might consult the useful study by Margenau, 1950.)

The abstract structure of an unobservable state space – a space of possible $E$-states – and a set of probability distributions of behavior contingent on the state, as in the derived Markov chain above, lead to technical problems of estimation of parameters. With high-speed computers now routinely available, however, this difficulty may not be as severe now as it once was. For theoreticians, the logic of the approach has an attraction that should not be deterred by foreseeable difficulties in parameter estimation. But it should not be thought that *every* problem involving social structure is being recommended for immediate treatment in terms of this method. There is no such implication intended. Social structure can and should be studied in many ways. Thus, $E$-state structuralism suggests one procedure that more formally minded theoreticians will want to consider when they go about formulating explanations for structural phenomena. In the broad context of the various ideas treated in this book, $E$-state structuralism should be regarded as one way to implement generative structuralism.

### *4.9.3. Toward further developments*

Some further ramifications of this synthesized approach to formulating problems in general theoretical sociology deserve some discussion.

One ramification is how expectation states researchers might employ the method. To convert an expectation states theory into an $E$-state structuralist model requires that the transition from the actor–situation unit to the social system be more fully realized. The state of the system should be a set of relations among the acting units, exhibiting over-time change with some possible set of social structures as one outcome. This transition from unit to system is not at present fully carried out in most expectation states research. The convenience of the experimental laboratory, where a single actor can be exposed to a manipulated social situation, has had the effect of keeping much of the theorizing at the actor–situation level. Yet, in principle, it should be quite possible to move to the coupling procedure and to the dynamics of a genuine system of interaction. A relation between two actors in *E*-state structuralism is a pair of *E*-states, one per actor. Expectation advantages (Berger, Fisek, and Norman, 1977; see also Berger, Wagner, and Zelditch, 1985) might serve as *E*-states, thereby producing a quantitative state space. For a pair of actors, the state space is the $x$–$y$ plane. The mechanisms dealt with in EST should produce a series of changes of state, with behavior as a function of state and a feedback loop from behavior to state. For three or more actors, in principle, the same conceptual structure should hold. A social network, for the analysis of the type of problem related to the emergence of a power and prestige structure, is represented as a set of relations such that each relation is a pair of expectation advantages. With the symmetry of status characteristics theory that reduces the relation to one degree of freedom, each relation is represented by a single quantitative state. Then the social network is represented by a matrix of such states, each matrix corresponding to a pattern. The possible social structures are among the equivalence classes of such matrix patterns of expectation advantage states; these structures might not always be hierarchical. Merely having a concept of a matrix state space is not of major interest, however. It is the trajectories of over-time matrix states that should become the focus of analysis, as depending on the configuration of parametric conditions (as described in Chapter 2). For some such conditions, the equilibrium pattern states would be hierarchical. For other conditions, the attractors of the expectation advantage processes might be orbits or oscillations in state space or even exhibit the phenomenon of strange attractors studied in recent chaos theory. In short, the quantitative state space construct now available to expectation states researchers suggests the possibility of exciting new developments, provided that the analysts go beyond the basic actor–situation model to treat the implied network process.

A second set of developments might be based on relating the *E*-state procedures to other constructs and models discussed in prior chapters. The relatively formal character of the *E*-state construct, so that it is not severely constrained by embeddedness in a particular conceptual scheme, suggests that some such connections might be made. There is no guarantee, however, that the connection is pragmatically important in any particular case.

In Chapter 3, action theory was treated in terms of formal developments centered around three representation principles dealing with, respectively, normative control, interpretive procedures, and behavioral adaptation. All three are candidates for relation to the *E*-state method and, for that matter, to expectation states theory.

First, the *E*-state method might be conjoined with the cybernetic hierarchy model of analytical action theory. For a two-level dynamic normative control hierarchy model of the actor, the *E*-state concept proliferates into at least four distinct concepts, each a construct, not an observable. This is because, as discussed in Chapter 3, each level is described in dual terms intrinsic to normative control: (actual, ideal). One level consists of the pair (actual expectation, norm), the other of (actual evaluation, value). Explicitly defining and treating these constructs as components of a complex state description of an actor with an observable "output" or behavioral term is the general idea. This means that the derived steady-state equations of the dynamic normative control process do not relate various scale measures to each other. They function in a different way. In fact, this functioning would be quite close to what Parsons envisioned in his analytical work. But the complexity here is also quite forbidding. Probably the best strategy would involve thought experiments by computer rather than extensive analytical work. The main question would be whether some simplified theoretical models could be treated in such a way that the coupling of two-level cybernetic hierarchy models, each with the multidimensional *E*-state description indicated here, yields results that can be compared with records of over-time observable behavior. In principle, it seems quite likely that this can be done. The number of free parameters involved, however, suggests that an enormous freight of unobservable quantities and relations is involved in the passage to the predictions. What this might mean is that no model of this type is really testable without enormously rich data so that parameters can all be estimated and yet with degrees of freedom left to see if predictions that might be wrong are in fact *not* wrong. It is an open question as to how far one can go in this direction with analytical action theory.

Second, consider interpretive procedures and structural–generative action theory. Might these ideas be connected with *E*-state structuralism? Since the latter arises by a unification of methods from experimental and network research programs, a certain amount of scepticism is warranted. But if *E*-states are content free so far as phenomenology is concerned, they fit the bill so far as ethnomethodology is concerned. For despite its heritage in the ideas of Husserl, ethnomethodology is not really concerned with any essences of consciousness. When Schutz decided to explore the natural attitude in depth, he took a route quite opposite from that promulgated by Husserl.[16] Garfinkel goes below the surface structure of interaction when he posits "background expectancies" (interpretive procedures) such as the et cetera principle. It is true that when it is pointed out to people that they are incessantly using such a principle, it is plausible for them to agree; but this is not the same as saying that in their use of the principle, each episode of use is a deliberate and self-conscious act. Far from it. Like fundamental grammatical rules, interpretive procedures are cognitive and generative without being brought to explicit consciousness. So they have been treated in Chapter 3 as taking the form of productions that, in turn, are not phenomenological in the sense of being objects of consciousness. This suggests that interpretive procedures are *E*-states in the particular form of production rules. As in the case of dynamic normative control hierarchies, so here in the case of reality constructors, the coupling procedure and the deployment of some version of *E*-state structuralism in relation to these concepts of the actor are speculative thoughts about possibilities, not reports of even tentative efforts.

Let me turn now to the possible connection of *E*-state structuralism to the adaptively rational action model. Recall the general character of the adaptive behavior model. The state of the actor is described in terms of a probability distribution over a menu of actions, and the probabilities are changed as a function of the sanctioning significance of situational social events. The actor, episode by episode, adjusts these action propensities as a function of payoffs, positive or negative sanctions. Intuitively, what one would suppose is that the actor is forming a connection between the possible situated actions and their outcomes in terms of sanction significance. Let us explore this idea a bit.

A typical such connection might be: Action *A* in situation *S* leads to a reward (an event with a positive-sanction significance). In fact, Homans's theory finds it impossible to carry through any cogent analysis without invoking the concept of expectation in forms such as "the reward the actor expected." So, intuitively, the empirical phenomena to which the adaptive behavior model was applied are those for which we would like to have an expectation-type construct.

This suggests that *E*-states would be summing up relevant aspects of experience that connect situated action to the sanction meanings of interactive events. Now, our general formal technique for the representation of the connection between situation and action is the production rule. So such *E*-states could be thought of as incipient (i.e., possibly highly transient) production rules with attached sanction significance terms. But how could this idea be related to the adaptive behavior model with its state of the actor as a probability distribution over actions? The probabilities could be thought of as attached to incipient production rules, all of which have the same ostensible situation term. The coupling of actors in the adaptive process has a plurality of possible outcomes, as we saw in the examples of Chapter 3. One of these can be the case in which each actor gravitates toward a stable mode of behavior, in which case each has adapted to the situation in the form of a single production rule. The two rules, one per actor, fit together in the context of the sanction significance of their interaction such that a stable relation is generated. Under other parametric conditions, the process can generate probabilistic production rules so that the actions exhibit stochastic variability with fixed probabilities. Under still other conditions, even this stochastic stability will not be generated.

Although this discussion links production rules, adaptive behavior, and emergent social structure, it does not show how this linkage can be formally articulated to the *E*-state theoretical method. One suspects that attempting such a formal statement would amount to a passage into some combination of the stimulus-sampling foundation of the adaptive behavior model with one of the more recent computational models of mind. Such a combination involving behavioral, cognitive, and social constructs would be a continuation of the brief discussion in Chapter 3 concerning the foundations of Homans's theory with the *E*-state method brought into the picture. Since most of the issues would not be sociological in the sense of referring to social structure, the worthwhileness of such an effort is open to question. It is the sort of project one might well want to leave to cognitive scientists.

Another approach might be worthwhile from the point of view of general theoretical sociology. It will be recalled that in concluding Chapter 3 attention was drawn to the promise of rational choice theory in its sociological context. In thinking about the axioms set out in Section 4.9.1 that define the particular theoretical model, we are naturally led to wonder how to apply the model to cases where not "attack" but some other behavior is relevant. Retaining the dominance focus, whatever the mode of behavior (e.g., gestural or verbal coercive attempt) according to Axiom 6, primates and humans select targets for domination by some random mechanism. This is the generalized baseline model assumption of the particular model. We have already seen that it is likely to be the source of empirical difficulties in accounting for the path as contrasted with the equilibrium outcome. Also, it is really not capturing the full potential of the *E*-state procedure as to its action side. So another form of baseline model might be used. The natural candidate is rational choice. Theoretical methods employed in that tradition might be applied to create simple optimization models. This would embed nonstructuralist action considerations within the overall constraint of the structural axioms. For instance, a specific idea would be: The target of a domination encounter is selected by a mechanism that maximizes the expected increment in rank, considering the effects on bystanders. Experience with such models might create a new theoretical method bridging *E*-state structuralism and rational choice theory. As always, the spirit of the approach would be one of formalization and unification in a context of approximations and idealizations.

The upshot of this discussion is that the *E*-state method, precisely because of its abstract generality, can be related to each of the actor–situation models described in Chapter 3. Yet these speculative remarks also suggest that the more complex the action model, the less the scientific payoff that is likely to come from the attempt to utilize the $E$-state method. In turn, this suggests the formal research problem of attempting to link $E$-state models to rational choice theory.

## 4.10. Summary

Structuralism is defined by presuppositions framing its conceptual orientation. It demands social relational data that provide information about social interactions or types of ties between social units. This is the empirical operations rule. It also demands that theories treat social relations as such. This is the theoretical model rule. From the standpoint of this book, it can be considered the negation of a mode of aggregation that characterizes much of sociological research, namely, over the social units as in standard survey research (and related forms of research individualism). In fact, even a relational focus can fail to realize the full meaning of network thinking if it amounts to an aggregation over conceptually isolated pairs. Thus, the network analysis branch of structuralism requires related relations. Even if only one type of relation is studied, such as acquaintanceship, it requires data in the form of related pairs of acquaintances such that there are paths of ties in a network.

Such social networks can be treated as biased nets. This is the representation principle that has defined the analytical framework of much of this chapter. Formally it leads to the derivation of a formula that recursively generates the tracing statistics interpretable in terms of paths of social–integrative ties. Diffusion processes, which can be understood as processes in networks, are more important for general theoretical sociology than is often recognized. Institutionalization, in the sense of the spread of a scheme of typifications (and corresponding interaction generators), can be construed as diffusion from local subnetwork to local subnetwork using paths of integrative ties. Thus, diffusion in networks is a conceptual link between the formalized interpretive sociology of Chapter 3 and the current network models.

A critical feature of such integrative ties is their strength. Granovetter's weak-ties theory was formalized in the biased net framework and shown to imply a dilemma of integration: For a given density of ties, the stronger the local integration, the weaker the global connectivity.

An episode of unification was provided in this chapter when the weak-ties theory was articulated to Blau's macrostructural theory. First, the macrostructural theory was formalized within the biased net framework. The image of structural properties as defined over distributions – properties such as heterogeneity, inequality, and consolidation of dimensions – is linked to a concept of integration defined in terms of rates at which direct integrative ties exist between subpopulations of nodes that are systemwide collectivities such as professionals and blue-collar workers or blacks, whites, and Hispanics. The link to interpretive theory is that these are based on typification schemes that define types of social objects in the system. In the present context they are types of nodes. The relevant bias parameter concerns homophily. Based on this formalization, the principles of macrostructural theory are derivable as word versions corresponding to derived formulas. Although both weak-ties theory and macrostructural theory treat integration, they treat it differently; the former in terms of connectivity of the whole integration structure or network, the latter in terms of rates of pairwise integrative relations between different types of nodes in a given typification scheme or dimension of differentiation. Yet it proved possible to unify the two theories. The key instrumental step was formalization of each within the same analytical framework defined by the principle that social networks are biased nets. An application to small worlds illustrates how particular models can be constructed that combine ideas of macrostructural theory and the social networks subtradition.

Finally, in the preceding section, the idea was to introduce generativity into structuralist model building. There, *E*-state structuralism was devised by drawing together certain procedural components and orientations from two distinct research subtraditions within general theoretical sociology: expectation states research and social networks research. Stated abstractly, *E*-state structuralism is a theoretical procedure or method that combines the explanatory power derived from a focus on process formulated in terms of *E*-states with the structural focus on networks. The procedure was illustrated by showing how one could generate as a consequence of a set of axioms a result corresponding to a previously discovered empirical regularity, namely, that animal groups tend toward hierarchy. In this way, the theory illustrates the conception of explanation discussed in Chapter 1. It preserves some features of the positivist conception of what scientific explanation means but embeds it in a realist philosophical model grounded in the idea of devising models such that one can generate the phenomenon of interest. It is an example of the entire approach of generative structuralism.

# Summary

With the following outline summary, I conclude this episode in what Whitehead has called the adventure of ideas. I have set out a generative structuralist conception of general theoretical sociology. In Chapter 1, the focus was metatheoretical: the structure of theory was treated as a meaning control hierarchy, exhibiting change that might be progressive under certain conditions, including the more effective implementation of specified cognitive operative ideals for the form of theory and of explanation in sociology. In Chapter 2, the focus was on the dynamics of linkage creation and dissolution in a social network, with social structure as an emergent outcome. Chapter 3 stressed action representation principles and their role in the development of theoretical models focused on problems of social structure. Analytical action theory suggested the vision of a network of socially coupled dynamical normative control systems. Structural–generative theory aims to forge a link between this vision and the stress on actors as embodying and interpreting institutional forms through tacit social knowledge processes. Adaptive rationality theory develops in detail the implications of social coupling of actor models. Chapter 4 presented one development within structuralism, focused on biased networks, which permitted an illustration of the idea of a unification dynamic based on tradition and formalization. It also set out the theoretical method of *E*-state structuralism, along with its illustrative use in theory formulations that might embody generative structuralism.

The following statements provide a compact summary of some of the key ideas – principles, problems, procedures, models, and so forth – presented in the previous four chapters. They are numbered to correspond to chapters, but there is no direct correspondence between sections of the chapters and the numbering of the statements given here.

## 1. A philosophy of general theoretical sociology

1.1. General theoretical sociology is a single comprehensive research tradition.

1.1.1. The various lines of theory developed from the classics are intersecting and communicating subtraditions.

1.1.2. There are several emerging do's and don'ts of the comprehensive tradition: (a) social network representations, (b) explicit principles of action, and (c) micro–macro linkage and other integrative theoretical work within and across theoretical frameworks.

1.1.3. The core problems of general theoretical sociology have to do with the emergence, stability, comparison, and change of social structures.

1.1.4. The comprehensive tradition has a corresponding generalized process worldview. The key idea is recursive generativity.

1.2. A positivist model of theory structure can be embedded within an instrumentalist model of theory that functions as an operative cognitive ideal in the pursuit of the aims of general theoretical sociology.

1.2.1. Ideally, a theoretical system takes the form of a hierarchical meaning control structure with four levels: (a) general presuppositions, (b) a representation principle, which initiates a framework for the analysis of a class of empirical phenomena based on a mode of formal representation, (c) theoretical models instantiating the mode of representation, and (d) invariants found in the process of empirically identifying and testing theoretical models.

1.2.2. The positivist idea of a theoretical system as an empirically interpreted mathematical axiomatic system fits into this structure as an optional and often important component at level (b) or (c) in 1.2.1.

1.2.3. Comprehensive theories are those that are of wide scope and allow us to construct innumerable theoretical models of the type specified through the associated representation principle.

1.3. A positivist model of theoretical explanation can be embedded within a realist philosophical model that functions as another cognitive ideal in general theoretical sociology.

1.3.1. Ideally, theoretical explanation takes the form of constructing models that have generativity. If a regularity statement for some body of data is to be explained theoretically, this requires constructing a model of a generative mechanism (or system of rules) that accounts for the form of the data that prompted the regularity statement.

1.3.2. The valid element in the positivist view is that, where possible, theoretical models should be derived within comprehensive theories that constrain their form.

1.3.3. There are three modes of generativity in theoretical model building: (a) combining mechanisms to define generators of dynamical systems; (b) combining rules to define generative grammars for conceptualized cultural totalities; and (c) a hybrid mode that combines elements of (a) and (b), focusing on production rules that generate dynamics involving knowledge states.

1.3.4. Four rules are suggested for guidance as operative cognitive ideals for constructing generative theoretical models in mathematical terms, given a framework defined by a representation principle: (a) Study conceptually simpler model objects first, (b) state simple postulates and derive complex outcomes, (c) formulate models in the small with implied recursive generativity, and (d) employ the state space approach so that observables are expressed as functions of the state.

## 2. Dynamical social systems and the key problems

2.1. The system idea has had two contexts of deployment in science: domain-specific system theories and general systems theories.

2.1.1. Problems of domain-specific social systems are the central concern of theoretical sociology.

2.1.2. General systems theorizing takes two forms: (a) comprehensive systems theories and (b) mathematical systems theories, one of which is dynamical systems theory.

2.1.3. Theoretical sociology can draw upon both comprehensive systems contributions and mathematical systems developments, especially dynamical systems.

2.2. The key components of a dynamical system are the behavior manifold (of all possible states and conditions of the system) and the generator (of process in state space). This is an implementation of the first mode of generativity.

2.3. Because endurance is problematic from a process worldview, equilibrium and stability are important features of dynamic analysis. The equilibrium concept is embedded within a dynamical systems framework and is a key feature of theoretical analysis.

2.4. The dynamical system, as studied over the whole behavior manifold, yields a complete portrait of the real dynamic possibilities, including the possible stable equilibrium states.

2.5. The concept of a dynamical social system combines two formal ideas: social network and dynamic system. We then obtain a formalized conception of four key theoretical problems and corresponding theorem types. The underlying conception is that general theoretical sociology deals with the ways in which logical possibilities are constrained so as to constitute only certain social structures and dynamical transformations as really possible. Theorems deal with such possibilities, not with the actual world directly.

2.5.1. Type 1 theorems concern the existence of social structures, enduring states of social interaction networks: They describe the content (which may be empty, unique, or multiple) of the set of possible social structures under varying parametric conditions.

2.5.2. Type 2 theorems concern the conditions of stability of social structures: Taken together with Type 1 conditions, they formulate whether or not and to what extent uniquely, social order is really possible under various parametric conditions.

2.5.3. Type 3 theorems concern the comparison of stable social structures: They state how social order varies with parametric conditions.

2.5.4. Type 4 theorems concern the change of social structures, including both smooth and catastrophic change, whether endogenously generated through fast–slow feedback loops or exogenously generated.

2.6. Drawing on the Pareto–Homans contribution to social systems thinking in sociology, we can define a general dynamical social system with two component subsystems: an adaptation and an integration subsystem.

2.6.1. Each subsystem is a dynamical system coupled to the other. One corresponds to the Marxian material basis; the other corresponds to Durkheimian depth sociology. But both Marx and Durkheim saw mutual dependence as intrinsic to them.

2.7. Examples of the four theorem types exist in the Pareto–Homans–Simon subtradition of general theoretical sociology that, through Homans, also intersects the Durkheimian depth sociological tradition.

2.7.1. The nonlinear analysis illustrates how catastrophic changes, corresponding to social structuration and destructuration, arise in the study of theoretical models with the results stated in Type 4 theorems.

2.7.2. Durkheimian social generativity is a concept in the spirit of unification: It combines the positivistic idea, from Durkheim, that social facts cause social facts – interpreted dynamically – and the realist idea that explanation requires a generative mechanism.

2.7.2.1. In a tentative spirit, one can distinguish the problems of general theoretical sociology from those arising by analogy with the problem of explaining Durkheim's law of suicide. Theoretical models that provide answers to these problems are generative but take social structural conditions as parametric and aim to show that the dynamics of some phenomenon $X$ adjusts to the prevailing conditions of social structure (attractor state of network). Such theoretical model building was termed *the theoretical sociology of X*.

2.7.3. Functional analysis involves a generative account of how necessary conditions for social order (existence and stability of social structures) framed in parameter space are themselves generated.

2.8. The critical analysis of the models studied within this framework shows that two conceptual problems exist. This leads to at least two conceptual needs for the advance of general theoretical sociology starting from a process foundation.

2.8.1. There is seen to be a conceptual need for principles of action from which social generators can be derived.

2.8.2. There is a conceptual need for a mode of analysis that retains the focus on relations in the theoretical study of possible social structures.

2.8.3. A perfected account of dynamical social systems involves methodological holism in that the object of theoretical interest is the social system, but also involves methodological individualism in that the ultimate source of Durkheimian social generativity is the interaction of individual actors.

2.9. The tradition of general theoretical sociology involves a recursive process of self-definition in which we modify our understanding of our mission in each generation, building on the transformations effected earlier. We focus on social structure and transform the meaning of that focus through a recursive generative process of producing sociology.

## 3. Action theory and social order

3.1. Among the proliferating lines of development of action theory as a subtradition of general theoretical sociology, three branches can be delineated reasonably clearly: (a) analytical action theory, centered around the contributions of Parsons; (b) interpretive sociology, including ideas of Mead, Blumer, Schutz, Berger and Luckmann, Garfinkel, and Giddens; and (c) adaptively rational action theory, primarily based on the work of Homans and Emerson, with its ambiguous link to rational choice theory, where we have the work of Coleman and others.

3.2. Three theoretical systems are initiated based on the three branches of action theory discussed. Each has certain presuppositions, involves a fundamental action representation principle, and may serve as a framework within which formal theoretical models are formulated and invariants found.

3.2.1. Analytical action theory: The control principle of action in its negative-feedback form states that an actor in a situation is a dynamical normative control system in the sense of control systems theory. Behavior is the control of internally meaningful inputs through comparison processes involving operative ideals at various levels of control.

3.2.2. Interpretive sociology: The control principle of action in its computational model form states that an actor in a situation is an information-processing system and a unit act is an episode of computational control.

3.2.2.1. The computational model of mind asserts that mental structures are programlike entities in two possible states: latent, as physically embodied symbol structures in memory, or active, as generative of thought and behavior.

3.2.2.2. Production systems are such programlike entities. The model instantiates the realist philosophical account of scientific explanation. Structural–generative action theory is a formalized interpretive sociology based on production systems.

3.2.3. Adaptively rational action theory: The principle of adaptively rational action states that an actor in a situation changes action propensities over time in response to the sanction significance of action consequences for that actor. This is the behavioral formulation of the theory.

3.3. Some implications and conceptual aspects of these three formal frameworks can be developed.

3.3.1. Analytical action theory:

3.3.1.1. An actor's behavior is generated through a multilevel cybernetic control hierarchy with operative ideals at four levels of dynamic normative control: values, norms, goals, and operations.

3.3.1.2. Classical polarities of voluntarism and constraint, internal and external, and the like are shown to be aspects of feedback loops in a normative control system.

3.3.1.3. The generic form or template for social generativity is derivable. It is a matrix of social couplings in the sense of "horizontal" input–output couplings of hierarchical dynamic normative control systems representing the actors.

3.3.1.4. Conjectured theorems on social order state necessary conditions for stable social substructures in terms of types of common values.

3.3.1.5. Interpenetration of normative control systems of actors, through sharing such values, is a basis for social relational wholes whose immediate parts are the actors and whose overlapping subparts are the value parameters of the relation.

3.3.1.6. The AGIL scheme can be given a dynamical systems interpretation and linked to the control principle of action. The social order problem is then addressed in terms of a theorem conjecture relating types of generated social relations to types of social values in the context of the problem of the existence of attractor states of coupled multilevel dynamic normative control systems.

3.3.1.7. The AGIL scheme can be used to state special analytical perspectives within general theoretical sociology, both "theoretical sociology of" in type and modes of structuralism.

3.3.2. Structural–generative action theory:

3.3.2.1. The production principle asserts that an institution, as a class of normal forms of interaction based on typification schemes, is generated through a socially distributed production rule system and through the use of universal interpretive procedures.

3.3.2.2. Structural–generative action theory also is integrative in spirit, seeking articulation with the analytical action-theoretical framework, focusing on the structure of social action systems.

3.3.3. Adaptively rational action theory:

3.3.3.1. There are two types of theories of adaptively rational action: (a) a dynamic utility approach in which, in the small, each actor changes action in the direction of increasing utility (a rational choice gradient dynamic) and (b) a behavioral approach in which probabilistic dispositions are altered through the sanction significance of the consequences of actions taken.

3.3.3.2. Using the theoretical procedure of coupling actor models, as applied to the behavioral theory of adaptively rational action, we obtain a derived social interaction generator in which each actor's action has sanction significance for the other.

3.3.3.3. The problems of deriving and studying the properties of the implied equilibria, the possible structures, are studied with computer assistance, that is, simulation. The deductive development of complexity from initially simple action models implies that the proof of theorems is replaced by computer studies of sampled possibilities and subsequent tentative general statements corresponding to the theorem types.

3.4. Conceptual and formal difficulties arise throughout this effort because many of the ideas are complex and difficult to formalize. Some of them are not easily connected to observations. Although it is too soon to speak of unification of the strands of (formalized) action theory, the principles are not necessarily inconsistent, and one can exhibit certain integrative efforts, as is illustrated in structural–generative action theory. In addition, strands of thought not covered in Chapter 3 may prove important in such integrative efforts, especially rational choice theory in its sociological forms.

## 4. Structuralism and unification

4.1. There are various kinds of structuralism related to the modes of generativity.

4.2. In the sense discussed in Chapter 4, structuralism is a vast advancing front of research based on two presuppositions that can be put into the form of rules.

4.2.1. One rule, the theoretical model rule, states that theoretical models should be about social relations and not about individuals as such.

4.2.2. The second rule, the empirical operations rule, states that social relations must constitute data and not constitute merely a mentioned but unmeasured background of analysis.

4.2.3. There are two main branches of structuralism: macrostructuralism and social network analysis.

4.3. One formal framework within the social network analysis branch of structuralism is based on the representation principle that social structures are biased networks. It is a mode of network representation specially aimed at large-scale social systems with respect to their integration or communal networks.

4.3.1. Through the concept of a tracing process, the biased network mode of analysis tries to incorporate a processual point of view into structural analysis.

4.4. From a dynamical social systems standpoint, the biased acquaintanceship network is an integrative substructure through which various flows occur treated as diffusion processes.

4.4.1. In one such diffusion process, emotional states flow in a social system. Another is institutionalization in the sense of spread of schemes of typification across social subnetworks. This relates to Giddens's social order conception.

4.5. A strength-of-weak-ties theorem is derivable for such biased networks and is associated with a dilemma of social integration involving a trade-off between local and global integration.

4.6. Various formal theories in the social networks tradition coordinate to the biased net representation principle and the associated models. Some of them are special cases.

4.7. Macrostructuralism, represented by Peter Blau's macrosociological theory, can be formalized within the biased net framework. Principles of the theory are simply properties of derived formulas.

4.8. A synthesis of formal weak-ties theory and formal macrostructural theory is an instance of unification-driven theorizing in sociology and leads to applications in the form exemplified by a small-worlds model.

4.9. To advance structuralism, one needs to add generative mechanisms that explain how social structures arise and change under various conditions. Linking this idea to Chapter 3, the generative mechanism should arise in the context of some action basis.

4.9.1. An effort in this direction was made through the procedure of *E*-state structuralism. This is an episode of unification at the level of presuppositions and procedures: The presuppositions and procedures of structuralism are linked to those of the expectation states research program.

4.9.2. *E*-state structuralism is instantiated in a theoretical model that generatively explains the emergence of hierarchy in small animal groups.

4.10. Various other recent developments in theoretical sociology relate to the efforts of Chapter 4 and, indeed, of this book.

# Notes

## Chapter 1 A philosophy of general theoretical sociology

1 Perhaps the subtradition that is reflected least in this book is Collins's conflict tradition and Marxian historical materialism. But this is not a matter of principle, but a simple result of limited investigations by one person. In particular, this book does not treat dynamic macrostructural models, although it recognizes them as essential to the advance of general theoretical sociology. But it is precisely in that area that the conflict tradition and the Marxian historical materialist variant within it are most useful. Nevertheless, in Chapter 2 I try to show how the framework developed there exhibits a Marxian materialist aspect as well as a Durkheimian integration focus.

2 Collins (1985) argues that the ritual solidarity wing of the Durkheimian tradition and at least the analytical wing of the conflict tradition have advanced cumulatively. Whatever the merit of this claim, in his own work Collins (1975, 1981) is now our premier example of someone committed to a unification dynamic. My main quarrel with Collins is twofold. First, his image of theory has been too much shaped by the regression equation image he protests against. Second, his purposeful neglect of the contributions of Pareto, Parsons, Homans, Merton, and Blau (a neglect related to the first problem) is an unfortunate blind spot in his vision of the field. In his most recent work, however, Collins (1988) has moved beyond the regression image.

3 This idea moves the positivistic tradition closer to contemporary realism, as I shall indicate in the next section. In Fararo (1973) the concepts of ''meaning postulate'' and ''exact concept'' (drawn from Carnap, 1956), the idea of ''systematic and empirical meaning'' (drawn from Hempel, 1952), and ''axiomatization within set theory'' (drawn from Suppes, 1957) were adopted, and extensive illustrations of their use in mathematical sociology were given. Model building, in the scientific sense, was linked to the metamathematical meaning of model. This axiomatic underpinning of mathematical sociology, however, was blended with a mode of thought derived from Toulmin (1953), Kuhn (1970), general systems thinking, and my own experience with model building. I adopted a ''cybernetic'' or control hierarchy view of the wider structure of theorizing in a discipline along with a dynamic conception of theory change. The reader need not be familiar with all these complex historical pathways of axiomatics and how I made use of them in the past in order to comprehend the philosophical viewpoint elaborated in this chapter.

4 The ''received view'' of theory structure (Suppe, 1977) defined rules of correspondence in a way that glossed over the distinction between interpretation and identification. In my usage, an interpretation is too general to do the work of supplying empirical instances and an identification is too contextual to do the work of supplying a theoretical interpretation. My use of ''correspondence rule'' for the more specific level is not common in the philosophical literature.

5 In the simplest cases, the mathematical objects comprising the abstract model are finite, and so specific finite sets of observations realize them. However, in more significant scientific theories, the ''spaces'' involved in models are infinite. Thus, there can be no case of the structural possibilities in such an abstract model actually corresponding to a set of empirical instances. All we can obtain empirically is a finite set. For instance, in the case of rational choice with respect to

probabilistic mixtures of pure alternatives, the model represents a complex evaluative capacity of human beings that is infinite in its implications for actualization (Fararo, 1973:Sect. 20.6). Generally speaking, theoretical analysis requires abstract models with aspects that go far beyond the relevant data.

6 These terms can be applied even in nonformal contexts where the representation element then refers to an abstract conceptual scheme, such as Parsons's AGIL scheme, or to an even more general "perspective," such as functionalism, symbolic interactionism, or the like.

7 In the case of perspectives or nonformal conceptual schemes defining frameworks, the models are instantiations of these meaning frameworks to more specific cases or classes of phenomena. In this sense, there is a "functionalist model of stratification" and a "symbolic interactionist model of deviance." Of course, in the case of representational principles that map a domain of empirical phenomena into a mathematical formalism, the models are mathematical models. As another variant, if the representational principle maps the phenomena into some programming language that is the basis for simulations of the phenomena, then the model level involves the construction of particular simulation programs. This approach characterizes some work in contemporary cognitive science, for instance.

8 Some readers might argue that given the nonhomogeneous character of what I call a representation principle, any such entity implies a category of abstract mathematical models defined by a set of axioms. The point, however, is that seldom in the history of science has the use of mathematics in theorizing been on the basis of *explicitly stated axiomatic systems.* Even when one is aware of the elegance and power of axiomatics, it does not follow that in every theoretical context one will use a strictly axiomatic procedure as defined earlier. Most of this book does *not* adopt the axiomatic procedure in any strict sense, although it is mathematical and very definitely postulates a number of representation principles.

9 That is, to the theoreticians using a theory, the mathematics is either essential to express the ideas of the theory or it is not. Most of general theoretical sociology as a research tradition consists of theories such that theoreticians do not feel that some formalization or other is so satisfactory as to ever after make its use essential. This is the key important point made by Hayes (1984) in writing about mathematical models and theoretical interests in sociology.

10 The term *directed graph* is often used if the lines are directed, as when relations are not symmetric, but I use the term *graph* for both directed and undirected cases.

11 This statement was not derived from a process model, and in this sense it is defective. This remark is elaborated in Section 1.4.

12 This is a different issue, obviously, than that relating to the influence of statistical models in sociology. On the latter, see Turner (1987).

13 There are a number of problematic aspects of this covering law model of explanation (Keat and Urry, 1982). A thorough discussion of these problems is beyond the scope of this chapter and not really required for my purposes.

14 This is drawn from the account in *Time Magazine,* October 24, 1983.

15 I am much indebted to Collins for drawing attention to this set of ideas in his various works, but the nomenclature Durkheimian depth sociology is my own. Collins refers to this body of ideas as defining a "ritual solidarity model."

16 In continuous-time models this statement needs amendment, but this is a minor point in this context. Also, the mechanism can be probabilistic as well as deterministic.

17 I first used this term in Fararo (1969a,b). Boudon (1974, 1981) closely follows the logic of generating processes in his accounts of the nature of sociological explanation.

18 A longer treatment may be found elsewhere (Fararo, 1987a).

19 Without paradox, in a mathematical framework one can have the structural stability together with change of state. This is indicated by movements along an attractor branch in the discussion in Chapter 2 of group process.

20 For instance, a mode of thought based on regression equations might claim to implement analytical realism since it relates variables representing aspects of a concrete phenomenon. But regression equations are not representations of generative mechanisms.

21 A third premise relates to the method of study of science. The positivist took the role of the abstract formal theorist. The role definition is to construct and study idealized formal language systems with the tools of modern symbolic logic and to explicate scientific concepts within such formalized language schemes. Carnap (1955) is the prototypical such positivist philosopher of science.

22 A third wing consists of historical realists such as Laudan (1977). This is a post-Kuhnian development concerned with the dynamics of science and the interplay of the content and the social structure of science. This wing especially opposes the third premise of positivist philosophy of science, described in note 21.

23 Recent discussions of this issue pose it as "realism versus empiricism," as in the papers in Churchland and Hooker (1985), which deal with issues framed in van Fraasen (1980).

24 Are there any social science examples of theory structure that satisfy the conception of a comprehensive theory of social phenomena in mathematical form? An approximation is given by game theory with the intended interpretation as applicable to any system of social interaction. So interpreted, game theory is a comprehensive theory, and game-theoretical models can be, and have been, constructed with games (e.g., game matrices or game trees) as model objects. The corresponding representational principle is simply this: A system of social interaction is a game. But from the perspective of work on the problems of general theoretical sociology, game-theoretical model building by sociologists has been limited. Instead, specialized fields such as public choice and analytical Marxism have made use of game-theoretical methods. Sociologists have favored more empirical routes of inquiry, although some have taken a theoretical route close to the spirit of game theory (e.g., Coleman, 1973, 1986). In Fararo (1973) I devoted nearly a quarter of the text to an exposition of game theory as a theory of institutional or rule-governed interactive choice situations. I took the theoretical problems that motivate game theory to be those of defining successively more comprehensive concepts of rationality, leading up to a cooperative rationality in social action. I wondered in writing what to make of game models (Fararo, 1973:630), although I tried to link the ideas to interpretive sociology (Sect. 22.7). The dual focus on *choice* and on *institutional structure* is what makes game theory so attractive. Boudon (1981) uses game-theoretical ideas very effectively. Related discussions occur in Sections 3.6 and 3.7 of the present volume.

## Chapter 2. Dynamical social systems and the key problems

1 In this most recent work, Collins (1988) shows strong signs of adopting a systems perspective. Giddens (1984) uses the term *system* but not in the context of dynamical systems thinking.

2 Section 4.9 has an application to a nonhuman interactive setting.

3 In Fararo (1972a) an effort was made to use a dynamical systems framework to describe mathematically the "field of status dynamics" and to study some specific theoretical models. The main conceptual difficulty with the approach was that it was not sufficiently centered on problems of social structure as defined in this chapter. It did not embody generative *structuralism*.

4 Sociologists too strongly influenced by the Popperian model of science may doubt the significance of a nonfalsifiable identity in scientific theorizing. But as Schelling (1978:Ch. 2) points out, they are often vital for theory development.

5 There is a somewhat more general form of (2.3.1) in which the right-hand side is replaced by $\mathbf{f}(\mathbf{x}, \mathbf{c}, \mathbf{t})$. This is not a trivial point, but to elucidate the fundamental ideas with the more general form would be forbiddingly difficult.

6 In a one-dimensional instance, $dx/dt = f(x, c)$ can be written in the form $dx = f(x,c)dt$. Then, for small $dt$, $x' = x + dx$. When the continuous-time generator takes the value zero at some state $x$, then $dx = 0$ and so $x' = x$, and the same state is preserved. Such a state is then labeled $x^E$ and called an equilibrium state.

7 Also, in the next chapter, the more general idea of *steady state* is introduced, with most of the idea carrying over to that context. For the present, a steady state may be thought of as a moving equilibrium: Imagine that the parameter changes incessantly so that a (stable) equilibrium state will incessantly adjust to this change.

8 The more complex conceptual apparatus of dynamical systems theory necessary to discuss here extends the notion of attractor to the cycles themselves. The advantage of this is that not only particular states of the system but entire modes of behavior in state space are regarded as generalized equilibrium conditions with attractor properties if the process gravitates toward them and repellor properties if the process moves away from them. There is still another mode of asymptotic behavior of the system, called chaos, in which all the trajectories eventually stay in a bounded region of state space but where there is what amounts to randomness within the region. For details on the complexities of definition and analysis of attractors of the limit cycle and chaotic type, see Thompson and Stewart (1986). Thus, the generalized conception proposed in the text in what follows is that social structures are attractors of dynamical social systems of any one of three types: attractor states, attractor cycles, and strange attractors. Attractors of the limit cycle type have an intuitive precedent in contemporary sociological theory, namely the "orbits" in AGIL space discussed by Parsons, Bales, and Shils (1953).

9 More generally, the conditions are in reference to the existence of three types of potential attractors, as in note 8.

10 In practice, the values of parameters are unknown but are estimated in the process of applying and testing the model. For methods, problems, and examples of estimation of differential equation models in sociology, see Doreian and Hummon (1976), as well as Tuma and Hannan (1984).

11 Focus on the full manifold is sometimes called *global dynamics* in the dynamical systems literature. For a nontechnical account, see Gleick (1987).

12 See, also, Pareto (1980) for an abbreviated version of the major work and see Finer (1966) for a selection of Pareto's writings from a number of works.

13 We realize today, or we should, that analogy is not something to run away from: It is a source of insights, metaphors, and models that help orient us to our subject matter and stimulate creative theorizing. This point is the core of one of the modern realist philosophies of science, as discussed in Sections 1.4 and 1.6. Analogies can be employed at various levels of scientific activity. Spencer (1967), e.g., made beautiful use of the biological analogy. Doubters should reread his essay, reproduced in Parsons et al. (1961:139–143). Spencer's analogy, between society and the organism, leads to the statement of principles of a conceptual framework that becomes independent of the source of the analogy in terms of its validation in the subject matter domain.

14 The relevance is also in terms of what Parsons calls the general action system level of analysis, as discussed in Chapter 3.

15 The first-order vs. second-order concepts in Homans's sense must be distinguished from a similar terminological contrast introduced by Schutz, which will be discussed in Chapter 3.

16 But if interaction in this sense is like time in physics, are there mechanisms that employ amount of time as a critical feature? In thermodynamics, we have: "The greater the time (i.e., the duration since some initial time), the greater the order lost by a closed system." The basic entropy principle says that in a closed system entropy can only increase (order decrease as distinctions such as hot and cold pass into homogeneity). The statement in quotes, which resembles the way Homans employs the concept of interaction in specifying mechanisms, is a consequence of the entropy principle but not quite a statement of it. This suggests that with a more sophisti-

cated theoretical system this type of statement would be derived rather than assumed. Again, in learning theory, the number of trials in a trial-and-error learning process is a critical variable. Yet no axiomatic learning theory includes an axiom about the sheer number of trials. Instead, the axioms are about the single episode of learning (or not) and the *deductions* are about the recursive application of this axiom to the situation produced by its application in every single trial. (See, e.g., Atkinson and Estes, 1963.) This is close to Homans's own later viewpoint (Homans, 1974) in which a statement such as ''the greater the frequency of interaction, the greater the strength of positive sentiments'' is regarded, in a qualified way, as following from the fundamental principles of behavior as applied to persons in interaction. Put in model terms, such a statement is a reading-off of a property of a model object as generated by the mechanisms defining a theoretical model. For instance, the average probability $P(t)$ of an error as a function of the trial $t$ is seen to be a decreasing function of $t$: The greater the number of trials, the lower the chance of error. The general point relates to the fact that generators are set up ''in the small'' with derivations ''in the large'' (Fararo, 1973:Sect. 8.9). See Section 3.6 for a use of this idea in the context of initiating analysis from an actor–situation model and deriving the generator of a dynamical social system model.

17 So what is (under some conditions) generated by the dynamical system connecting the elements of interaction, activities, and sentiments consists (at least) in the membership *roles* of the specified persons in *collectivities* (groups) with their own *norms*. These three structural elements (role, collectivity, norm) plus one (value) constitute the four types of social structural elements in one of the conceptual schemes of Parsons. (See Parsons et al., 1961:41–44.) This is only one of a large set of at least partial correspondences between Homans and Parsons. (See also note 19.) Although in the context of discussing Homans it is natural to think of a relatively small system and so of a single group with various subgroups, for general purposes this is too restrictive. The point is that under certain conditions, the network of interactions may be such that a single group with various subgroups may *not* be generated. Even when a single collectivity is generated and maintained, the subgroups may exhibit the property of constituting (among other things) an arena of conflict. For instance, a society can be an arena of conflict (of its constituent subcollectivities) as well as a single collectivity. The two features are *structural aspects* that may be maintained (or not) in a single dynamical social system.

18 Each person counted as one of the set of members of a particular generated or given group also may be a member of other groups. Thus, social interaction generates the property that persons may belong to multiple groups and groups may share persons. This is the ''duality'' or social interpenetration of individuals and groups (Breiger, 1974; Fararo and Doreian, 1984). From this point of view, the conceptualized family of all social systems in which a person is included yields a family of membership roles that stand in various structural relations. This entity can be studied from the standpoint of a dynamical system where the referent is an individual and the theoretical model is social systemic. This point is developed with conceptual rigor by Bates and Harvey (1975:Pt. 4). Also, any such person can be treated as the referent of other system concepts, such as personality treated as a dynamical system. However, for the treatment of the core problems of general theoretical sociology, which concern social structure, individual personality is not an endogenous component. Employing Pareto's procedural analogy, ''pure sociology'' may be supplemented with personality theory in its applications, where the real social system phenomena are more closely approximated by taking personality states and mechanisms into account. A further discussion of these matters occurs in Chapter 3.

19 Homans (1950:Ch. 16) also has a place for Parsons's goal attainment function as linked to organization and authority. So, despite the reservations that Homans (1950:268–273) expresses about functional theory in anthropology, his own work presents outstanding examples of analyses of social dynamics with respect to four functional dimensions or problems: adaptation to the environment, integration of persons with each other, latent pattern maintenance of the emergent

structures, and collective goal attainment through organization and authority. In short, he treats the Parsonian canonical four functions in terms of a frame of reference that is a nonmathematical dynamical systems point of view. The four-function scheme is stated in dynamical systems terms in Section 3.3.

20 Arbitrarily large-scale systems are characterized as biased networks in Chapter 4.

21 The derivative of a vector is the vector of derivatives of the components. The derivative of a matrix is the matrix of derivatives of the entries, where each is a function of time.

22 Actually, what is meant here is called *regular* equivalence in the technical literature.

23 Each of the next two chapters introduces principles at the framework level and some procedures at the theoretical model level that add to the depth of the formal approach of this volume. Chapter 3 adds principles of action and the theoretical procedure of coupling actor models to generate interaction models, whereas Chapter 4 adds network principles and procedures that become especially relevant when the social systems treated are vast in size.

24 For a useful discussion of trade offs in theoretical model building, see Heckathorn (1984).

25 Not surprisingly, given the exposure to Henderson, Whitehead, and Pareto, Talcott Parsons (1954:215) employs the same early model of the nature of analytical theory as an analogue to a system of differential equations. See Section 3.3 for a discussion of Parsons's ideas in dynamical systems terms.

26 I discuss Giddens's theory in Section 3.4.1 and offer further discussion in Chapter 4 of ideas related to his version of the problem of social order.

27 This does not mean that chaos is irrelevant to general theoretical sociology but only that I myself have not yet absorbed it sufficiently to feel confident in applying it to theoretical model building.

28 This particular "do" is strongly emphasized as the primary theoretical rationale for social networks thinking in the survey paper by Marsden and Laumann (1984).

29 I use the term *one-sided* to remind the reader of Marx's discussion of the relational character of such entities as labor and capital (Ollman, 1976).

30 Block models are hypotheses about a reduced structural form based on grouping positions that are sufficiently similar in their pattern of relations to all other positions. (See Burt, 1980.)

31 Interdependence without direct interaction occurs when the relevant situational conditions of an actor are altered by the results of actions of others. Such interdependent sets of actions can be generative of emergent effects that are unintended by any of the actors. This point is emphasized in various works by Raymond Boudon. See, e.g., Boudon (1981). An important example is given by dynamic segregation models constructed by Schelling (1971).

32 This accounts for the considerable attention given to the logic of triad configurations among social network researchers during the 1970s. See, e.g., Holland and Leinhardt (1977b) and Chase (1980), as well as Chapter 4 of the present volume.

## Chapter 3. Action theory and social order

1 Formalization of ideas in what I call analytical action theory is addressed in several papers by Hayes (1980, 1981, 1984).

2 An act that is an intrinsic means to one end can be a symbolic means to another end.

3 Above this bottom level all the transformations involve aggregations or syntheses of neural currents that take on increasingly more complex subjective significance as Powers interprets them. In Whiteheadian (1929) general process terms, each transformation is a prehension with its initial datum (input) as an aspect of the objective datum, the nexus of other actualities. But any prehension has a subjective form, which is *how* that initial datum is felt by the subject of the prehension. Through the successive syntheses, the Whiteheadian–Powers hierarchy of control *generates* the higher levels. Consciousness is the prehension (input reading) of a high but still lower-level synthesis consisting of a difference between a proposition and indicated particulars that are the

logical subjects of the proposition. The lowest-level entities in Whitehead and in Powers are physical prehensions. This generativity of consciousness from a base in physical prehensions presupposes a cybernetic hierarchy as the complex internal processual structure of brain–body functioning. It also presupposes that subjectivity is not an emergent phenomenon: By general metaphysical assumption, any prehension has a ''how-it-feels'' aspect, although not all prehensions have occasions of human beings as their subjects so that most feelings are alien to us.

4 McPhail and Wohlstein (1986) show that the control system model set out by Powers is applicable to the conceptualization of collective behavior.

5 I follow closely the model formulated by Powers (1973: Appendix).

6 Apparently antinormative behavior, such as theft, cheating, and the like, does not contravene the basic control system model. The cheater has his or her own operative ideals by which the situation is altered in accordance with certain ends that others do not accept. (The implied problem of order will be discussed later.)

7 The model stated here assumes a strict linear order of the levels of control. For instance, the goal level is set by the output from the norm level and has no direct connection to the value level. This follows Powers (1973) in his basic model, where each of the higher levels directly controls only the level just below. One might consider generalizing this model to allow direct as well as indirect control of goals through outputs from the value level.

8 The nomenclature throughout follows Parsons closely except for this last usage of *mental model* for cognitive integration or synthesis. I do not believe Parsons suggested any terminology here because through most of his career, he did not interpret the action adaptation dimension as the cognitive dimension. The shift toward the cognitive interpretation was initiated by Lidz and Lidz (1976).

9 Figure 2.1 is misleading in one respect because it suggests uniqueness. For instance, in that figure there is a unique equilibrium value of $y$ for each possible value of $x$. The analytical situation is more like that in Figure 2.6, where there is a region of $x$ values where no $y$-equilibrium exists and a region where multiple $y$-equilibria exist. One should envision a generalization of the single fold in Figure 2.6 to a repeated pattern of folds so as to yield multiple attractor and repellor branches. If the dependence is mutual, as in the social state variables we are considering here, then an analogous picture holds in the other direction. When the intersections of the two complex graphs of dependence are considered, the attractor points of the whole are those that are attractors from both points of view. Thus the economic structure exercises a ''veto power'' (Ashby, 1963:83) over the possible overall social structures; but so does the political structure, the communal structure, and the fiduciary structure. As Ashby (1963:83) puts it, ''*No state (of the whole) can be a state of equilibrium unless it is acceptable to every one of the component parts*, each acting in the conditions given by the other.''

10 In terms of Parsons's (1960) model, these states of the pattern variables of affective neutrality versus affectivity and performance versus quality characterize the symbolism employed in the instrumental activity. Approximately, this is technological knowledge as an element of the culture of the group.

11 Again, in Parsons's (1960) model, these states of the pattern variables of affective neutrality versus affectivity and performance versus quality characterize a symbolic medium. In this instance, the medium seems to be an emotionally toned symbolism of group identity.

12 One could include affective neutrality and performance within this rational cluster.

13 One could include affectivity within this cluster and, for completeness but without easy interpretability, also quality.

14 For a useful discussion of the foundations of the AGIL scheme, see Baum (1976).

15 For instance, the ''production of culture'' (Peterson, 1979) seems to fit here. See also Robertson (1988). Note also that AGIL dimensions can be taken in pairs to define dynamical systems, by analogy with the sociocultural case treated in Section 2.10.2.

16 One major limitation of the general dynamical social action system is revealed in this discussion, however. The treatment of **b** does not include any dynamical subsystem for change of **b**. From the Paretan standpoint of analytical abstraction, this is not a conceptual problem. But the empirical significance of group size and of material technology, elements conceptually within **b,** does suggest an important conceptual limitation of theory guided only by analytical action theory.

17 The idea of model building centered on stating recursive rule systems was an essential point of the pioneering book by Miller, Galanter, and Pribram (1960). Spradley (1972) collected together a diverse set of conceptual and empirical efforts in this direction.

18 Artificial intelligence uses of production systems are discussed by Nilsson (1977). For another example of their use in cognitive science, see Anderson (1983).

19 Bates and Harvey (1975) use this idea of latent state without formally writing down action production rules. Their term for such a rule is *norm*. The terminological problem with regard to norms, production rules, and interpretive procedures or "rules" as understood in ethnomethodology is one that plagues efforts in this area.

20 Recent work in cognitive psychology has stressed parallel distributed processing (Rumelhart et al., 1986). The relevant brain network models are "subcognitive" and treat the Newell–Simon production system level as a kind of surface structure that contrasts with the deeper subcognitive processing. This idea retains but revises the computational model of mind discussed in Section 1.4.2. It is possible that in the future the analogy between distributed parallel processing in neural networks and distributed parallel processing in social networks might be exploited; the same mathematical and simulation techniques may apply.

21 Other institutional identities such as <woman> are omnirelevant, to use Garfinkel's nice term, i.e., status assignments that are carried from situation to situation. Durkheim's concept of the individual as a sacred being in modern societies is a hypothesis about a typified entity <individual>. Goffman (1967) follows up this idea with the deduction that since sacred things must be treated in special ways, there must exist rules of conduct that embody ritual behavior toward selves, one's own and other's. In Goffman's sense, <self> is a primary component of the sacred institution <individual>.

22 The productions discussed here are slight modifications of what was called the deviation counteraction generator in Fararo and Skvoretz (1984a).

23 For further discussions of negative feedback and computational models, see Fararo and Skvoretz (1984a, 1986a).

24 Of course, some deviation counteraction can be institutionalized action so that specific types of actors are called upon in specific types of situation to perform the functions in this deviation counteraction process. This includes official interpretations of actions as obligatory and the like. Also, the official interpretive actions thus institutionalized will be kept on track (or not, in the unstable case) by the general monitoring production system.

25 Probably the most important line of research today that has the potentiality of integrating these two formalisms in the context of empirical research on interaction is that originated by David Heise, whose theory was described earlier. Possible connections between Heise's affect control theory and the production system approach are discussed by Skvoretz and Fararo (1988) and by Smith-Lovin (1987), who also relates the ideas to the sophisticated cognitive science work of Carley (1985). For many years, Heise's work focused on affect control in terms of a quantitative and empirically identified negative-feedback model. More recently, through adopting the techniques of knowledge engineers writing down expert systems, Heise (1988) constructed a framework and a computer program for computer-assisted analysis of event sequences generated through production system models of everyday social knowledge.

26 To explain how human beings acquired the capacities or powers described by such principles means to invoke a general biosocial evolutionary framework. This is itself quite a significant task, but it does not negate using known or reasonably conjectured general principles of action

as starting points for deriving models of interaction. Among recent writers on theory, Boudon (1981) has expressed the logic of methodological individualism with particular force and clarity.

27 Homans (1974) argues for a correspondence between the two in the sense that the preference structures (represented by utility functions) assumed by economic theory are psychological structures generated through adaptive behavioral processes in given environments. But his main theory, in terms of the nature of the generator of dynamics, is drawn from the behavioral tradition.

28 In turn, Emerson's work has been a strong influence on the contributions of other theorists, especially Cook (Cook and Emerson, 1978) but also other "exchange theorists" (Cook, 1987).

29 A relevant discussion of rational action may be found in March and Simon (1958:Ch. 6).

30 Details on such mathematical complexities are fully discussed by Sternberg (1963). The adaptive behavior process starts from a very simple idea but yields two general outcomes: (1) the bifurcation upon bifurcation generated by the linear operators, which yields diversification of action by experience, and (2) the nonlinear operator for the average process. The latter has the potentiality of yielding surprising results since nonlinear phenomena are those that may yield multiple equilibria, with possible catastrophes as discussed in Chapter 2 as well as possible strange attractors or chaos.

31 Bush and Mosteller (1955:Ch. 2) devote one chapter to showing how a stimulus-sampling theory logically implies that the operators on action probabilities must be linear. A similar approach is taken by Atkinson and Estes (1963). The equations used here are a special case, chosen as especially appropriate for correspondence with the subtradition of work by Homans and Emerson with regard to its model of individual action. The required axiomatic basis asserts that a situation corresponds to a collection of stimulus patterns and the effective stimuli are a random sample of these patterns. That is, the actor is a sampler of situation patterns and the sampling model is random (for instrumental–philosophical reasons of simplicity and fertility of consequences that can be tested). To relate probability distributions over actions in different situations, Luce (1959) proposed a general probabilistic choice axiom. The axiom implies a ratio scale over the space of choice. Luce's theory is stated rather fully, and an empirical test in a sociological measurement context (job prestige) is reported in Fararo (1973:Ch. 11). In the present context, the relevant point is that when Luce applies his choice theory to the dynamic adaptation problem, he obtains a nonlinear operator model. He also shows how the linear operator model drops out as a special case when certain conditions hold. Thus, from this wider standpoint on the foundations of the dynamics of adaptive action through choices from varying sets of alternatives relevant in various occasions, the linear operator model is a first approximation to the nonlinear model.

32 Homans states, "For all action taken by persons, the more often a particular action of a person is rewarded, the more likely the person is to perform that action" (1974:16).

33 An important axiom of Homans's theory treats emotional reactions accompanying the comparison of actual and expected outcomes. The key point is the generation of a new kind of behavior when a "shift" is felt to have occurred, i.e., when the actual is not the same as expected. This new behavior is aggressive or approving toward the agency of the perceived shift in contingent reaction. This suggests the following idea, which I do not try to write down formally. Consider the class of all possible situations in which the shift occurs one way or the other. The set of action alternatives for these situations are two *expressive behaviors,* approval and aggression. The actor may learn to suppress aggression (via high negative sanction probabilities following aggressive behavior) or to express it (via high reward probabilities following aggressive behavior). Similarly, the actor may learn to display approval or to inhibit it. Thus there is a *secondary adaptive process* over a presumed series of such situations wherein the adaptation equations generate expressive behavior. Current probabilities are then transformed (with distinct parameters, say, $c$ and $d$ rather than $a$ and $b$). As Homans (1974:39) puts it, the result is that such behaviors become at one and the same time emotional and voluntary. Homans's stimulus similarity axiom is readily

comprehended within the general axioms of stimulus sampling theory (see note 31), one family of models of which comprises the adaptive behavior equations treated here.

34 Indeed, in another context, Parsons makes clear that in the same *highly generalized sense* he agrees with Homans that all social interaction is exchange (Parsons and Smelser, 1956:10, note 2). The same cited passage agrees with Homans (1967) that the law of supply and demand is a special case of the more general paradigm of action and reaction. Analytical action theory, however, is not based on the presupposition that an assumption base in adaptive behavior (even with its emotional elements) is sufficient for general comprehensive theoretical purposes.

35 I am drawing on a contribution by Lave and March (1975:Sect. 6.6). Another example of this type of utilization of the Bush–Mosteller model is provided by England (1973).

36 As will be discussed, this result is obtained through simulation studies. Using a table of random numbers, we generate the initial event and change the state via the equations; then we generate another event with the updated state, compute the change in state and generate another event and so forth.

37 See Rapoport (1960, 1983) on this role of formal theoretical model building in science. For an illustration of such what-if thinking in sociology with a large-scale model, see Boudon (1974). In the latter case, it turned out that purely analytical investigations could be undertaken to validate the conjectured generalities from the computational thought experiments, as is shown in Fararo and Kosaka (1976).

38 For the single-actor model, approximation arguments, yielding approximations to the recursion in average probabilities, permit an equation to be derived for the asymptotic behavior: It is quadratic, implying *two* average equilibrium states. See Bush and Mosteller [1955:Formula (13.28)] for details.

39 Willer and Anderson (1981) stress the role of coercion in institutionalized settings such as the classical capitalist factory. They argue that coercion is outside the scope of Homans's framework. This seems unlikely, given the great generality of the action–reaction conception, its essential isomorphism with the double contingency of the action framework, its representation in the coupled adaptive behavior model, and such results as those obtained here where we readily can generate unequal exchange. However, a serious analysis of coercion in terms of the present model has not been undertaken; it is possible that there are certain unintended but real limitations in this regard.

40 In fact, one can define multilevel networks in which the successive nodes start with production rules, followed by systems of productions representing roles, followed by systems of roles representing positions, and so forth. The logic is exactly as defined in Bates and Harvey (1975) and also shown with production rules as the ultimate nodes in Fararo and Skvoretz (1986a).

41 Another satisfying aspect of such rational choice models is that they embody the interpretation-of-action principle, as I call it (Fararo, 1973:653). This is an interpretive procedural rule of everyday life; namely, in a simplified form, "People choose according to their preferences, given what they know or believe about possible outcomes." This is a reflexive principle, applying to each person as self-interpretive actor and to each observer of the action, including the sociologist (who, in turn, understands what we might call "theory construction action" in the same terms).

42 See, e.g., the combination of formal theoretical, simulation and empirical studies undertaken by Markovsky (1987) and Markovsky, Willer, and Patton (1988). For useful overviews of many other recent developments in sociological theory, see Ritzer (1988) and Collins (1988).

## Chapter 4. Structuralism and unification

1 For example, the recent book edited by Wellman and Berkowitz (1988) appears in a series entitled *Structural Analysis in the Social Sciences*. The series editor, Mark Granovetter, describes

the scope (on the page facing the title page) as including ''approaches that explain social behavic and institutions by reference to relations among such concrete social entities as persons an organizations. This contrasts with at least four other popular strategies: (1) reductionist attempt to explain by a focus on individuals alone; (2) explanations stressing the causal primacy o abstract concepts such as ideas, values, mental harmonies and cognitive maps (what is ofter called 'structuralism' on the Continent should be sharply distinguished from structural analysis in the present sense, although Claude Levi-Strauss' early work on kinship is much closer to it); (3) technological and material determinism; (4) explanations that take 'variables' to be the mair concepts of analysis, as for the 'structural equation' models that dominated much 1970s sociology, where the 'structure' is that connecting variables rather than concrete social entities. The methodological core of structural analysis is the 'social network' approach.''

2 A powerful polemical argument on structuralism as contrasted with individualism is given by Mayhew ([illegible]).

3 The reader may consult Chapter 2 for the distinction between slow and fast dynamics. A slow dynamic in parameter space induces a fast dynamic in state space, which may include abrupt changes in type of attractor state occupied. This language and the accompanying intuitions arise in the context of catastrophe analysis (Fararo, 1978).

4 The ideas here relate to other random baseline models for structural analysis developed by sociologists. They differ in that in this approach the random baseline is only the methodological starting point for the construction of the theoretically significant types of models that include bias parameters, to be described shortly. For an argument in favor of the purely random baseline approach to demonstrating sociological theorems, see Mayhew (1984) and also see the special issue of the same journal for other discursive articles on baseline models. Also, the term *density* is most often used to refer to the proportion of all possible ties that actually exist in a network. Calling this quantity $d$, it is the contact density divided by $N-1$. For a discussion of network sampling to estimate $d$, see Erickson and Nosanchuk (1983).

5 A somewhat different interpretation might be given in which the generative process itself is one of random encounters constrained by the bias parameters and the density. Skvoretz (1985) explores a simulation model of such a process. By contrast, the interpretation here is that some real social structure already exists and a tracing process with given density reveals an aspect of that structure. Also, Skvoretz (in press) treats problems of estimation of parameters and empirical testing of biased net models.

6 A more complex version of formula (4.4.2) is developed in Fararo and Skvoretz (1987). The same qualitative conclusions hold for this simpler model.

7 For another treatment of Lévi-Strauss's ideas in terms of structural balance see Abell (1970). Also relevant is the extension of the balance concept so as to allow cycles of different lengths to have different weights (Norman and Roberts, 1972).

8 The logic of formula (4.4.2) is extendable to this case after first writing down the more complex version of the formula mentioned in note 6. That is, we integrate over terms involving $f(s)$ and $\sigma(s, s')$ where $f(s)$ is the probability density function of the strength variable and $\sigma(s, s')$ is the closure bias as a function of the pair of strengths of ties of members of a pair to a third party. The weak-ties axiom becomes a statement about the function $\sigma(s, s')$ to the effect that as the strengths of the ties increase, so does the bias toward closure in the triad.

9 For the present unification task, however, I shall concentrate only on the heterogeneity element. Success in that respect, if attained, will then serve as the launching point for further unification efforts.

10 More generally, as indicated in note 8, each tie could be assigned a quantitative strength, and the closure bias is then expressed as varying with this strength. A related point is that a network with multiplexity bias can be defined (Fararo and Skvoretz, in press). Such a type of bias parameter

relates very closely to interlock among qualitatively different kinds of relations and also to the pattern variable diffuseness–specificity.

11 For an elaboration of the state space approach to probabilistic model building in sociology, see Fararo (1973). For an extended empirical example of a contrast between the inadequacy of Markov models framed in terms of observables versus the empirical adequacy of a state space formulation, see Cohen (1963). The particular model constructed by Cohen is postulated as such rather than logically derived within a comprehensive theoretical framework whose assumptions constrain the form that the process model can take. Models with the latter property have been called ''theoretical construct models'' in a study (by Berger et al., 1962) aiming to clarify the functions of models in the social sciences. See Ashby (1963) for a discussion of ''machines with input'' and the principle of state determination. See Margenau (1950) and more recently van Fraasen (1980) for philosophies of science geared to the state space approach. A realist theory of explanation orients us to model generative structures that we think are generating the observables, whereas empiricist philosophers stress predictive accuracy. What the discussion shows is that these two criteria, predictive accuracy with respect to observables and models of unobservable generative mechanisms, over time may lead to the identical scientific behavior under some conditions.

12 The presentation in Sections 4.9.1 and 4.9.2 draws upon portions of Fararo and Skvoretz (1986b).

13 In fact, EST can be regarded as a branch of the action theory tradition. Berger and other senior members of the core group were trained at Harvard at the height of Parsons's work on analytical action theory and of Bales's work with small group processes. They combined certain elements from these programs with other elements. The combination is a unique cluster with a time-extended and productive history of theory and research.

14 One exception illustrating a path crossing is the important paper by Fisek (1974), whose work constitutes one of several background elements for the procedure to be described in this section.

15 The readily available article by Fararo and Skvoretz (1986b) provides a mathematically explicit treatment of examples, of the derivation of the transition probability matrix of the process, and of the equivalence class procedure described in what follows.

16 I am grateful to Turner (1986:328) for his clarifying interpretation of the relationship of Schutz to Husserl.

# References

Abell, Peter. 1970. "The Structural Balance of the Kinship Systems of Some Primitive Peoples." Pp. 359–366 in *Introduction to Structuralism,* edited by M. Lane. New York: Basic.

1984. "Comparative Narratives: Some Rules for the Study of Action." *Journal for the Theory of Social Behaviour* 14:309–331.

Abraham, Ralph H., and Christopher D. Shaw. 1981. *Dynamics: The Geometry of Behavior* (4 Vols.). Santa Cruz, Calif.: Aerial.

Alexander, Jeffrey C. 1978. "Formal and Substantive Voluntarism in the Work of Talcott Parsons: A Theoretical and Ideological Reinterpretation." *American Sociological Review* 43:177–198.

1982. *Theoretical Logic in Sociology.* Vol. 1. *Positivism, Presuppositions, and Current Controversies.* University of California Press.

(ed.). 1985. *Neofunctionalism.* Beverly Hills, Calif.: Sage.

Alexander, Jeffrey C., Bernhard Giesen, Richard Münch, and Neil J. Smelser (eds.). 1987. *The Micro–Macro Link.* Berkeley: University of California Press.

Allee, W. C. 1938. *The Social Life of Animals.* New York: Norton.

Allison, Paul D. 1978. "Measures of Inequality." *American Sociological Review* 43:865–880.

Anderson, Bo. 1979. "Cognitive Balance Theory and Social Network Analysis: Remarks on Some Fundamental Theoretical Matters." Pp. 453–469 in *Perspectives in Social Networks,* edited by P. W. Holland and S. Leinhardt. New York: Academic.

Anderson, John R. 1983. *The Architecture of Cognition.* Cambridge, Mass.: Harvard University Press.

Arrow, Kenneth J., and F. H. Hahn. 1971. *General Competitive Analysis.* San Francisco: Holden-Day.

Ashby, W. Ross. 1963 [1956]. *An Introduction to Cybernetics.* New York: Wiley.

Atkinson, Richard C., and William K. Estes. 1963. "Stimulus Sampling Theory." Chapter 10 in *The Handbook of Mathematical Psychology,* Vol. 2, edited by R. D. Luce, R. R. Bush, and E. Galanter. New York: Wiley.

Axelrod, Robert. 1984. *The Evolution of Cooperation.* New York: Basic.

Axten, Nick, and Thomas J. Fararo. 1977. "The Information Processing Representation of Institutionalized Social Action." Pp. 35–77 in *Mathematical Models of Sociology,* edited by P. Krishnan. Keele, UK: Sociological Review Monograph 24. Reprinted 1979. Totowa, N.J.: Rowan & Littlefield.

Axten, Nick, and John Skvoretz. 1980. "Roles and Role-Programs." *Quality and Quantity* 14:547–583.

Babloyantz, Agnessa. 1986. *Molecules, Dynamics, and Life.* New York: Wiley-Interscience.

Barchas, Patricia R. (ed.). 1984. *Social Hierarchies: Essays toward a Sociophysiological Perspective.* Westport, Ct.: Greenwood Press.

Bartholomew, David J. 1982. *Stochastic Models for Social Processes,* 3rd ed. New York: Wiley.

Bates, Frederick L., and Clyde C. Harvey. 1975. *The Structure of Social Systems.* New York: Gardner Press. Reprinted 1986. Melbourne, Fla.: Krieger.

Baum, Rainer. 1976 ''Communication and Media.'' Pp. 533–556 in *Explorations in General Theory in Social Science,* Vol. 2, edited by J. Loubser, R. Baum, A. Effrat, and V. Lidz. New York: Free Press.

Bellah, Robert N. 1973. ''Introduction'' in *Emile Durkheim on Morality and Society,* Chicago: University of Chicago Press.

Bellman, Richard. 1961. *Adaptive Control Processes: A Guided Tour.* Princeton, N.J.: Princeton University Press.

Benton, Ted. 1977. *Philosophical Foundations of the Three Sociologies.* Boston: Routledge & Kegan Paul.

Berger, Joseph, Bernard P. Cohen, J. Laurie Snell, and Morris Zelditch, Jr. 1962. *Types of Formalization.* Boston: Houghton Mifflin.

Berger, Joseph, M. Hamit Fisek, and Robert Z. Norman. 1977. ''Status Characteristics and Expectation States: A Graph-theoretical Formulation.'' Pp. 91–171 in *Status Characteristics and Social Interaction,* edited by J. Berger, M. H. Fisek, R. Z. Norman, and M. Zelditch, Jr. New York: Elsevier.

Berger, Joseph, David Wagner, and Morris Zelditch, Jr. 1985. ''Introduction: Expectation States Theory. Review and Assessment.'' Pp. 1–71 in *Status, Rewards, and Influence,* edited by J. Berger and M. Zelditch, Jr. San Francisco: Jossey-Bass.

Berger, Peter, and Thomas Luckmann. 1966. *The Social Construction of Reality.* New York: Doubleday.

Berkowitz, Stephen D. 1981. *An Introduction to Structural Analysis: The Network Approach.* Toronto: Butterworth.

Bernard, H. Russell, and Peter D. Killworth. 1979. ''A Review of Small-World Literature.'' *Sociological Symposium* 28:87–100.

Bershady, Harold J. 1973. *Ideology and Social Knowledge.* New York: Wiley.

Blau, Peter M. 1964. *Exchange and Power in Social Life.* New York: Wiley.

1977. *Inequality and Heterogeneity: A Primitive Theory of Social Structure.* New York: Free Press.

Blau, Peter M., Terry C. Blum, and Joseph E. Schwartz. 1982. ''Heterogeneity and Intermarriage.'' *American Sociological Review* 47:45–62.

Blau, Peter M., and Joseph E. Schwartz. 1984. *Crosscutting Social Circles: Testing a Macrostructural Theory of Intergroup Relations.* New York: Academic.

Blumer, Herbert. 1969. *Symbolic Interactionism: Perspective and Method.* Englewood Cliffs, N.J.: Prentice-Hall.

Boden, Margaret. 1980. *Jean Piaget.* New York: Penguin.

Bonacich, Philip. 1987. ''Power and Centrality: A Family of Measures.'' *American Journal of Sociology* 92:1170–1182.

Bott, Elizabeth. 1955. ''Urban Families: Conjugal Roles and Social Networks.'' *Human Relations* 8:345–383.

Boudon, Raymond. 1974. *Education, Opportunity, and Social Inequality.* New York: Wiley.

1981. *The Logic of Social Action: An Introduction to Sociological Analysis.* Boston: Routledge & Kegan Paul.

Boulding, Kenneth. 1956. ''General System Theory – The Skeleton of Science.'' *General Systems Yearbook* 1:11–17.

Boyd, John P. 1969. ''The Algebra of Group Kinship.'' *Journal of Mathematical Psychology* 6:139–167.

Breiger, Ronald L. 1974. ''The Duality of Persons and Groups.'' *Social Forces* 53:181–190.

Breiger, Ronald L., and Philippa E. Pattison. 1986. "Cumulated Social Roles: The Duality of Persons and Their Algebras." *Social Networks* 8:215–256.

Buckley, Walter. 1967. *Sociology and Modern Systems Theory*. Englewood Cliffs, N.J.: Prentice-Hall.

(ed.). 1968. *Modern Systems Research for the Behavioral Scientist: A Sourcebook*. Chicago: Aldine.

Bunge, Mario. 1973. *Method, Model and Matter*. Boston: Riedel.

Burt, Ronald S. 1980. "Models of Network Structure." *Annual Review of Sociology*, Vol. 6.

1982. *Toward a Structural Theory of Action*. New York: Academic.

1987. "Social Contagion and Innovation: Cohesion versus Structural Equivalence." *American Journal of Sociology* 92:1287–1335.

Bush, Robert R., and Frederick Mosteller. 1955. *Stochastic Models of Learning*. New York: Wiley.

Carley, Kathleen. 1985. "An Approach for Relating Social Structure to Cognitive Structure." *Journal of Mathematical Sociology* 12:1–26.

Carnap, Rudolf. 1955. "Logical Foundations of the Unity of Science." Pp. 42–62 in *International Encyclopedia of Unified Science*, Vol. 1, Part 1, edited by O. Neurath, R. Carnap, and C. Morris. Chicago: University of Chicago Press.

1956 [1947]. *Meaning and Necessity*, enlarged edition. Chicago: University of Chicago Press.

Cartwright, Dorwin, and Frank Harary. 1956. "Structural Balance: A Generalization of Heider's Theory." *Psychological Review* 63:277–293.

Chase, Ivan D. 1980. "Social Process and Hierarchy Formation in Small Groups: A Comparative Perspective." *American Sociological Review* 45:905–924.

1982a. "Behavioral Sequences During Dominance Hierarchy Formation in Chickens." *Science* 216:439–440.

1982b. "Dynamics of Hierarchy Formation: The Sequential Development of Dominance Relationships." *Behavior* 80:218–240.

Chomsky, Noam. 1957. *Syntactic Structures*. The Hague: Mouton.

1965. *Aspects of the Theory of Syntax*. Cambridge, Mass.: MIT Press.

Churchland, Paul M., and Clifford A. Hooker (eds.). 1985. *Images of Science: Essays on Realism and Empiricism*. Chicago: University of Chicago Press.

Cicourel, Aaron V. 1973. *Cognitive Sociology*. Baltimore, Md.: Penguin.

Cobb, Loren. 1981. "Stochastic Differential Equations for the Social Sciences." Pp. 37–68 in *Mathematical Frontiers of the Social and Policy Sciences*, edited by L. Cobb and R. Thrall. Boulder, Colo.: Westview.

Cohen, Bernard P. 1963. *Conflict and Conformity: A Probability Model and Its Application*. Cambridge, Mass.: MIT Press.

1980. *Developing Sociological Knowledge*. Englewood Cliffs, N.J.: Prentice-Hall.

Coleman, James S. 1964. *An Introduction to Mathematical Sociology*. New York: Free Press.

1973. *The Mathematics of Collective Action*. Chicago: Aldine.

1986. *Individual Interests and Collective Action: Selected Essays*. Cambridge: Cambridge University Press.

Coleman, James S., Elihu Katz, and Herbert Menzel. 1957. "The Diffusion of an Innovation Among Physicians." *Sociometry* 20:253–270.

Collins, Randall. 1975. *Conflict Sociology*. New York: Academic.

1981. "On the Micro-Foundations of Macrosociology." *American Journal of Sociology* 86:984–1014.

1985. *Three Sociological Traditions*. New York: Oxford University Press.

1987. "Interaction Ritual Chains: The Micro-Macro Connection as an Empirically Based Theoretical Problem.'' Pp. 193–206 in *The Micro-Macro Link,* edited by J. Alexander, B. Giesen, R. Münch, and N. Smelser. Berkeley, Calif.: University of California Press.

1988. *Theoretical Sociology.* San Diego: Harcourt Brace Jovanovich.

Cook, Karen S., and Richard M. Emerson. 1978. ''Power, Equity and Commitment in Exchange Networks.'' *American Sociological Review* 43:721–739.

(ed.). 1987. *Social Exchange Theory.* Newbury Park, Calif.: Sage Publications.

Coser, Lewis. 1956. *The Functions of Social Conflict.* New York: Free Press.

D'Abro, A. 1951 [1939]. *The Rise of the New Physics,* Vol. 1. New York: Dover.

Dahrendorf, Ralf. 1959. *Class and Class Conflict in Industrial Society.* Stanford, Calif.: Stanford University Press

Davis, James A. 1967. ''Clustering and Structural Balance in Graphs.'' *Human Relations* 20:181–187.

De Waal, Frans. 1982. *Chimpanzee Politics: Power and Sex Among the Apes.* New York: Harper & Row.

Dewey, John. 1938. *Logic: The Theory of Inquiry.* New York: Holt.

Dodd, Stuart, E. D. Rainboth, and Jiri Nehnevajsa. 1955. *Revere Studies in Social Interaction.* Public Opinion Laboratory, University of Washington, Seattle.

Doreian, Patrick. 1986. ''Measuring Relative Standing in Small Groups and Bounded Social Networks.'' *Social Psychology Quarterly* 49:247–259.

Doreian, Patrick, and Norman P. Hummon. 1976. *Modeling Social Processes.* New York: Elsevier.

Duncan, Otis Dudley. 1984. *Notes on Social Measurement: Historical and Critical.* New York: Russell Sage Foundation.

Duncan, Otis Dudley, and Leo F. Schnore. 1959. ''Cultural, Behavioral, and Ecological Perspectives in the Study of Social Organization.'' *American Journal of Sociology* 65:132–146.

Durkheim, Emile. 1915. *The Elementary Forms of the Religious Life.* New York: Free Press.

1951. *Suicide.* New York: Free Press.

1964[1933]. *The Division of Labor in Society.* New York: Macmillan.

1974. *Sociology and Philosophy.* New York: Free Press.

Elster, Jon. 1985. *Making Sense of Marx.* Cambridge: Cambridge University Press.

Emerson, Richard M. 1981. ''Social Exchange Theory.'' Pp. 30–65 in *Social Psychology: Sociological Perspectives,* edited by M. Rosenberg and R. H. Turner. New York: Basic.

England, J. Lynn. 1973. ''Mathematical Models of Two-Party Negotiations.'' *Behavioral Science* 18:189–197.

Erickson, Bonnie H., and T. A. Nosanchuk. 1983. ''Applied Network Sampling.'' *Social Networks* 5:367–382.

Etzioni, Amitai. 1968. *The Active Society: A Theory of Societal and Political Processes.* New York: Free Press.

Faia, Michael A. 1986. *Dynamic Functionalism: Strategy and Tactics.* ASA Rose Monograph. Cambridge: Cambridge University Press.

Fararo, Thomas J. 1969a. ''The Nature of Mathematical Sociology.'' *Social Research* 36:75–92.

1969b. ''Stochastic Processes.'' Pp. 245–260 in *Sociological Methodology 1969,* edited by E. F. Borgatta. San Francisco: Jossey-Bass.

1972a. ''Dynamics of Status Equilibration.'' Pp. 183–217 in *Sociological Theories in Progress,* Vol. 2, edited by J. Berger, M. Zelditch, Jr., and B. Anderson. New York: Houghton Mifflin.

1972b. ''Status, Expectations and Situation.'' *Quality and Quantity* 6:37–98.

1973. *Mathematical Sociology.* New York: Wiley. Reprinted 1978. Melbourne, Fla.: Krieger.

1976. ''On the Foundations of the Theory of Action in Whitehead and Parsons.'' In *Explorations in General Theory in Social Science,* Vol. 1, edited by J. Loubser, R. Baum, A. Effrat, and V. Lidz. New York: Free Press.

1978. "An Introduction to Catastrophes." *Behavioral Science* 23:291–317.

1981a. "Social Activity and Social Structure: A Contribution to the Theory of Social Systems." *Cybernetics and Systems* 12:53–81.

1981b. "Biased Networks and Social Structure Theorems." *Social Networks* 3:137–159.

1983. "Biased Networks and the Strength of Weak Ties." *Social Networks* 5:1–11.

1984a. "Neoclassical Theorizing and Formalization in Sociology." In *Mathematical Ideas and Sociological Theory,* edited by T. J. Fararo. New York: Gordon & Breach.

1984b. "Catastrophe Analysis of the Simon-Homans Model." *Behavioral Science* 29:212–216.

1987a. "Concrescence and Social Order: Process Philosophical Foundations of Sociological Theory." Pp. 77–121 in *Current Perspectives in Social Theory,* Vol. 8, edited by J. Wilson. Greenwich, Ct.: JAI Press.

1987b. "Generativity in Theoretical Model-Building." Pp. 137–170 in *Advances in Group Processes: Theory and Research,* Vol. 4, edited by E. J. Lawler and B. Markovsky. Greenwich, Ct.: JAI Press.

Fararo, Thomas J., and Patrick Doreian. 1984. "Tripartite Structural Analysis." *Social Networks* 6:141–175.

Fararo, Thomas J., and Kenji Kosaka. 1976. "A Mathematical Analysis of Boudon's IEO Model." *Social Science Information* 15:431–475.

Fararo, Thomas J., and John Skvoretz. 1984a. "Institutions as Production Systems." *Journal of Mathematical Sociology* 10:117–181.

1984b. "Biased Networks and Social Structure Theorems, II." *Social Networks* 6:223–258.

1986a. "Action and Institution, Network and Function." *Sociological Forum* 1:219–250.

1986b. "*E*-State Structuralism." *American Sociological Review* 51:591–602.

1987. "Unification Research Programs: Integrating Two Structural Theories." *American Journal of Sociology* 92:1183–1209.

1988. "Dynamics of the Formation of Stable Dominance Structures." In *Status Generalization,* edited by M. Webster and M. Foschi. Palo Alto, Calif.: Stanford University Press.

In press. "The Biased Net Theory of Social Structures and the Problem of Integration." In *Sociological Theories in Progress,* Vol. 3, edited by J. Berger, M. Zelditch, Jr., and B. Anderson. Newbury Park, Calif.: Sage.

Fararo, Thomas J., and Morris Sunshine. 1964. *A Study of a Biased Friendship Net.* Syracuse, N.Y.: Syracuse University Youth Development Center and Syracuse University Press.

Feld, Scott. 1982. "Social Structural Determinants of Similarity." *American Sociological Review* 47:797–801.

Fienberg, Stephen E., M. M. Meyer, and Stanley Wasserman. 1985. "Statistical Analysis of Multiple Sociometric Relations." *Journal of the American Statistical Association* 80:51–67.

Finer, S. E. (ed.). 1966. *Vilfredo Pareto: Sociological Writings.* New York: Praeger.

Fisek, M. Hamit. 1974. "A Model for the Evolution of Status Structures in Task-Oriented Discussion Groups." Pp. 53–83 in *Expectation States Theory: A Theoretical Research Program,* edited by J. Berger, T. L. Connor, and M. H. Fisek. Cambridge, Mass.: Winthrop. Reprinted 1982. Lanham, Md.: University Press of America.

Foster, Caxton C., Anatol Rapoport, and Carol J. Orwant. 1963. "A Study of a Large Sociogram, II: Elimination of Free Parameters." *Behavioral Science* 8:56–65.

Freeman, Linton C. 1979. "Centrality in Social Networks. I. Conceptual Clarification." *Social Networks* 1:215–239.

1984. "Turning a Profit from Mathematics: The Case of Social Networks." *The Journal of Mathematical Sociology* 10:343–360.

Freeman, Linton C., Thomas J. Fararo, Warner Bloomberg, Jr., and Morris Sunshine. 1963. "Locating Leaders in Local Communities: A Comparison of Some Alternative Approaches." *American Sociological Review* 28:791–798.

Freese, Lee (ed.). 1980a. *Theoretical Methods in Sociology: Seven Essays*. Pittsburgh: University of Pittsburgh Press.

Freese, Lee. 1980b. ''Formal Theorizing.'' Pp. 187–212 in *Annual Review of Sociology*, Vol. 6. Palo Alto, Calif.: Annual Reviews.

Friedkin, Noah. 1980. ''A Test of Structural Features of Granovetter's Strength of Weak Ties Theory.'' *Social Networks* 2:411–422.

Galtung, Johan. 1966. ''Rank and Social Integration: A Multidimensional Approach.'' Pp. 145–198 in *Sociological Theories in Progress*, Vol. 1, edited by J. Berger, M. Zelditch, Jr., and B. Anderson. New York: Houghton Mifflin.

Garfinkel, Harold. 1967. *Studies in Ethnomethodology*. Englewood Cliffs, N.J.: Prentice-Hall.

Giddens, Anthony. 1984. *The Constitution of Society: Outline of the Theory of Structuration*. Berkeley: University of California Press.

Gleick, James. 1987. *Chaos: Making a New Science*. New York: Viking.

Goffman, Erving. 1959. *The Presentation of Self in Everyday Life*. New York: Doubleday.

1967. *Interaction Ritual*. New York: Doubleday.

Granovetter, Mark S. 1973. ''The Strength of Weak Ties.'' *American Journal of Sociology* 78:1360–1380.

1978. ''Threshold Models of Collective Behavior.'' *American Journal of Sociology* 83:1420–1443.

1979. ''The Theory-Gap in Social Network Analysis.'' Pp. 501–518 in *Perspectives in Social Network Research*, edited by P. W. Holland and S. Leinhardt. New York: Academic.

1982. ''The Strength of Weak Ties: A Network Theory Revisited.'' Pp. 105–130 in *Social Structure and Network Analysis*, edited by P. V. Marsden and N. Lin. Beverly Hills, Calif.: Sage.

1985. ''Economic Action and Social Structure: The Problem of Embeddedness.'' *American Journal of Sociology* 91:481–510.

Granovetter, Mark S., and Roland Soong. 1983. ''Threshold Models of Diffusion and Collective Behavior.'' *Journal of Mathematical Sociology* 9:165–179.

Habermas, Jürgen. 1971. *Knowledge and Human Interests*. Boston: Beacon.

1981. *Reason and the Rationalization of Society*, Vol. 1 of *The Theory of Communicative Action*. Boston: Beacon.

Hacking, Ian. 1983. *Representing and Intervening*. Cambridge: Cambridge University Press.

Harary, Frank, Robert Z. Norman, and Dorwin Cartwright. 1965. *Structural Models: An Introduction to the Theory of Directed Graphs*. New York: Wiley.

Harré, Rom. 1970. *The Principles of Scientific Thinking*. London: Macmillan.

Harré, Rom, and Paul Secord. 1973. *The Explanation of Social Behavior*. Totowa, N.J.: Littlefield.

Hayes, Adrian C. 1980. ''A Semi-formal Explication of Talcott Parsons' Theory of Action.'' *Sociological Inquiry* 50:39–56.

1981. ''Structure and Creativity: The Use of Transformational-Generative Models in Action Theory.'' *Sociological Inquiry* 51:219–239.

1984. ''Formal Model Building and Theoretical Interests in Sociology.'' Pp. 107–123 in *Mathematical Ideas and Sociological Theory*, edited by T. J. Fararo. New York: Gordon & Breach.

Heckathorn, Douglas D. 1984. ''Mathematical Theory Construction in Sociology: Analytic Power, Scope, and Descriptive Accuracy as Trade-offs.'' Pp. 77–105 in *Mathematical Ideas and Sociological Theory*, edited by T. J. Fararo. New York: Gordon & Breach.

Heider, Fritz. 1946. ''Attitudes and Cognitive Organization.'' *Journal of Psychology* 21:107–112.

1958. *The Psychology of Interpersonal Relations*. New York: Wiley.

Heise, David. 1979. *Understanding Events: Affect and the Construction of Social Action*. Cambridge: Cambridge University Press.

1986. ''Modeling Symbolic Interaction.'' Pp. 291–284 in *Approaches to Social Theory*, edited by S. Lindenberg, J. S. Coleman, and S. Nowak. New York: Russell Sage Foundation.

1988. "Modeling Event Structures." In *Cognitive Science and Sociology*, special issue of *The Journal of Mathematical Sociology*, edited by D. Heckathorn. Vol. 14, No. 2.

Hempel, Carl G. 1952. *Fundamentals of Concept Formation in Empirical Science*. Chicago: University of Chicago Press.

1965. *Aspects of Scientific Explanation and Other Essays in the Philosophy of Science*. New York: Free Press.

Hirsch, Morris W., and Stephen Smale. 1974. *Differential Equations, Dynamical Systems, and Linear Algebra*. New York: Academic.

Hogarth, Robin M., and Melvin W. Reder (eds.). 1986. *Rational Choice: The Contrast Between Economics and Psychology*. Chicago: University of Chicago Press.

Holland, Paul W., and Samuel Leinhardt. 1977a. "Transitivity in Structural Models of Small Groups." Pp. 49–66 in *Social Networks: A Developing Paradigm*, edited by S. Leinhardt. New York: Academic.

1977b. "A Method for Detecting Structure in Sociometric Data." Pp. 411–432 in *Social Networks: A Developing Paradigm*, edited by S. Leinhardt. New York: Academic.

1981. "An Exponential Family of Probability Distributions for Directed Graphs." *Journal of the American Statistical Association* 76:33–50.

Homans, George C. 1950. *The Human Group*. New York: Harcourt, Brace & World.

1967. *The Nature of Social Science*. New York: Harcourt, Brace & World.

1974 [1961]. *Social Behavior: Its Elementary Forms*, rev. ed. New York: Harcourt Brace Jovanovich.

1984. *Coming to My Senses: The Autobiography of a Sociologist*. New Brunswick, N.J.: Transaction.

Jaeckel, Martin. 1971. "Coleman's Process Approach." Pp. 236–275 in *Sociological Methodology 1971*, edited by H. L. Costner. San Francisco: Jossey-Bass.

Jasso, Guillermina. 1978. "On the Justice of Earnings: A New Specification of the Justice Evaluation Function." *American Journal of Sociology* 83:1398–1419.

1980. "A New Theory of Distributive Justice." *American Sociological Review* 45:3–32.

1986. "A New Representation of the Just Term in Distributive Justice Theory: Its Properties and Operation in Theoretical Derivation and Empirical Estimation." *Journal of Mathematical Sociology* 12:251–274.

Kaplan, Abraham. 1964. *The Conduct of Inquiry*. San Francisco: Chandler.

Katzner, Donald W. 1983. *Analysis Without Measurement*. Cambridge: Cambridge University Press.

Keat, Russell, and John Urry. 1982. *Social Theory as Science*, 2nd ed. Boston: Routledge & Kegan Paul.

Kemeny, John G., and J. Laurie Snell. 1962. *Mathematical Models in the Social Sciences*. Cambridge, Mass.: MIT Press.

Kleinbach, Russell L. 1982. *Marx via Process: Whitehead's Potential Contribution to Marxian Social Theory*. Washington, D.C.: University Press of America.

Kuhn, Alfred. 1974. *The Logic of Social Systems*. San Francisco: Jossey-Bass.

Kuhn, Thomas S. 1970 [1962]. *The Structure of Scientific Revolutions* (2nd enlarged ed.). Chicago: University of Chicago Press.

Lane, Michael (ed.). 1970. *Introduction to Structuralism*. New York: Basic.

Laszlo, Ervin. 1972. *Introduction to Systems Philosophy*. New York: Harper & Row.

Laudan, Larry. 1977. *Progress and Its Problems: Towards a Theory of Scientific Growth*. Berkeley: University of California Press.

Lave, Charles A., and James G. March. 1975. *An Introduction to Models in the Social Sciences*. New York: Harper.

Leinhardt, Samuel (ed.). 1977. *Social Networks: An Emerging Paradigm*. New York: Academic.

Lenski, Gerhard, and Jean Lenski. 1982. *Human Societies: An Introduction to Macrosociology*, 4th ed. New York: McGraw-Hill.

Leplin, Jarrett (ed.). 1984. *Scientific Realism*. Berkeley: University of California Press.

Lévi-Strauss, Claude. 1963. *Structural Anthropology*. New York: Basic.

Levine, Donald N. (ed.). 1971. *Georg Simmel on Individuality and Social Forms*. Chicago: University of Chicago Press.

Lidz, Charles W., and Victor Meyer Lidz. 1976. "Piaget's Psychology of Intelligence and the Theory of Action." Pp. 195–239 in *Explorations in General Theory in Social Science*, edited by J. Loubser, R. Baum, A. Effrat, and V. Lidz. New York: Free Press.

Lindenberg, Siegwart. 1983. "An Assessment of the New Political Economy." *Sociological Theory* 3:99–114.

1986. "How Sociological Theory Lost Its Central Issue and What Can Be Done About It." Pp. 19–24 in *Approaches to Social Theory*, edited by S. Lindenberg, J. S. Coleman, and S. Nowak. New York: Russell Sage Foundation.

Lockwood, David. 1964. "Social Integration and System Integration." Pp. 244–256 in *Explorations in Social Change*, edited by George K. Zollschan and Walter Hirsh. London: Routledge.

Lopreato, Joseph. 1984. *Human Nature and Biocultural Evolution*. Boston: Allen & Unwin.

Lorrain, François, and Harrison C. White. 1971. "Structural Equivalence of Individuals in Social Networks." *Journal of Mathematical Sociology* 1:49–80.

Lucas, George R., Jr. (ed.). 1986. *Hegel and Whitehead: Contemporary Perspectives on Systematic Philosophy*. Albany: State University of New York Press.

Luce, R. Duncan. 1959. *Individual Choice Behavior*. New York: Wiley.

Luhmann, Niklas. 1976. "Generalized Media and the Problem of Contingency." Pp. 507–532 in *Explorations in General Theory in Social Science*, Vol. 2, edited by J. Loubser, R. Baum, A. Effrat, and V. Lidz. New York: Free Press.

Lukes, Steven. 1977. *Essays in Social Theory*. New York: Columbia University Press.

McPhail, Clark, and Ronald T. Wohlstein. 1986. "Collective Locomotion as Collective Behavior." *American Sociological Review* 51:447–463.

Mann, Leon. 1969. "Queue Culture: The Waiting Line as a Social System." *American Journal of Sociology* 74:340–354.

March, James G., and Herbert A. Simon. 1958. *Organizations*. New York: Wiley.

Margenau, Henry. 1950. *The Nature of Physical Reality*. New York: McGraw-Hill.

Margolis, Howard. 1982. *Selfishness, Altruism and Rationality: A Theory of Social Choice*. Chicago: University of Chicago Press.

Markovsky, Barry. 1987. "Toward Multilevel Sociological Theories: Simulations of Actor and Network Effects." *Sociological Theory* 5:100–115.

Markovsky, Barry, David Willer, and Travis Patton. 1988. "Power Relations in Networks." *American Sociological Review* 53:220–236.

Marsden, Peter V., and Edward O. Laumann. 1984. "Mathematical Ideas in Social Structural Analysis." Pp. 53–76 in *Mathematical Ideas and Sociological Theory*, edited by T. J. Fararo. New York: Gordon & Breach.

Marx, Karl, and Friedrich Engels. 1972. *The German Ideology*. New York: International.

Mayer, Thomas. 1975. *Mathematical Models of Group Structure*. Indianapolis: Bobbs-Merrill.

Mayhew, Bruce H. 1980. "Structuralism Versus Individualism: Part 1, Shadowboxing in the Dark." *Social Forces* 59:335–375.

1984. "Baseline Models of Sociological Phenomena." *Journal of Mathematical Sociology* 9:259–281.

Mead, George Herbert. 1934. *Mind, Self and Society: From the Standpoint of a Social Behaviorist*. Chicago: University of Chicago Press.

1936. *Movements of Thought in the Nineteenth Century*. Chicago: University of Chicago Press.

1938. *The Philosophy of the Act*. Chicago: University of Chicago Press.

Mehan, Hugh, and Houston Wood. 1975. *The Reality of Ethnomethodology*. New York: Wiley.

Merton, Robert K. 1968 [1949]. *Social Theory and Social Structure,* enlarged ed. New York: Free Press.

Miller, George A., Eugene Galanter, and Karl H. Pribram. 1960. *Plans and the Structure of Behavior*. New York: Holt.

Miller, James Grier. 1978. *Living Systems*. New York: McGraw-Hill.

Mintz, Beth, and Michael Schwartz. 1985. *The Power Structure of American Business*. Chicago: University of Chicago Press.

Münch, Richard. 1982. ''Talcott Parsons and the Theory of Action. II. The Continuity of the Development.'' *American Journal of Sociology* 87:771–826.

Nadel, S. F. 1957. *The Theory of Social Structure*. London: Cohen & West.

Newcomb, Theodore M. 1953. ''An Approach to the Study of Communicative Acts.'' *Psychological Review* 60:393–404.

Newell, Allen, and Herbert A. Simon. 1972. *Human Problem Solving*. Englewood Cliffs, N.J.: Prentice-Hall.

Nilsson, Nils J. 1977. *Principles of Artificial Intelligence*. Palo Alto, Calif.: Tioga.

Norman, Robert Z., and Fred S. Roberts. 1972. ''A Measure of Relative Balance of Social Structures.'' Pp. 358–391 in *Sociological Theories in Progress,* Vol. 2, edited by J. Berger, M. Zelditch, Jr., and B. Anderson. New York: Houghton Mifflin.

Nowakowska, Maria. 1973. ''A Formal Theory of Actions.'' *Behavioral Science* 18:393–416.

Ollman, Bertell. 1976. *Alienation,* 2nd ed. New York: Cambridge University Press.

Olsen, Marvin E. 1978. *The Process of Social Organization,* 2nd ed. New York: Holt, Rinehart & Winston.

Pareto, Vilfredo. 1935 [1920]. *The Mind and Society*. Translation by A. Bongiorno and A. Livingston. New York: Harcourt Brace.

1980 [1920]. *Compendium of General Sociology,* abridged version of *The Mind and Society,* by G. Farina. Minneapolis: University of Minnesota Press.

Parsons, Talcott. 1937. *The Structure of Social Action*. New York: Free Press.

1951. *The Social System*. New York: Free Press.

1954 [1949]. *Essays in Sociological Theory,* rev. ed. New York: Free Press.

1960. ''The Pattern Variables Revisited: A Response to Professor Dubin's Stimulus.'' *American Sociological Review* 25:467–483.

1966. *Societies: Evolutionary and Comparative Perspectives*. Englewood Cliffs, N.J.: Prentice-Hall.

1969. *Politics and Social Structure*. New York: Free Press.

1977. *Social Systems and the Evolution of Action Theory*. New York: Free Press.

1978. *Action Theory and the Human Condition*. New York: Free Press.

Parsons, Talcott, Robert F. Bales, and Edward A. Shils. 1953. *Working Papers in the Theory of Action*. New York: Free Press.

Parsons, Talcott, and Edward A. Shils. 1951. ''Values, Motives, and Systems of Action.'' Pp. 47–275 in *Toward a General Theory of Action: Theoretical Foundations for the Social Sciences,* edited by T. Parsons and E. A. Shils. New York: Harper.

Parsons, Talcott, Edward A. Shils, Kaspar D. Naegele, and Jesse R. Pitts (eds.). 1961. *Theories of Society*. New York: Free Press.

Parsons, Talcott, and Neil J. Smelser. 1956. *Economy and Society*. New York: Free Press.

Peterson, Richard A. 1979. ''Revitalizing the Culture Concept.'' Pp. 137–166 in *Annual Review of Sociology,* Vol. 5. Palo Alto, Calif.: Annual Reviews.

Pool, Ithiel de Sola, and Manfred Kochen. 1978. ''Contacts and Influence.'' *Social Networks* 1:5–51.

Popper, Karl R. 1959. *The Logic of Scientific Discovery*. New York: Basic.

Powers, Charles H., and Robert A. Hanneman. 1983. ''Pareto's Theory of Social and Economic Cycles: A Formal Model and Simulation.'' Pp. 59–89 in *Sociological Theory 1983*, edited by R. Collins. San Francisco: Jossey-Bass.

Powers, William T. 1973. *Behavior: The Control of Perception*. Chicago: Aldine.

Rapoport, Anatol. 1951. ''Nets with Distance Bias.'' *Bulletin of Mathematical Biophysics* 13:85–91.

1956. ''The Diffusion Problem in Mass Behavior.'' *General Systems Yearbook:* 1:48–55.

1957. ''Contributions to the Theory of Random and Biased Nets.'' *Bulletin of Mathematical Biophysics* 19:257–277.

1960. *Fights, Games and Debates*. Ann Arbor: University of Michigan Press.

1966. *Two Person Game Theory: The Essential Ideas*. Ann Arbor: University of Michigan Press.

1968. ''Systems Analysis: General Systems Theory.'' Pp. 452–458 in *International Encyclopedia of the Social Sciences*, Vol. 15. New York: Macmillian.

1983. *Mathematical Models in the Social and Behavioral Sciences*. New York: Wiley.

Rapoport, Anatol, and William J. Horvath. 1961. ''A Study of a Large Sociogram.'' *Behavioral Science* 6:279–291.

Rawls, John. 1971. *A Theory of Justice*. Cambridge, Mass.: Harvard University Press.

Ritzer, George. 1988. *Sociological Theory*, 2nd ed. New York: Knopf.

Robertson, Roland. 1988. ''The Sociological Significance of Culture: Some General Considerations.'' *Theory, Culture & Society* 5:3–23.

Roemer, John (ed.). 1986. *Analytical Marxism*. Cambridge: Cambridge University Press.

Rumelhart, David E., James L. McClelland, and the PDP Research Group. 1986. *Parallel Distributed Processing: Explorations in the Microstructures of Cognition* (2 vols.). Cambridge, Mass.: MIT Press.

Samuelson, Paul A. 1964 [1947]. *Foundations of Economic Analysis*. New York: Atheneum.

Schelling, Thomas C. 1971. ''Dynamic Models of Segregation.'' *Journal of Mathematical Sociology* 1:143–186.

1978. *Micromotives and Macrobehavior*. New York: Norton.

Schutz, Alfred. 1973. *Collected Papers: Vol. I. The Problem of Social Reality*. The Hague: Martinus Nijhoff.

Simon, Herbert A. 1957. *Models of Man*. New York: Wiley.

Skvoretz, John. 1983. ''Salience, Heterogeneity and Consolidation of Parameters.'' *American Sociological Review* 48:360–375.

1984. ''Languages and Grammars of Action and Interaction: Some Further Results.'' *Behavioral Science* 29:281–297.

1985. ''Random and Biased Networks: Simulations and Approximations.'' *Social Networks* 7:225–261.

In press. ''Social Structure and Intermarriage: A Reanalysis.'' In *Structures of Power and Constraint: Papers in Honor of Peter M. Blau*, edited by C. Calhoun, M. Meyer, and W. R. Scott. Cambridge: Cambridge University Press.

Skvoretz, John, and Thomas J. Fararo. 1980. ''Languages and Grammars of Action and Interaction: A Contribution to the Formal Theory of Action.'' *Behavioral Science* 25:9–22.

1986. ''Inequality and Association: A Biased Net Theory.'' Pp. 29–50 in *Current Perspectives in Social Theory*, Vol. 7, edited by J. Wilson and S. McNall. Greenwich, Ct.: JAI Press.

1988. ''Action Structures and Sociological Action Theory.'' In *Cognitive Science and Sociology*, special issue of *The Journal of Mathematical Sociology*, edited by D. Heckathorn. Vol. 14, No. 2.

1989. ''Connectivity and the Small World Problem.'' In *The Small World*, edited by M. Kochen. Norwood, N.J.: Ablex.

Skvoretz, John, Thomas J. Fararo, and Nick Axten. 1980. "Role Programme Models and the Analysis of Institutional Structure." *Sociology* 14:49–67.

Smith-Lovin, Lynn. 1987. "Affect Control Theory: An Assessment." Pp. 171–192 in *Analyzing Social Interaction: Advances in Affect Control Theory,* edited by L. Smith-Lovin and D. R. Heise, special issue of *The Journal of Mathematical Sociology,* 13/1–2.

Solomonoff, Ray, and Anatol Rapoport. 1951. "Connectivity of Random Nets." *Bulletin of Mathematical Biophysics* 13:107–117.

Spencer, Herbert. 1967 [1898]. *The Evolution of Society: Selections from Principles of Sociology,* edited by R. Carneiro. Chicago: University of Chicago Press.

Spradley, James P. (ed.). 1972. *Culture and Cognition: Rules, Maps, and Plans.* New York: Chandler.

Sternberg, Saul. 1963. "Stochastic Learning Theory." Chapter 9 in *The Handbook of Mathematical Psychology,* Vol. 2, edited by R. D. Luce, R. R. Bush, and E. Galanter. New York: Wiley.

Stinchcombe, Arthur L. 1968. *Constructing Social Theories.* New York: Harcourt Brace Jovanovich.

1983. *Economic Sociology.* New York: Academic.

Suppe, Frederick (ed.). 1977. *The Structure of Scientific Theories.* Urbana: University of Illinois Press.

Suppes, Patrick. 1957. *Introduction to Logic.* Princeton, N.J.: Van Nostrand.

1969. *Studies in the Methodology and Foundations of Science: Selected Papers from 1951 to 1969.* New York: Humanities Press.

Suppes, Patrick, and Richard C. Atkinson. 1960. *Markov Learning Models of Multiperson Interactions.* Palo Alto, Calif.: Stanford University Press.

Tarski, Alfred. 1946 [1941]. *Introduction to Logic and to the Methodology of the Deductive Sciences,* 2nd ed. New York: Oxford University Press.

Thibaut, John W., and Harold H. Kelley. 1959. *The Social Psychology of Groups.* New York: Wiley.

Thom, Rene. 1975. *Structural Stability and Morphogenesis.* Reading, Mass.: Benjamin.

Thomas, George, John Meyer, Francisco Ramirez, and John Boli. 1987. *Institutional Structure: Constituting State, Society, and the Individual.* Beverly Hills, Calif.: Sage.

Thompson, J. M. T., and H. B. Stewart. 1986. *Nonlinear Dynamics and Chaos: Geometrical Methods for Engineers and Scientists.* New York: Wiley.

Toulmin, Stephen. 1953. *The Philosophy of Science.* London: Hutchinson.

1961. *Foresight and Understanding: An Enquiry into the Aims of Science.* New York: Harper.

Travers, Jeffrey, and Stanley Milgram. 1969. "An Experimental Study of the Small World Problem." *Sociometry* 32:425–443.

Tuma, Nancy Brandon, and Michael T. Hannan. 1984. *Social Dynamics: Models and Methods.* Orlando, Fla.: Academic.

Turner, Jonathan H. 1984. *Societal Stratification: A Theoretical Analysis.* New York: Columbia University Press.

1986. *The Structure of Sociological Theory,* 4th ed. Chicago: Dorsey Press.

Turner, Jonathan H., and Leonard Beeghley. 1981. *The Emergence of Sociological Theory.* Homewood, Ill.: Dorsey Press.

Turner, Stephen P. 1987. "Underdetermination and the Promise of Statistical Sociology." *Sociological Theory* 5:172–184.

van Fraasen, Bas. 1980. *The Scientific Image.* Oxford: Clarendon Press.

van Parijs, Philip. 1981. *Evolutionary Explanation in the Social Sciences: An Emerging Paradigm.* Totowa, N.J.: Rowman & Littlefield.

von Neumann, John, and Oscar Morgenstern. 1947 [1944]. *The Theory of Games and Economic Behavior,* 2nd ed. Princeton, N.J.: Princeton University Press.

Wagner, David G. 1984. *The Growth of Sociological Theories.* Beverly Hills, Calif.: Sage.

Wagner, David G., and Joseph Berger. 1985. "Do Sociological Theories Grow?" *American Journal of Sociology* 90:697–728.

Waller, W. W., and R. Hill. 1951. *The Family: A Dynamic Interpretation.* New York: Dryden.

Warner, W. Lloyd. 1959. *The Living and the Dead: A Study in the Symbolic Life of Americans.* New Haven, Ct.: Yale University Press.

Weber, Max. 1978. *Economy and Society. Part 1. Conceptual Exposition.* Berkeley: University of California Press.

Wellman, Barry. 1983. "Network Analysis: Some Basic Principles." Pp. 155–200 in *Sociological Theory 1983*, edited by R. Collins. San Francisco: Jossey-Bass.

Wellman, Barry, and S. D. Berkowitz (eds.). 1988. *Social Structures: A Network Approach.* Cambridge: Cambridge University Press.

White, Harrison C. 1963. *An Anatomy of Kinship.* Englewood Cliffs, N.J.: Prentice-Hall.

1981. "Production Markets as Induced Role Structures." In *Sociological Methodology 1981*, edited by S. Leinhardt. San Francisco: Jossey-Bass.

White, Harrison C., Boorman, Scott A., and Ronald L. Breiger. 1976. "Social Structure from Multiple Networks, I. Blockmodels of Roles and Positions." *American Journal of Sociology* 81:730–780.

Whitehead, Alfred North. 1925. *Science and the Modern World.* New York: Macmillan.

1927. *Symbolism: Its Meaning and Effect.* New York: Macmillan. Reprinted 1959. New York: Capricorn.

1929. *Process and Reality,* corrected ed. New York: Free Press.

1933. *Adventures of Ideas.* New York: Macmillan.

Whyte, William F. 1943. *Street Corner Society.* Chicago: University of Chicago Press.

Wiener, Norbert. 1948. *Cybernetics.* Cambridge, Mass.: MIT Press.

Willer, David. 1984. "Analysis and Composition as Theoretic Procedures." Pp. 23–51 in *Mathematical Ideas and Sociological Theory: Current State and Prospects,* edited by T. J. Fararo. New York: Gordon & Breach.

1986. *Theory and the Experimental Investigation of Social Structures.* New York: Gordon & Breach.

Willer, David, and Bo Anderson (eds.). 1981. *Networks, Exchange and Coercion: The Elementary Theory and Its Applications.* New York: Elsevier (distributed by Greenwood Press, Westport, Ct.).

Wilson, John. 1983. *Social Theory.* Englewood Cliffs, N.J.: Prentice-Hall.

Wippler, Reinhard, and Siegwart Lindenberg. 1987. "Collective Phenomena and Rational Choice." Pp. 135–152 in *The Micro-Macro Link,* edited by J. Alexander, B. Giesen, R. Münch, and N. Smelser. Berkeley: University of California Press.

Wittgenstein, Ludwig. 1958 [1953]. *Philosophical Investigations,* 2nd ed. Oxford: Blackwell.

Wrong, Dennis H. 1961. "The Oversocialized Conception of Man in Modern Sociology." *American Sociological Review* 26:183–193.

Zee, Anthony. 1986. *Fearful Symmetry: The Search for Beauty in Modern Physics.* New York: Macmillan.

Zeeman, E. C. 1976. "Catastrophe Theory." *Scientific American* 234(4):65–83. (Unabridged version appears in Zeeman, 1977.)

1977. *Catastrophe Theory: Selected Papers 1972–1977.* Reading, Mass.: Addison-Wesley.

Zetterberg, Hans. 1966 [1954]. *Theory and Verification in Sociology,* 3rd enlarged ed. Totowa, N.J.: Bedminster.

# Index of names

# Index of subjects

**Other books in the Arnold and Caroline Rose Monograph Series of the American Sociological Association**

J. Milton Yinger, Kiyoshi Ikeda, Frank Laycock, and Stephen J. Cutler: *Middle Start: An Experiment in the Educational Enrichment of Young Adolescents*

James A. Geschwender: *Class, Race, and Worker Insurgency: The League of Revolutionary Black Workers*

Paul Ritterband: *Education, Employment, and Migration: Israel in Comparative Perspective*

John Low-Beer: *Protest and Participation: The New Working Class in Italy*

Orrin E. Klapp: *Opening and Closing: Strategies of Information Adaptation in Society*

Rita James Simon: *Continuity and Change: A Study of Two Ethnic Communities in Israel*

Marshall B. Clinard: *Cities with Little Crime: The Case of Switzerland*

Steven T. Bossert: *Tasks and Social Relationships in Classrooms: A Study of Instructional Organization and Its Consequences*

Richard E. Johnson: *Juvenile Delinquency and Its Origins: An Integrated Theoretical Approach*

David R. Heise: *Understanding Events: Affect and the Construction of Social Action*

Ida Harper Simpson: *From Student to Nurse: A Longitudinal Study of Socialization*

Stephen P. Turner: *Sociological Explanation as Translation*

Janet W. Salaff: *Working Daughters of Hong Kong: Filial Piety or Power in the Family?*

Joseph Chamie: *Religion and Fertility: Arab Christian–Muslim Differentials*

William Friedland, Amy Barton, and Robert Thomas: *Manufacturing Green Gold: Capital, Labor, and Technology in the Lettuce Industry*

Richard N. Adams: *Paradoxical Harvest: Energy and Explanation in British History, 1870–1914*

Mary F. Rogers: *Sociology, Ethnomethodology, and Experience: A Phenomenological Critique*

James R. Beniger: *Trafficking in Drug Users: Professional Exchange Networks in the Control of Deviance*

Jon Miller: *Pathways in the Workplace: The Effects of Race and Gender on Access to Organizational Resources*

Andrew J. Weigert, J. Smith Teitge, and Dennis W. Teitge: *Society and Identity: Toward a Sociological Psychology*

Michael A. Faia: *Dynamic Functionalism: Strategy and Tactics*

Joyce Rothschild-Whitt. Allen Whitt: *The Cooperative Workplace: Potentials and Dilemmas of Organizational Democracy and Participation*

Severyn T. Bruyn: *The Field of Social Investment*

Guy E. Swanson: *Ego Defenses and the Legitimation of Behaviour*

Liah Greenfeld: *Different Worlds: A Sociological Study of Taste, Choice and Success in Art*

Thomas K. Rudel: *Situations and Strategies in American Land-Use Planning*

Percy C. Hintzen: *The Costs of Regime Survival: Racial Mobilization, Elite Domination and Control of the State in Guyana and Trinidad*

John T. Flint: *Historical Role Analysis in the Study of Religious Change: Mass Educational Development in Norway, 1740–1891*

Judith R. Blau: *The Shape of Culture: A Study of Contemporary Cultural Patterns in the United States*

Fred C. Pampel and John B. Williamson: *Age, Class, Politics, and the Welfare State*